flavors

the junior league of san antonio

Making Time to Make a Difference

The Junior League of San Antonio, Inc. is an organization of women committed to promoting voluntarism and to improving the community through the effective action and leadership of trained volunteers. Its purpose is exclusively educational and charitable. This is a special 80th anniversary edition of *Flavors*.

Copyright © 1978 by The Junior League of San Antonio, Inc.
All Rights Reserved

ISBN 0-9610416-0-9
Library of Congress Catalogue Card Number 77-88731
Printed in the United States of America

First Edition 1978 — 15,000 Copies
Second Edition 1979 — 15,000 Copies
Third Edition 1981 — 15,000 Copies
Fourth Edition 1983 — 15,000 Copies
Fifth Edition 1987 — 15,000 Copies
Sixth Edition 2003 — 10,000 Copies

Manufactured by
Favorite Recipes® Press
an imprint of

FRP™

P.O. Box 305142
Nashville, Tennessee 37230
800-358-0560

Flavors Cookbook Information:

The Junior League of San Antonio, Inc.
723 Brooklyn Avenue
San Antonio, Texas 78215
210 225 1861 ext 45
210 225 6832 fax
www.jlsa.org

Introduction

Bienvenidos — welcome — to *Flavors* and San Antonio. Stroll down our wonderful, winding river and sample our history; then taste the delights that only so cosmopolitan a city, rich in history and diverse cultures, can produce. Where else can you discover the bustle and excitement of big city life slowed and enhanced by the graceful amble of a river throughout its center? It is this mixture of new and old, metropolis and village, that makes San Antonio a special place in which to live, visit, and eat. The tantalizing smells of Fiesta with its pots of Mexican chili, Irish stew, French onion soup, Spanish paella, Italian lasagne, Greek meatballs, Creole gumbo, Western barbeque, Texas wild game, Indian curries, Oriental delicacies, Russian borsch, and German sausage may all be found within these pages. The only thread of similarity you will find making these dishes typically San Antonio is the inevitable dash of picante or Mexican spice.

Flavors was compiled for you with love and care. Almost three thousand treasured recipes were received from Junior League and Bright Shawl members and their friends. The Cookbook Committee and volunteer testers selected those which seemed unique and most appropriately representative of this melting pot of independence in which we live. Each recipe has been tested and edited to insure accuracy and excellence. Recipes have been carefully worded to be complete but as concise as possible; therefore, it is not necessary to grease, peel, cover, etc. unless specifically indicated in the directions. It is assumed, however, that all oven temperatures mean preheated. The word "divided" following an ingredient indicates that this ingredient will be used more than once in the recipe in the amounts specified in the directions.

The section entitled "Pilon" — that something extra when nothing more is expected — is a collection of party ideas and menus to last all year that will tempt your taste buds and provide beginnings for your own ideas each month.

Flavors is dedicated to our testers without whom it could never have been written and to our husbands and families who endured both feast and famine for three years depending upon the stage of production. We hope your enjoyment in using *Flavors* will be as great as ours was in creating it.

The Junior League of San Antonio, Inc.
2003 *Flavors* Cookbook Committee

Chairman
Michelle Parchman

Sustaining Advisor
Milby Hartwell

Treasurer
Avery O'Hare

Marketing
Pily Jenkins

Sales, Marketing and Distribution Committee

Melissa Barnett
Kimberly Blackburn
Erica Bochantin
Nicole Boyd
Haley Buchman
Katherine Buzzini
Amy Case
Karen Chase
Ann Bohl Deacon
Betsy Dose
Earl Fae Cooper Eldridge
Julie Faulkner
Stacy Foerster
Karen Greenwood
Delaina Harrison
Pamela Johnson
Jennifer Jones
Lee Ann Jones
Laurie Kaplan

Jessie Kardys
Lisa Keller
Manda Kelley
KaRynn Kolm
Veronica Lozano
Amy McLin
Tina Mencio
Kim Nourie
Laura Peel
Denise Reams-White
Diane Shaw
Bunkie Shed
Maria Smith
Verr Bateman Soltes
Lisa Westmoreland
Kori Williams
Adrianne Frost Winter
Lisa Wolff

The Junior League of San Antonio, Inc.
Charlotte Hopson
Judith Miller

Special Thanks to Our Advisors
Bracewell & Patterson, L.L.P.
Padgett, Stratemann & Co., L.L.P.

Table of Contents

The Junior League of San Antonio, Inc.
Board of Directors 2003–2004

President, KaRynn Kolm

President-Elect, Karen Greenwood

Treasurer, Avery O'Hare

Treasurer-Elect, Rebecca Dumas

Recording Secretary, Tiffany Mills

Community Council Chair, Terri Herbold

Fund Development Council Chair, Melissa Barnett

Marketing Council Chair, Bunkie Shed

Membership Development Council Chair, Tammy Dullnig

Placement Chair, Michelle Kocurek

Research and Development Council Chair, Shannon Moravits

Member-at-Large, Michelle Parchman

Member-at-Large, Jill Ruggles

Strategic Planning Chair, Tina Magness

Bylaws Parliamentarian, Lisa Wolff

Sustaining Advisor, Kathy Griesenbeck

Headwaters of the San Antonio River

"The San Antonio Spring may be classed as of the first water among the gems of the natural world. The whole river gushed up in one sparkling burst from the earth. It has all the beautiful accompaniments of a smaller spring, moss, pebbles, seclusion, sparkling sunbeams, and dense overhanging luxuriant foliage. The effect is overpowering."

A Journey Through Texas.   Frederick Law Olmstead, 1857.

Daffodil Dip

1	hard-boiled egg	2	tablespoons finely chopped onion
½	cup mayonnaise	1	clove garlic, minced
8	ounces cream cheese, softened	1	tablespoon anchovy paste
½	cup finely chopped fresh parsley		Dash of pepper

Sieve yolk and white of egg separately. Gradually add mayonnaise to cream cheese, mixing until well blended. Add parsley, egg white, onion, garlic, anchovy paste, and pepper, mixing well. Sprinkle with egg yolk. *Serve with raw vegetables or crackers, or use to stuff fresh mushrooms.*

Mrs. Jess Lewis Mayfield (Joyce Elaine Musselman)

Cream Cheese Dip

3	ribs celery		Mayonnaise
1	medium onion	¾	cup finely chopped pecans
1	large green pepper	1	clove garlic, minced
18	ounces cream cheese	1	cup heavy cream

Grind celery, onion, and pepper in meat grinder. Mix cheese with some mayonnaise until soft and creamy. Add pecans, garlic, and ground vegetables. Refrigerate for several hours. Before serving, add cream until dip is desired consistency. *Makes a good sandwich spread when made with less cream.*

Mrs. Chalmer K. McClelland (Dodie West)

Billye's Dip for Vegetables

1	clove garlic, pressed		Black pepper to taste
½	teaspoon dry mustard	3	tablespoons snipped chives
1	teaspoon Worcestershire sauce	⅓	cup snipped fresh parsley
2	tablespoons anchovy paste	1	cup mayonnaise
3	tablespoons tarragon wine vinegar	½	cup sour cream

Combine all ingredients and refrigerate at least 8 hours. Serve with raw vegetables.

Mrs. Fred C. Lepick, Jr. (Morgia Howard)

Hot Artichoke Dip

1 cup grated Parmesan cheese
1 cup mayonnaise

14 ounces artichoke hearts, drained and chopped

Mix all ingredients thoroughly. Broil until hot. Serve with crackers. *May also be served cold.*
Serves 6-8.
Mrs. Richard Bennett (Leslie Ann Wilson)

Quick Spinach or Braunschweiger Dip

2 10 ounce packages frozen chopped spinach, cooked and drained, or 1 roll Braunschweiger, at room temperature
1 package Lipton Onion Soup Mix

1 pint sour cream
Dash of Tabasco sauce
1 tablespoon Worcestershire sauce, optional

Mix all ingredients thoroughly. *Spinach dip may also be used as stuffing for tomatoes or as filling for an omelet, and is good hot or cold.*
Serves 8-10.
Mrs. Frank J. Siebenaler (Louise)

Sausage Stroganoff Dip

1 clove garlic
2 pounds bulk sausage
3 tablespoons flour
2 cups milk
2 large onions, chopped
1 6 ounce can mushrooms
½ stick butter

2 teaspoons soy sauce
2 tablespoons Worcestershire sauce
Salt and pepper to taste
Paprika to taste
2 cups sour cream
Melba toast or chips

Rub a large skillet with garlic, heat, and brown sausage. Pour off grease as it accumulates and break up sausage with a fork. Sprinkle sausage with flour and add milk. Simmer until slightly thickened and set aside. Sauté onions and mushrooms in butter until onions are tender. Add onions, mushrooms, and seasonings to sausage mixture. Cook until mixture bubbles, remove from heat, and add sour cream. Keep hot in a chafing dish and serve with melba toast or large chips. *To double recipe, use only three onions. Men especially love this dip and it is a nice change from picadillo. Leftover dip can be served over rice for dinner.*
Freezes well before adding sour cream.
Mrs. Pierce Sullivan (Mary Wallace Kerr)

Picadillo

2	pounds lean ground beef or venison	3	canned jalapeño chilies, chopped
4	tablespoons olive oil	½	cup raisins
2	onions, finely chopped		Salt and pepper to taste
1	clove garlic, crushed		Pinch of ground cinnamon
2	apples, peeled, cored, and chopped		Pinch of ground cloves
1	14½ ounce can tomatoes with onion and green pepper	2	ounces slivered almonds

In a large skillet, brown meat in 3 tablespoons oil. Add onion and garlic and brown. Add remaining ingredients, except the almonds, and simmer for 20 minutes. Sauté almonds in 1 tablespoon oil until golden, add to other ingredients, and cook 2 minutes. *Serve with large Fritos as a dip or as a main dish with rice. Picadillo resulted from the merging of Spanish cookery with Aztec cuisine, and with variations is enjoyed throughout Latin America.*
Serves 6.
Mrs. Eleanor Weed

Straw Hat Dip

1	pound ground beef	½	teaspoon salt
1	onion, chopped	¼	teaspoon pepper
1	clove garlic, minced		Dash of Tabasco sauce
1	15 ounce can kidney beans		Mozzarella cheese, grated
1	10 ounce can Rotel tomatoes and green chilies		Stuffed green olives, sliced
			Tostados

Brown ground beef with onion and garlic. Add kidney beans, tomatoes, and seasonings. Simmer for 45 minutes. Place dip in a chafing dish, top with cheese and olives, and serve with tostados.
Serves 8.
Mrs. John Oppenheimer (Evelyne Ehrich)

Hot Beany Cheese Dip

1	pound Cheddar or Colby cheese	1	11 ounce can refried beans
1	6 ounce can Frito Bean Dip, plain or jalapeño		

Grate cheese into saucepan. Add bean dip and beans. Melt slowly, stirring until combined. Serve hot. *Traditionally, any cowboy who can resist this recipe is given two weeks off with pay to rest and regain his senses.*
Serves 8.
Mrs. Porter Drolla (Molly Porter)

Chili con Queso Dip

1	cup chopped onion	1	10 ounce can Wolf Brand chili without beans
2	tablespoons butter		
1	10 ounce can Rotel tomatoes and green chilies	4	tablespoons Pace Picante Sauce, optional
½	teaspoon cumin seeds	1	4 ounce can chopped green chilies, optional
1	pound Velveeta cheese		
12	ounces Cheddar cheese, cubed		

Sauté onion in butter. Add tomatoes, mashing large pieces. Add cumin, cheese, chili, picante sauce, and green chilies, and cook until cheese is melted. *May also be served over chalupa shells which have been spread generously with refried beans.*
Makes 6 cups.
Mrs. George M. McDougall (Frances L. Hoffman)

Hot Shrimp Cheese Dip

1	10¾ ounce can cream of shrimp soup	1	4 ounce can mushrooms
		1	4½ ounce can shrimp
1	6 ounce roll garlic cheese	1	tablespoon lemon juice

Combine all ingredients in a double boiler and cook until cheese is melted. Serve hot in chafing dish with melba toast rounds or chips.
Serves 8.
Mrs. Thomas R. Benesch (Jane Bickham)

Shrimp and Crab Dip

16	ounces cream cheese, softened	½	teaspoon cream style horseradish
1	tablespoon milk		
1	cup crabmeat	¼	teaspoon salt
1	cup cooked, peeled cocktail-sized shrimp		Dash of pepper
2	tablespoons finely chopped onion	⅓	cup sliced almonds, toasted

Blend cream cheese with milk. Add all other ingredients, except almonds, and mix well. Spoon into casserole, sprinkle with almonds, and bake at 375° for 15 minutes. Serve hot.

Mrs. Joe J. Lodovic, Jr. (Jeanne Spencer)

Carl's Tuna Dip

1	7 ounce can solid white tuna, drained and flaked	1	envelope Good Seasons Italian dressing
12	ounces sour cream	1	hard-boiled egg, chopped
2	teaspoons lemon juice	2	tablespoons Pace Picante Sauce

Mix all ingredients in a bowl. Serve chilled with crackers or chips.
Yields 2 cups.
Mrs. Christopher Goldsbury, Jr. (Linda Pace)

Paresa (par ē′ sa)

6	pounds freshly ground lean sirloin	Juice of 4-6 lemons, optional
3	pounds sliced American cheese, finely diced	Generous amounts of salt and coarsely cracked pepper
4-5	onions, finely diced	Assorted crackers

Mix ingredients thoroughly, but carefully, since cheese should remain chunky. Spread generously on crackers. *Serve very fresh. It will keep no more than 2 days. This is a German specialty, eaten in good quantity with beer. You can even have the butcher make some at a grocery store in Castroville, Texas.*
Serves 30-40.
Mrs. William W. Coates, III (Sue Schoeneck)

Pinwheel Surprise

1	package crescent rolls
3	ounces or more cream cheese, softened

Separate rolls into triangles and place on a pizza pan with the points toward the center. Press dough together to cover pan and bake according to package directions. Cool and spread with cheese. Top in circular rows with any combination of the following ingredients:

olives	mushrooms	shrimp	crumbled bacon
crab	anchovies	onion	sieved egg
ham	pimiento	celery	pepperoni

To serve, slice in wedges as you would pizza.
Serves 8.
Mrs. Franklin C. Redmond (Jeanne Martinak)

Ripe Olive Spread

8   ounces cream cheese, softened
½   cup Hellmann's mayonnaise
4½ ounces chopped ripe olives

1   bunch green onions and tops,
    finely chopped
Assorted crackers or party rye bread

Mix cream cheese and mayonnaise by hand. Combine with olives and onions. Serve as a spread with assorted crackers or with party rye bread. May be doubled. *Too easy to be so good!*
Serves 6-8.
Mrs. Elkin McGaughy (Barbara Crossette)

Curry Canapé

1½ cups grated sharp Cheddar cheese
1   scant cup chopped ripe olives
¼-½ cup chopped green onions
½   cup mayonnaise

1   tablespoon curry powder or
    to taste
Bread rounds, buttered and toasted

Mix first 5 ingredients and spread on bread rounds. Broil until bubbly.
Yields 5 dozen.
Mrs. Fred Bramlette (Lida Lee Denney)

Braunschweiger Spread

8   ounces Braunschweiger
2   tablespoons grated onion
3   tablespoons salad dressing or
    mayonnaise

2   tablespoons sweet pickle relish
1   hard-boiled egg, sieved, or
    chopped parsley

Let Braunschweiger come to room temperature. Mix well with onion, dressing, and relish. Shape and chill 6 hours. Garnish with egg or parsley.

Mrs. Richard Nevitt (Patty)

Chicken Almond Pâté

10	ounces Swanson's boned chicken	3	tablespoons sherry
1	stick butter, softened	2	teaspoons lemon juice
½	cup coarsely chopped onion	Tabasco sauce to taste
1	clove garlic, minced	4	ounces slivered almonds, toasted

Purée all ingredients, except almonds, in blender until smooth. Refrigerate in a bowl for several hours until firm. Remove from bowl, shape, and decorate with almonds. Chill 2-3 hours. *May be prepared a day ahead or frozen without the almonds.*
Serves 6. Freezes.
Mrs. Patrick S. Chumney (Candes Parker)

Easy Pâté

¼	cup minced onion	1	stick butter, softened
3	tablespoons butter	1	teaspoon salt
1½	pounds chicken livers	⅛	teaspoon pepper
½	cup dry sherry	¼	teaspoon nutmeg
½	cup heavy cream	Paprika to taste

Sauté onion until soft in 3 tablespoons butter. Add chicken livers and cook quickly until all the pink has disappeared. Purée onion and liver in blender or food processor. Add remaining ingredients and blend on low speed until creamy. Chill well.
Serves 10.
Mrs. Robert E. Fawcett, Jr. (Ann Ingrum)

Glynne's Mock Pâté

1½	sticks butter	⅓	cup cognac or bourbon
2	pounds liverwurst, smoked gooseliver, or Braunschweiger	1	tablespoon fresh thyme or ½ tablespoon dried thyme
¾	cup chopped fresh parsley		

Cream butter, add meat, and mix well. Add seasonings and chill. *This may be shaped in a ball, covered with seasoned cream cheese, and topped with caviar. Mock pâté, as well as seasoned cream cheese mixed with capers, is good spread on very thin slices of ham which are then rolled and cut in half.*

Mrs. Huard Hargis Eldridge (Earl Fae Cooper, Jr.)

Shrimp Pâté

5	5 ounce cans shrimp	⅔	cup mayonnaise
⅓	cup minced onion	¼	teaspoon white pepper
1	stick butter, melted	5	dashes Worcestershire sauce
1	tablespoon prepared horseradish	4	dashes Tabasco sauce
1	teaspoon salt		Parsley
3	tablespoons lemon juice		

Drain shrimp, reserving several for garnish. In a blender, combine all ingredients except those for garnish, and blend well. This should make a stiff paste. Pack it firmly into a 3 cup mold, and chill 4-5 hours until firm. Unmold and garnish with parsley and whole shrimp. *Serve with toast rounds.*
Serves 12.
Mrs. Monte D. Tomerlin (Jacqueline R. Beretta)

Liptauer Cheese

1	pound cream cheese	2	teaspoons caraway seed
½	cup sour cream	1	tablespoon paprika
1	stick butter, softened	¼	teaspoon salt
1	small onion, quartered		Tabasco sauce to taste
2	teaspoons capers		Worcestershire sauce to taste
1	tablespoon anchovy paste		

Soften cream cheese in blender. Add remaining ingredients and blend until smooth. May be molded and is better if made the day before. *Serve with melba toast or rye wafers.*
Freezes.
Mrs. Monte D. Tomerlin (Jacqueline R. Beretta)

Tarama

4-5 ounces carp roe caviar	10-12 slices white bread, crusts removed
1½-2 tablespoons finely grated onion	Juice of 2-3 lemons or more to taste
1¼-2 cups imported olive oil, divided	

Mash carp roe and add grated onion. Add a little of the olive oil and beat thoroughly to a smooth paste. Dip bread into water, squeeze out excess, and tear in small bits. Add bread to roe mixture alternately with olive oil and lemon juice. Beat until cream colored. *Serve as an hors d'oeuvre with unsalted crackers or chips, or spread on small toast triangles.*

Mrs. James W. Nixon, Jr. (Kiki)

Red Caviar Mousse

1 envelope gelatin
2 tablespoons cold water
½ cup boiling water
4 ounces red caviar
3 cups yogurt

3 cups mayonnaise
1 tablespoon lemon juice
1 tablespoon Worcestershire sauce
2 tablespoons onion juice

Soften gelatin in cold water. Dissolve gelatin in boiling water. Mix with remaining ingredients, pour into a mold, and chill until set. *Serve with sesame crackers.*

Mrs. Robert Sawtelle (Terry Emerson)

Russian Caviar Mousse

1 envelope gelatin
2 tablespoons cold water
½ cup boiling water
1 tablespoon lemon juice
1 tablespoon Worcestershire sauce
2 tablespoons mayonnaise

2 cups sour cream
⅛ teaspoon dry mustard
4-5 ounces Russian caviar, preferably black
Watercress, optional
Toast rounds or crackers

Soften gelatin in cold water for 5 minutes. Dissolve gelatin in boiling water. Add lemon juice and Worcestershire sauce. Combine mayonnaise and sour cream. Add gelatin mixture, mustard, and caviar, and mix thoroughly. Pour into a mold and chill at least 5 hours. Unmold, garnish with watercress, and serve with toast rounds. *May be prepared a day ahead. Very different and delicious.*

Mrs. Patrick H. Swearingen, Jr. (Gail Hall)

Crab à la Chauveaux

6 ounces crabmeat, fresh or canned
8 ounces cream cheese, softened

1 12 ounce bottle Heinz Chili Sauce

Rinse crab and remove any filament or shell. Spread the cream cheese evenly over the bottom of a paper plate or shallow round serving dish. Pour the chili sauce over the cheese and sprinkle with crabmeat. *Serve with Ritz crackers.*

Mrs. Tony Chauveaux (Kathryn Williams)

Cheese Ball

12	ounces cream cheese	1	2¾ ounce bottle capers, drained
1	stick margarine	½	medium onion, grated
2	tablespoons anchovy paste		Chopped fresh parsley

Mix the first 5 ingredients together. Roll in parsley.

Mrs. Howard E. Lancaster (Betty Lain)

Chutney Cheese Ball

8	ounces cream cheese	¼	teaspoon dry mustard
1	teaspoon or more curry powder		Paprika
½	cup Major Grey's Chutney, chopped		Unsalted peanuts, chopped

Cream cheese, curry powder, chutney, and mustard. Chill slightly and form into desired shape. Cover with paprika and peanuts. Flavors blend if prepared in advance.

Mrs. Amalda Nevitt

Roquefort Ring

1	envelope gelatin	1½-2 tablespoons grated onion
¼	cup cold water	4-5 stuffed olives, chopped
6	ounces Roquefort cheese	Salt to taste
6	ounces cream cheese, softened	White pepper to taste
½	cup heavy cream	

Sprinkle gelatin into cold water and allow to soften for 10 minutes. Stir over hot water until dissolved. Set aside to cool. Press Roquefort cheese through a sieve into a bowl and blend in cream cheese. Stir in gelatin mixture, cream, onion, olives, salt, and pepper. Pour into a 2½-3 cup ring mold and chill. Stir gently once or twice until set. Unmold and serve.
Serves 8.
Mrs. George A. Kampmann (Wister Howell)

Texas Cheese Ball

1	6 ounce roll Kraft garlic cheese	1	tablespoon finely chopped parsley
1	6 ounce roll Kraft smoked cheese	1	tablespoon chili powder
4	ounces bleu cheese	1	tablespoon Worcestershire sauce
8	ounces cream cheese		Dash of Tabasco sauce
6	ounces finely chopped pecans, or ¾ cup	3	cloves garlic, finely minced
		¼-½	cup grated onion

Bring cheeses to room temperature. Mix pecans, parsley, and chili powder, and place on wax paper. Using a mixer, blend cheeses with Worcestershire, Tabasco, garlic, and onion. Form into a ball, and roll in the pecan mixture.

Mrs. E. S. Christilles (Mildred)

Tomato Cheese Log

1	cup drained canned whole tomatoes	2	cloves garlic, crushed
8	ounces cream cheese, softened	1	teaspoon salt
8	ounces Cheddar cheese, grated	⅛-¼	teaspoon cayenne pepper
1	stick butter or margarine, softened	8	ounces chopped walnuts
½	cup chopped onion		Tomato for garnish

Combine tomatoes, cheeses, butter, onion, garlic, salt, and cayenne. Beat with an electric mixer until smooth. Spoon out onto a large piece of wax paper and roll to form a log. Freeze 1 hour or until firm. Cover with chopped walnuts and garnish with bits of tomato. May be prepared ahead. *Serve with melba toast rounds and assorted crackers. Leftovers, if any, are great for sandwiches.*

Mrs. Louis Veil

Escargots à la Bourguignonne

1⅓	sticks butter, softened	⅓	teaspoon salt
1½	teaspoons dried parsley	⅛	teaspoon pepper
1	teaspoon garlic powder	2	dozen escargots
⅓	teaspoon dried green onions	2	dozen shells

Mix butter and spices together. Put escargots in shells and fill shells with butter mixture. Place in a baking pan. Bake at 350° for 10-15 minutes. *Serve with small slices of hot French bread as the first course at dinner or as hors d'oeuvres. The escargots of Burgundy are known throughout the world as being the most succulent, thus à la bourguignonne.*
Serves 4.
Mrs. G. Milton Johnson (Ellen Bond Zimmerman)

Fish Puffs

2	pounds firm, white fish such as bass or redfish	1	teaspoon pepper
½-⅔	cup cornstarch	1-2	tablespoons dry sherry or rice wine
2	tablespoons salt	2	egg whites
			Peanut oil

Cut fish into 1 inch cubes. Place in a nonmetallic bowl or dish and cover with a generous amount of cornstarch. Add salt, pepper, and enough sherry to make it pasty. Mix until all the pieces are well coated. Chill at least 1 hour. Just before serving, stiffly beat egg whites and coat the fish pieces. Fry, a few at a time, in hot peanut oil until light brown. Do not overcook or the puff of the egg whites will be lost. Serve immediately.

Mrs. Frates Seeligson (Martita Rice)

Crabmeat Canapé Patrice

	Melted butter	1	pound crabmeat, flaked
1	loaf Pullman bread, crusts removed and sliced horizontally at bakery, or sandwich bread	2	ounces Pinot Chardonnay or Chablis
½	cup finely chopped shallots		Salt to taste
2	tablespoons olive oil		White pepper to taste
1	cup medium cream sauce	2	teaspoons chopped parsley

Brush melted butter on both sides of bread before cutting into desired shapes for canapé bases. Toast under broiler on one side only. Bases may be made several days ahead and frozen. Sauté shallots in oil until tender. Blend in cream sauce. Add crabmeat, wine, salt, and pepper. Cook 8 minutes over low heat, sprinkle with parsley, and allow to cool. Spread on untoasted side of canapé bases, bake at 325° for 5 minutes, and serve. *Leftover bread may be browned to make croutons. This canapé is a real party stopper and never fails to disappear immediately.*
Serves 20.
Mrs. Richard E. Whiting

Crab Appetizer

6   hot dog buns, halved and buttered
1   cup canned or fresh crabmeat
¼   cup finely chopped onion
¼   cup finely chopped celery

½   cup mayonnaise
¾   cup grated Cheddar cheese, divided
Salt and pepper to taste

Toast buns until slightly brown. Mix crabmeat, onion, celery, mayonnaise, and ½ cup cheese together. Spread on buns and sprinkle with remaining cheese. Broil until heated. Cut in small sections for appetizer, or serve whole for a quick lunch.

Mrs. John B. Pipes (Virginia Lindsey)

Honey Dipped Shrimp

Shrimp, peeled and cleaned
Honey

Bacon

Wrap each shrimp with a slice of bacon and secure with a toothpick. Dip the shrimp in honey. Place over a hot charcoal fire for approximately 25 minutes, turning occasionally. Remove the shrimp when done, and dip once more in the honey. Return shrimp to the grill for 30 seconds. Remove the shrimp and serve immediately. *This recipe was given to me by the butcher at the Ize Box Meat Market.*

Mrs. Benjamin F. Swank, III (Susie Schroeder)

Marinated Shrimp

1¼   cups salad oil
¾   cup white vinegar
1½   teaspoons salt
2½   teaspoons celery seed
2½   tablespoons capers with juice

1   clove garlic, crushed
2   pounds cooked shrimp, peeled
3   medium onions, sliced
5   bay leaves
1½   tablespoons whole cloves

Mix first 6 ingredients. Layer the shrimp and sliced onions, crushing bay leaves and whole cloves over each layer. Pour oil mixture over shrimp and marinate for 24 hours, turning after 12 hours. *There is never enough as people don't stop eating it until it is all gone!*

Mrs. Jim B. Criscoe (Judy)

Barbara's Sherried Shrimp with Louis Sauce

1½   pounds uncooked shrimp, peeled and cleaned
¼-½ cup dry sherry
½   stick butter
½   teaspoon garlic salt

¼-½ cup grated Parmesan cheese
½   cup mayonnaise
1   tablespoon tomato paste
1   teaspoon Worcestershire sauce
1   teaspoon prepared mustard

Marinate shrimp in sherry for several hours. Melt butter over low heat, add shrimp and sherry, and sprinkle with garlic salt. Simmer 10-15 minutes or until shrimp turn pink. Do not overcook. Using a slotted spoon, remove shrimp and place on a teflon or greased baking sheet. Sprinkle cheese over shrimp and broil 2-3 minutes until cheese is lightly browned. Combine remaining ingredients to make sauce. Serve hot shrimp with cocktail picks and sauce.

Mrs. Huard Hargis Eldridge (Earl Fae Cooper, Jr.)

Panamanian Shrimp Ceviche

1½ pounds uncooked shrimp, peeled and cleaned
1   cup lemon juice
1   4½ ounce can roasted and peeled green chilies, drained, seeded, and chopped
½   cup minced green onions
2   large tomatoes, peeled, seeded, and chopped

1   teaspoon salt
¼   cup Bertolli olive oil
½   teaspoon aji (Panamanian pepper) or 1 jalapeño pepper, seeded and minced
1   clove garlic, minced
1   4 ounce jar pimiento, drained and minced

Cut shrimp in pieces. Combine shrimp with lemon juice, cover, and refrigerate for 2 hours. Mix with remaining ingredients and marinate overnight. Drain. Adjust seasonings and serve chilled. *This is a delicious appetizer and lends itself well to your own creative urges such as the addition of oregano or other herbs.*

Mrs. Robert E. Schorlemer (Ann Kalb)

Ceviche de México

2   pounds firm, white fish fillets such
    as red snapper or bass
18 limes juiced, or 1½ cups
3   large onions, chopped
4   large tomatoes, peeled and chopped
1   bunch fresh cilantro, chopped,
    or dried coriander to taste
1   medium jar stuffed green olives

1   7 ounce can mild jalapeños or
    8 mild jalapeños, chopped
3   tablespoons olive oil
3   tablespoons vinegar
1   teaspoon black pepper
1   teaspoon ground oregano
1   teaspoon ground cumin

Cut fish in ½ inch cubes and cover with lime juice in a nonmetallic bowl. Layer onions, tomatoes, cilantro, olives, and jalapeños. Do not mix. Add oil, vinegar, pepper, oregano, and cumin. Cover and refrigerate overnight. One hour before serving mix thoroughly and return to refrigerator.
Serves 12.
Mrs. Earl Hobbs Chumney, Jr. (Barbara Sue Christian)

Ceviche

10   fillets of fresh trout, skinned, or
     2½ pounds
1½-2 cups fresh lime juice
4   tomatoes, peeled and finely chopped
3   green peppers, finely chopped
2   small hot peppers, finely chopped
2   onions, finely chopped

2   tablespoons olive oil
Dash of Tabasco sauce
¼   teaspoon ground cloves
1   tablespoon salt
¼   cup chopped parsley
1   teaspoon oregano

Cut trout fillets into bite-sized pieces. Place in a flat dish, cover with lime juice, and refrigerate 4-5 hours. Drain and pat dry with paper towels. Combine fish with remaining ingredients and refrigerate at least 5 hours or preferably overnight. *Serve individually on leaf lettuce with a wedge of lime and crackers.*
Yields 8 cups. May be halved.
Mrs. John H. Wood, Jr. (Kathryn Holmes)

Mini Egg Fu Yung

3 eggs
½ cup chopped water chestnuts
½ cup chopped bean sprouts
⅓ cup chopped green onions
1 6½ ounce can tuna, drained and flaked
¼ teaspoon salt
⅛ teaspoon pepper
Soy sauce
Chinese mustard

In a medium bowl, beat eggs until light and fluffy. Fold in vegetables and tuna. Add salt and pepper, mixing well. Drop by tablespoon onto a lightly oiled hot griddle or skillet to make a small pancake. Cook on both sides until lightly browned. Serve hot with soy sauce and Chinese mustard.
Yields 2 dozen.
Mrs. George Rice, Jr. (Martha Lewis)

Ratitos

1 7 ounce can jalapeños, whole with stems
1 pound shrimp, cooked, peeled, and chopped; or 1 pound crabmeat; or ½ pound Cheddar cheese, grated
1 cup buttermilk
½ cup flour, divided
¼ cup + 2 tablespoons cornmeal, divided
Salt and pepper to taste

Slit each pepper on one side and remove seeds, leaving stems in place. Stuff with shrimp. Mix buttermilk, ¼ cup flour, 2 tablespoons cornmeal, salt, and pepper to make batter. Mix ¼ cup flour with ¼ cup cornmeal to make flour mixture. Dip each stuffed pepper in batter, roll in flour mixture, dip again in batter, and again in flour mixture. Deep fry until golden brown. Serve hot. *Jalapeños will look like a small mouse with the stem as a tail.*

Mr. Ken Harrell

Flaquitos

½ pound hot bulk sausage
½ pound ground beef
1 cup oil
1 dozen tortillas
¾ cup grated sharp cheese
Salt to taste
Picante sauce to taste

Brown sausage and ground beef in frying pan; drain. Heat oil in a separate skillet over medium high heat. Fill each tortilla with 1 tablespoon meat mixture and 1 tablespoon cheese. Roll tortilla and place seam side down in hot oil and hold until bottom hardens and will not separate. Turn and fry until crisp. Drain, salt, and serve with picante sauce.
Yields 12 flaquitos.
Mrs. J. Burton Barnes (Libba McClelland)

Jalapeño Pie

4   jalapeños, seeded
⅓   cup chopped water chestnuts
10   ounces Cheddar cheese, grated

1/16 teaspoon salt or Cheesoning
4   eggs, beaten

Preheat oven to 300°. Slice jalapeños into strips. Pave an 8-9 inch nonmetallic pie plate with jalapeño strips in a spoke wheel pattern. Sprinkle water chestnuts over jalapeños and cover with cheese. Using a spatula, press cheese lightly over the other 2 layers. Sprinkle with salt. Swirl eggs over pie surface so that seasoning blends through layers. Place pie on middle oven rack and bake for 25-30 minutes. Turn heat off and open oven door. After about 10 minutes, remove to a cooling rack. Cut in wedges and serve either hot or at room temperature. Cover and refrigerate any unused portion and heat before serving.

Mr. Ralph Rowntree

Mary Margaret's Green Chili Hors d'Oeuvres

1   4 ounce can green chilies
1   10 ounce stick Cracker Barrel
     sharp Cheddar cheese, grated
3   eggs, beaten
1   tablespoon mustard

1   teaspoon Worcestershire sauce
Dash of Tabasco sauce
Salt and pepper to taste
Paprika to taste

Remove seeds from chilies and drain. Layer in a greased 6 x 9 pan. Mix cheese, eggs, mustard, Worcestershire, Tabasco, salt, and pepper. Pour over chili peppers. Bake at 350° for 25 minutes. Sprinkle paprika on top. Cut into bite-sized squares and serve hot.
Yields 25-30 squares.
Mrs. Richard E. Dullnig (Sue Dunning)

Pinwheel Sausage Roll

1   package crescent rolls
12   ounces bulk sausage, at room
     temperature

Divide dough into 4 rectangles and divide sausage into 4 parts. Spread sausage on rectangles and roll in jelly roll fashion. Chill in freezer until each roll may be easily sliced into 9-10 pinwheels. Bake according to package directions. Drain on paper towels before serving.
Yields 36 pinwheels. Does not freeze well before baking.
Mrs. Wilbur F. Littleton, Jr. (Jean Richards)

Tamale Delights

6	tamales	1	pound bacon

Cut tamales into bite-sized pieces. Wrap each piece with ½ slice bacon. Broil until bacon is crisp, turning frequently. Serve hot.
Serves 8.
Mrs. Monte D. Tomerlin (Jacqueline R. Beretta)

Tiropita

12	eggs	1	pound butter, melted and divided
1	pound Feta cheese, crumbled	½	pound filo pastry
1	pound Gruyère cheese, grated		

Beat eggs until thick. In a separate bowl, combine cheeses with 1 cup melted and cooled butter. Add eggs and mix well. Brush remaining butter on 18 pastry sheets. Line an 11 x 14 x 2 pan with 10 of the sheets and add cheese mixture. Top with 8 remaining sheets of pastry. Bake at 350° for 30 minutes or until golden brown. Cut in squares and serve warm. *Expensive, but absolutely delicious!*
Yields 16 squares.
The Cookbook Committee

Place thin slices of hard salami on a rack over a shallow pan, generously cover with freshly grated Parmesan cheese, and bake at 300° until crispy. Drain well on paper towels.

Cheese Puffs

12	2 inch bread rounds	1	egg yolk, well beaten
¼	pound Cheddar cheese, grated	1	egg white, stiffly beaten
¼	teaspoon baking powder		

Toast bread rounds on one side only. Combine grated cheese, baking powder, and egg yolk. Fold in egg white. Spread on untoasted side of bread rounds. Place under broiler for a few minutes until hot and puffed. *Great as is or flavored according to your taste.*
Yields 12 cheese puffs.
Mrs. Richard H. Eckhardt (Mary Webb)

Mary's Cheese Squares

1	large loaf Pullman white bread, unsliced	2	sticks butter, at room temperature
1	pound Old English cheese, at room temperature	1	teaspoon Worcestershire sauce

Trim off crusts and cut bread into 1 inch cubes. Combine remaining ingredients thoroughly in mixer. Ice each cube on five sides. Place on baking sheet, plain side down. Freeze for 15 minutes, transfer to airtight container, and return to freezer. When ready to serve, remove number desired, and bake on baking sheet at 350° for about 10 minutes or until the sheen disappears. Do not brown. Serve hot. *These are fabulous and well worth the effort. This recipe came from my sister-in-law, Mary Folbre Pinnel, a former San Antonio Junior League President.*
Yields 5 dozen.
Mrs. Thomas W. Folbre (Polly McShane)

Cheese Melbas

White bread
Parmesan cheese, grated
Hellman's mayonnaise

Paprika
Thinly sliced onion, optional

Trim crust from slices of bread. Cut each slice into 4 squares or other shapes. Mix equal parts of cheese and mayonnaise and spread on bread squares. Sprinkle with paprika and bake at 400° until slightly brown. *This recipe may be varied by drying bread rounds briefly in a slow oven and placing a very thin slice of onion between two layers of the cheese mixture.*
Serves 8.
Mrs. T. Maxey Hart, Jr. (Mary "Mimi" Bond Austin)

Chicken Nuggets

3	whole boneless chicken breasts	1	teaspoon dried thyme or ¼ teaspoon powdered thyme
½	cup dried bread crumbs		
¼	cup grated Parmesan cheese	1	teaspoon dried basil
2	teaspoons Accent	1	stick butter, melted
1	teaspoon salt		

Cut each breast into 6-8 pieces, about 1½ inches in size. Combine bread crumbs, cheese, Accent, salt, and herbs. Dip chicken in melted butter and then in crumbs. Shape into nuggets. Place in single layer on foil lined baking sheet. Bake at 400° for 15-20 minutes.
Serves 4-6 as main course or 12 as hors d'oeuvres.
Mrs. Beverly Wheatley (Beverly Annette Klaver)

Ham Rolls

24 finger rolls or miniature bolillos	2 tablespoons prepared mustard
1 pound cooked ham, finely ground, or 3 cups	¼ cup finely chopped celery
	¼ cup pickle juice
3-4 tablespoons coarsely ground sour pickles	¾ stick butter, melted

Lay each roll flat on a cutting board and cut off end points with a serrated knife so that roll will stand up when sliced in half. Using a small, sharp knife or grapefruit knife, remove centers of rolls and further hollow out with a cocktail fork. Set aside rolls, toast and crumble the centers, and measure ¾ cup crumbs. Grind and measure the ham and pickles. Put bread crumbs through grinder to absorb remaining juice. Toss ham, pickles, and crumbs lightly with mustard, celery, and pickle juice using 2 forks. Dip edge of each roll into melted butter, spooning a few drops of butter into each cavity. Fill rolls lightly, but generously, with the ham mixture. Stand rolls side by side in a 9 x 13 x 1½ casserole. Rolls may be frozen at this point. Bake at 350° for 20 minutes or until thoroughly heated and browned.

Note Albert and Jane Maury Maverick's ham rolls have been a favorite in San Antonio for 100 years. The recipe originated during the post-Civil War days at Piedmont, the hospitable Maury home at Charlottesville, Virginia, when Virginia ham and other food was scarce. Albert Maverick, a son of Samuel Augustus Maverick, Yale law graduate, who signed the Texas Declaration of Independence as a delegate from the Alamo and whose name found its way into the American language, met Jane Maury when he was a student at the University of Virginia. They brought the recipe here when they came from their honeymoon trip in 1877 on one of the first trains to arrive in San Antonio. During their 70 years of marriage, ham rolls were a favorite at their table in their homes on Avenue E, where President Benjamin Harrison was a guest at the time of the first Battle of Flowers parade, and Sunshine Ranch, where as many as 150 illustrious guests, children, and grandchildren would gather for their traditional Sunday suppers. The recipe has been prized by their descendents, including more than 25 daughters, granddaughters, and great-granddaughters who have been members of the Junior League of San Antonio.

Mrs. Robert S. Morris (Lillian Maverick Padgitt)

In researching Ham Rolls, the Cookbook Committee discovered that each branch of the Maverick family has its own version of this recipe. Feel free to discover your individual variation. This recipe was tested using a food grinder, but it may be prepared with a blender or a food processor.

Granny's Toast Snack

1	loaf extra thin Pepperidge Farm white or wheat bread	1	stick butter, melted Parmesan cheese, grated

Trim crusts from bread and cut slices in half. Brush butter on one side. Sprinkle Parmesan on top. Toast in 300° oven until slightly brown. Keeps well in an airtight container.
Serves 10.
Mrs. W. Carlton Church, III (Ann Webb Schoenfeld)

Cheese Sticks

8	hot dog buns	1	3 ounce jar Kraft grated Romano cheese
1	stick butter or margarine, melted		

Cut each hot dog bun into 8 lengthwise strips. Brush all sides with melted butter. Sprinkle top with cheese and carefully transfer to baking sheet. Bake at 200° for 20-40 minutes until light brown and crisp. Store in airtight container. Best if heated before serving. *Fun to serve upright like bread sticks.*
Yields 64 sticks.
Mrs. William W. Coates, III (Sue Schoeneck)

Hot Cheese Cookies

2	sticks margarine, softened	1	teaspoon salt
½	pound extra sharp Cracker Barrel cheese, grated		Shake of Romano or Parmesan cheese
1	cup nuts (sunflower seeds, almonds, pecans, poppy seeds, pepitas, sesame seeds, or any combination)		Dash of garlic salt, optional
		¼-½	teaspoon cayenne pepper
		1	heaping teaspoon paprika
2	cups flour	1	heaping teaspoon dried parsley

Mix ingredients by hand or with mixer. Dough will be very stiff. Roll into 4 thin logs in waxed paper. Chill or freeze. When ready to use, slice into thin rounds and place on greased baking sheets. Bake at 350° for 10-12 minutes or until golden brown.
Yields 60.
Mrs. Hall Street Hammond (Patricia Wilcox)

Cheese Straws

1	stick butter, softened	1	teaspoon Tabasco sauce
1	pound New York State cheese, grated	¼	teaspoon paprika
1	teaspoon salt	2	cups cake flour or 1½ cups all purpose flour

Cream butter and cheese. Add remaining ingredients and blend. Roll out on lightly floured surface and cut in thin strips. Place on greased baking sheet and bake at 300° for 30-35 minutes. *This is a favorite given to me by my mother, Nadine (Mohm) Swallow.*
Serves 20.
Mrs. Milton Wagenfuehr (Betty Swallow)

Carol's Lace

Monterey Jack cheese   Teflon cookie sheet

Preheat oven to 350°. Cut cheese into 1-1½ inch squares, ¼ inch thick. Place on teflon sheet about 2 inches apart and bake at 350° for 5 minutes or until edges are slightly brown. Cool and remove with a spatula. *Sprinkle with paprika if desired.*

Miss Elizabeth M. Ridenhower

Peanut Butter Logs

1	loaf day-old, extra thin sandwich bread	1	cup peanut butter
1	cup graham cracker crumbs	1	cup cooking oil

Trim crusts off bread and cut each slice into 6 strips. Toast strips and crusts at 250° until dry, but not brown. Roll or grind crusts into crumbs and mix with graham cracker crumbs. Beat oil into peanut butter. Dip toasted strips into peanut butter mixture and lay on rack over foil or waxed paper to drip. Dip each in crumb mixture and dry in refrigerator on tray or rack over paper. Store in airtight container. *It's a messy recipe, but fun. Children love to help with the dipping.*
Yields 120 sticks.
Mrs. William W. Coates, III (Sue Schoeneck)

Squash Chips

| 2 | acorn squash | Salt to taste |
| | Peanut oil | Ground ginger to taste |

Peel and seed squash. Slice paper thin and soak in ice water for 1 hour. Drain and pat dry. Fry in deep, 400°F oil until brown and crisp. Drain and sprinkle with salt and a little ginger. Serve hot.
Serves 4.
Mrs. Frates Seeligson (Martita Rice)

Arkansas Hot Pepper Pecans

1	cup pecans	½	teaspoon salt
2	tablespoons butter, melted	6	dashes Tabasco sauce
2	teaspoons soy sauce		

Spread pecans evenly in a casserole or on a baking sheet and cover with butter. Bake at 300° for 25-30 minutes or until lightly browned. Mix soy sauce, salt, and Tabasco and stir into toasted pecans. Let stand at least 30 minutes and drain on paper towels. Pecans will keep for months in a tightly covered container. *This recipe was created as the result of many experiments using pecans from our orchard in Arkansas and is our favorite.*

Mrs. Jack T. Williams, II (Jane Yeaton)

Acapulco Jicama

| 1 | medium-sized jicama or yam bean | 2 | tablespoons chili powder |
| ⅓ | cup fresh lime juice | 2 | tablespoons Lawry's seasoned salt |

Peel and thinly slice the jicama. Do not prepare this in advance as it dries out. In one bowl put the lime juice, and in another bowl mix the chili powder and the seasoned salt. Dip jicama in the lime juice, then in the salt and chili powder mixture. Close your eyes and you're in Acapulco! *The texture of jicama is similar to a water chestnut, and the Mexicans often use it as a substitute. It can be thinly sliced and added to green beans.*
Serves 12.
Mrs. Travis Bailey (Martha Wiggins)

Dilled Carrots

1	pound carrots	1	tablespoon salt
½	onion, sliced	1	teaspoon dill seed
⅛	teaspoon cayenne pepper	1	cup vinegar
1	clove garlic	1	cup water
1	scant teaspoon sugar		

Scrape carrots and cut in thin strips. Combine carrots with onion and spices. Boil vinegar and water. Pour over carrot mixture. Set out overnight. Spoon carrots into a jar and refrigerate.

Mrs. Tony Chauveaux (Kathryn Williams)

Italian Marinated Vegetables

8	ounces button mushrooms, drained	1½	cups wine vinegar
1	green pepper, cut in bite-sized strips	1	teaspoon sugar
1	carrot, sliced crosswise	1½	teaspoons salt
1	head cauliflower, broken into flowerets	½	teaspoon pepper
1	pound can artichoke hearts, cut into fourths	2	teaspoons oregano, crushed
		2	teaspoons tarragon, crushed
12	small white onions or 6-8 green onions with 1 inch of their tops	½	cup salad oil
		½	cup olive oil
½	cup stuffed olives		Cherry tomatoes
			Minced parsley

Combine all vegetables, except tomatoes and parsley, in a large bowl. Heat vinegar and stir in seasonings. Cool slightly, combine with oils, pour over vegetables, and mix well. Cover and refrigerate for 24 hours before serving, stirring occasionally. Drain vegetables and arrange in a lettuce-lined bowl. Garnish with cherry tomatoes and sprinkle with minced parsley. Provide cocktail picks for spearing.
Serves 10.
Mrs. Edward E. DeWees, Jr. (Rebecca Ruth Davis)

Puerto Vallarta Teaser

6	unripened bananas	1	pound bacon

Peel and slice bananas into 1 inch pieces. Wrap each piece in ½ slice bacon and secure with a toothpick. Broil for 20 minutes or until bacon is done, turning once. Serve immediately. *Slices of bacon may be partially cooked before wrapping bananas.*
Serves 12-16.
Mrs. J. Ross Crawford (Judith Claire Bennett)

Stuffed Artichokes

4	artichokes	6	cloves garlic, minced
2	cups Progresso Italian bread crumbs	¼	cup grated Romano cheese
4	strips uncooked bacon, chopped	½	cup olive oil, divided
		½	cup water

Cut stems off artichokes, rinse, and turn upside down to drain. Combine bread crumbs, bacon, garlic, cheese, ¼ cup olive oil, and enough water to make mixture stick together lightly. With a teaspoon, stuff each leaf with a little of the mixture until entire artichoke is full. Do not remove choke. Dribble remaining olive oil over the stuffed artichokes. Put artichokes in a pot with 1 inch water. Cook, covered, for 45-60 minutes over low heat or until you can pull a leaf out easily. Serve hot as hors d'oeuvres or as part of main course. *These may be stuffed a day ahead to save time.*

Mr. Ben Adams

Spinach Balls

2	10 ounce packages frozen chopped spinach	¾	cup butter or margarine, melted
2	cups Pepperidge Farm Herb Seasoned Stuffing	½	cup grated Parmesan cheese
1	cup finely chopped onion	1	tablespoon garlic salt
6	eggs, beaten	½	teaspoon thyme
		1	tablespoon black pepper

Cook spinach according to directions and drain thoroughly. Add remaining ingredients and mix well. Pinch off and roll into bite-sized balls. Freeze. When ready to use, thaw slightly and bake at 350° for 20 minutes. Serve immediately. **Yields 65-70 balls. Freezes before baking.**
Mrs. Charles R. Jones

Tempura

1	egg	1¼	cups flour
1¼	cups water		Vegetable oil

Mix egg, water, and flour. Dip any of the following seafoods or vegetables in batter and fry in hot oil until crisp:

shrimp	onion	eggplant	mushrooms
lobster	green beans	sweet potato	green pepper

Serve with soy sauce, sweet and sour sauce, and hot mustard. Equal parts of soy sauce and lime juice also make a good dip.

Mrs. Harry Brusenhan (Laura)

Antipasto Misto

Antipasto
1	6 ounce package thinly sliced mozzarella, cut in half	6	hard-boiled eggs, halved
½	pound salami, casing removed and thinly sliced	¼	pound mushrooms
24	cherry tomatoes	1	14 ounce can artichoke hearts, drained
9¾	ounces solid white tuna	1	large onion, thinly sliced
1	tin anchovies, drained	16	ounces sliced beets, drained
1	4½ ounce can large ripe olives, drained	1	4 ounce jar pimiento strips, drained

Marinade
¾	cup olive oil	½	teaspoon dry mustard
¼	cup vinegar	½	teaspoon oregano
½	teaspoon salt	¼	teaspoon cracked pepper
½	teaspoon sugar	2	tablespoons capers

Antipasto Place a slice of cheese on each slice of salami, roll, and secure with a toothpick. Arrange separate ingredients in slightly overlapping rows in a shallow baking dish. Vegetables should not be layered or mixed.

Marinade Mix all the ingredients and pour over antipasto. Refrigerate for 8 hours before serving.
Serves 12.
Mrs. Edgar M. Duncan (Linda Wyatt)

Magnificent Mushrooms

⅔	cup chopped onion	1	egg, beaten
1	tablespoon + ½ stick butter, divided	1	tablespoon chopped parsley
1	pound large mushrooms	1	tablespoon flour
¼	pound ground beef	⅔	cup dry white wine
2	cloves garlic, finely chopped, divided	½	teaspoon dry mustard
½	teaspoon oregano	1	tablespoon lemon juice
Salt and pepper to taste		⅔	cup sour cream
		½	cup grated Parmesan cheese

Sauté onions in 1 tablespoon butter. Separate mushroom stems from caps, and chop stems. In remaining butter, sauté stems, beef, and 1 clove garlic until browned. Season with oregano, salt, and pepper. Add ½ of the onions, the egg, and ½ tablespoon parsley, and mix thoroughly. Stuff mushroom caps with mixture. Put caps in buttered baking dish and bake at 350° for 30 minutes. Prepare a sauce with remaining onions and parsley, garlic, flour, wine, dry mustard, and lemon juice. Cook until smooth and thickened, and add sour cream. Remove mushrooms from oven, put a little of the sauce into each cap, sprinkle with cheese, and broil until browned. Serve immediately.
Serves 10-12.
Mrs. Edgar M. Duncan (Linda Wyatt)

Mushroom Squares

5	slices sandwich bread	¼	cup shredded Swiss cheese
Butter		2	tablespoons salad dressing or
4	ounces mushroom stems and pieces, drained and chopped		mayonnaise
		1	tablespoon dried parsley flakes
4	slices bacon, cooked and crumbled	Dash of salt	

Trim crusts from bread and cut bread into quarters. Butter bread and place on a baking sheet buttered side down. Mix the remaining ingredients and spoon a small amount on bread squares. These may be prepared a day ahead, covered, and refrigerated. When ready to serve, bake at 400° for 7 minutes.
Yields 20 squares.
Mrs. Gordon W. Sixty

Mushroom Sandwiches

8	ounces fresh mushrooms, finely chopped	1	cup light cream
		2	tablespoons minced chives
3	tablespoons butter	1	teaspoon lemon juice
3	tablespoons flour	1-2	drops Tabasco sauce, optional
¾	teaspoon salt	1	loaf sandwich bread, crusts removed
¼	teaspoon Accent	Melted butter	

Sauté mushrooms in 3 tablespoons butter for 2 minutes. Blend in flour, salt, Accent, and cream. Stir until thickened and add chives and lemon juice. Roll each bread slice between wax paper until very thin. Spread 1 tablespoon of mixture on each slice of bread and roll. May be frozen at this point or refrigerated up to 24 hours. Dip in melted butter and toast. Cut in half for appetizer or leave whole to accompany soup or salad.
Freezes.
Mrs. Donald Krause (Neal)

Marinated Mushrooms

Whole button mushrooms in jars or canned French mushrooms, drained	La Martinique French Dressing
	Parsley

Marinate mushrooms in dressing. Chill for at least 24 hours turning several times. Drain and serve garnished with parsley. Use cocktail picks for spearing.

Mrs. George Johnston Ames (Annabell Ellen Sweeney)

Hot Pickled Mushrooms

¾-1 pound small fresh mushrooms
6   tablespoons olive oil (no substitution)
3   tablespoons white vinegar
1   teaspoon oregano leaves
1   teaspoon salt
½   teaspoon sugar

¼   teaspoon pepper
¼   cup sliced onion
2   tablespoons pimiento
1   clove garlic, sliced
Several jalapeño peppers

Rinse and trim stems from mushrooms. Pat dry. Cover with boiling water and let stand for 1 minute. Drain. Immerse in ice water until chilled. Drain again. Mix remaining ingredients. Pour over mushrooms, cover, and chill at least 24 hours. *These keep for several weeks in refrigerator.*

Mrs. Julian Craven (Eleanor)

Party Meatballs in Sour Cream Sauce

Meatballs
1   pound lean ground beef
½   cup soft bread crumbs
½   cup milk
1   egg, slightly beaten

½   cup grated Parmesan cheese
2   tablespoons dried minced onion
1   teaspoon salt
½   teaspoon pepper

Sour Cream Sauce
2   tablespoons butter or margarine
¼   cup flour
1   10½ ounce can beef consommé

½   cup sour cream
1   4 ounce can mushrooms
¼   cup dry white wine

Meatballs   Mix all ingredients thoroughly and shape into 1 inch balls. Place on baking sheet and bake at 400° for 12 minutes.

Sour Cream Sauce   Melt butter and blend in flour. Gradually stir in consommé, sour cream, juice from mushrooms, and wine. Stir until thickened. Add meatballs and mushrooms. Cover and simmer for 15 minutes. Serve in chafing dish. *Meatballs may also be served with sauce over rice, and they are good combined with spaghetti sauce.*

Freezing instructions   Cool meatballs on baking sheet 15 minutes after cooking. Place in freezer for 50 minutes, remove, and place in freezer containers.
Yields 35 meatballs.
Mrs. Robert N. Campbell, Jr. (Jacqueline Covo)

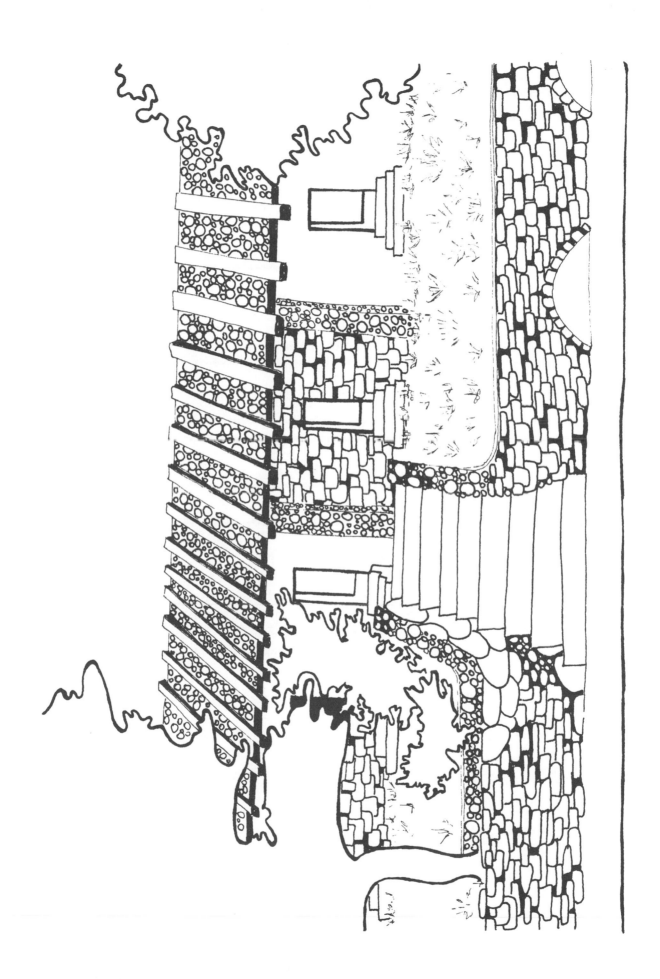

Bath House in Brackenridge Park

"Near the park's north end the river has been walled and floored to provide a public swimming pool. In this manner the river of Spanish dons has been turned to modern man's pleasure."

San Antonio's River.   Louise Lomax, 1948.

"The temperature of the river is of just that agreeable elevation that makes you loth to leave a bath, and the color is the ideal blue. Few cities have such a luxury. The streets are laid out in such a way that a great number of houses have a garden extending to the bank, and so a bathing-house, which is in constant use."

A Journey Through Texas.   Frederick Law Olmstead, 1857.

"The temperature of the water is nearly the same all the year through — neither too hot nor too cold for bathing — and it is seldom that a day passes in which all the inhabitants do not enjoy the healthy and invigorating luxury of swimming. I say all — for men, women, and children can be seen at any time in the river, splashing, diving, and paddling about like so many Sandwich Islanders. The women in particular are celebrated for their fondness for bathing, and are excellent swimmers."

Narrative of the Texan Sante Fé Expedition.   George Wilkins Kendall, 1844.

Tomato Sip

2	10½ ounce cans beef bouillon	½	teaspoon salt
3	cups canned tomato juice	½	teaspoon sugar
2	lemon slices	¼	teaspoon Accent
6	whole cloves	2	tablespoons sherry
⅛	teaspoon dried basil		

In a large saucepan, combine bouillon, tomato juice, lemon, cloves, and basil. Simmer for 5 minutes and strain. Stir in salt, sugar, Accent, and sherry. Serve hot in mugs.
Serves 10.
Mrs. Kaye E. Wilkins (Sidney Howell)

Hot Cranberry Punch

⅓	cup brown sugar	1	quart cranberry juice cocktail
½	cup water	16	ounces pineapple juice
½	teaspoon cloves	⅛	teaspoon salt
¼	teaspoon allspice		Lemon juice, optional
¼	teaspoon cinnamon		Slices of orange or lemon
⅛	teaspoon nutmeg		Butter pats

Combine sugar, water, and spices in a saucepan and bring to boil. Add juices and return to boil. Serve hot with slices of oranges or lemons floating on top. Have small butter pats available to melt in individual servings. Rum, vodka, or gin may be added. *This punch has been popular in cold weather at children's birthday parties, Christmas teas, and in the evening with liquor added.*
Yields 16 portions.
Mrs. Middleton S. English (Shirley Fitch)

Wassail

7	quarts water	4	sticks cinnamon
2	cups sugar	10	tea bags
1	cup lemon juice	2	cups any type fruit juice, fresh,
1	tablespoon whole cloves		frozen, or canned

Bring first 5 ingredients to a boil and turn off heat; add tea and fruit juice. Steep for 5 minutes and discard tea bags. May be served hot or cold, but hot is preferable as it makes such a spicy smell in the house while heating. Serve in punch bowl. *Bernardine Rice, who is a third generation resident of the South Presa Street historic district, serves this at her annual Christmas party. Economical and delicious.*
Yields 31 cups. Keeps indefinitely.
Mrs. Lewis Fairchild Fisher (Mary Maverick McMillan)

Mexican Punch

2   12 ounce cans frozen orange juice,
    diluted as directed
1   46 ounce can pineapple juice
2   .24 ounce packages cherry Koolaid

Juice of 1 lemon
1   28 ounce bottle ginger ale
2   tablespoons vanilla
1   tablespoon almond flavoring

Mix all ingredients. Fill punch bowl with crushed ice. Pour mixture over ice.
Yields more than 1 gallon.
Mrs. Raymond Judd

*For flavor and color, use cranberry juice ice cubes in tea and other summer
drinks.*

Spicy Orange Tea

4   tablespoons orange peel
5   2 inch cinnamon sticks, partially
    broken

2½ tablespoons whole cloves
¼   pound pekoe tea, or 2 cups
Honey or sugar to taste

Bake only the colored part of orange peel, not the white, at 200° for 1½ hours
or until dried. Blend with cinnamon, cloves, and tea and brew as you would
for regular tea, being sure not to brew longer than 5 minutes. Strain and serve
hot with honey or sugar. Dried tea may be blended and allowed to stand to
develop flavor. *This makes a nice gift when placed in a tea cup and sealed with
plastic wrap.*
Yields 2½-3 cups.
Mrs. Hall Street Hammond (Patricia Wilcox)

Spiced Apple Punch

1   quart water
3   Constant Comment tea bags
¼   cup sugar

2   cups cider or apple juice
Apple slices, fresh or frozen

Boil water, add tea, cover, and steep 5 minutes. Remove tea bags and stir in
sugar until dissolved. Add cider. Reheat and garnish with apple slices.
Serves 10-12.
Mrs. Walter Mathis Bain (Sue Howell)

Margaritas

3   parts tequila
1   part triple sec or Cointreau
1   part fresh lime juice

1   part fresh lemon juice
Salt

Mix all ingredients except salt. Dip glass in mixture, then salt, being careful not to get salt inside glass. Fill glass with crushed ice and margarita mixture.

Mr. William E. Fitch

Frozen Margaritas

1   6 ounce can frozen lime juice
6   ounces triple sec or Cointreau
9   ounces tequila

Crushed ice
Salt, optional

Combine liquid ingredients in blender. Add crushed ice and blend. Serve in salt-rimmed glasses.

Mr. Ken Harrell

Wine Margaritas

| 1 part fresh lime juice | 6 parts Chablis |
| 1½ parts triple sec | Salt, optional |

Combine liquid ingredients in pitcher. Serve in salt-rimmed glasses over crushed ice.

Mrs. Rex Watson (Ginger Jensen)

Apéritif de Jurbise

| 1 orange with rind that has not been artificially colored | 1 bottle of wine, red or white |
| 25-30 lumps of sugar | |

Peel the orange so that some of the pulp adheres. In a quart jar place the orange peel, sugar, and wine. Allow to set in a cool, dark corner for 30 days. Decant and serve as an apéritif. *I obtained this recipe from my "femme de menage" when I lived in the little town of Jurbise, Belgium. It is a poor man's apéritif and modulates the most ordinary wine.*

Mrs. F. R. Veach, Jr. (Dorothy Ann)

Peyton's Sherry Cobbler

Juice of ½ lemon	Cocktail sherry
1 teaspoon sugar	1 maraschino cherry
Dash of bitters, optional	1 orange slice, halved

Fill a highball glass, goblet, or Pilsner beer glass with crushed ice. Mix lemon juice, sugar, and bitters, and pour over ice. Fill glass with sherry. Garnish with cherry and a thin slice of orange. Serve with a straw.
Serves 1.
Ellen Fowlkes

Chi-Chi

1½ ounces vodka	½ ounce milk
2 ounces pineapple juice	1 ounce lemon juice
1 ounce coconut syrup	Crushed ice

Put all ingredients in blender for about 5 seconds. *Decorate with pineapple on rim of glass.*
Serves 1.
Mrs. Benjamin Bennett

Mint Julep

1 teaspoon sugar
3 fresh mint leaves
2 drops crème de menthe
1 jigger (1½ ounces) sour mash bourbon
1 pony (1 ounce) dark rum
Crushed ice
Bourbon
Fresh mint

Each Mint Julep must be prepared in an individual tumbler. Combine the sugar and the mint in a tumbler with a small amount of water. Muddle the mint with a spoon using the sugar as an abrasive. Add crème de menthe, bourbon, and rum. Cover tumbler with plastic wrap, and refrigerate overnight. When ready to drink, fill tumbler with crushed ice and bourbon. Garnish with fresh mint. *Obviously wicked! This was given to me years ago by Asa Beach, Jr. and is the best I have ever tasted.*
Serves 1.
Mr. Huard Hargis Eldridge

Moscow Mule

Crushed ice
1 jigger vodka
Juice of ¼ lime or to taste
Ginger beer

Fill a metal mug, preferably a copper one, with crushed ice. Add vodka, lime juice, and enough ginger beer to fill.
Serves 1.
Mr. Edward E. DeWees, Jr.

Naval War College Old Fashioneds

2 ounces simple syrup*
1 fifth bourbon
½ ounce cherry juice from maraschino cherries
Peel from 1 lemon
14 drops bitters
Orange slices, halved
Maraschino cherries

Combine ingredients, except orange slices and cherries, in a quart jar and let stand for at least 24 hours. Peel may then be removed or left in mixture indefinitely. Shake or stir well before using the first time. Further mixing is never necessary. To serve, put 2 ounces of mixture in an old fashioned glass, add ice, and no more than 4 ounces water. Garnish with orange slice and cherry.

*To make simple syrup Add 1 part water to 2 parts sugar and boil gently for about 1 minute (½ cup sugar and ¼ water makes 4 ounces).

Colonel George Privette

Orange Blossoms

6   ounces gin
1   6 ounce can frozen orange juice
    concentrate

Dash of almond extract
Fresh mint

Combine ingredients in a blender, add ice to fill, and blend thoroughly. Serve in champagne glasses or punch cups garnished with sprigs of mint. *Inexpensive gin may be used.*
Serves 4-6.
Mrs. Walter J. Buzzini, III (Minnette London)

Red Roosters

1   pint vodka
1   6 ounce can frozen orange
    juice concentrate

1   quart cranberry juice
Juice of 1 lemon

Mix all ingredients in a plastic container and freeze. Just before serving, whirl a few seconds in the blender.

Mrs. Howard Hasting

Ramos Gin Fizz

3   tablespoons confectioners' sugar
3-4 drops orange flower water
Juice of ½ lime
Juice of ½ lemon
1   jigger gin

1   egg white
½   glass crushed ice
2   tablespoons light cream
1   ounce club soda

Mix all ingredients in blender. Serve immediately in a tall glass. *This is the recipe used at the Cadillac Bar in Nuevo Laredo, Mexico.*
Serves 1
Mrs. Kenneth Reed Bentley (Carol Jane Case)

Tomato Flip

1   46 ounce can tomato juice
1   6 ounce can frozen orange juice
    concentrate

6   ounces vodka

Mix all ingredients and chill. Serve over ice. *A different drink to serve for brunch, one that ladies will enjoy.*

Mrs. Mason Matthews

Strawberry or Peach Daiquiris

16 ounces frozen strawberries or
    peaches, partially thawed
1   6 ounce can frozen daiquiri mix or
    limeade

6   ounces light rum
1-2 handfuls crushed ice

Combine all ingredients in blender and blend well. *A beautiful, delicious summertime drink.*
Serves 4-6.
Mr. John A. Bitter, III

Banana Pizazz

6   cups water
4   cups sugar
1   12 ounce can frozen orange juice,
    diluted as directed
5   ripe bananas
2   lemons with peeling, quartered
    and seeded

1   46 ounce can pineapple juice
3-6 32 ounce bottles ginger ale, regular
    or diet, chilled
Rum, optional

Heat water and sugar until sugar is dissolved. Combine bananas and lemons in blender with a little sugar water and blend thoroughly. Mix all ingredients except ginger ale. Freeze in ring molds. Thaw 1 hour before serving. At the last minute add 3 bottles ginger ale and stir. As the rings melt add remaining ginger ale as needed. *For extra pizazz add rum.*
Serves 50.
Mrs. Lewis Fairchild Fisher (Mary Maverick McMillan)

Boula

1   carton frozen fruit, preferably
    strawberries

1   cup brandy or cognac
2   bottles of champagne, chilled

In a punch bowl, marinate fruit in brandy or cognac for 1-2 hours. When ready to serve, add chilled champagne. *May be served over ice.*

Dr. Melvin L. Thornton

Sangria

1	lemon	4	ounces brandy
1	lime	4	ounces light rum
1	apple		Orange slices, optional
1	gallon red Burgundy		

Juice the lemon and lime and slice the rinds. Slice apple, but do not peel. Combine ingredients and refrigerate all day. Sliced oranges may be added, if desired. *This is a good sangria for those who do not like sweet drinks. Men are sure to enjoy it.*

Mrs. Alfred E. McNamee (Josephine McClelland)

Equal parts of Fresca and red wine with a slice of orange make a good, light, quick sangria.

White Sangria

1	orange, sliced and seeded	½	cup sugar
1	lemon, sliced and seeded	2	bottles white Burgundy
1	lime, sliced and seeded	1	quart club soda
2	whole cinnamon sticks	1	cup vodka, optional
½-1	cup brandy		

Place fruit and cinnamon sticks in a bowl and add brandy. Cover and refrigerate at least 4 hours or overnight if possible. Add sugar, fruit, and brandy mixture to wine. Chill for at least 2 hours. When ready to serve, remove cinnamon sticks, add club soda, and vodka. Pour over crushed ice in stemmed goblets. *Maraschino cherries add even more color to this delightful drink which also may be served in a clear punch bowl.*

Mrs. Tony Chauveaux (Kathryn Williams)

Mama's Eggnog

1	dozen eggs, separated	1½	cups heavy cream
1½	cups sugar	1½	cups light cream
2	cups bourbon		Nutmeg

Beat egg whites until stiff. Set aside. Beat egg yolks until cream colored and add sugar slowly. When blended, add bourbon and cream. Fold in the egg whites carefully and sprinkle the top with nutmeg.
Serves 8-10.
Mrs. Gerry Allan Solcher (Sally Sethness)

Old South Eggnog

12	eggs, separated	2	teaspoons vanilla
4	cups confectioners' sugar, divided	1	quart heavy cream
2	cups bourbon	1	tablespoon nutmeg
1	cup rum		

Beat egg yolks until cream colored. Continue beating and add 2 cups sugar, bourbon, rum, and vanilla. Beat cream until it stands in peaks and add 1 cup sugar. Beat egg whites until stiff, and add 1 cup sugar. Mix together in a punch bowl. Garnish with nutmeg. Serve immediately. *This very thick eggnog originated in Alabama and is a Christmas tradition with our family.*
Yields 40 servings.
Mrs. John Watson

Good bourbon is a must for eggnog.

Coffee Punch

1	quart strong coffee	½	teaspoon ground cloves
1	gallon vanilla or coffee ice cream	4	tablespoons brandy, rum,
4	teaspoons vanilla		whiskey, or Kahlúa
1	teaspoon ground cinnamon		

Mix all ingredients in a large punch bowl. *This recipe can be easily halved or quartered.*

Mrs. Anne Covington Phelps

For the best iced coffee, use ice cubes made from coffee.

Roman Punch

| 1 | quart lemon sherbet | 1 | split of champagne, chilled |
| 1 | cup choice rum | | |

Place lemon sherbet in a chilled bowl. Slowly mix rum into sherbet. Quickly add the champagne and serve in sherbet glasses.
Serves 8-10.
Mrs. Walter J. Buzzini, III (Minnette London)

Christmas Morning Milk Punch

1	pint or more coffee ice cream	¼	cup light rum
1	cup milk	1	jigger brandy
½	cup bourbon		Nutmeg

Mix first 5 ingredients in blender. Serve in punch cups with a dash of nutmeg on top.
Serves 4.
Mrs. Jon Grant Ford (Nancy Archer)

Red Hot Toddies

4	32 ounce bottles cranberry apple drink	2	oranges, quartered
¼	cup red hot cinnamon candies	1	fifth bourbon

Pour juice into a 24 cup percolator. Place candies and oranges in coffee basket and percolate as for coffee. Remove basket and stir in bourbon. Serve in mugs. *Great on a cold and cozy evening!*
Serves 18.
Mrs. J. Ross Crawford (Judith Claire Bennett)

Velvet Hammer

1	part Cointreau	1	part crème de cacao
1	part cognac	1	part light cream

Mix briefly in blender and pour over cracked ice in a champagne glass. *This is an excellent after dinner drink.*

Mr. John Kampmann Meyer

Kahlúa

4	cups sugar	1	fifth vodka
2	ounces instant coffee	1	vanilla bean
2	cups water		

Blend sugar and coffee. Add water and heat until dissolved. Add vodka. Cut vanilla bean in pieces putting equal amount in each quart bottle. Let stand 2 weeks.
Yields 2 quarts.
Mrs. Elmer A. Haile

Hot Wine Punch

1	6 ounce can frozen orange juice concentrate	2	cups port wine, red or white
1	6 ounce can frozen pink lemonade concentrate	½	cup honey
		1	orange, sliced
4	6 ounce cans water	1	lime, sliced
			Cinnamon sticks

Mix ingredients, except cinnamon sticks, and heat. Serve in a mug to which a cinnamon stick has been added. *Great on a cold winter evening instead of cocktails.*
Serves 6-8.
Mr. Alfred L. Shepperd

Vodka Wassail Bowl

	Whole cloves	10	cinnamon sticks
3	large oranges	2	cups vodka
1	gallon apple juice	¼	cup brandy
½	cup lemon juice		

Insert cloves in oranges, place in shallow pan, and bake at 350° for 30 minutes. Heat apple juice in a large kettle until bubbles form around the edges. Add lemon juice, cinnamon sticks, and baked oranges. Simmer, covered, for 30 minutes. Remove from heat; add vodka and brandy, mixing well. Serve warm in a punch bowl. *Serve with cream cheese on pumpernickel, thin slices of smoked salmon, cucumber sandwiches, and coffee.*
Serves 36.
Mrs. Jon Grant Ford (Nancy Archer)

Irish Coffee

1	tablespoon brown sugar	1½	tablespoons lightly whipped cream, flavored with sugar and vanilla
1½	ounces Irish whiskey		
3½-4	ounces hot coffee		

Put brown sugar in bottom of stemmed glass or cup. Add whiskey and fill with coffee. Top with cream. *Good, easy, winter dessert or after dinner drink.*
Serves 1.
Mr. Huard Hargis Eldridge

Mexican Coffee

24	cups hot coffee	1	cup Kahlúa or Kahlúa with brandy, to taste
16	ounces or more piloncillo		
3	ounces Mexican chocolate		Whipped cream or vanilla ice cream

In a large container or coffee urn, combine coffee, piloncillo, and chocolate, stirring until piloncillo and chocolate are dissolved. Add Kahlúa. Taste and adjust seasonings. Serve in demitasse cups with whipped cream for hot coffee and with ice cream for cold coffee.

Alternate Method 1   Substitute a 1 pound can of Hershey's chocolate syrup and cinnamon to taste for the piloncillo and Mexican chocolate.

Alternate Method 2   Substitute 2 cups of sugar, 3 squares of unsweetened chocolate, and cinnamon to taste for the piloncillo and Mexican chocolate.

Tasting is a must! The amount of sugar, chocolate, cinnamon, and Kahlúa should vary according to the time of day and type of food you wish to serve with this coffee.

Mrs. Harold Vexler (Esther)

New Orleans Café Brûlot

1	orange peel, cut into 1 x ⅛ inch strips	6	whole cloves
1	lemon peel, cut into 1 x ⅛ inch strips	1	2 inch cinnamon stick
		1	cup cognac
5	lumps sugar	½	cup curaçao
		2	cups fresh, strong coffee

Six hours before serving, combine all ingredients, except coffee, and cover. When ready to serve, heat the mixture and pour into a warmed chafing dish. Ignite. Slowly stir and pour coffee in a thin stream until the flames die. Ladle the café brûlot into demitasse cups and serve at once.
Serves 6-8.
Dr. Joe McFarlane, Jr.

Cafe Mystique

Strong, cold coffee	2	rounded tablespoons dry malt mix
Kahlúa or bourbon		Whipped cream
Ice cubes	1½	teaspoons brown sugar, optional

Fill blender beaker with ⅓ coffee, ⅓ Kahlúa, and ⅓ ice. Add malt mix. Blend and pour over ice. Top with whipped cream. Add brown sugar if using bourbon.

Mr. Don Strange

Mill Race Studio

"A somewhat 'lost looking' San Antonio River moves cautiously around one corner of a small stone building near Brackenridge Park Golf Links...This building was the second pumphouse constructed by the San Antonio Water Works Company in 1878."

"When the waterworks abandoned this pumphouse its fascinating story was just beginning. In 1925, Gutzon Borglum, the late sculptor, famed for his carvings on South Dakota's Rushmore Mountain, discovered the empty pumphouse and secured permission from the City Water Board to use it as his studio. He worked in it until 1937."

San Antonio's River.   Louise Lomax, 1948.

Chilled Cream of Avocado Soup

2   10¾ ounce cans cream of chicken soup
1   cup puréed avocado

1   cup light cream, chilled
¼   teaspoon white pepper
Chopped chives

Bring soup to a boil, remove from heat, and chill. Add avocado. When ready to serve, stir in cream and pepper. Pour into cups and sprinkle with chopped chives.
Serves 10.
Mrs. Edward E. DeWees, Jr. (Rebecca Ruth Davis)

Cold Avocado Soup

¼   cup minced onion
2   tablespoons butter
2   tablespoons flour
3   cups chicken broth
2   tablespoons lemon juice
1   teaspoon cream style horseradish

¼   teaspoon curry powder
Salt to taste
White pepper to taste
2   large avocados, sliced
1   cup milk
1   cup light cream

Sauté onion in butter until soft, add flour, and stir 1 minute. Add chicken broth and simmer for 15 minutes. Add next 5 ingredients and pour into a blender. Add avocados and blend until smooth. Stir in milk and cream. Serve hot or cold.
Serves 6.
Mrs. Kaye E. Wilkins (Sidney Howell)

Curried Apple Soup

½   stick butter
½   cup chopped onion
½   cup chopped celery
2½   cups chicken stock
1   tablespoon curry powder
2   tablespoons cornstarch
2   egg yolks, slightly beaten

1   cup heavy cream, heated
2   firm eating apples, divided
Salt to taste
Freshly ground pepper to taste
Lemon juice
Paprika

Melt butter; add chopped onion and celery. Cook until soft but not brown. Stir in chicken stock and curry powder. Add cornstarch mixed with a little water. Bring to a boil and simmer for 8 minutes. Add egg yolks to cream and stir gradually into soup. Remove from heat immediately. Blend mixture with 1 peeled, cored, and diced apple until smooth. Season with salt and freshly ground pepper. Chill. Peel, core, and dice remaining apple and sprinkle with lemon juice to prevent discoloring. Just before serving, stir in diced apple. Serve very cold in chilled bowls. Top with a sprinkle of paprika.
Serves 4.
Mrs. R. C. Wright

Cool as a Cucumber Soup

2 tablespoons chopped shallots, fresh or frozen
2 tablespoons butter
2 medium cucumbers, peeled and chopped
2 10¾ ounce cans chicken broth
3 tablespoons Minute tapioca

1 tablespoon red wine vinegar
Salt and pepper to taste
½ teaspoon dill, or to taste
12 ounces sour cream or low fat yogurt
Sprigs of fresh dill or toasted slivered almonds

Sauté shallots in butter until soft. Add remaining ingredients, except sour cream, and simmer about 30 minutes or until cucumbers are tender. Purée in blender. Add sour cream and stir until very smooth. Chill and serve garnished with dill or almonds.
Serves 4-6.
Mrs. Frates Seeligson (Martita Rice)

Cucumber Spinach Soup

1 bunch green onions, sliced
2 tablespoons butter
4 cups cucumbers, peeled and diced
3 cups chicken broth
1 cup chopped fresh spinach

½ cup peeled, sliced potatoes
Salt and pepper to taste
Lemon juice to taste
1 cup light cream

Sauté onions in butter until softened. Add all other ingredients, except cream, and simmer until potatoes are tender. Purée mixture in blender, pour into a bowl, and stir in cream. Chill for several hours before serving.
Serves 8.
Mrs. Robert L. Cook (Sandra Mueller)

Cold Spinach Soup

½ medium onion, chopped, or 1 cup
2 tablespoons butter
2 tablespoons flour
¾ cup chicken broth
¾ cup light cream

1 10 ounce package fresh or frozen spinach, cooked and drained
¼ teaspoon Accent
⅛ teaspoon white pepper
Salt to taste

Sauté onion in butter until tender, but not brown. Add flour and cook 2-3 minutes. Gradually add broth and cream, stirring constantly until mixture thickens. Stir in spinach. Purée in blender, add seasonings, and chill.
Serves 4-5.
Mrs. James Neal Martin (Susan Vandever Hammond)

Fresh Tomato Soup

1	cup minced onion	2	tablespoons tomato paste
2	cloves garlic, minced	2	tablespoons cornstarch
2	tablespoons butter	½	cup heavy cream
2	pounds ripe tomatoes, peeled, seeded, and chopped	¼	cup snipped dill or 1 teaspoon dried
3¼	cups chicken broth, divided		Salt and pepper to taste

Sauté onion, garlic, and butter until onion is soft. Add tomatoes and 1 cup broth. Simmer 20 minutes. Add 2 cups more broth, tomato paste, and cornstarch dissolved in ¼ cup broth. Bring liquid to a boil over high heat. Reduce heat and simmer, stirring occasionally, for 10 minutes or until thickened. Cool, force through a sieve, and chill overnight. Just before serving, stir in cream, dill, and seasonings.
Serves 6-8.
Mrs. Robert L. Cook (Sandra Mueller)

To garnish gazpacho, use chopped hard-boiled eggs, cold minced chicken, minced shrimp, cubed ham, or slices of avocado. For a different flavor add cumin, and for a creamier texture add sour cream.

Gazpacho

1	cup peeled, finely chopped fresh tomato	2	tablespoons olive or vegetable oil
½	cup finely chopped green pepper	½	teaspoon Worcestershire sauce
½	cup finely chopped celery	1	teaspoon salt
½	cup finely chopped cucumber	¼	teaspoon pepper
¼	cup finely chopped onion	¼	cup V-8 juice
2	teaspoons finely chopped parsley	1¾	cups tomato juice
1	small clove garlic, minced		Few drops hot sauce, optional
2½	tablespoons wine vinegar		Sour cream
			Finely chopped chives

Combine all ingredients except sour cream and chives. Chill thoroughly and serve in chilled cups or bowls. Top with sour cream and sprinkle with chives. *This recipe can be multiplied.*
Serves 4.
Mrs. Myron Chrisman (Marilyn Allen)

Curried Potato Pea Soup

1   10¾ ounce can cream of potato
     soup
1   10¾ ounce can green pea soup
14   ounces chicken broth
1   teaspoon curry powder

1   teaspoon celery salt
1   cup light cream
Sour cream
Chives or watercress, chopped

Combine soups and broth in a blender and whirl until smooth. Add curry powder and celery salt and heat. Cool, add cream, and refrigerate. When ready to serve, top with sour cream and a sprinkle of chives or watercress. Serves 10-12.
Mrs. Richard H. Eckhardt, Jr. (Judith Thomas)

Vichyssoise

1   2⅝ ounce package Knorr Leek soup
1   pound potatoes, pared and cut
     into ½ inch pieces, or 2 cups
½   teaspoon salt
Dash of white pepper

2   13 ounce cans chicken broth
2   cups milk
1   cup light cream, chilled
½   cup snipped chives

Prepare leek soup according to package directions, using only 2 cups water. Add potatoes, salt, pepper, and chicken broth. Simmer, covered, for 45 minutes until potatoes are very soft. Put mixture through blender, 2 cups at a time, until smooth. Heat milk until bubbles form around edges, remove from heat, and add to soup mixture. Mix well and chill at least 6 hours. Before serving, add cream, mix well, sprinkle with chives, and serve surrounded by ice.
Serves 12.
Mrs. Jack Harvey, Jr. (O'Linda Boggess)

Ripe Olive Soup

3   cups chicken stock or broth
1   cup pitted ripe olives
1   tablespoon grated onion
1   small clove garlic, minced
2   eggs

2   cups light cream
⅓   cup sauterne
Worcestershire sauce to taste
Salt to taste
Lemon slices

Simmer chicken stock with olives, onion, and garlic for 15 minutes. Beat eggs with cream, gradually stir in olive mixture, and return to saucepan. Heat and stir until it almost boils. Remove from heat and cool. Stir in sauterne, Worcestershire, and salt. Purée in blender and refrigerate. Serve in chilled mugs garnished with lemon slices.
Serves 6.
Ms. Jessica Bell

Hot Avocado Soup

6	ounces frozen Calavo guacamole	8	green onion tops, chopped
2	10¾ ounce cans cream of chicken soup	1	teaspoon chili powder
2	tablespoons lemon juice	1	avocado, coarsely chopped
1½	cups milk		Hot buttered croutons or chives, optional

Place guacamole, chicken soup, lemon juice, and milk in blender. Blend for 10 seconds. Heat in a saucepan with onion tops and chili powder. When hot, add avocado and serve topped with croutons or chives.
Serves 8.
Mrs. Donald M. Greer, Jr. (Anne Lindsay)

Split Pea Soup

1	large onion, chopped		Salt to taste
4	ribs celery, chopped		Freshly ground pepper to taste
2	ounces pork fat	3-4	lean ham hocks
1-2	tablespoons chopped fresh parsley or 1-2 teaspoons dried parsley	1	cup diced ham, optional
		1	16 ounce package split peas
1	clove garlic, minced	2	quarts water
1	carrot, chopped	1	teaspoon Tabasco sauce

Sauté onion and celery in fat. Add parsley, garlic, carrot, salt, and pepper. Add ham hocks, ham, split peas, and water. Simmer 2-3 hours or until thoroughly cooked. Add more water if necessary. Correct seasonings and add Tabasco. *This is best prepared ahead.*
Makes 3 quarts.
Mrs. Huard Hargis Eldridge (Earl Fae Cooper, Jr.)

Frijole Soup

1	pound pinto beans	1	16 ounce can tomatoes
½	pound salt pork	2	10¾ ounce cans chicken broth
½	cup chopped onion		Salt and pepper to taste
1	clove garlic, minced		Muenster cheese
6	tablespoons olive oil		Sour cream

Cook beans with salt pork until tender. Drain beans, reserving water. Purée beans in blender, adding reserved water as needed. Sauté onion and garlic in olive oil. Add tomatoes and cook for 10 minutes. Add beans and chicken broth and simmer 20 minutes. Place a slice of cheese in each bowl, pour soup over cheese, and top with sour cream.
Serves 6-8.
Mrs. George Campbell (Kathryn Cage)

Black Bean Soup

1	pound black beans	Tabasco sauce to taste	
1-2	quarts chicken stock	Salt and pepper to taste	
1	large meaty ham bone, fat removed, or 1 large or 2 small ham hocks	2	tablespoons Worcestershire sauce
¼-½	pound salt pork	2	large green peppers, chopped
1	cup chopped onions	1	large tomato, peeled and chopped
1	bay leaf	1	clove garlic, pressed
½	cup chopped celery with tops	Sherry to taste	
1	6 ounce can tomato paste	Lemon slices	
6	chilies serranos, chopped and seeded, optional		

Rinse beans and cover with chicken stock or use half stock and half water. At least 2 quarts of liquid will be needed. Add ham bone and salt pork and simmer for about 6 hours. Remove bones and put mixture, about 1 cup at a time, into blender to purée. Return mixture to pot and add remaining ingredients except sherry and lemon. Add more broth or water, if necessary. Simmer slowly at least 2 more hours. Add sherry just before serving and float a lemon slice on top of each serving.
Yields ½ gallon. Freezes.
Mrs. Edgar M. Duncan (Linda Wyatt)

Caldo Gallego
"Hot Pot from Galicia"

1½-2 cups dried navy beans, soaked overnight		3-4	potatoes, peeled and chopped, or 4 cups
1	large ham hock	1	10 ounce package frozen chopped turnip greens
2-3	cloves garlic, minced	3	teaspoons salt
2	large onions, chopped, or 2 cups	1	teaspoon pepper

In a large soup kettle, cook beans, ham hock, and garlic for 3 hours. When beans are tender, add remaining ingredients. Continue cooking until vegetables are tender. Serve hot. *I acquired this recipe during our 3 years in Spain. This is really a peasant soup served most often in Galicia and might be called "Spanish soul food". It is economical, hearty, and very filling. Men love it! The turnip greens really make it special and the soup can be watered down, reheated, and just gets better!*
Serves 6-8.
Mrs. S. G. Southworth, Jr.

Sopa de Lentejas

3-4 strips bacon or 4-5 tablespoons
    bacon drippings
1 large onion, chopped, or 1 cup
1 16 ounce can tomatoes

2-3 cloves garlic, mashed
½ pound lentils
Salt and pepper to taste
Tabasco sauce to taste

Sauté bacon, onion, tomatoes, and garlic in a soup pot until onion is tender. Add lentils and enough water to cover by 2 inches. Cook, covered, over low heat for 1-2 hours, stirring occasionally to prevent scorching. Add more water if too dry or thick. When lentils are very tender, mash or blend ½-¾ of lentil mixture. Mix with remaining lentils. If you prefer a smoother soup, purée all lentils. Season with salt, pepper, and Tabasco. *Lentils take less time to prepare than pintos so this may be prepared on short notice. This recipe is from the Copper Canyon Lodge in Creel, Mexico.*

Mrs. Charles Richard Eyster (Agnes Christian Welsh)

French Onion Soup

5 cups thinly sliced yellow onions,
    or 1½ pounds
3 tablespoons butter or margarine
1 tablespoon vegetable oil
1 teaspoon salt
¼ teaspoon sugar
3 tablespoons flour
3 10½ ounce cans beef bouillon,
    boiling

3 cups boiling water
½ cup dry white wine
Salt and pepper to taste
16 slices toasted French bread*
    or 2 cups croutons
½ cup grated Parmesan cheese
2 ounces Swiss cheese, slivered
1 tablespoon grated onion
1 tablespoon butter, melted

Cook onions slowly with butter and oil in a heavy, covered, 4 quart saucepan for 15 minutes. Stir in 1 teaspoon salt and the sugar. Increase heat to moderate and cook, uncovered, 35-40 minutes, stirring often, until onions are a deep golden brown. Sprinkle with flour and stir 3 minutes. Remove from heat, add bouillon and water, and blend well. Add wine, salt, and pepper, and simmer, partly covered, about 35 minutes longer. Pour over toast rounds and serve with grated Parmesan cheese.

Variation After adding wine, salt, and pepper, bring to a boil, pour into an oven proof tureen, and stir in Swiss cheese and grated onion. Float toast rounds on top of soup and sprinkle Parmesan cheese and melted butter over toast. Bake at 325° for 20 minutes. Broil for 1-2 minutes or until top is lightly browned. Serve at once.

*To toast French bread Slice bread ½-1 inch thick, place on baking sheet, and bake at 325° about 30 minutes or until thoroughly dried out and golden brown.
Serves 8.
Mrs. Lee Quincy Vardaman (Jane McCurdy)

Lettuce Soup

½ stick butter or margarine
½ cup chopped green onions
¼ cup chopped parsley
1 10½ ounce can beef broth
1 cup water

1 head lettuce, or 7 cups of leaves
1 cup light cream
1 teaspoon salt
⅛ teaspoon pepper
½ teaspoon dried leaf tarragon

Melt butter in large saucepan; add onions and parsley. Cook over medium heat until onions are tender. Stir in beef broth, water, and lettuce. Cover and simmer 25 minutes. Purée in blender or food mill. Return to saucepan and stir in remaining ingredients. Serve hot or cold.
Serves 6.
Mrs. Judson H. Phelps, Jr. (Clytie Thomas)

Mrs. Young's Spicy Farm Soup

1 quart water
1 46 ounce can tomato juice
1 small cabbage, coarsley shredded
3 ribs celery, chopped
2 tablespoons chili powder
¼ cup chopped onion
Salt to taste
1 green pepper, diced

1-2 bay leaves
3 tablespoons Worcestershire sauce
2 chicken bouillon cubes
2 beef bouillon cubes
½ teaspoon garlic salt or to taste
1 10 ounce package frozen broccoli
1 10 ounce package frozen cauliflower

Boil all ingredients, except broccoli and cauliflower, for 30 minutes. Then add the broccoli and cauliflower, and boil 20 minutes longer. *Keeps well in refrigerator. This soup hits the spot served with corn bread on a cold day.*
Makes 4 quarts.
Mr. Earl Fae Cooper

Borsch

1-2 pounds beef stew meat or soup bones
3 quarts water
1 8 ounce can beets, chopped
1 small head cabbage, shredded
3 carrots, chopped

4 tomatoes, quartered
1 rib celery, chopped in large pieces
1 medium onion, quartered
Salt and pepper to taste
8 ounces sour cream

Cover meat with water, bring to a boil, and simmer for 1 hour. Add remaining vegetables and simmer, covered, for at least another 2 hours. Serve in individual bowls with a spoonful of sour cream in each bowl. *Given to us by our Russian instructor who at one time was a page to the last Russian tzar.*
Serves 10-12.
Mrs. David B. Person (Bobbie Ann Harper)

Sopa Poblano

¼	pound lean pork, cubed	1	small zucchini, thinly sliced
1	tablespoon vegetable oil	3	tablespoons tomato purée
½	medium onion, chopped	1	quart chicken stock
1	ear of fresh corn, kernels removed and cob scraped	Salt to taste	
1	chili poblano, thinly sliced	1	ripe avocado, diced
		¼	cup Parmesan cheese

Sauté pork in oil over medium heat until browned, stirring frequently. Add onion, corn, chili poblano, zucchini, tomato purée, and chicken stock. Simmer 20 minutes or until vegetables are tender. Just before serving, add salt, avocado, and cheese.
Serves 4.
Miss Michelle Renee Knight

Pop's Peppered Soup

1½	pounds brisket	½-1	teaspoon freshly cracked pepper
10	cups water	Salt to taste	
5	ounces Rotel tomatoes and green chilies	½	cup dried barley
2	tablespoons chopped onion	1	10 ounce package frozen mixed vegetables
1	tablespoon La Choy Brown Gravy Sauce or Bovril	1	10 ounce package frozen cut okra

Trim ¾ of the fat from brisket and discard. Cut brisket in 1 inch cubes and boil slowly for 1½ hours in 10 cups water. Add tomatoes, onion, gravy sauce, pepper, and salt. Cook barley separately according to package directions for 30 minutes, drain, and rinse. Add to soup mixture along with frozen vegetables and cook 30 minutes. Adjust seasonings if necessary.
Serves 6.
Mrs. Alex Weil, III (Penny Speier)

Monterey Jack Cheese Soup

½	cup finely chopped onion	1½	cups medium white sauce
½	cup peeled and diced tomato	1½	cups milk
2	whole canned green chilies, chopped	¼	teaspoon salt
½	clove garlic, minced	Dash of pepper	
1	cup chicken stock	1½	cups grated Monterey Jack cheese

Combine onion, tomato, chilies, and garlic in a saucepan with chicken stock and simmer until vegetables are tender. Remove from heat and slowly stir in white sauce. Return to low heat and gradually add milk, salt, pepper, and cheese, stirring constantly until cheese is melted.
Serves 4.
Mrs. Vivian Cochran

Cheese Zucchini Soup

4 slices bacon
½ cup finely chopped onion
¼ cup chopped green pepper
2½ cups zucchini, cut in ¼ inch slices
1 tablespoon chopped pimiento
1 cup water
1½ teaspoons salt, divided

½ stick butter
¼ cup flour
¼ teaspoon pepper
2½ cups milk
½ teaspoon Worcestershire sauce
1 cup grated Cheddar cheese

Fry bacon until crisp and remove from pan. Sauté onion and pepper in bacon drippings. Add squash, pimiento, water, and ½ teaspoon salt. Cover, bring to a boil, and simmer 5 minutes. Melt butter in a 3 quart saucepan and stir in flour, 1 teaspoon salt, and pepper. Remove from heat and stir in milk and Worcestershire sauce. Boil 1 minute, stirring constantly. Remove from heat, add cheese, and stir until melted. Mix all ingredients together except bacon. Heat before serving and garnish with crumbled bacon.
Serves 6.
Mrs. John Henry Tate, II (Toby McClelland)

Cheese Soup

1 cup grated carrots
1 cup minced celery
½ cup minced onion
1½ quarts chicken stock
2 cups milk
2 sticks butter

1 cup flour
¾-1 pound sharp Cheddar cheese, grated
1 teaspoon salt
½ teaspoon white pepper
3 tablespoons Worcestershire sauce

Boil carrots, celery, and onion in chicken stock until tender. Add milk and set aside. Melt butter in a large skillet or saucepan. Add flour, cooking and stirring until well blended. Add stock mixture, continuing to cook until smooth. Add cheese, salt, pepper, and Worcestershire, stirring until cheese is melted. Serve hot.
Yields 1 gallon.
Mrs. Richard F. Halter (Beverly Francis)

Minestrone

2 pounds beef soup bones
3 pounds chuck or shoulder, cut in bite-sized pieces
1 28 ounce can tomatoes in purée or juice
1 15 ounce can tomato sauce
Celery tops
2 medium onions, quartered
¼ cup chopped parsley
1 tablespoon or more salt
2 teaspoons basil leaves, crushed
½ teaspoon pepper
¼ teaspoon garlic powder

2 bay leaves
3-4 beef bouillon cubes
Dash of Tabasco sauce
2 cups sliced celery
2 cups sliced carrots, parboiled
6-8 ounces uncooked shell macaroni, or 2 cups
1½ pounds fresh green beans, snapped and parboiled, or three 9 ounce packages frozen Italian green beans
1 10 ounce package frozen peas
1 16-20 ounce can white or red kidney beans

Place soup bones and beef in an 8-10 quart soup kettle and add enough water to cover meat and bones. Bring to boil and skim surface of liquid if desired. Add tomatoes, tomato sauce, celery tops, onions, parsley, salt, basil, pepper, garlic powder, and bay leaves. Bring to a boil again, reduce heat, cover, and simmer several hours or until meat is tender. Cool. Remove meat from bones and place that meat plus the other pieces of meat aside and strain the liquid. Return meat to liquid and add bouillon cubes and Tabasco. Refrigerate. The preceeding may be done a day ahead. Remove any excess fat that has hardened from the top. Add remaining ingredients, except kidney beans, and simmer, covered, 15-20 minutes or until macaroni is tender. Stir in kidney beans, heat until bubbly, and serve.
Serves 12.
Mrs. Ben Foster, Jr. (Raye Boyer)

Surprise Soup

1 10¾ ounce can tomato soup
1 10¾ ounce can split pea soup
1 10½ ounce can beef bouillon

1 soup can milk
2 tablespoons Worcestershire sauce
Curry powder to taste

Combine all ingredients and heat. Serve hot or cold.
Serves 8.
Mrs. Frederick C. Groos, Jr. (Martha Grace Bailey)

Chunky Potato Soup

6 medium potatoes, peeled and diced
2 tablespoons butter
1 medium carrot, diced
¼ cup finely chopped onion
2 tablespoons flour
1 quart milk

2 tablespoons finely chopped parsley
1 tablespoon salt
½ teaspoon seasoned salt
¼ teaspoon Accent
¼ teaspoon cayenne pepper
1 chicken bouillon cube

Cook potatoes in boiling salted water until tender and drain. Melt butter in a 3 quart kettle until golden brown. Add carrot and onion. Cover and cook until tender. Remove from heat, blend in flour, and stir in milk. Add ½ of the potatoes. Mash remaining potatoes. Add to soup with seasonings and bouillon cube. Heat until steaming hot.
Serves 6.
Mrs. James W. Pressley

Hot Spinach Soup

⅓ cup minced green onions
3 tablespoons butter
4 cups packed thinly shredded spinach leaves
½ teaspoon salt
½ teaspoon pepper

3 tablespoons flour
5½ cups canned chicken broth, boiling
2 egg yolks
½ cup heavy cream
Watercress, optional

Sauté onions slowly in butter in a covered saucepan for 5-10 minutes until tender, but not brown. Stir in spinach leaves, salt, and pepper. Cover and cook slowly about 5 minutes, or until tender. Sprinkle in flour and stir over moderate heat for 3 minutes. Remove from heat. Blend in chicken broth, return to heat, and simmer 5 minutes. If not served immediately, set aside uncovered. Reheat to simmer before proceeding. Beat egg yolks and cream in a large mixing bowl. Very slowly beat 1 cup of soup mixture into egg and cream mixture. Gradually blend in remaining soup. Return soup to saucepan and stir over moderate heat 1-2 minutes. Decorate servings with sprigs of watercress.
Serves 8.
Mrs. Charles Michael Montgomery (Gladys Fae Cooper)

Vegetable Soup for a Group

1½ pounds meaty beef shanks
1 pound stew meat
3 quarts water
2 tablespoons + 2 teaspoons salt, divided
½ teaspoon pepper
Celery leaves
2 large onions
Bouquet garni:
    2 bay leaves, crumbled
    ¼ teaspoon oregano
    ¼ teaspoon thyme
    ¼ teaspoon turmeric
½ cup chopped parsnips

1½ cups diced potatoes
1 cup diced carrots
½ cup diced turnips
½ pound green beans, cut into ½ inch pieces
1 quart shredded cabbage
½ cup sliced zucchini
2 16 ounce cans tomatoes
1 teaspoon sugar
1 12 ounce can corn
1 10 ounce package frozen peas
¼ teaspoon thyme
Alphabet noodles, optional

Place beef in a kettle with 2½ quarts water. Add 1 tablespoon salt, pepper, celery leaves, and 1 chopped onion. Place ingredients for bouquet garni in a metal tea egg or in a piece of cheesecloth tied securely. Add to kettle and simmer 3 hours. Remove celery leaves. Take out meat, remove bones, and cut meat into bite-sized pieces. Return to stock. Add parsnips, potatoes, carrots, turnips, green beans, cabbage, 1 chopped onion, and 1 tablespoon salt. Simmer 1 hour. Add zucchini, tomatoes, sugar, corn, peas, thyme, 2 cups water, and 2 teaspoons salt. Cook for 1 hour or more. Remove bouquet garni. If using noodles, it may be necessary to add 1-2 cups water.
Yields 5½ quarts.
Mrs. Edgar M. Duncan (Linda Wyatt)

A dash of cinnamon is a nice addition to avgolemono just before serving.

Avgolemono
Lemon and Egg Soup

6 cups chicken broth
¼ cup manestra or rice
1 teaspoon salt

3 egg whites
3 egg yolks, beaten
¼ cup fresh lemon juice

Combine broth, manestra, and salt in a large saucepan. Bring to a boil, reduce heat, cover, and simmer about 20 minutes or until the manestra is just tender. Remove pan from heat. Beat egg whites until stiff, and slowly add the egg yolks, continuing to beat. Beat in the lemon juice and slowly stir in about 2 cups of the hot broth. Pour egg mixture into the broth mixture, place over low heat, stirring constantly to prevent curdling. Serve immediately.
Serves 6.
Mrs. William W. Flannery (Magdalene Anthony)

Wonton Soup

10	7 x 7 inch wonton or egg roll sheets*, or ½ pound	4-5	water chestnuts, minced
½	cup pork, minced or ground	½	teaspoon salt
½	cup fresh shrimp, minced or ground	1	teaspoon sherry
1	tablespoon chopped green onion	½	teaspoon M.S.G.
4-5	mushrooms, minced	7-10	cups chicken broth, boiling
			Leaf spinach or green onion tops, shredded

Cut each wonton sheet into 3½ inch squares. Combine remaining ingredients, except broth and greens, to make filling. With 1 corner of square facing you, place ½ teaspoon of filling in this corner. Fold toward center twice, then bring right and left corners to center, sealing with a drop of water. When complete, each wonton will resemble a nurse's cap. Drop wontons in boiling soup and cook until they float, add ½ cup cold water or soup, and allow wontons to float again before removing. To serve, place 2 wontons in each bowl with about ⅓-½ cup broth and garnish with greens.

*To make wonton sheets   Mix 1 cup flour, ½ teaspoon salt, and 1 egg, and knead until smooth. Cover dough with a damp cloth for 30 minutes. Roll dough paper thin. Yields 40 3½ inch squares.

Mrs. Harry Brusenhan (Laura)

Wonton sheets are frequently filled with pork and seafood mixtures, but for a new twist try filling them with a sweet mixture. Purée dates in a blender with enough orange juice to make a paste. On each 3½ inch wonton square, place a spoonful of date mixture, roll diagonally, twist the ends as you would cellophane on hard candies, and seal with a drop of water. Fry in deep, hot oil until golden and roll in confectioners' sugar.

Egg Drop Soup

1½	quarts chicken broth	1	teaspoon or more soy sauce
1	egg	2	teaspoons chopped chives
2	tablespoons cold water		

Bring broth to a rolling boil. With a fork, beat egg and cold water until thoroughly mixed. Pour this slowly into the boiling broth, stirring constantly. Egg mixture may also be dropped in broth through a sieve. Season the soup with soy sauce and add chives. Soup may be prepared ahead and reheated. *Quick and easy! Serve in small soufflé dishes or custard cups placed in a straw basket filled with twigs to resemble a nest.*
Serves 8.
Mrs. Antonio Ponvert (Anne Duncan)

Tortilla Soup

1	medium onion, chopped	1	10¾ ounce can tomato soup
1	jalapeño pepper, chopped	1½	cans water
2	cloves garlic, minced	1	teaspoon ground cumin
2	tablespoons oil	1	teaspoon chili powder
2	pounds stew meat, optional	1	teaspoon salt
1	14½ ounce can tomatoes	½	teaspoon lemon-pepper seasoning
5	ounces Rotel tomatoes and green chilies	2	teaspoons Worcestershire sauce
		3	tablespoons Tabasco sauce
1	10½ ounce can beef broth	4	tortillas, cut in 1 inch squares
1	10¾ ounce can chicken broth	¼	cup grated Cheddar cheese

Sauté the first 5 ingredients in a large kettle. Add remaining ingredients, except tortillas and cheese, and simmer for 50 minutes. Add tortillas and cook 10 minutes. Pour into mugs and sprinkle with cheese. *With your first sip you will leave your chair, but quickly sit down and continue to sip. Hot but good!* **Serves 6-8.**
Mrs. Gilbert Lehne (Elvie)

Sopa de Tortilla

2	10¾ ounce cans Campbell's Chicken Broth, diluted according to instructions	1	teaspoon chopped onion
		3	small cloves garlic, minced
½	cup chopped celery	1	teaspoon chopped parsley
1	teaspoon chili powder	1	tablespoon olive oil
1	small tomato, peeled, seeded, and chopped	1	medium package (6¾ ounce) Doritos, regular flavor
		1	cup grated sharp Cheddar cheese

Boil broth, celery, and chili powder until celery is tender. Fry tomatoes, onion, garlic, and parsley in oil until onion is soft. Add tomato mixture to broth. Break the Doritos into medium pieces and add to soup, boiling briefly until the Doritos are soft. Add cheese just before serving.

Mr. Jack Beretta

Quick Delicious Clear Chicken Soup

2	13 ounce cans chicken broth	4	ounces very dry sherry

Heat broth to boiling and add sherry. Turn off heat and keep broth on burner for 2 minutes. Serve in mugs at once. *Good with sandwiches or for buffet brunch.* **Serves 6.**
Mrs. Helen Brooks Purifoy (Suzie)

Chicken Cheese Soup

1	whole chicken breast	1	10¾ ounce can cream of chicken
2	cups water		soup
⅓	cup diced celery	½	cup milk
⅓	cup diced carrots	½	cup grated sharp cheese
⅓	cup chopped onion		

Boil chicken breast in water for 20 minutes, or until tender. Remove chicken, cut into pieces, and reserve 1 cup of the broth. Add vegetables to broth and simmer, covered, for 10 minutes or until tender. Gradually stir in soup, milk, chicken, and cheese.
Serves 6.
Mrs. William J. Lyons (Bernice Beyer)

Creole Chicken Gumbo

1	5 pound hen	½	teaspoon fresh thyme
1	large onion, quartered	1	10 ounce package frozen cut okra
4	outside ribs celery with tops, divided		or 2 cups fresh okra, sliced, cooked, and drained
2	bay leaves	¼	cup chopped fresh parsley
Pinch of rosemary, crumbled		1	16 ounce can tomatoes
2-3	pounds raw shrimp	2	cups V-8 juice
1	small onion, quartered	Salt to taste	
Dash of cayenne pepper		Dash of Tabasco sauce	
2	green peppers, chopped	Cooked rice	

Boil hen with the large onion, 2-3 ribs celery, 1 bay leaf, and rosemary. When chicken is tender, remove, bone, and cut into pieces. Strain broth, discarding all but the bay leaf, and reserve 6 cups liquid. Cook shrimp with the small onion, remaining celery, cayenne pepper, and remaining bay leaf until pink. Drain immediately, cool, clean, and set aside. Heat reserved chicken broth and add green peppers, thyme, okra, parsley, tomatoes, V-8, and salt. Simmer approximately 30 minutes, stirring occasionally. Add chicken, shrimp, and Tabasco. Adjust seasonings and serve hot over a small amount of rice.
Serves 8.
Mrs. Charles H. Randall (Jane)

San Antonio Gumbo

6	tablespoons flour	Salt and pepper to taste
5	tablespoons bacon drippings	2 pounds raw shrimp, peeled
2	onions, finely chopped	2 7½ ounce cans king crabmeat or
1½	cups finely chopped celery	three 6 ounce packages frozen
1	clove garlic, pressed	crabmeat
1	28 ounce can tomatoes	1-2 10 ounce packages frozen cut okra
1	15 ounce can tomato sauce	3 tablespoons Worcestershire sauce
5	cups water	1 teaspoon chili powder

In a large, heavy kettle, brown flour in bacon drippings until dark brown. This takes a long time. Add onions, celery, and garlic and cook until onions are transparent and slightly browned. Add tomatoes, tomato sauce, water, salt, and pepper and boil over medium heat for about 1 hour. Add seafood and okra. Cook about 30 minutes or until desired thickness is obtained. Add Worcestershire and chili powder and continue to cook 5-10 minutes. *Serve over Mexican Rice (see index).*
Serves 25. Freezes.
Mrs. Hubert W. Green, Jr. (Leah Tritt)

Seafood Gumbo

1	10¾ ounce can clam chowder	1 large onion, finely chopped and
1	10¾ ounce can chicken gumbo	sautéed in 2 tablespoons butter
1	10¾ ounce can tomato soup	Salt and pepper to taste
1	10¾ ounce can chicken broth	Dash of hot sauce
3	cups of any combination of:	Herbs to taste
	fish chunks	1 10 ounce package frozen chopped
	shrimp, fresh or frozen	okra, thawed
	crabmeat	
	oysters	

Combine all ingredients. Heat until mixture begins to boil, immediately turn down heat, and simmer for 10-15 minutes.
Serves 6-8.
Mrs. Kip McKinney Espy (Sally Searcy Kleberg)

Crab Soup

1   10¾ ounce can cream of tomato soup
1   10¾ ounce can green pea soup
2   cups fresh or canned crabmeat

1-2   soup cans light cream or milk, depending on desired thickness
2   tablespoons sherry or to taste
Cooked rice, optional

Mix all ingredients, except rice, and stir well. Heat slowly in a saucepan over medium heat, stirring occasionally. Serve with a spoon of rice on top. *Good with Paprika Crackers (see index).*
Serves 6.
Mrs. David Keedy (Gladys Dimock)

Quahog Clam Chowder

1   slice bacon, chopped
¼   cup chopped onion
1   medium potato, peeled and diced
½   cup water
1   6½ ounce can chopped clams and juice
1   scant teaspoon salt
¼   teaspoon sugar

Pepper to taste
Thyme to taste
Rosemary to taste
1   tablespoon butter
1   tablespoon flour
½   cup milk
¼ -½ cup light cream

Fry bacon until crisp. Add onion and cook until golden. Add diced potatoes and water. When potatoes are cooked, add clams, juice, and seasonings. Make a cream sauce with butter, flour, and milk. Combine sauce with potato mixture and cool. Just before serving, add cream and heat to a simmer. *This is a specialty on Nantucket Island where originally only Quahog clams were used in this chowder.*
Serves 2.
Mrs. O. Elliott Ursin

Oyster Stew Savarin

½   stick butter or margarine
1   teaspoon Worcestershire sauce
Dash of paprika
1   quart raw oysters

1½ quarts milk
1½ teaspoons salt
Dash of pepper

Melt butter in a deep saucepan. Add Worcestershire and paprika, stirring until smooth. Add oysters and oyster liquor. Cook over low heat until edges of oysters curl. Add milk, salt, and pepper. Heat thoroughly, but do not boil.
Serves 6.
Mrs. Benjamin Wyatt

Lone Star Brewery

"When the Teuton colonists came in the forties they brought their music and thrift and love of home and good lager. A brewery was soon a first class paying investment."

Glamorous Days.   Frank Bushick, 1934.

The old Lone Star Brewery was purchased in 1972 by the San Antonio Museum Association. Since that time the brewery office, pictured on the preceeding page, has burned. The remaining restored buildings provide a home for the San Antonio Museum of Art.

Crisp Salad Greens

The Bright Shawl Tearoom, owned and operated by the Junior League of San Antonio and known for its crisp salad greens, recommends the following procedure.

Lettuce   This green should be washed and placed with the water that clings to the leaves into plastic bags or wrapped in damp towels. When it is thoroughly chilled, it may be torn and again refrigerated in bags or damp towels. Never cut greens for a salad; the leaves should always be torn apart.

Spinach   This delicate green bruises easily. Wash spinach only when ready to use, or it will develop a burned look at the edges of its leaves. To store, remove the stems, tear into pieces, and place in plastic bags. Just before using spinach, wash it thoroughly to remove all the sand and shake it as dry as possible.

Lettuce and spinach should not be combined until they are ready to be served.

Mrs. Vernon Gibson (Cecelia)

Add salt to a tossed salad just before serving as it breaks down the crispness of the vegetables.

Caesar Salad

1 clove garlic, crushed	Cracked pepper to taste
1 head romaine, torn into pieces	¼ teaspoon dry mustard
Juice of 1-1½ lemons	Parmesan cheese to taste
1 egg	Croutons to taste
2 tablespoons olive oil	1 2 ounce tin anchovies

Rub a wooden salad bowl with garlic, allowing a small portion to remain in the bowl, and add lettuce. In a separate bowl, combine lemon juice, egg, and olive oil and stir quickly with a fork. Pour over lettuce and add pepper, dry mustard, cheese, and croutons. Separate the whole anchovies and lay them individually in the salad. Sprinkle liberally with cheese and toss. *This was my mother's recipe. I have never tasted a Caesar salad as delicious!*
Serves 4.
Mrs. Kenneth Reed Wynne (Paula Gay Edwards)

For an unusual buffet salad, try "Lettuce Tortillas". Make available to your guests large outer leaves of Boston bibb lettuce, a selection of seasoned mayonnaises, and a variety of vegetables. Vegetables should be served in long strips either partially cooked or canned. Roll your own tortillas by spreading leaf with seasoned mayonnaise and roll around choice of vegetables.

Wilted Watercress or Garden Lettuce

4   bunches watercress, or enough to
    fill 1 large bowl
6   green onions, chopped
4   hard-boiled eggs, chopped

Salt and pepper to taste
¾   cup bacon drippings
6   tablespoons wine vinegar

Wash watercress carefully and chop in fairly large pieces. Add onions and eggs. Season with salt and pepper. Pour hot drippings over mixture and add heated vinegar. Serve at once.
Serves 12.
Miss Cora Alice Perry

Mandarin Spinach Salad

Fresh spinach
Hard-boiled egg, chopped
Mandarin orange slices
Bacon bits
1   cup oil
¾   cup sugar

⅓   cup catsup
¼   cup vinegar
2   tablespoons Worcestershire sauce
1   small onion, grated
Salt to taste

In a large salad bowl combine spinach, egg, oranges, and bacon bits. Blend remaining ingredients until sugar is dissolved and pour over the spinach mixture. *The dressing portion of this recipe yields enough for four 10 ounce packages of spinach.*

Mrs. Eugene T. Standley (Elizabeth W. Stuart)

For a new twist to an old favorite, substitute grapefruit sections for the mandarin orange sections in spinach salad.

Spinach Salad

1   cup fresh spinach, torn into pieces
Red onion slices
½   ounce bleu cheese, crumbled

2   teaspoons salad oil
½   teaspoon lemon juice
Salt and pepper to taste

Combine ingredients and toss. *This is a delicious salad that is not too high in calories.*
Serves 1.
Mrs. Howard E. Lancaster (Betty Lain)

Fresh Spinach Salad

1   egg
1   tablespoon grated Parmesan cheese
1   clove garlic, crushed
1½   teaspoons Dijon mustard
Salt and pepper to taste
½   cup salad oil

½   cup lemon juice
1½   pounds fresh spinach, stems removed
3   hard-boiled eggs, chopped
2   strips crisp bacon, crumbled
Fresh chives, chopped

In a jar, mix together thoroughly 1 egg, cheese, garlic, mustard, salt, pepper, salad oil, and lemon juice. Shake and chill. Tear spinach into pieces, sprinkle with chopped eggs and bacon, and toss with dressing. Garnish with chives. Serves 6-8.
Mrs. Fred C. Lepick, Jr. (Morgia Howard)

Spinach Salad Oriental

1¼   pounds fresh spinach, torn into pieces
½   pound bacon, fried crisp and crumbled
2   cups water chestnuts, drained
1   cup bean sprouts
1   red onion, sliced

4   hard-boiled eggs, chopped
1   cup salad oil
½   cup vinegar
¾   cup sugar
2   teaspoons salt
⅓   cup catsup

Combine first 6 ingredients in a large bowl and set aside. Combine remaining ingredients and whirl in blender. Pour amount desired over salad. Leftover dressing may be kept in refrigerator.
Serves 8.
Mrs. Robert Callaway

Hot Bacon Dressing over Spinach

3   slices bacon, cut in small pieces
2½   tablespoons olive oil
1   medium onion, thinly sliced
1   tablespoon flour
1   tablespoon sugar
1   teaspoon dry mustard
¼   cup vinegar

1   cup water
1   10 ounce package fresh spinach, washed, dried, and torn in small pieces
Salt and pepper to taste
1   hard-boiled egg, sliced
Croutons

Fry bacon until crisp, reserving 2½ tablespoons drippings. Add oil to drippings and sauté onion. Combine flour, sugar, and dry mustard, and add to onion mixture. Gradually add vinegar and water and cook, stirring constantly until thickened. Serve over spinach, season with salt and pepper, and garnish with bacon, egg, and croutons.
Serves 6.
Mrs. Edgar M. Duncan (Linda Wyatt)

Julia's Special Salad

14-16 ounces canned artichoke hearts
¼ pound fresh spinach
1 head romaine, torn in pieces
1 head endive, torn in pieces
1 cup mayonnaise
2 tablespoons capers
2 cloves garlic, crushed
¼ cup beef bouillon
½ teaspoon curry powder
Dash of Worcestershire sauce
Dash of Tabasco sauce
1 tablespoon dry mustard

Combine artichokes and greens in a large salad bowl. Mix remaining ingredients and pour over salad. Toss. *My mother, Julia Cage, is known far and wide as the best salad maker. This is one of her favorites. It is really delicious and different!*
Serves 10-12.
Mrs. George Campbell (Kathryn Cage)

Artichoke Rice Salad

1 package chicken flavored rice or brown rice cooked in chicken broth
4 green onions, chopped
½ green pepper, chopped
18 pimiento stuffed green olives, sliced
2 jars marinated artichoke hearts and the oil from 1 jar or canned artichoke hearts marinated in Italian dressing
¼ teaspoon curry powder
1⅓ cups mayonnaise

Cook rice according to package directions, omitting butter. Cool, add remaining ingredients, and mix well.
Serves 5-6.
Mrs. Frank J. Siebenaler (Louise)

Asparagus Vinaigrette

2 teaspoons salt
1 teaspoon cracked pepper
1 teaspoon paprika
½ teaspoon sugar
½ teaspoon dry mustard
¼ teaspoon cayenne pepper
¼ cup vinegar
1 cup olive or vegetable oil
2 tablespoons finely minced green pepper, fresh or dried
1 tablespoon chopped parsley
2 tablespoons sweet pickle relish
1 tablespoon chopped chives
1 tablespoon capers
2 cans asparagus
Pimiento strips

Combine all ingredients, except asparagus and pimiento, in a jar and shake well. Pour over asparagus. Marinate at least 4 hours. Serve garnished with pimiento strips. *May be served hot or cold.*
Yields 1¼ cups vinaigrette.
Mrs. Robert Lee Brusenhan, Jr. (Lollie Wright)

Mother's Stuffed Celery

1	stalk celery	2	whole pimientos, well drained
½	pound Cheddar cheese	3	tablespoons Durkee's Salad
1	cup pecans		Dressing

Separate the celery into ribs. Grind together, or finely mince, the celery heart, cheese, pecans, and pimiento. Mix well with Durkee's dressing. The mixture should be stiff. Be sure ribs of celery are very dry before filling each rib with this mixture. Reconstruct a stalk of celery by rolling tightly in foil or plastic, and refrigerate to set. When ready to serve, use a sharp knife to make ½ inch slices crosswise. *This recipe is a Christmas tradition in my family.*
Serves 10.
Mrs. Ernst Louis Goodrich

Avocado halves rubbed with lime juice, filled with caviar, topped with sour cream mixed with a small amount of mayonnaise, and sprinkled with chopped hard-boiled egg make an easy but elegant salad.

Philomena's Spanish Cole Slaw

1	cup salad oil	¼	teaspoon white pepper
1	cup white vinegar	2	pounds green cabbage, shredded
¼	teaspoon instant horseradish	1	pound red cabbage, shredded
1	cup sugar	2	green peppers, finely chopped
2	tablespoons salt	1	large onion, diced
2	tablespoons celery seed	1	2 ounce jar pimientos, slivered
¾	teaspoon black pepper	1	carrot, grated

Combine the first 8 ingredients and boil rapidly for 1 minute. Mix thoroughly and combine with vegetables. Refrigerate several hours or overnight before serving. This recipe is party size and it can be successfully halved, eliminating the red cabbage if you prefer. *Looks delicious served in a clear glass bowl or your favorite wooden salad bowl. This is true Texas fare served with brisket, ribs, barbecued chicken, or game, along with beans and corn bread.*
Serves 12-14.
Mrs. Carlos Perry (Jan)

Old-Fashioned Cauliflower Slaw

1	cup mayonnaise or salad dressing	1	large head cauliflower, separated into flowerets and thinly sliced
1	cup sour cream	1	cup thinly sliced radishes
1	package garlic-cheese salad dressing mix	¼	cup sliced green onions
4	teaspoons caraway seeds	½	cup chopped watercress or parsley

Mix the first 4 ingredients in a bowl and refrigerate. Mix remaining ingredients, combine with mayonnaise mixture, and chill 2-3 hours. The mayonnaise mixture may be prepared ahead and the vegetables combined, but they should not be mixed together more than 2-3 hours before serving. *Good served in the summer with barbecued meat. It's a crisp, cold vegetable dish and is a nice substitute for potato salad.*
Serves 8-10.
Mrs. William W. Coates, III (Sue Schoeneck)

Marinated Vegetable Medley

3	cups sliced zucchini	Lettuce
3	cups sliced mushrooms	Natural Swiss cheese, cut in strips
½	cup sliced green onions	Summer sausage, cut in strips
1	cup pitted ripe olives	
1	8 ounce bottle Italian or Caesar dressing	

Combine zucchini, mushrooms, green onions, and olives. Pour dressing over vegetables. Cover and refrigerate 3-4 hours, stirring occasionally. Serve on a bed of lettuce garnished with cheese and sausage. *This is a delicious main dish for luncheons or light suppers.*
Serves 6-8.
Patricia J. Lewenthal

Delilah's Yogurt Salad

8	ounces plain yogurt (not Swiss style)	1	teaspoon chopped mint, optional
1½	tablespoons vinegar	½	teaspoon salt
1	tablespoon chopped green onion	¼	teaspoon sugar
1	tablespoon chopped parsley	2	medium cucumbers, peeled and sliced lengthwise, then crosswise

Combine yogurt with vinegar and seasonings, then add cucumber slices. Chill well before serving. *Excellent with lamb, curry, or Middle Eastern dishes.*

Mrs. Robert Buchanan (Sara "Sally" Ware Matthews)

Onion Salad

2   large Bermuda onions, thinly sliced   Lettuce
⅔   cup sugar   Cherry tomatoes
1   package Good Seasons French
    dressing, mixed with lemon juice
    instead of vinegar

Cover onions with water and boil for 1 minute. Drain in a colander and quickly place in a bowl of ice water. Let stand for 15 minutes. Mix sugar and dressing, shaking thoroughly. Drain onions, add dressing, cover, and chill for at least 2 hours. Place onions on lettuce leaves and garnish with cherry tomatoes. *Serve with Paprika Crackers which are saltines that have been spread with butter, sprinkled with paprika, and toasted. Excellent with wild game and ham.*
Serves 6-8.
Mrs. John H. Foster (Phoebe)

Hearts of Palm Salad

¼   cup salad oil   ⅛   teaspoon dry mustard
1   tablespoon finely chopped green   1   hard-boiled egg, finely chopped
    onion   1   tablespoon chopped pimiento
1   tablespoon snipped parsley   1   14 ounce can hearts of palm,
1   tablespoon vinegar   chilled, drained, and cut into
1   teaspoon lemon juice   strips
¼   teaspoon seasoned salt   Boston lettuce

In a jar, combine oil, onion, parsley, vinegar, lemon juice, salt, and dry mustard. Cover and shake vigorously to blend. Add egg and pimiento, mixing well. Place hearts of palm on a bed of lettuce and serve with dressing.
Serves 4.
Mrs. James M. Cavender, III (Judith Gosnell)

Picnic Potato Salad

18	large potatoes, or 12 pounds	¼	cup prepared mustard
1	pound bacon	1½	cups sweet pickle relish
4	hard-boiled eggs	1	teaspoon M.S.G.
2	medium onions, chopped	2	teaspoons salt
2	ribs celery, chopped	1	4 ounce jar diced pimientos,
4	cups Hellmann's mayonnaise		drained

Boil potatoes about 1 hour or until they may be easily pierced with a fork. Drain, cool slightly, peel, and cut into ¾ inch cubes. Fry bacon, drain and crumble, reserving drippings. Pour hot drippings over potatoes, and mix gently until all the potatoes are coated and the grease is absorbed. Chop 3 hard-boiled eggs, add to potatoes, and save the other to slice for garnish. Add the remaining ingredients and mix lightly. Refrigerate overnight.
Serves 40-50.
Mr. Huard Hargis Eldridge

Dissolve 2 envelopes of gelatin in ½ cup water and add to your favorite chilled potato salad mixture. Line loaf pans with foil and thin slices of ham. Add salad mixture and chill. Unmold and garnish. Serve sliced.

Hot Dutch Potato Salad

½	pound bacon, cut in 1 inch pieces	Dash of pepper
2	tablespoons flour	4 large potatoes, pared, cooked,
2	tablespoons sugar	and sliced
1	teaspoon dry mustard	½ cup chopped celery
⅔	cup vinegar	⅓ cup chopped green onions and tops
⅔	cup water	1 pound link kiolbassa or venison
1	teaspoon salt	sausage, cooked and sliced

Fry bacon, drain and crumble, reserving ⅓ of the drippings. Combine drippings, flour, sugar, and mustard in saucepan, stirring until smooth. Add vinegar and water. Cook over medium heat, stirring constantly until thickened. Remove from heat and add salt and pepper. Arrange ½ of the potatoes in a shallow, oblong baking dish. Sprinkle with ½ of the celery, green onions, and bacon; then cover with ½ of the dressing. Repeat a second layer and bake at 350° for 25 minutes. The last 5 minutes sprinkle sausage over the top.
Serves 6.
Mr. Benjamin Wyatt

Tabouli

1	cup coarse cracked wheat, bulgur #2 grind	¼	cup olive oil
3-4	large tomatoes, chopped		Juice of 1½ lemons
4-8	cups coarsely chopped parsley		10-20 mint leaves, chopped
2	bunches green onions, chopped		Salt to taste
1	4½ ounce can chopped ripe olives		Cracked pepper to taste

Soak cracked wheat in cold water to cover for ½ hour; it will expand. Add tomatoes, parsley, green onions, and olives and mix well. Sprinkle with olive oil and lemon juice. Add mint, salt, and pepper. *Especially good with grilled meats.*
Serves 8.
Mrs. Kamal Abouzeid (Mary Pyman)

Sauerkraut Salad

1½	cups sugar	½	cup chopped celery
1	cup vinegar	½	cup chopped onions
32	ounces sauerkraut	½	cup chopped green pepper
½	cup shredded carrots		

Heat sugar and vinegar until sugar is dissolved, but do not boil. Drain sauerkraut, add the liquid to sugar and vinegar, and mix well. Pour this mixture over sauerkraut combined with remaining ingredients and set aside to cool. This will keep several weeks in refrigerator.

Mrs. James K. Ellis

Fire and Ice Tomatoes

¾	cup vinegar	⅛	teaspoon cayenne pepper
¼	cup water	1	teaspoon salt
¼	cup sugar	1	green pepper, sliced
1½	teaspoons dry mustard	1	onion, sliced
1½	teaspoons celery seed	6	tomatoes, peeled and sliced
⅛	teaspoon pepper		

Combine the first 8 ingredients and bring to a boil. Pour over pepper, onion, and tomatoes, and chill for 24 hours. *This is good to take on a picnic, layered in a jar.*
Serves 6.
Mrs. Robert L. Cook (Sandra Mueller)

Easy and Beautiful Salad

Tomato slices
Fresh mushroom slices
Artichoke hearts
Red onion slices
Green onions
Green pepper rings

Dill weed
Sesame seeds
Avocado slices
Fresh parsley, chopped
La Martinique French Dressing

Early in the day, using a large glass bowl, layer all ingredients except parsley and avocado. Add French dressing, cover, and refrigerate. Just before serving, arrange avocados on salad and sprinkle with parsley. Gently spoon dressing from bottom of bowl over salad and serve.

Mrs. Charles Parish, Jr. (Betty Caldwell)

Molded Spinach Salad

3   10 ounce packages frozen spinach
1½ envelopes gelatin
¼   cup water
1   10½ ounce can consommé
3   hard-boiled eggs, chopped
1   cup mayonnaise

1   tablespoon vinegar
1   tablespoon lemon juice
1   teaspoon horseradish or any
    picante sauce
Salt and pepper to taste

Cook spinach without water. Dissolve gelatin in water and add to heated consommé. Mix spinach with eggs, mayonnaise, and seasonings. Add consommé mixture to spinach. Put in a ring mold and chill.
Serves 6-8.
Mrs. James D. Folbre, Jr. (Jane Shotts)

Cottage Cheese Vegetable Mold

2   tablespoons gelatin
1   cup cold water
½   cup mayonnaise
2   cups creamed cottage cheese
⅓   cup vinegar
1   10 ounce package frozen chopped
    broccoli, cooked and drained

1   tablespoon minced onion
1   teaspoon salt
¼   teaspoon pepper
½   cup finely chopped carrots
½   cup finely chopped celery
½   cup sliced raisins, optional
Parsley

Soak gelatin in cold water about 5 minutes. Heat and stir until gelatin is dissolved. Combine mayonnaise, cottage cheese, and vinegar. Blend well with a beater. Add gelatin and stir. Add remaining ingredients, except parsley, and mix lightly. Pour into a lightly oiled 5½ cup mold. Chill until firm. Unmold and garnish with parsley.
Serves 8.
Mrs. Orvis Meador, Sr.

Emerald Salad

1   3 ounce package lime gelatin
¾   cup boiling water
¾   cup shredded, unpeeled cucumber
2   teaspoons grated onion

1   cup mayonnaise
1   cup cream style small curd cottage
    cheese
⅓   cup blanched, slivered almonds

Dissolve gelatin in water and cool until slightly set. Combine cucumber and onion, drain well, and mix with remaining ingredients. Add to gelatin, and pour into molds which have been rinsed in cold water or into an 8 inch pan. Chill overnight. *Perfect St. Patrick's Day recipe.*
Serves 6-8.
Mrs. William B. Schiller

Molded Guacamole Salad

1   cup boiling water
1   3 ounce package lemon gelatin
⅔   cup cold water
1   cup mashed avocado
2   teaspoons lemon juice
Dash of Tabasco sauce
3   tablespoons chopped onion

½   teaspoon sugar
Salt and pepper to taste
½   cup canned tomatoes, drained
    and chopped
¼   cup sour cream or ¼ cup sweet
    pickle relish, drained
¼   cup mayonnaise

Pour boiling water over gelatin and stir until dissolved. Add cold water and chill until slightly thickened. Fold remaining ingredients, except mayonnaise, into slightly thickened gelatin. Spoon into 8 individual molds and chill until firm. Unmold and top with a dollop of mayonnaise. *Especially good with any chicken entrée.*
Serves 8.
Mrs. C. B. Carraway

Tomato Confetti Salad

1   3 ounce package lemon gelatin
1   cup boiling water
1   10¾ ounce can tomato soup
Juice of 1 lemon
3   ribs celery, finely chopped

2   ounces slivered almonds
¼   cup chopped green pepper
¼   cup chopped onion
Salt to taste
Cracked pepper to taste

Dissolve gelatin in water. Add soup and lemon juice. Cool and fold in remaining ingredients. Pour into a greased ring mold. *Serve garnished with parsley and a good, tart mayonnaise.*
Serves 4-6.
Mrs. Arthur M. Eldridge

Tomato Soup Aspic

1	teaspoon gelatin	1	cup mayonnaise
¼	cup cold water	1	tablespoon Worcestershire sauce
1	10¾ ounce can tomato soup	1	teaspoon Tabasco sauce
9	ounces cream cheese, at room temperature	2	teaspoons salt, divided
		¾	cup cubed cucumber
1	tablespoon grated onion	½	cup chopped celery
1	teaspoon lemon juice	½	pint sour cream

Soften gelatin in water. Heat soup in a double boiler, add cream cheese, and whip until smooth. Add gelatin, stir until dissolved, and cool. Add onion, lemon juice, mayonnaise, Worcestershire, Tabasco, and 1 teaspoon salt, mixing well. Pour in a mold and chill until firm. At serving time, unmold and top with a dressing made by adding cucumbers, celery, and 1 teaspoon salt to sour cream.
Serves 10.
Mrs. Fred Bramlette (Lida Lee Denney)

Molded Gazpacho Salad with Avocado Cream

Gazpacho Salad

2	envelopes gelatin	½	cup finely chopped green onion
4½	cups tomato juice, divided	¾	cup finely chopped green pepper
¼	cup wine vinegar	¾	cup peeled, finely chopped cucumber, drained
1	clove garlic, crushed		
2	teaspoons salt	¼	cup finely chopped pimiento
¼	teaspoon pepper		Parsley
Dash of cayenne pepper			
2	large tomatoes, peeled, chopped, and drained		

Avocado Cream

⅓	cup mashed avocado	½	teaspoon salt
½	cup sour cream		Dash of cayenne pepper

Gazpacho Salad Soften gelatin in 1 cup tomato juice for 5 minutes. Heat until mixture simmers and gelatin is dissolved. Remove from heat and add remaining tomato juice, vinegar, garlic, salt, pepper, and cayenne. Chill until mixture begins to set. Fold in tomatoes, onion, green pepper, cucumber, and pimiento. Pour into a greased 6 cup ring mold. Chill about 3 hours or until firm. Unmold salad, garnish with parsley, and serve with Avocado Cream.

Avocado Cream Combine ingredients and blend well. *This recipe is particularly popular with men.*
Serves 6-8.
Mrs. Elkin McGaughy (Barbara Crossette)

Christmas Salad Ring with Sour Cream Dressing

2   1 pound cans sliced pickled beets
1   6 ounce package lemon or orange gelatin
¼   cup finely minced onion
½   teaspoon salt
⅛   teaspoon allspice

1   teaspoon +1 tablespoon prepared horseradish, divided
3   tablespoons lemon juice
½   cup sour cream
½   cup mayonnaise

Drain liquid from beets and measure, adding enough water to make 3½ cups. Cut beets into strips and set aside. In a saucepan combine the gelatin, beet liquid, onion, salt, allspice, and 1 teaspoon horseradish. Stir over medium heat until gelatin is dissolved. Remove from heat, stir in lemon juice, and chill until syrupy. Add beets to gelatin mixture. Pour into a 2 quart mold and chill until set. Unmold and serve with a dressing made by combining sour cream, mayonnaise, and 1 tablespoon horseradish. If a ring mold is used, place bowl of dressing in center.
Serves 8-12.
Mrs. Frank E. Rouse

Cranberry Grape Salad

1   pound fresh cranberries
2   cups sugar
2   cups Tokay grapes, halved and seeded
1   13¼ ounce can pineapple tidbits, drained

1   cup miniature marshmallows, optional
¾   cup chopped pecans
½   pint heavy cream, whipped

Grind cranberries or chop in blender. Add sugar and refrigerate overnight. Drain cranberries and add grapes, pineapple, marshmallows, and pecans. Fold cream into mixture and refrigerate. *A delicious salad for Thanksgiving or Christmas turkey dinners.*
Serves 12-16.
Mrs. Walter Mathis Bain (Sue Howell)

Honey Orange Salad

4   seedless oranges, peeled and sliced
2   tablespoons honey

½   cup shredded coconut
½   cup pecans, toasted

Combine oranges, honey, and coconut. Chill 30 minutes. Just before serving, add pecans. This does not keep well overnight.
Serves 6.
Miss Elizabeth Avenengo

"Texasize" Fruit Bowl

1   13¼ ounce can pineapple tidbits
2   11 ounce cans mandarin oranges
1   cup grapes, halved
2-3   bananas
1   pint fresh strawberries

3   tablespoons lemon juice
¼   teaspoon almond flavoring
1   22 ounce can peach pie filling
Fresh mint

Drain canned fruit and combine with fresh fruit. Mix lemon juice and almond flavoring with pie filling, stir in fruit, and chill 3-4 hours. Serve in a crystal bowl and garnish with mint.
Serves 8.
Mrs. James W. Curtis (Mildred Kay Fisher)

Minted Melon Bowl

1½   cups orange juice
½   cup sugar
1   tablespoon grated lemon rind
1   tablespoon lemon juice

¼   cup crushed mint leaves
3   cups cantalope balls
3   cups honeydew melon balls
Watermelon balls, optional

Combine the first 5 ingredients in a saucepan. Place over low heat and stir until sugar is dissolved. Bring to a boil, remove from heat, and cool. Combine melon balls in a large bowl. Strain syrup over melon balls. Chill several hours or overnight. Serve garnished with mint sprigs.
Serves 8.
Mrs. Jon Grant Ford (Nancy Archer)

Cut honeydew and cantalope into wedges. Using a melon ball cutter, cut 3 balls of melon from each wedge and place into the opposite fruit. Serve with mint sauce.

Applesauce Surprise

1   3 ounce package raspberry gelatin
1   cup boiling water
15   ounces applesauce

2   teaspoons lemon juice
½   cup chopped pecans
Mayonnaise or sour cream

Combine gelatin with water, add remaining ingredients, except mayonnaise, and chill until set. Top with mayonnaise or sour cream.
Serves 4.
Mrs. Arthur M. Eldridge

Cranberry Port Salad with Cream Cheese Sauce

1	16 ounce can jellied cranberry sauce		3	ounces cream cheese, at room temperature
1	6 ounce package raspberry gelatin			Light cream
½	cup cold water			Celery salt
2	cups cranberry juice, heated			Tabasco sauce
¾	cup port wine			Worcestershire sauce
½-¾	can water chestnuts, chopped			Onion juice

Heat cranberry sauce until almost liquid. Soften gelatin in cold water and dissolve in hot cranberry juice. Add cranberry sauce and stir until both gelatin and sauce are dissolved. Stir in port and pour into 10 lightly oiled individual salad molds. Refrigerate until partially set. Add water chestnuts and refrigerate until congealed. Make a sauce by thinning the cream cheese with cream and seasoning to taste with the remaining ingredients. *This salad may also be served with homemade mayonnaise.*
Serves 10.
Mrs. Virginia P. Sinclair (Virginia Phillips)

Daiquiri Salad

8	ounces cream cheese, softened			Few drops of green food coloring
1	3¼ ounce package instant vanilla pudding		20	ounces crushed pineapple
⅔	cup daiquiri mix		10	maraschino cherries

Mix all ingredients, except cherries, in blender. Freeze in a square pan until partially congealed. Distribute cherries evenly over salad and return to freezer until firm. Cut into squares, each with a cherry on top.
Serves 10.
Mrs. James Donnell (Leighton Collier)

Sea Foam Salad

2	pounds 5 ounces canned pears		1	cup heavy cream, whipped
1	3 ounce package lime gelatin			Mayonnaise to taste
6	ounces cream cheese			Grenadine to taste
2	tablespoons light cream			

Drain pears and bring 1 cup of the liquid to a boil. Dissolve gelatin in boiling liquid and cool. Mix cream cheese with light cream, add gelatin, and beat with electric mixer until blended. Chill until partially thickened. Mash pears and drain well. Fold pears and whipped cream into gelatin mixture. Pour into a mold and chill. Serve with mayonnaise mixed with grenadine.
Serves 10.
Mrs. George V. Burkholder (Gretchen Schneider)

Grapefruit Salad with Pineapple Dressing

Salad
4   large grapefruit
1   14¼ ounce can crushed pineapple
1   6 ounce package lemon gelatin
9   ounces cream cheese

Cream or mayonnaise
½   cup chopped pecans
Pomegranate seeds, optional

Dressing
2   eggs, well beaten
½   cup sugar
½   teaspoon salt
1½ tablespoons flour
1   cup pineapple juice from drained
     pineapple, heated

1   tablespoon butter
Juice of 1 lemon
½   pint heavy cream, whipped

Salad   Halve grapefruit, scrape out all fruit and juice into a bowl and reserve shells. Drain pineapple and reserve 1 cup of juice for dressing and the remainder for gelatin. Prepare gelatin according to package directions using reserved fruit juices for liquid and chill. Remove membrane from grapefruit and break fruit into pieces. When the gelatin is partially set, add the pineapple and grapefruit. Thin the cream cheese to a spreading consistency by adding cream. Add nuts to cheese mixture. Fill each grapefruit shell with a layer of gelatin, then cheese mixture, and another layer of gelatin. Chill until thoroughly congealed. Cut each shell in half, sprinkle with pomegranate seeds, and serve with pineapple dressing.

Dressing   In a saucepan combine eggs, sugar, salt, and flour. Add pineapple juice and cook, stirring until mixture thickens. Remove from heat, add butter and lemon juice, and chill. Fold cream into chilled mixture. *May be prepared ahead.*
Serves 16.
Mrs. Robert Beall

Molded Cream Cheese Salad

1   3 ounce package lime gelatin
½   cup boiling water
1   3 ounce package pimiento cream
     cheese, diced
3   ounces cream cheese, diced
1   cup pineapple juice

⅛   teaspoon salt
¾   cup pineapple chunks
½   cup broken pecans
½   cup chopped green pepper
Cherry tomatoes

Mix gelatin and water. Add cheeses to gelatin mixture and stir until most of cheese has dissolved. Add remaining ingredients except cherry tomatoes. Pour into 1 quart mold and refrigerate for 2-3 hours. Garnish with cherry tomatoes.
Serves 6-8.
Mrs. Richard Knight, Jr. (Darleen)

Spiced Peach Salad

1   28 ounce can spiced peaches
1   teaspoon cinnamon
6-8 whole cloves
1   6 ounce package orange gelatin
¼   cup sherry
½   teaspoon salt

1   6 ounce can frozen orange juice
    concentrate
½   teaspoon ginger
3   ounces cream cheese, broken into
    pieces

Drain liquid from peaches and measure, adding enough water to dissolve gelatin as the package directs. Boil liquid with cinnamon and cloves for 2-3 minutes. Remove cloves and dissolve gelatin in hot liquid. Add sherry, salt, orange juice, ginger, and cream cheese. Put the mixture in blender and whirl until cream cheese is well blended. Remove stones, cut peaches into pieces, and add to the liquid mixture. Pour into a 6 cup mold and refrigerate until set. *Serve with ham or poultry.*
Serves 10-12.
Mrs. Wilbur F. Littleton, Jr. (Jean Richards)

Strawberry Cream Squares

1   6 ounce package strawberry gelatin
2   cups boiling water
2   10 ounce packages frozen
    strawberries
1   13½ ounce can crushed pineapple,
    drained

2   large ripe bananas, finely diced
1   cup sour cream
½   cup chopped pecans, optional

Dissolve gelatin in water. Add strawberries, stirring occasionally until thawed. Add pineapple and bananas. Pour half of mixture in an 8 x 8 x 2 pan and chill until firm. Spread evenly with sour cream. Pour remaining half of mixture over sour cream and chill again. Cut into squares. Top with dollops of sour cream and sprinkle with chopped pecans.
Serves 9.
Mrs. Carl A. Nentwich (Carol Ann Cory)

Holiday Mold

1   tablespoon gelatin
¼   cup hot water
1   pint large curd cottage cheese

6   ounces cream cheese
Pinch of salt
1   pint heavy cream, whipped

Dissolve gelatin in hot water and cool. Work cheeses together with a beater. Add salt and gelatin. Fold in whipped cream and pour into a chilled ring mold. *Pretty served with homemade cranberry sauce in the middle.*

Mrs. Lyman W. Webb (Page Parker)

Crystallized Ginger Salad

1   20 ounce can pineapple chunks
     in syrup
2   tablespoons gelatin
4   tablespoons cold water
½   cup sugar
⅛   teaspoon salt
16   ounces ginger ale
2   tablespoons lemon juice
½   pound Malaga or green grapes,
     halved and seeded

1   orange, peeled and cut in pieces
1   grapefruit, peeled and sectioned
½   pound crystallized ginger,
     chopped
Lemon juice to taste
Paprika to taste
Hellmann's mayonnaise to taste

Drain pineapple and bring ½ cup of the liquid to a boil. Dissolve gelatin in cold water, add boiling pineapple liquid, and stir until the gelatin is dissolved. Add sugar, salt, ginger ale, and 2 tablespoons lemon juice. Chill until almost set. Fold pineapple chunks into chilled gelatin mixture with the grapes, orange, grapefruit, and ginger. Pour into a mold and chill. Add lemon juice and paprika to mayonnaise and whip with a fork. Unmold salad and garnish with mayonnaise.

Mrs. Pressly Shafer, Jr. (Margaret Fauntleroy)

Skins are easily removed from citrus fruits by pouring boiling water over the whole fruits and allowing them to stand for 5 minutes before peeling.

Imperial Salad

2   ripe bananas, mashed
¾   cup sugar
1   8 ounce can crushed pineapple
2   tablespoons chopped maraschino
     cherries

½   cup chopped pecans
2   tablespoons lemon juice
1   pint sour cream

Mix all ingredients together and freeze.
Serves 6-8.
Mrs. Keith Wurzbach

Curried Chicken Salad

2	cups cooked chicken, cut in large chunks	¼	cup capers
1½	cups sliced celery	½	cup French dressing
1½	cups cooked rice	½	cup sour cream
½	cup sliced almonds, toasted	1	teaspoon salt
		1	teaspoon curry powder

Combine chicken, celery, rice, almonds, and capers. Blend French dressing, sour cream, salt, and curry powder. Mix all ingredients and refrigerate. *May be served with chopped eggs, crumbled bacon, chutney, coconut, or peanuts, as for curry.*
Serves 8-10.
Mrs. Richard H. Eckhardt (Mary Webb)

Chutney Chicken Salad

1	cup Hellmann's mayonnaise	2	13¼ ounce cans pineapple chunks, drained
½	cup chopped chutney		
1	teaspoon curry powder	2	cups diagonally sliced celery
2	teaspoons grated lime peel	1	cup sliced green onions
¼	cup fresh lime juice	½	cup whole blanched almonds, toasted
½	teaspoon salt		
4	cups diced, cooked white meat of chicken		Crisp greens

Combine mayonnaise, chutney, curry powder, lime peel, lime juice, and salt in a large bowl and blend well. Add chicken, pineapple, celery, onions, and almonds. Mix well and serve on crisp greens. *May be prepared a day ahead and will keep several days if you do not add the dressing. Always add the almonds just before serving.*
Serves 6-8.
Mrs. Pierce Sullivan (Mary Wallace Kerr)

South of the Border Salad

3	carrots, scraped	¼	cup minced onion
	Chicken broth	¼	cup chopped green onions
1	large potato	½	cup chopped celery
4	cups cold, cooked, cubed chicken	1	tablespoon chopped parsley
1	medium green pepper, chopped	1	cup homemade mayonnaise
1	4 ounce can chopped green chilies, drained		Salt and pepper to taste

Cook carrots in chicken broth 10-15 minutes, cool, and chop. Boil potato in chicken broth about 30 minutes or until done, cool, peel, and cube. Add remaining ingredients to carrots and potatoes, mixing well. Chill before serving.

Lena Torres

Paella Salad

1   6 ounce package yellow or saffron
    rice
2   tablespoons tarragon vinegar
⅓   cup vegetable oil
1⅛ teaspoons salt, divided
⅛   teaspoon dry mustard
¼   teaspoon Accent
2½ cups diced, cooked chicken

1   tomato, peeled and chopped
1   green pepper, chopped
½   cup cooked green peas
¼   cup minced onion
⅓   cup finely sliced celery
1   tablespoon chopped pimiento
Crisp salad greens

Cook rice according to package directions. Mix together vinegar, oil, ⅛ teaspoon salt, dry mustard, and Accent. Immediately pour over cooked rice. Let
stand at room temperature until cool. Add chicken, 1 teaspoon salt, and remaining ingredients except salad greens. Toss lightly to mix and refrigerate for
2-3 hours. Serve on crisp salad greens. *May be prepared ahead. Great for
gourmet picnics.*
Serves 6.
Mrs. Middleton S. English (Shirley Fitch)

Mexican Chef Salad

1   pound ground beef
4   teaspoons ground cumin
Salt to taste
2   teaspoons cracked pepper
1   small head lettuce, torn into pieces
1   large tomato, chopped
1   avocado, chopped

1   small onion, minced
½   cup grated Cheddar cheese
1   cup coarsely crushed Fritos
1   15 ounce can kidney beans, heated
    and drained
Buttermilk type salad dressing
Picante sauce to taste

Brown beef, drain excess grease, and add cumin, salt, and pepper. In a large
bowl, toss lettuce, tomato, avocado, onion, cheese, and Fritos. Add beef and
beans. Toss with dressing and serve with picante sauce.

Variation   Substitute ranch style beans which have been drained, washed,
and chilled for the kidney beans; and 1½-2 10 ounce cans of Old El Paso
chopped green tomatoes and chilies for the buttermilk type dressing.
Serves 4.
Mrs. Monte D. Tomerlin (Jacqueline R. Beretta)

Corned Beef Salad

1 3 ounce package lemon gelatin	1 cup chopped cucumber
1¾ cups hot water	1 cup minced onion
1 cup mayonnaise	2 hard-boiled eggs, chopped
1 12 ounce can corned beef, minced	1 teaspoon horseradish
1 cup chopped celery	Olives

Dissolve gelatin in water and cool until thickened. Stir in mayonnaise, corned beef, celery, cucumber, onion, eggs, and horseradish. Put in a greased mold, decorate with olives, and refrigerate overnight.
Serves 12.
Mrs. John F. Loyd (Annette Emerson)

Tuna Cashew Salad

1 9¼ ounce can solid white meat tuna	⅔ cup mayonnaise
1 cup diced celery	1 tablespoon curry powder, optional
¼ cup chopped green onions	1 tablespoon lemon juice
2 tablespoons capers or sliced olives	Cantaloupe or pineapple rings
½ cup cashew nuts	Red tip lettuce

Mix tuna, celery, green onions, capers, and cashew nuts in a large bowl. Set aside. Combine mayonnaise, curry powder, and lemon juice. Pour over tuna mixture, toss, and chill. Serve on cantaloupe or pineapple rings on a bed of lettuce.
Serves 4.
Mrs. Ted Thomas (Nell Ezell)

Shrimp and Crab Salad

2 cups cooked, peeled shrimp, cut in pieces	¾ cup Kraft Creamy French Dressing
2 cups crabmeat	2 cups chopped celery

Combine shrimp and crabmeat and marinate in French dressing. Add celery and mix well.
Serves 8-10.
Mrs. Henry W. Sebesta, Jr. (Patricia Klaver)

For company fare, place a thin bed of shredded lettuce 3-4 inches in diameter on each plate. Center a tomato slice on the lettuce and top with an artichoke bottom. Spoon salad mixture into artichoke, garnish with whole shrimp and strips of pimiento, and top with mayonnaise. Sprinkle chopped, hard-boiled egg over the outer circle of lettuce. Et voilá, shrimp and crab salad that looks as good as it tastes.

Seafood Tomato Aspic Supreme

1   10¾ ounce can tomato soup
12 ounces V-8 juice
8   ounces cream cheese
4   tablespoons gelatin
½   cup water
Salt to taste
1   tablespoon Tabasco sauce
1   cup Hellmann's mayonnaise
¾   cup chopped green pepper
¾   cup chopped celery
¼   cup chopped green onion tops

1   2 ounce bottle pimiento stuffed
    green olives, finely sliced
2   avocados, mashed
1   medium onion, chopped
Squeeze of lemon
1   tablespoon parsley flakes
1   pound cooked shrimp, peeled,
    cleaned, and cut into bite-sized
    pieces
1   6 ounce can Blue Plate crabmeat,
    flaked

Heat soup, juice, and cream cheese. Strain to remove any remaining lumps of cheese. Dissolve gelatin in water and add to soup mixture. Add remaining ingredients and chill. *This salad is pretty garnished with artichoke hearts, pickled cucumbers, and ripe olives. Serve with thin bacon flavored crackers or finger sandwiches.*
Serves 12.
Mrs. Irene S. Zipp

Crab or Shrimp Mold

1   tablespoon gelatin
¼   cup cold water
¾   cup tomato juice, heated
3   ounces cream cheese, at room
    temperature
¾   cup mayonnaise
½   teaspoon salt

2   tablespoons lemon juice
⅓   cup finely diced green pepper
1   cup diced celery
1½ teaspoons grated onion
½   pound crabmeat or shrimp
Crisp salad greens

Soften gelatin in cold water, dissolve in tomato juice, and cool. Cream the cheese until very smooth, blend with mayonnaise, and stir into tomato juice mixture. When mixture has thickened slightly add remaining ingredients, except salad greens, and pour into individual molds. Chill until firm. Unmold on crisp salad greens.
Serves 8.
Mrs. William W. Beuhler

Shrimp Mold

11   ounces cream cheese
3   tablespoons mayonnaise
½   package gelatin, dissolved in
     2 tablespoons cold water
1½ tablespoons lemon juice
1   pound cooked shrimp, finely
     chopped

½   cup finely diced celery
1   onion, finely grated
2   hard-boiled eggs, finely diced
Salt and pepper to taste
2   teaspoons Tabasco sauce
Parsley

Combine the first 4 ingredients. Add remaining ingredients, except parsley, and pour into a lightly oiled mold. Refrigerate until set and garnish with parsley. *This mold may also be served with crackers as an hors d'oeuvre.*
Serves 12 for salad, 24 for hors d'oeuvre.
Mrs. Walter Hale, III (Janin Sinclair)

Salmon Mousse with Dill Sauce

Salmon Mousse
2   envelopes gelatin
½   cup water
1   10¾ ounce can tomato soup
9   ounces cream cheese
½   cup chopped olives
½   cup chopped celery
½   cup chopped onion
1   tablespoon capers

½   cup chopped green pepper
1   cup mayonnaise
5   drops Tabasco sauce
1   teaspoon Worcestershire sauce
Juice of 1 lemon
1   15½ ounce can sockeye (red)
     salmon, drained and flaked, or
     other seafood

Dill Sauce
1   egg
1   teaspoon salt
Pinch of pepper
Pinch of sugar
4   teaspoons lemon juice

1   teaspoon grated onion
2   tablespoons finely cut fresh dill or
     1 tablespoon dried dill
1½ cups sour cream

Salmon Mousse Soften gelatin in water. Heat soup to boiling and stir in gelatin until dissolved. Pour over cream cheese and beat until smooth using a mixer or blender. Stir in remaining ingredients. Pour into a 2 quart mold greased with mayonnaise. Chill at least 3 hours or preferably overnight. Serve with Dill Sauce.

Dill Sauce Beat egg until fluffy. Stir in remaining ingredients, and chill.

This mousse may be unmolded on a bed of lettuce and garnished with sliced hard-boiled eggs and thin slices of cucumber. If a fish mold is used, make cucumber "scales" and use an olive for the "eye"
Serves 8.
Mrs. Richard T. Davis (Mary Catherine "Buzzy" McClure)

Lila's Salad Dressing

½ cup salad oil
½ cup garlic wine vinegar
¼ cup sugar or to taste

1 tablespoon Lawry's seasoned salt
1 tablespoon lemon juice
Pepper to taste

Combine ingredients, shake well, and store covered in refrigerator.

Mrs. James Michael Bell (Marion Dewar)

Lemon Herb Salad Dressing

1 cup safflower oil
⅓ cup fresh lemon juice
1 teaspoon salt
¼ teaspoon pepper

¼ teaspoon basil
¼ teaspoon oregano
¼ teaspoon thyme or tarragon
1 clove garlic, minced

Blend together in a bowl or shake in a jar until thoroughly mixed.

Mrs. Robert Buchanan (Sara "Sally" Ware Matthews)

Mama's Favorite Dressing

½ cup vegetable oil
3 tablespoons white vinegar
1 teaspoon salt
¼ teaspoon black pepper

1 tablespoon sugar
2 tablespoons finely grated onion
¼ cup Heinz chili sauce

Mix all ingredients lightly in shaker. *Serve on salad of sliced tomatoes, asparagus, and grapefruit slices.*
Serves 4.
Mrs. Jeremiah Handy (Patricia Fullingim)

Dione Lucas' Salad Dressing

1 teaspoon kosher salt
½ teaspoon freshly cracked white pepper
½ teaspoon freshly cracked black pepper
¼ teaspoon dry mustard
1 tablespoon Worcestershire sauce

2 teaspoons fresh lemon juice
1 tablespoon tarragon vinegar
½ teaspoon garlic which has been chopped in salt
2 tablespoons French olive oil
6 tablespoons oil, safflower or peanut
1 egg, beaten

Combine ingredients. Serve at room temperature. *Dressing is sufficient to coat 2-3 heads of romaine or Boston lettuce.*

Mrs. Donald McGregor Jacobs (Bonnie Sue Dilworth)

A red sheep on the package indicates true Roquefort cheese.

Roquefort Dressing

8 ounces Roquefort cheese, divided
¾ cup buttermilk
3½ cups Hellmann's mayonnaise
¼ cup white vinegar
3 tablespoons sugar

½ teaspoon salt
¾ teaspoon Accent
½ teaspoon garlic powder
¼ teaspoon white pepper

Beat 4 ounces of the cheese with buttermilk until smooth. Add mayonnaise, vinegar, and seasonings. Crumble remaining cheese and stir into dressing. *Stores indefinitely.*
Yields approximately 1 quart.
Mrs. John C. Mitchell (Marthanne Warren)

Blanco Special Dressing

1	cup vegetable oil	1	teaspoon pepper
1	cup white vinegar	1	teaspoon dry mustard
1	cup catsup	1	onion, grated
1	cup sugar	¾	cup grated Cheddar cheese
1	teaspoon salt		

Combine ingredients, except cheese, and simmer 5 minutes. Cool, add cheese, and refrigerate. *Delicious served on avocados.*
Yields 1 quart.
Mrs. George A. Kampmann (Wister Howell)

Rodeo Shake-Up Salad Dressing

3	ounces bleu cheese, crumbled	¼	teaspoon pepper
2	hard-boiled eggs, finely chopped	¼	teaspoon dry mustard
1	tablespoon grated onion	⅓	cup tarragon vinegar
1	teaspoon paprika	1	cup salad oil
1	teaspoon salt		

Place ingredients in a jar, shake well, and refrigerate.
Yields 2 cups.
Mrs. William W. Coates, III (Sue Schoeneck)

Savory Salad Dressing

1	ripe avocado, coarsely mashed	½ cup olive oil
2	small tomatoes, diced and drained, optional	¼ cup wine vinegar
2	teaspoons grated onion	Salt and pepper to taste
1½-2	tablespoons anchovy paste	Lettuce, torn into pieces

Combine the first 7 ingredients and toss with lettuce. *This dressing should be served the same day it is prepared.*

Mrs. Lewis Fairchild Fisher (Mary Maverick McMillan)

Copper Kettle Salad Dressing

6	tomatoes, cut in wedges	2	teaspoons sugar
4	tablespoons olive oil	3	teaspoons salt
4	tablespoons lemon juice	½	teaspoon pepper
⅛	teaspoon turmeric	2	green onions with tops, chopped
¾	teaspoon cumin	1	cup pitted ripe olives, chopped
2	tablespoons chopped parsley		Mixed greens

Mix all ingredients, except greens, and refrigerate 4-8 hours. Toss with mixed greens just before serving. *This recipe is from the Copper Kettle Restaurant in Aspen, Colorado.*
Serves 8.
Mrs. Robert L. Cook (Sandra Mueller)

Renee's Salad Dressing

2	tablespoons olive oil	1	teaspoon celery seed
1⅜	cups vegetable oil	½	teaspoon thyme
½	cup tarragon vinegar	1	clove garlic
2	tablespoons lemon juice	1	cup heavy cream, whipped
1	tablespoon chopped onion		Mixed greens
1	teaspoon chopped chives		Onion rings, optional
2	teaspoons sugar		Avocado slices, optional
3	teaspoons salt		

Place ingredients, except cream, greens, onion rings, and avocado, in a blender and whirl 30 seconds. Fold cream into the mixture. Toss well with mixed greens so every leaf is coated. Onion rings and avocado slices may be added to the salad. *This dressing originated at Renee's French Restaurant located on Main Avenue in the 1930's. It is a good dressing without the cream, but stronger so must be used sparingly.*
Yields 2 cups.
Mrs. Pressly Shafer, Jr. (Margaret Fauntleroy)

Parsley Dressing

½	cup chopped parsley	1	cup vegetable oil
4	cloves garlic	½	cup vinegar
½	cup sugar	1	teaspoon salt

Whirl all ingredients in blender.
Yields 2 cups.
Mrs. John Oppenheimer (Evelyne Ehrich)

Zippy Slaw Dressing

1	cup Hellmann's mayonnaise	3-4	tablespoons sugar, white or brown
5	teaspoons prepared mustard		Sliced cabbage
2	tablespoons white vinegar		

Combine the first 4 ingredients, stirring until sugar is dissolved. Make at least 1 hour before serving. Pour over sliced cabbage. *This dressing keeps for weeks in the refrigerator.*
Yields approximately 1 cup.
Mrs. Kenneth L. Farrimond (Susan Redwine)

Green Goddess Salad Dressing

1	cup mayonnaise	2-3	teaspoons tarragon vinegar
2-3	tablespoons finely chopped onion	1	clove garlic, crushed
1	teaspoon chopped parsley	1	2 ounce tin anchovies, mashed

Thoroughly mix ingredients and refrigerate. *This dressing keeps well for a week.*
Yields approximately 1 cup.
Mrs. William B. Culverwell (Sally Powell)

Buttermilk Salad Dressing

3	tablespoons cornstarch	2	teaspoons dehydrated minced garlic
2½	teaspoons dehydrated minced onion	½	teaspoon black pepper
1	teaspoon salt	¾	cup grated Romano cheese
2	teaspoons dried parsley	1	quart Hellmann's mayonnaise
2	teaspoons Accent	2	cups buttermilk

Combine the first 8 ingredients, mixing well. Stir in mayonnaise and buttermilk. *This dressing may also be used as a dip, and it will keep 2-3 months in the refrigerator.*

Mrs. Neal Marks (Alice)

Russian Dressing

1 quart mayonnaise	6 hard-boiled eggs, chopped
1 12 ounce bottle chili sauce	Juice of 1 lemon
2 tablespoons grated onion	Salt to taste
2 tablespoons capers	3-4 ounces evaporated milk, optional
½ cup chopped ripe olives	

Mix all ingredients. If a thinner dressing is preferred, add milk. Chill before serving. *This dressing keeps well in the refrigerator for 2 months.*
Yields approximately 6 cups.
Mrs. Weir Labatt, III (Laura Martin)

Mayonnaise

2 egg yolks	¼ teaspoon paprika
1 teaspoon salt	Dash of cayenne pepper
1 teaspoon sugar	5 tablespoons lemon juice
1 teaspoon dry mustard	2 cups vegetable oil

Using a mixer or blender, beat egg yolks until thickened. Beat in remaining ingredients except oil. Continuing to beat, gradually add the oil a few drops at a time. *This mayonnaise has a pretty color because of the paprika. It may be omitted if a whiter mayonnaise is preferred.*

Mrs. Dorothy Swain

Celery Seed Dressing

1 teaspoon dry mustard	1 teaspoon onion juice
1 teaspoon salt	4 tablespoons vinegar
1 teaspoon paprika	1 cup salad oil
⅓ cup sugar or honey	1 teaspoon whole celery seeds

Place all ingredients, except oil and celery seeds, in blender. Blend at low speed and add oil gradually. When well blended and thick, stir in celery seeds. *Especially good over fruit salad.*
Yields 1 cup.
Mrs. Lyman W. Webb (Page Parker)

Mary Lou's Poppy Seed Dressing

¾   cup sugar
1   teaspoon salt
1   teaspoon prepared mustard
½   cup white wine vinegar
1   clove garlic

1½   teaspoons onion juice
1   cup vegetable oil
2   teaspoons poppy seeds
8   ounces softened cream cheese, optional

Beat all ingredients until thick. For a thicker dressing add cream cheese and whirl in blender until smooth. *This wonderful dressing for fruit salads was served at the Kappa House while I was at the University of Texas.*

Mrs. Edgar M. Duncan (Linda Wyatt)

Bombay Dressing

1   cup mayonnaise
1   8 ounce can crushed pineapple
1   teaspoon curry powder

¼   cup raisins
1   tablespoon dried minced onion
Pineapple juice, optional

Combine ingredients and shake well. If a thinner dressing is preferred, add juice. Refrigerate until raisins and onions are softened. *Lila Vultee gave me this excellent dressing recipe for chicken salad or fruits.*

Mrs. James Michael Bell (Marion Dewar)

Honey Fruit Salad Dressing

⅔   cup sugar
1   teaspoon dry mustard
1   teaspoon paprika
1   teaspoon celery seed
¼   teaspoon salt

5   tablespoons vinegar
1   tablespoon lemon juice
⅔   cup honey
1   teaspoon grated onion
1   cup salad oil

Mix the dry ingredients in a blender. Add remaining ingredients and blend.

Mrs. Paul Sanders (Effie Mae Russell)

The Ursuline

"I must give you some details of the Convent of San Antonio. This house is very well provided in many respects for a new foundation and a new country...The exterior of our Convent is wonderfully respectable for Texas...The river is about as far from the hall door as San Antonio's walk is from back-door. It is many feet below the level of our Convent. Our lawn is planted with young trees; all new to us and of which we do not yet know names. Beyond the lawn is the vegetable and fruit garden. Pumpkins, haricots, apricots, tomatoes...and melons in abundance."

From a letter to the Convent in Waterford, Ireland, 1852-1853.

Legend is that when The Ursuline was built, clocks were installed on the south, east, and west sides but not on the north. The reason for this was that the city went no farther north than this building. The clock on the south side has since been removed.

Cheese Soufflé

3	tablespoons butter	½	teaspoon dry mustard
3	tablespoons flour		Cayenne pepper to taste
1	cup milk	3	eggs, separated
¼	teaspoon salt	1	cup packed, grated Cheddar cheese
⅛	teaspoon paprika		

Melt butter and add flour, stirring until bubbly. Gradually add milk and seasonings, stirring constantly until sauce thickens. Stir in beaten eggs yolks and cook 1 minute. Add cheese and stir until slightly melted. Beat egg whites until stiff and fold lightly into cooled cheese mixture. Pour into a 1 quart soufflé dish and bake at 325° for 30 minutes or until firm. *Extremely easy to make!*
Serves 4.
Mrs. Richey Wyatt (Eloise Richey)

Cheese Soufflé for Two

¼	stick butter or margarine	¼	teaspoon salt
1	tablespoon flour		Cayenne pepper to taste
½	cup scalded milk	2	eggs, separated
¾	cup grated Cheddar cheese		

Melt butter, add flour, and let bubble, stirring constantly. Add milk, cheese, salt, and pepper, stirring until cheese is melted. Allow mixture to cool slightly, then stir in egg yolks. Fold stiffly beaten egg whites carefully into mixture. Pour into a well buttered 7 inch soufflé dish or two 4 inch dishes and set in shallow pan of water. Bake at 350° for 30-45 minutes depending on size of dish. Serve immediately. *Goes well with a tossed salad and an English muffin.*
Serves 2.
Mrs. T. Graves Keithly

Cheese Dreams

1	cup grated Cheddar cheese	3	tablespoons mayonnaise
	Minced onion to taste, optional	2	tablespoons Durkee's dressing
	Dash of Tabasco sauce	8	bread slices or rounds
	Dash of Worcestershire sauce		Butter

Mix cheese, onion, Tabasco, Worcestershire sauce, mayonnaise, and Durkee's dressing. Spread mixture between slices of bread in sandwich fashion. Toast under broiler on one side. Turn, butter, and toast other side. Serve with buttered side up. *These are wonderful with fruit salad or soup for lunch or in bread rounds for tea. Those of us from Nashville grew up on Cheese Dreams.*

Mrs. Charles Parish, Jr. (Betty Caldwell)

Secret Enchiladas

5   tablespoons oil
6   tablespoons flour
2   tablespoons chili powder
3   cloves garlic, minced
1   8 ounce can tomato sauce
1   teaspoon Wilson's BV Paste
    (Beefer Upper)
1¼ teaspoons cumin seeds
5½ cups boiling water

1½ teaspoons salt
Shortening or vegetable oil
16 tortillas
8   ounces Swiss cheese, grated
8   ounces Monterey Jack cheese, grated
8   ounces sharp Cheddar cheese, grated
1   medium onion, chopped
Salt to taste

Heat 5 tablespoons oil and stir in flour. Add chili powder, garlic, tomato sauce, BV paste, and cumin. Slowly add boiling water and salt. Simmer 1 hour. While sauce is cooking, heat enough shortening to measure ½ inch in the bottom of a skillet. Immerse tortillas for about 30 seconds, turning once. Tortillas must not get crisp and must remain pliable. Mix cheeses and onion. Spoon some of the cheese mixture into each tortilla, reserving some cheese for topping. Roll tortillas and place seam side down in a greased baking dish. Sprinkle reserved cheese mixture over enchiladas. The enchiladas may be covered and refrigerated at this point. Before baking, cover enchiladas with sauce, and bake at 350° until cheese is melted.

Mrs. Strauder Nelson, Jr. (Carolyn Moffitt)

Avocado Enchiladas

2   slices bacon, diced
2½ pounds canned tomatoes, mashed
2   hot peppers, minced
2   cloves garlic, minced
Salt and pepper to taste

Butter and Crisco
1   pound yellow cheese, grated
2   large onions, grated
4   medium avocados, mashed
24 tortillas

Sauté bacon. Add tomatoes, peppers, garlic, salt, and pepper. Cook slowly until mixture thickens. The consistency of the sauce should be such that only a little remains on the tortilla. Water may be added if necessary. Melt enough butter and Crisco to measure ½ inch in the bottom of a skillet. Soften tortillas in heated butter mixture, dip in tomato sauce, covering tortilla completely, and remove to a plate. Fill each tortilla with some of the cheese, a sprinkling of onion, and about 1 teaspoon of mashed avocado. Roll and place seam side down in 2 greased 8 x 12 baking dishes. Sprinkle remaining cheese over top and cover with remaining sauce. Bake at 300° for 25 minutes.
Serves 8.
Mrs. O. J. Solcher, Jr. (Elizabeth McAllister)

Queso de Dios

8	ounces sharp Cheddar cheese	12	ounces canned green chilies
8	ounces mild Cheddar cheese	3	cups sour cream
8	ounces Monterey Jack cheese		

Slice cheeses in ½ inch strips. In a 5 x 8 x 1½ casuela (Mexican clay baking dish) or any oven proof serving dish, layer in the following order: sharp cheese, chilies, sour cream, mild cheese, Jack cheese, chilies, and sour cream. Repeat layers. Bake at 375° for 30 minutes. *Good quality cheese is a must. Recipe was developed by the "instinct" method while living in Tucson, Arizona, where unique Mexican food may be found. Serve as a side dish with Mexican food or as a dip.*
Serves 8.
Mr. Comer M. Alden, Jr.

Green Chile Casserole

1	4 ounce can chopped green chilies	½	cup flour
½	pound Cheddar or Longhorn cheese, grated	1	teaspoon salt
2	eggs, beaten	1½	cups milk

Layer chilies and cheese in buttered 1½ quart casserole. Mix eggs, flour, salt, and milk, and pour over chile-cheese layers. Bake at 350° for 50-55 minutes. Serve immediately. *This dish has local flavor and goes well with many brunch or luncheon menus.*
Serves 6-8.
Mrs. Lee Quincy Vardaman (Jane McCurdy)

Cheese 'n Eggs

2	slices bread	4	eggs, beaten
1	cup water		Salt and pepper to taste
1	cup grated cheese		

Place bread in skillet. Pour water over bread and add cheese. Stir constantly over low heat until well mixed and the cheese is melted. Add eggs, salt, and pepper to bread and cheese and stir until done. Serve immediately. *This recipe takes 5 minutes to prepare and is delicious for breakfast or a light supper with fruit or green salad.*
Serves 2.
Mrs. Emil K. Moore

Cheese Fondue

12 ounces natural Swiss cheese, grated	1 tablespoon cornstarch
8 ounces Gruyère cheese, grated	1 tablespoon water
12 ounces dry white wine	Dash of Kirsch or brandy
1 small clove garlic, crushed	Day-old or oven dried bite-sized pieces of French bread
Salt and pepper to taste	

In fondue pot, place cheeses, wine, garlic, salt, and pepper. Heat, stirring constantly with a wooden spoon, until cheese is melted. Cheese and wine will remain somewhat separated. Blend cornstarch with water and pour into cheese mixture. Continue stirring for 4-5 minutes until mixture is thickened. Add Kirsch and lower flame. Stir occasionally as the mixture will continue to thicken. Serve with French bread. *Everyone has a favorite cheese fondue recipe. This is ours, given to us by the chef at the Hotel du Cerf in Chesieres-Villars, a ski resort, in the province of Vaud, Switzerland.*
Serves 4.
Mrs. Richard H. Eckhardt (Mary Webb)

The following dish is an ancient one. Two hundred years ago, some cooks began calling it "Rarebit", apparently because this sounded more refined. The name is actually a culinary joke. When a hunter's bag was poor, a Welsh housewife cooked cheese instead of rabbit.

Mushroom Rabbit with Beer

¼ stick butter	1 teaspoon salt
12 ounces Cheddar cheese, grated, or 3 cups	¾ teaspoon paprika
1 cup + 1 tablespoon beer, divided	1 cup sliced fresh mushrooms
1½ teaspoons dry mustard	Toasted bread triangles
	Green onions, finely chopped

In the top of a double boiler, over simmering water, melt butter. Add grated cheese and as the cheese melts, gradually stir in 1 cup beer. Combine 1 tablespoon beer with mustard, salt, and paprika. Stir the seasonings into the cheese when it is melted and smooth. Add mushrooms and cook the rabbit for 2 minutes. Serve at once over toasted bread triangles and garnish with green onions. *Fresh oysters may be added along with the mushrooms, if desired. This dish also is delicious served over hot corn bread.*
Serves 6-8.
Mrs. Alex Weil, III (Penny Speier)

Quiche for a Crowd

To prepare quiche for a crowd, line a 9 x 13 casserole with two recipes for pie crust and prebake according to package directions or recipe instructions. If no instructions for prebaking are available, 450° for 8-10 minutes is recommended. A partially baked pie shell will assure you of an edible crust all the way around. This step is also recommended for dessert pies.

Baked as well as unbaked pie shells freeze beautifully. A basic quiche filling may be made a day ahead and blended briefly just before using. Most quiche ingredients may also be prepared ahead; cheese grated, bacon fried, onions sautéed, ham sliced, etc. All you need to do is assemble and bake the day of the party. Quiche is also good at room temperature and therefore makes elegant picnic fare. *Especially festive when prepared in individual pie tins.*

The Cookbook Committee

Quiche Moselle

1	9 inch deep dish pastry shell or 2 8 inch pastry shells	¼	cup chopped onion
		¼	stick butter
1	cup thinly sliced summer sausage (2 inch diameter), cut in half	1	tablespoon flour
		3	eggs, beaten
1	cup grated Swiss cheese	1¼	cups light cream
1	cup grated Cheddar cheese	¼	cup Moselle wine
1	cup sliced fresh mushrooms		

Bake pastry shell at 450° for 6 minutes or until lightly browned. Remove from oven and cool. Reduce heat to 325°. Scatter sausage over bottom of shell. Combine cheeses and sprinkle over sausage. Sauté mushrooms and onions in butter until soft; stir in flour. Blend together eggs, cream, and wine; add to mushroom mixture. Pour carefully over cheese. Bake at 325° for 40-45 minutes, or until set. Let cool 10-15 minutes. You may prepare the entire recipe in advance with the exception of adding the eggs, cream, and wine mixture. Refrigerate until ready to bake and then add the liquids. This quiche may also be made without a pie shell. *The quiche can be served as a main dish, hors d'oeuvre, or at a picnic.*
Serves 4-6.
Mrs. Middleton S. English (Shirley Fitch)

Quiche Jardinière

1 9 inch deep dish pastry shell
2 tablespoons finely chopped green pepper
2 tablespoons minced onion
¼ stick butter or margarine, divided
½ cup cherry tomatoes, sliced ¼ inch thick
Flour

Pinch of thyme
1 cup grated Swiss cheese
3 eggs
1⅓ cups light cream
1 teaspoon seasoned salt
Pinch of cayenne pepper
3 green pepper rings
3 cherry tomatoes, halved
Freshly ground black pepper

Prick bottom of pastry shell with fork. Bake at 400° for 8 minutes, remove from oven, and cool. Sauté peppers and onions in 1 tablespoon butter until golden, remove, and set aside. Add remaining butter to skillet. Dredge tomato slices in flour and quickly sauté. Drain on paper towels. Arrange tomato slices on bottom of pastry shell. Sprinkle with thyme, pepper, onions, and cheese. Beat eggs; stir in cream, seasoned salt, and cayenne pepper. Pour over filled pastry shell. Garnish top with pepper rings and tomato halves. Bake at 375° for 40 minutes or until knife inserted in center comes out clean. Remove from oven and grind pepper over quiche. Let stand 10 minutes before serving.
Serves 6.
Mrs. Benjamin Wyatt

Chicken Quiche

Crust
1 stick butter or margarine
1 3 ounce package cream cheese

1 cup flour
1 teaspoon salt

Filling
2 whole chicken breasts, cooked and cut into pieces
⅓-½ cup chopped ham
½ cup grated Swiss cheese, or more if desired

2 cups light cream
3 eggs
Salt and pepper to taste
Pinch of nutmeg

Crust   Cut margarine and cheese into flour and salt, pat together, and chill. Roll out to fill a 9 inch deep dish pie plate or 10 inch quiche pan. Bake at 450° for 10 minutes. If pastry shell is to be frozen, bake at 500° for 10 minutes. *Crust shrinks and bubbles. To avoid this, fill crust with dry beans or raw rice before cooking. Beans and rice may be saved and used again for the same purpose.*

Filling   Place chicken and ham in pastry shell. Sprinkle with cheese. Beat together cream, eggs, and seasonings. Pour egg mixture over filled pastry shell. Bake at 375° for 30-35 minutes or at 325° for 45 minutes if pastry shell was frozen.
Serves 4.
Mrs. Thomas Pawel (Nancy Emma Ray)

Commerce Street Bridge

"Spanish and German used to be spoken about as much as English. Over the bridges that spanned the River at principal crossings as late as the 70's, there were sign boards in three languages reading:

Walk your horse over this bridge, or you will be fined.

Schnelles Reiten uber diese Brucke ist verboten.

Anda despacio con su caballo, o teme la ley."

Glamorous Days. Frank Bushick, 1934.

Easy Eggs Benedict

1	10¾ ounce can cream of chicken soup or ½ can cream of chicken soup + ½ can cream of mushroom soup	¼	cup milk
		½	stick butter
		3	English muffins, split and buttered
½	cup mayonnaise	6	thin slices ham
1	tablespoon + 1 teaspoon lemon juice	6	eggs, poached

Heat soup, mayonnaise, lemon juice, milk, and butter until butter melts. Stir until smooth. Toast English muffins. Top with ham slices and poached eggs. Cover with sauce and serve immediately. *Good and easy!*
Serves 6.
Mrs. Sandra Harley Carey

Chutney Eggs

12	hard-boiled eggs	⅓	cup finely chopped Major Grey's Chutney
6	slices bacon, fried and crumbled	3-4	tablespoons Hellman's mayonnaise

Cut eggs in half lengthwise and remove yolks. Mash and add bacon, chutney, and mayonnaise. Stuff egg whites with yolk mixture. A pastry tube may be used. *Serve as a canapé with cocktails. All will be eaten!*
Makes 24 halves.
Mrs. Ralph L. Marx

Eggs Pacific

12	hard-boiled eggs, sliced		Dash of pepper
1	pound shrimp, cooked and peeled	1	tablespoon dry white wine
3	tablespoons butter	1	tablespoon capers, drained
3	tablespoons flour	2	tablespoons chopped parsley
1⅔	cups light cream	¼	teaspoon thyme
2	teaspoons prepared mustard	½	cup grated Swiss cheese
1	teaspoon salt		

Butter a 2 quart baking dish or 6 individual baking dishes. Arrange half the eggs on the bottom. Sprinkle shrimp over eggs and top with remaining egg slices. Melt butter and stir in flour; cook 1 minute without browning. Gradually add cream, stirring with wire whip. Blend well. Stir in mustard, salt, pepper, wine, capers, parsley, and thyme. Pour sauce over eggs; sprinkle with cheese and bake at 425° for 15 minutes or until bubbly. If individual dishes or shells are used, place them on baking sheet and reduce baking time to 10 minutes.
Serves 6.
Mrs. George Bickham Grieder (Joanne Ugland)

To peel hard-boiled eggs, cover briefly with cold water, drain, and shake from side to side in the pan until shells are thoroughly crushed. Even the freshest eggs will be no problem!

Creole Eggs

¾	cup water	1	tablespoon margarine
½	cup chopped green pepper	2	tablespoons flour
¼	cup chopped onion	1	cup evaporated milk
½	cup chopped celery	6	hard-boiled eggs, sliced
1	teaspoon salt, divided	½	cup soft bread crumbs
½	teaspoon pepper, divided	1	tablespoon margarine, softened
1¼	cups tomato sauce	½	cup grated Parmesan cheese

Bring water to boil. Add green pepper, onion, celery, ½ teaspoon salt, and ¼ teaspoon pepper and continue to boil for 10 minutes. Add tomato sauce and boil 5 minutes longer. Make a white sauce by melting margarine in a saucepan and blending in the flour. Slowly stir in the milk; add ½ teaspoon salt and ¼ teaspoon pepper. Cook until thickened. Add eggs to the white sauce and pour into a 2 quart casserole. Cover with tomato mixture. Top with mixture of bread crumbs, softened margarine, and cheese. Bake at 400° for 15-20 minutes. *Perfect for brunch or luncheon. This is good with fresh fruit and hard rolls.*
Serves 8.
Mrs. Armand D. Cox, Jr.

Christmas Morning Casserole

4 slices bacon	½ cup flour
½ pound dried beef, chopped	1 quart milk
4 ounces canned mushrooms, drained	¼ teaspoon pepper
	16 eggs
1 large green pepper, chopped	1 cup Pet evaporated milk
1 stick butter, divided	Salt to taste

Sauté bacon and remove from skillet. Add beef, mushrooms (reserving some for garnish), green pepper, and ½ stick butter to bacon drippings. Stir in flour, 1 quart milk, and pepper, cooking slowly until mixture thickens to a cream sauce consistency. Mix eggs with evaporated milk, season with salt, and scramble in remaining butter. In a 3 quart round casserole, alternate layers of sauce and eggs, beginning and ending with sauce. Eggs must be completely covered with sauce. Garnish with mushrooms. Bake, covered, at 275° for 1 hour. *May be prepared a day ahead and refrigerated before baking.*
Serves 12.
Mrs. Albert Steves, IV (Martha Monier)

Easter Egg Casserole

½ stick butter	1 pound sharp Cheddar cheese, grated
¼ cup flour	
1 cup light cream	1½ dozen hard-boiled eggs, thinly sliced
1 cup milk	
¼ teaspoon thyme	1 pound bacon, fried and crumbled
¼ teaspoon marjoram	¼ cup finely chopped parsley
¼ teaspoon basil	Buttered bread crumbs

Melt butter and blend in flour. Add cream and milk gradually, stirring until thickened. Add herbs and cheese to sauce, stirring until cheese is melted. Use vegetable spray or butter to grease a 9 x 13 casserole. Make 3 layers of the following: sliced eggs, bacon, parsley, and cheese sauce. Top with bread crumbs. Bake at 350° for 30 minutes.
Serves 8-10.
Mrs. Patricia Beveridge (Patricia Preis)

Fideo

5 ounces vermicelli (fideo)	1 10 ounce can Rotel tomatoes and
3 tablespoons olive oil	green chilies
1 large clove garlic, minced	Salt to taste
2 green onions, chopped	Parmesan cheese to taste

Sauté vermicelli in olive oil until golden brown. Add garlic and onions. Sauté for 1 minute, add tomatoes and salt, cover, and cook over low heat for 8 minutes. This may be served with Parmesan cheese.
Serves 4-5.
Mrs. Paul R. Snow (Mary Lynn "Mimi" Fariss)

Pasta al Pesto

2 large cloves garlic	1 cup freshly grated Parmesan cheese
1 cup fresh basil leaves	½ cup pine nuts
1½ cups olive oil or ¾ cup olive oil	Salt, optional
and ¾ cup peanut oil or	16 ounces spaghetti, cooked and lightly
safflower oil	oiled

Purée garlic, basil, and oil in blender. Add cheese and nuts and continue to blend. Depending on the Parmesan, add salt to taste. Pour over hot spaghetti. *Good as a vegetable dip or poured over broiled fish, and may be used as a salad dressing by thinning with vinegar and oil.*
Serves 6-8. Sauce freezes.
Mrs. Lewis Tucker (Marjorie Stephenson)

Fettuccine

1 teaspoon McCormick garlic juice	¼ teaspoon poultry seasoning
¼ teaspoon paprika	1 teaspoon dried parsley
¼ teaspoon pepper	½ cup milk, warmed
8 ounces sour cream	12 ounces egg noodles, cooked
2 sticks butter or margarine	and drained
1 tablespoon grated Parmesan cheese	

Combine all ingredients, except milk and noodles, and heat until cheese and butter are melted. Add milk and noodles. Serve immediately.
Serves 6-8.
Judge John H. Wood, Jr.

Melt an extravagant amount of butter or margarine in an iron skillet, add 8-10 crushed saltine crackers, sauté until golden brown, and sprinkle over buttered pasta or green vegetables for a simply spectacular treat.

Pastitsio

10 tablespoons butter, divided	3 tablespoons tomato paste
¾ cup flour	½ cup water
4 teaspoons salt, divided	3 eggs, beaten
1 quart hot milk	1 pound elbow macaroni, cooked
3 eggs, lightly beaten	in water with 2 tablespoons salt
2 medium onions, chopped	and drained
2 pounds ground beef	1¾ cups grated Greek cheese,
½ teaspoon pepper	Kefalotiri or ricotta
½ teaspoon cinnamon	

Melt 6 tablespoons butter. Blend in flour and 1 teaspoon salt until smooth. Gradually add milk, stirring constantly. When thickened, add sauce very slowly to eggs, beating constantly so that eggs do not curdle. Set aside to cool. Sauté onions in 4 tablespoons butter until golden. Add beef, 3 teaspoons salt, pepper, and cinnamon, stirring until browned. Add tomato paste diluted with water and cook 5-10 minutes. Set aside. Combine eggs and macaroni. Spread ½ the macaroni mixture in a buttered 3-4 quart casserole and sprinkle with ½ cup cheese. Spread meat mixture over cheese, sprinkle with ½ cup cheese, add remaining macaroni, and sprinkle with ½ cup cheese. Bake at 350° about 10 minutes. Remove from oven, top with cream sauce, and sprinkle with remaining cheese. Bake 30 minutes or until browned.
Serves 8.
Mrs. S. Peter Lambros

Manicotti

Crêpes

1	cup milk	½	teaspoon salt
½	cup water	¾	cup flour
4	eggs	¼	cup wheat germ
¼	cup oil		Butter

Sauce
Italian tomato sauce with meat

Filling

¾-1 pound ricotta cheese	½ pound mozzarella cheese, sliced in strips
2 eggs, beaten	
3-4 tablespoons grated Parmesan cheese	Additional mozzarella and Parmesan cheese for topping
Salt and pepper to taste	

Crêpes Combine all ingredients, except butter, in blender and allow to stand for at least 1 hour. Brush a heated 4-6 inch pan with butter, pour in 1 tablespoon batter and quickly tilt pan to spread batter evenly. Cook until lightly browned on both sides. *Yields 12.*

Sauce Spread a thin layer of your favorite Italian tomato sauce with meat in a baking dish.

Filling Mix ricotta, eggs, Parmesan, salt, and pepper. Spread each crêpe with a portion of the filling and add a slice of mozzarella cheese. Roll crêpes and arrange ¼ inch apart on top of sauce. Spoon more of the sauce over the top. Sprinkle with additional grated mozzarella and Parmesan cheese. Bake at 300° for 15-20 minutes.
Serves 8.
Mrs. Charles Richard Eyster (Agnes Christian Welsh)

Spaghetti a la Chica Armondo

4	tomatoes, peeled, seeded, and chopped	1	pound mozzarella cheese, cubed
½	cup or more chopped fresh basil (no substitution)	1	pound cooked ham, cubed
		10-12	ripe olives, chopped
½	cup chopped fresh parsley	2	cloves garlic, minced
1½	cups olive oil	1	pound spaghetti, cooked
			Parmesan cheese, grated

In a bowl combine all ingredients except spaghetti and Parmesan. Cover and let stand at least 30 minutes. Just before serving, toss with hot spaghetti. Serve with Parmesan cheese. *This is surprisingly fresh and garden-like for a spaghetti dish.*
Serves 6-8.
Mrs. Lewis Tucker (Marjorie Stephenson)

Spaghetti Casserole

1½-2 pounds ground beef
1 onion, chopped
½ green pepper, chopped
32 ounces canned tomatoes
1 6 ounce can tomato paste
Salt and pepper to taste
Garlic salt to taste

1-2 tablespoons sugar
Pinch of oregano
1 10¾ ounce can tomato soup
¼ pound mushrooms, chopped and sautéed in 1 tablespoon butter
16 ounces spaghetti
1 pound Cheddar cheese, grated

Brown meat with onion and green pepper. Add tomatoes and tomato paste. Fill tomato paste can ½ full with water and add to mixture. Add seasonings, tomato soup, and mushrooms. Simmer for 20-30 minutes, stirring occasionally. Cook spaghetti, which has been broken into shorter lengths, in boiling salted water, drain, and add to meat mixture, mixing well. Remove from heat. Add ⅔ of cheese and stir until melted. Pour in a shallow casserole and top with remaining cheese. Bake at 325° for 45 minutes or until hot and bubbly. *This is a very rich, sumptuous spaghetti recipe that is easy to prepare and better made a day ahead. The perfect recipe for any large group and especially teenage parties.*
Serves 10-12. Freezes.
Mrs. Kaye F. Wilkins (Sidney Howell)

Lasagne

3 6 ounce cans tomato paste
3 6 ounce cans water
6 tablespoons olive oil
3 tablespoons Spice Islands Spaghetti Sauce Seasoning
¾ cup red Burgundy
1 16 ounce box lasagne noodles

2 quarts boiling salted water
1 pound lean ground beef
1 pound small curd cottage cheese
8 ounces mozzarella cheese, thinly sliced
½ cup grated Parmesan cheese

Combine the first 5 ingredients and simmer for 20 minutes. Cook noodles in water for 20 minutes or until tender, drain, and rinse in cold water. Sauté ground beef until lightly browned. In a 7 x 11 x 2 casserole, layer 3 times in the following order: noodles, cottage cheese, beef, sauce, and mozzarella cheese. Sprinkle with Parmesan cheese. Bake at 350° for 20 minutes, or until bubbly.
Serves 8.
Mrs. G. Milton Johnson (Ellen Bond Zimmerman)

Chicken Lasagne

¼ cup chopped pimiento
½ cup chopped green pepper
1 cup chopped onion
2 cloves garlic, minced
½ cup olive oil
2 cups cooked, chopped chicken
½ cup diced ham
1 cup cooked, chopped chicken livers, optional, or ½ cup more ham and ½ cup more chicken
4 8 ounce cans tomato sauce
2 6 ounce cans tomato paste

1 cup dry white wine
1 cup chicken broth
1 teaspoon salt
½ teaspoon pepper
½ teaspoon crushed basil
½ teaspoon oregano
1 cup frozen peas, optional
16 ounces lasagne noodles, cooked, drained, and rinsed
Ricotta cheese
Parmesan cheese, grated
Mozzarella cheese, grated

Sauté pimiento, green pepper, onion, and garlic in olive oil until soft. Add chicken, ham, chicken livers, tomato sauce, tomato paste, wine, broth, and seasonings. Cover and simmer for 30 minutes. Add peas and remove from heat. In a greased baking dish, layer 4 times in the following order: sauce, noodles, and cheeses. Bake at 350° for 30 minutes or until cheese is melted and bubbly.
Serves 8.
Mrs. Edgar M. Duncan (Linda Wyatt)

Spinach Lasagne

2 10 ounce packages frozen chopped spinach, thawed and drained
½ pound fresh Parmesan cheese, grated, or 2 cups
6 cups ricotta cheese or 6 cups cottage cheese + 3 beaten eggs
Salt to taste
Freshly ground pepper to taste
½ teaspoon ground nutmeg

16 lasagne noodles, cooked, drained, and rinsed
3-4 tablespoons vegetable oil
2 cloves garlic, minced
1 large yellow onion, chopped
3 cups tomato sauce
2 teaspoons sugar
½ teaspoon dried basil
½ teaspoon oregano

Butter a large, deep casserole with a cover and set aside. Mix spinach with 1½ cups Parmesan cheese, ricotta cheese, salt, pepper, and nutmeg. Spread about ⅓ cup of the mixture on each noodle. Roll each noodle up and stand on end in the casserole. Heat oil in a heavy skillet. Add garlic, onion, and 1 cup water. Bring to a boil and cook until all the water has boiled away and the onion is soft and transparent. Stir in tomato sauce, sugar, basil, oregano, and additional salt and pepper. Bring to a boil, reduce heat, and simmer for 5 minutes. Pour sauce over noodles, cover, and bake at 350° for 30 minutes. Before serving, sprinkle with the remaining Parmesan cheese.
Serves 8.
Mrs. Ben Foster, Jr. (Raye Boyer)

Noodle Casserole

8	ounces medium noodles	½	teaspoon salt
1	teaspoon vegetable oil	1	tablespoon or more grated onion
1	cup small curd or Lite-line Lowfat cottage cheese	¼	teaspoon Tabasco sauce
1	cup sour cream	2	tablespoons chopped pimiento
1	teaspoon Worcestershire sauce	1	tablespoon chopped green pepper
		½-¾	cup grated sharp cheese

Cook noodles according to package directions adding oil. Drain noodles and combine with remaining ingredients except sharp cheese. Place in a buttered 2 quart casserole and sprinkle with sharp cheese. Bake at 350° for 25-30 minutes or until brown. Let stand 10 minutes before serving. *Good to accompany Chicken with Duck Sauce (see index).*
Serves 8-10.
Mrs. Ralph L. Marx

Baked Macaroni with Cheese

4½	tablespoons butter	1	cup + 2 tablespoons light cream
6	tablespoons flour	1	pound macaroni, cooked and drained
1½	cups beef broth		
Salt and pepper to taste		1½	pounds Gruyère or Fontina cheese, grated
Paprika to taste			
1½	tablespoons Pace Picante Sauce	½	cup buttered bread crumbs

Blend butter with flour. Add the beef broth, seasonings, picante sauce, and cream. Cook in a double boiler about 10 minutes or until thick and smooth. Butter a 3 quart baking dish and arrange a layer of the macaroni on the bottom. Add a layer of cheese, a layer of macaroni, and another layer of cheese. Pour over this 1½ cups of the sauce. Add another layer of cheese, macaroni, and then more cheese. Top this with remaining sauce and another layer of macaroni and cheese. Sprinkle with bread crumbs. Bake at 350° for 10 minutes or until bubbly and brown on top.
Serves 8.
Mrs. Christopher Goldsbury, Jr. (Linda Pace)

Bowen's Island

"Temperatures in San Antonio being mild enough to suit outdoor recreation almost any day in the year, pleasure seekers could go to Bowen's Island at any time, reaching it by way of a bridge at the Old Mill Crossing. Years later the river channel was moved and its former bed filled in to make room for today's skyscraper, the Transit Tower."

San Antonio's River. Louise Lomax, 1948.

Pecan Pilaf

¾   cup pecans, coarsely chopped   1   teaspoon salt
2½ cups rice   5   cups chicken broth
½-¾ stick butter

Toast pecans until crisp at 325° for 15-20 minutes. In a heavy pan cook the rice in the butter until it is straw colored, stirring constantly. Add salt and chicken broth, mix well, and bring to a boil. Cover and cook over low heat about 15 minutes or until rice is tender and all broth is absorbed. You may place a clean towel between the pan and lid for a few minutes before serving to help absorb any excess moisture. Add nuts to rice and mix carefully. *This is absolutely fantastic with Chicken Mandarin (see index).*
Serves 8.
Mrs. Ferd C. Meyer, Jr. (Marcia Marron)

Browned Rice Oregano

3   strips bacon   1 large onion, chopped, or 1½ cups
1½ cups uncooked rice   1 teaspoon oregano, crushed
2   10½ ounce cans beef broth   1 teaspoon cumin seed, crushed

Fry bacon until crisp. Drain and crumble. Reserve 2 tablespoons bacon drippings. Add rice to drippings, stirring until well browned. Add broth, onions, spices, and bacon. Cover and cook 15 minutes.
Serves 6.
Mrs. George McDougall (Frances L. Hoffman)

Chinese Fried Rice

10	slices bacon	1	cup sliced mushrooms
3	tablespoons bacon drippings	2½	cups cooked white rice
½	cup chopped green onions and tops	2	tablespoons soy sauce
1	cup diced celery	1	egg, beaten

Fry bacon until crisp, drain, and crumble. Reserve 3 tablespoons bacon drippings. Add onions and celery; cook until almost tender, stirring frequently. Add mushrooms, rice, and soy sauce. Reduce heat and simmer about 10 minutes, stirring occasionally. Stir egg into rice mixture and cook only until egg is done. Sprinkle bacon over top of rice.
Serves 8.
Mrs. Frates Seeligson (Martita Rice)

Rice-Stuffed Zucchini

1	7-8 ounce package chicken flavored rice mix, prepared according to package directions	4	medium zucchini
		Salt to taste	
6	cups water	1	small tomato, peeled, seeded, and chopped
1½	teaspoons salt	½	cup grated Cheddar cheese

In a large saucepan over medium heat, bring 6 cups water and 1½ teaspoons salt to boil. Cut zucchini in half lengthwise, add to water, and cook 5-7 minutes until just crisp-tender. Drain immediately and cool under cold water. Using tip of teaspoon or grapefruit spoon, scoop out and discard seeds from zucchini halves, leaving shells about ¼-½ inch thick. Arrange zucchini halves in a row on a greased 9 x 13 baking dish and sprinkle with salt. Pile rice into zucchini halves; top each with some tomato and cheese. Bake at 375° for 10 minutes or until cheese melts and rice is hot. *Looks impressive, tastes good, and is fun to prepare.*
Serves 8.
Mrs. Bruce Weilbacher (Carolyn Hennessey)

Indian Rice

1	package Uncle Ben's Curried Rice	3	green onions, sliced
2	jars marinated artichoke hearts	8	stuffed green olives, sliced
⅓	cup mayonnaise		

Prepare rice according to package directions. Drain marinade from artichoke hearts and add to mayonnaise, mixing well. Cut artichoke hearts into small pieces. Add mayonnaise mixture, artichoke hearts, onions, and olives to rice. Toss lightly. *This may be served at room temperature. It does not have to be piping hot, and it is always a hit.*
Serves 4.
Mrs. Sol Schwartz (Joanie)

Spanish Rice

1	cup uncooked rice	2	tablespoons bacon drippings
1	onion, finely chopped	1	8 ounce can stewed tomatoes
1	large rib celery, chopped	1	10½ ounce can beef broth
1	green pepper, chopped	¼	cup sliced stuffed olives
½	cup sliced fresh mushrooms		

Sauté rice, onion, celery, green pepper, and mushrooms in bacon drippings until vegetables are tender. Drain stewed tomatoes and reserve liquid. Add broth to tomato liquid with enough water to equal 2 cups. Add tomatoes, olives, and liquid to rice. Cover and simmer 15-20 minutes.
Serves 6.
Mrs. Fred Groos (Jane Connor)

Spanish Rice Pronto

¼	cup bacon drippings	2	8 ounce cans tomato sauce
1	medium onion, thinly sliced	1	teaspoon prepared mustard
½	medium green pepper, sliced	1	teaspoon salt
1⅓	cups uncooked Minute rice	Dash of pepper	
1⅓	cups hot water		

Melt bacon drippings in a 10 inch skillet. Add onion, green pepper, and rice. Cook and stir over high heat until lightly browned. Add water, tomato sauce, and seasonings; mix well. Bring quickly to a boil, cover tightly, and simmer 10 minutes.
Serves 6.
Mrs. Thad Ziegler, Jr. (Patsy Battaglia)

Mexican Rice

½ pound chorizo or any highly seasoned sausage
½ cup chopped onion
1 clove garlic, minced
¼ cup finely chopped celery
½ cup peeled and chopped fresh tomato
¼ cup finely chopped green pepper
1 tablespoon chopped parsley

¾ cup uncooked rice
½ cup cubed, boiled potato, optional
¼ teaspoon ground cumin
1 tablespoon chili powder
½ cup currants or raisins
1¾ cups water
1½ cups chopped, salted peanuts
Salt and pepper to taste

Cook sausage over medium heat until it breaks into small pieces. Add onion, garlic, celery, tomato, green pepper, and parsley. Cook until vegetables are limp and tender. Add rice, potato, spices, currants, and water to vegetables. Cook for 5 minutes, mixing all ingredients well. Pour into a 2 quart casserole. Cover and bake at 350° for 35-40 minutes. Remove cover, sprinkle with peanuts, and bake 10 minutes.
Serves 4-6.
Mrs. Edgar M. Duncan (Linda Wyatt)

Mexican Green Rice Casserole

1½ cups uncooked rice
1 green pepper, chopped
2 poblano peppers, chopped
1 small green hot pepper, chopped, optional

1 onion, chopped
1 stick butter
1 cup sour cream
½ pound Monterey Jack cheese, grated

Cook rice and set aside. Sauté the peppers and onions in butter. Purée in blender. Add sour cream and continue to blend. In a 1½ quart casserole, layer half of each ingredient in the following order: rice, pepper-sour cream mixture, and cheese. Repeat layers. Bake at 350° for 20-30 minutes or until cheese is melted. *May be frozen before baking.*
Serves 8-10.
Mrs. Ben Hammond (Mimi Beach)

Exotic Rice

1¼ cups uncooked rice
½ stick butter
2½ cups chicken broth

½ cup almonds, toasted
¼ cup golden or white raisins
Salt and pepper to taste

Brown rice in butter. Add chicken broth, cover, and bake at 350° for 40 minutes. Add remaining ingredients and press into a buttered mold. Bake 10 minutes. Unmold carefully. *Center may be filled with fresh green beans, finely sliced and buttered.*
Serves 6-8.
Mrs. Robert Ownby

Savory Rice

1 stick butter
1 cup chopped onion
1 clove garlic, minced
7 ounces uncooked Minute rice
1 teaspoon summer savory

3 beef bouillon cubes
3 cups boiling water
4 ounces canned sliced mushrooms, drained, optional
1½ ounces grated Parmesan cheese

Melt butter in large skillet and add onion, garlic, rice, and summer savory. Sauté about 10 minutes. Dissolve bouillon cubes in boiling water. Add to rice mixture. Add mushrooms and cheese. Pour into greased 2 quart casserole. Cover and bake at 350° for 30 minutes. This may be served with additional Parmesan cheese. Serves 10.
Mrs. Paul A. Braymen (Judy Barnard)

Green Mountain Rice

⅔ cup uncooked long grain rice
½ cup finely chopped onion
1 tablespoon margarine
3 ounces cream cheese, softened

½ teaspoon salt
2 eggs
1½ cups milk
2 tablespoons snipped parsley

Cook rice. Sauté onion in margarine until tender, but not brown. In large mixing bowl blend cream cheese and salt. Beat in eggs, one at a time. Add milk and mix well. Stir in rice, onion, and parsley. Pour into greased casserole and bake at 350° for 35-40 minutes. Remove and let stand 5 minutes before serving. *Good with fish and chicken or under seafood Newburg.*
Serves 8.
Mrs. John H. Langston, Jr.

Easy Rice Casserole

1 cup uncooked long grain rice
1 10½ ounce can beef consommé
½ cup water
1 tablespoon fresh lemon juice

½ teaspoon Fines Herbes
1 teaspoon salt
½ stick butter

Combine ingredients. Cook in covered casserole for 1 hour at 350°. Stir once after first 30 minutes.
Serves 4.
Mrs. Kenneth Reed Wynne (Paula Gay Edwards)

Spanish Governor's Palace

"As Ignacio Perez purchased the property known today as the Governors' Palace, on the west side of Military Plaza, and made it his homestead, it is very likely that the place was occupied by his relative, the governor, and hence in relatively recent years, has the distinction of being properly called the Governors' Palace."

Presidio de Texas at the Place Called San Antonio.   Frederick Chabot, 1929.

Baked Trout with Sour Cream Sauce

4	10 ounce ocean trout fillets	1	teaspoon tarragon
12	ounces sour cream	1	teaspoon salt
4	tablespoons grated Parmesan cheese	1	cup garlic flavored croutons, crushed
1½	teaspoons paprika		Sprigs of fresh parsley

Place fillets in a casserole. Combine sour cream, Parmesan, paprika, tarragon, and salt and spread evenly over fish. Sprinkle croutons over fish and top with parsley. Bake at 350° for 30-45 minutes.
Serves 4.
Mrs. Christopher Stephen Young (French Anne Pruitt)

Trout Hudson

6-8	medium mushrooms, sliced	1½-2	pounds trout fillets
½	stick butter		Cracked pepper to taste
	Juice of 1½ lemons		Salt to taste
2	tablespoons sherry		

Sauté mushrooms in butter and lemon juice. Add sherry. Line a shallow baking pan with foil. Place fish, skin side down, on foil. Season fish with cracked pepper and salt lightly. Pour the mushroom mixture over fish and bake at 350° for 30 minutes.
Serves 2.
Mrs. George E. Dullnig (Margaret Rolle)

Trout Almondine

6	large trout or redfish fillets		Garlic salt to taste
	Juice of 2 lemons, divided		Pepper to taste
24	saltine crackers, crushed	¾	cup sliced almonds
2	sticks butter, divided	1	4 ounce can mushrooms, drained

Marinate fish in the juice of 1 lemon for 5 minutes. Coat fish with crackers and sauté in 1 stick butter for 3-5 minutes on each side. Place fish in a baking pan, sprinkle lightly with garlic salt and pepper, and top with remaining lemon juice. Sauté almonds and mushrooms in remaining butter and pour over fish. Bake at 300° for 20 minutes. Serve immediately.
Serves 6.
Mrs. Orvis E. Meador, Jr. (Jo Lynne Musselman)

Stuffed Flounder

1 cup chopped, cooked shrimp
2 tablespoons capers
2 hard-boiled eggs, chopped
¼ cup light cream
1 large flounder or other flat fish
2 tablespoons butter
2 tablespoons flour
1 cup milk
½ cup flaked crabmeat
1 large tomato, diced
Salt to taste
¼ teaspoon white pepper

Mix shrimp, capers, and eggs with enough cream to moisten and bind ingredients. Along the backbone of the fish, cut a large opening on each side, being careful not to go to the edge. Stuff fish with shrimp mixture and place in a buttered, shallow casserole. Melt butter, stir in flour, and add milk gradually, stirring constantly until thickened. Add crabmeat, tomato, salt, and pepper. Pour sauce over fish. Bake at 350° for 45-60 minutes or until the fish flakes easily when tested with a fork.
Serves 4.
Mrs. Ernest L. Brown, III (Connie Lentz)

Fish Fillets au Sharon

1 pound sole or flounder fillets
½ cup mayonnaise
2 green onions, finely chopped
2 tablespoons drained capers, finely chopped
2 tablespoons chopped fresh parsley
2 tablespoons lemon juice
¼ teaspoon ground white pepper
¼ teaspoon salt
Fresh parsley or sweet red pepper, sautéed in butter, for garnish

Spray a flat baking pan with vegetable spray or grease with mayonnaise. Place fish fillets in a single layer in pan. Make a tartar sauce by combining mayonnaise, onions, capers, parsley, lemon juice, white pepper, and salt. Cover fish with sauce. Bake at 400° for 10-20 minutes or until fish flakes easily. If there are 8 fillets to the pound, cook 10 minutes. If there are 4 fillets to the pound, cook 20 minutes. Do not overcook. Garnish with parsley or peppers. *An original recipe, named after a daughter who liked it very much.*
Serves 4.
Mrs. F. R. Veach, Jr. (Dorothy Ann)

Swiss Baked Fish Fillets

2	pounds frozen fish fillets, thawed	¾	teaspoon salt
1	cup sour cream	⅛	teaspoon pepper
½	cup slivered Swiss cheese	1	teaspoon prepared mustard
¼	cup finely chopped green onions		

Lightly grease a 2½ quart baking dish. Arrange fillets in baking dish. Mix remaining ingredients and spread over fillets. Bake at 450° for 20 minutes or until fish flakes easily with a fork. Brown under broiler for 1-2 minutes.
Serves 6.
Mrs. Charles Ralph Hardinge (Anne Kennerly Rumsey)

Fish in Cream Sauce

1	5 pound fish	1	stick butter, divided
1¼	cups stock	½	cup white wine
2	sprigs parsley	2	tablespoons flour
½	teaspoon thyme	1	cup heavy cream
¼	cup chopped celery with leaves	2	egg yolks
¼	cup coarsely chopped onion	¼	cup water
12	black peppercorns		Juice of ½ lemon
2	tablespoons chopped shallots		Cayenne pepper to taste
Salt and pepper to taste			

Bone fish and make a stock by combining the bones, head, and tail from fish with parsley, thyme, celery, onion, peppercorns, and enough water to cover. Simmer for 20-30 minutes and strain. Butter a baking dish just large enough to hold fish. Sprinkle fish with shallots, salt, and pepper. Place fish in pan, skin side down, and dot with 2 tablespoons butter. Combine ½ cup stock with wine and pour over fish. Cover with foil and bake at 450° for 10-15 minutes or until fish flakes. Melt 2 tablespoons butter in a saucepan, stir in flour, add ¾ cup stock, and simmer about 10 minutes. Drain liquid from fish into a separate saucepan, boil until reduced by half, and add fish stock sauce. Stir in cream and bring to boil. In another saucepan, combine egg yolks with water and beat with a whisk over low heat. Beat in lemon juice and remove from heat when mixture is slightly thickened. Gradually add 3 tablespoons melted butter, beat in fish sauce, and add cayenne. Pour over fish and broil until golden and lightly glazed.
Serves 4.
Mrs. Frates Seeligson (Martita Rice)

Fish Portuguese

1	cup chopped onion	1	teaspoon salt
½	cup chopped celery and tops	⅛-¼	teaspoon pepper
½	cup chopped parsley	¼	cup vegetable oil
2	pounds fish fillets (if frozen, dry well)	¾	teaspoon paprika
		2	8 ounce cans tomato sauce

Combine onion, celery, and parsley and spread in a large, shallow greased or teflon baking dish. Place fish in overlapping layers on the vegetables. Season with salt and pepper, drizzle with oil, and sprinkle with paprika. Bake at 375° for 10 minutes. Pour tomato sauce over fish and bake 30-35 minutes, basting occasionally.
Serves 6.
Mrs. Richard H. Eckhardt (Mary Webb)

Barbecued Salmon Steaks with Avocado Butter

Salmon Steaks

1	cup oil	¼	teaspoon marjoram
3	tablespoons lemon juice	½	teaspoon salt
2	teaspoons barbecue spice	⅛	teaspoon pepper
¼	teaspoon basil	6	salmon steaks, about ½ pound each

Avocado Butter

1	stick butter or margarine, softened	1	teaspoon Worcestershire sauce
¼	cup mashed avocado	½	teaspoon garlic salt
4	teaspoons lemon juice	½	teaspoon barbecue spice or chili powder
1	tablespoon chopped parsley		

Salmon Steaks   Place all ingredients, except the salmon, in a jar and shake well. Arrange salmon in a casserole, top with sauce, and cover. Refrigerate about 4 hours, turning occasionally. Drain ½ the sauce from salmon and reserve. Broil salmon 2 inches from heat for about 4 minutes, turn, and spoon on reserved sauce. Broil about 7 minutes or until fish flakes easily with a fork. Serve steaks topped with Avocado Butter.

Avocado Butter   Whip butter or margarine until fluffy and light. Fold in remaining ingredients, cover, and refrigerate. *Avocado Butter may also be used as an hors d'oeuvre spread.*
Serves 6.
Mrs. Edgar M. Duncan (Linda Wyatt)

Red Snapper New Orleans

1	whole red snapper, about 3 pounds	3-4	cups water
Salt and pepper to taste		Juice of 1 lemon	
2	onions, chopped, or 4 cups	2	pinches of thyme
4	tablespoons bacon drippings	3	bay leaves
5	tablespoons flour		

Season fish generously with salt and pepper and place in a roaster. Sauté onions in 3 tablespoons drippings until golden. Remove onions and set aside. Add remaining drippings and stir in flour, cooking until well browned. Add 3 cups water and continue to stir until blended. Pour over fish, adding additional water if necessary, to cover half of fish. Add onion and remaining ingredients. Cover and bake at 350° for 35 minutes. Remove cover and bake at 450° for 10 minutes, basting frequently. *May be garnished with lemon slices, paprika, and parsley.*
Serves 4-6.
Mrs. Archie S. Brown (Margaret Terrell)

Tuna Puff Sandwiches

1	6½ ounce can solid white meat tuna	2	tablespoons chopped green pepper
1½	teaspoons prepared mustard	3	English muffins or hamburger buns, split and toasted
¼	teaspoon Worcestershire sauce	6	tomato slices
¼	cup mayonnaise	½	cup mayonnaise
1½	teaspoons onion salt	¼	cup grated American cheese

Mix first 6 ingredients, mound onto muffins, and top with tomato slices. Combine ½ cup mayonnaise and cheese, spread over sandwiches, and broil until they puff. *You may substitute shrimp, crab, or lobster for tuna if you're not fighting inflation.*
Yields 6 halves.
Mrs. Ted Thomas (Nell Ezell)

Crabmeat Dijon

1	tablespoon chopped shallots	1	teaspoon chopped parsley
½	stick butter, divided	1	teaspoon chopped chives
⅓	cup Chablis	4	egg yolks
1¾	cups light cream, divided	Salt and pepper to taste	
1	pound lump crabmeat	1	tablespoon Dijon mustard

Sauté shallots in 3 tablespoons butter until tender. Add wine and cook until liquid is reduced by half. Stir in 1½ cups cream and add crabmeat, parsley, and chives. Beat egg yolks with ¼ cup cream. Remove crabmeat from heat and slowly add the egg yolk mixture, stirring constantly. Season with salt, pepper, and mustard. Bake in a 2 quart buttered casserole at 350° for 30 minutes. When ready to serve, top with 1 tablespoon butter. *This recipe came from the chef at the Jockey Club in Buenos Aires.*
Serves 12.
Mrs. Eyvind M. Verner (Mary Louise Ramsay)

Crab Cohagan

1   onion, chopped
½   green pepper, chopped
½   cup chopped celery
1   clove garlic, crushed
1   tablespoon chopped parsley
1   stick butter
1   pound crabmeat
⅔   cup light cream
2   tablespoons flour
¼   teaspoon thyme

1   hard-boiled egg, chopped
2   eggs, beaten
1½ tablespoons lemon juice
10 drops Tabasco sauce
½   teaspoon Worcestershire sauce
½   teaspoon salt
1   cup bread crumbs
1   stick butter, melted
1   cup mayonnaise
1½ teaspoons curry powder

Sauté onion, green pepper, celery, garlic, and parsley in 1 stick butter. Stir in crabmeat. Add cream mixed with flour, thyme, hard-boiled egg, beaten eggs, lemon juice, Tabasco, Worcestershire, and salt. Place mixture in ramekins, sprinkle with bread crumbs mixed with melted butter, and top with mayonnaise seasoned with curry. Bake at 375° for 15-20 minutes.
Serves 6.
Mrs. Paul A. Braymen (Judith Barnard)

Mama's Crab Newburg

4-5 cloves garlic, crushed
2   large onions, chopped
1   green pepper, chopped
1   stick butter
2   tablespoons flour
¼   teaspoon curry powder
1   13 ounce can evaporated milk

1   pound Old English cheese, grated
⅛   teaspoon cayenne pepper
¼   teaspoon Worcestershire sauce
¼   teaspoon pepper
Milk, optional
1   pound king crabmeat

Sauté garlic, onions, and green pepper in butter until tender. Stir in flour and curry powder. Add evaporated milk, cheese, and seasonings, stirring constantly. Additional milk may be added if the sauce is too thick. Gently stir in crab and continue to stir so the mixture does not burn. *This versatile recipe from my grandmother may be prepared substituting shrimp for crab and served over rice or spaghetti. It may also be used as a dip served either hot or cold.*
Serves 4-6. Freezes.
Mrs. William A. Jeffers, Jr. (Billie Jeanette Street)

Crab Casserole

2	tablespoons butter	1	cup grated Swiss cheese
2	tablespoons flour	2	egg yolks, beaten
1	cup milk or light cream	2	cups crabmeat
½	teaspoon salt	2	tablespoons melted butter
⅛	teaspoon pepper	¼	cup Ritz cracker crumbs

Melt butter and stir in flour. Add milk and stir until mixture boils and thickens. Cook about 3 minutes, stirring occasionally. Add salt, pepper, and cheese, stirring until cheese is melted. Remove from heat, add egg yolks, then crabmeat. Pour into a casserole. Mix melted butter and cracker crumbs together and sprinkle on top. Bake at 350° for 30 minutes. *This recipe was obtained while sitting in the White House kitchen with Zephra Wright, the family cook for the Johnsons for many years, and copying down every word that she spoke.*
Serves 8.
Mrs. James D. Price (Warrie Lynn Smith)

Crabmeat Elizabeth

1½	pounds large mushrooms	1	pound crabmeat
5-6	tablespoons butter or margarine, divided	⅓	cup Pickapeppa sauce
		¼	cup sherry
3	green onions, chopped	⅓	cup bread crumbs
2	tablespoons flour	½	cup grated Romano cheese
1	cup milk	½	cup chopped parsley
½	cup mayonnaise		

Sauté whole mushroom caps in 2-3 tablespoons butter. Drain and place in 1 large or 6 individual buttered baking dishes. Sauté green onions lightly in 1 tablespoon butter and set aside. Melt remaining butter and stir in flour. Add milk gradually, stirring until thickened. Add green onions, mayonnaise, crab, Pickapeppa, sherry, and bread crumbs. When mixture is hot, pour over mushrooms, and sprinkle with cheese and parsley. Bake at 350° for 20 minutes.
Serves 6.
Mrs. Robert R. Archer (Marian Lindsay)

Gallino's Crab Rockport

1	pound lump crabmeat	1	tablespoon Worcestershire sauce
1/3	cup finely chopped onion	1/2	teaspoon salt
1/2	cup finely chopped celery	1/4	teaspoon pepper
1	tablespoon chopped fresh parsley	3 1/2	teaspoons mayonnaise
1/3	cup finely chopped ripe olives		Paprika
1/2	cup finely crushed seasoned croutons		

Combine all ingredients, except paprika, mixing thoroughly. Place mixture into 4 buttered shells or ramekins, sprinkle with paprika, and bake at 325° for 30-40 minutes.
Serves 4.
Mr. Frank Gallino

Crab and Avocado Enchiladas

1/4	cup finely chopped onion	1/2	teaspoon salt
1/4	cup chopped ripe olives		Dash of pepper
1/4	cup fresh mushrooms, sliced		Crushed red pepper flakes to taste, optional
2	tablespoons butter		
10	ounces crabmeat, fresh, canned, or frozen	1	dozen tortillas
			Hot vegetable oil
1	ripe avocado, mashed	1	cup grated Cheddar cheese
1 1/2	cups sour cream, divided	1/2	cup sliced ripe olives

Sauté onion, chopped olives, and mushrooms in butter. Remove from heat and stir in crabmeat, avocado mixed with 1 cup sour cream, salt, pepper, and red pepper. Dip each tortilla in hot oil and drain on absorbent paper. Fill each tortilla with some of the crab mixture, roll, and place seam side down in a buttered 9 x 11 casserole. Cover with remaining sour cream, and sprinkle with cheese and sliced olives. Bake at 350° for 20 minutes and serve immediately.
This is a nice luncheon dish served with tomato aspic and bolillos. Never mind the calories, just eat and enjoy!
Serves 6.
Mrs. Frederick L. Thomson, III (Barbara South)

Hot Stuffed Avocados

6	tablespoons vinegar	¼	teaspoon celery salt
3	cloves garlic, sliced in half	⅛	teaspoon cayenne pepper
3	avocados, halved	1	tablespoon grated onion
2	tablespoons butter	2	cups cooked crabmeat, lobster,
2	tablespoons flour		shrimp, spam, ham, chicken,
1	cup light cream		or turkey
½	teaspoon Worcestershire sauce	½	cup grated Cheddar cheese
1¼	teaspoons salt		Toast "boats"*
⅛	teaspoon pepper		

Place 1 tablespoon vinegar and ½ clove garlic in each avocado half and let stand for 30 minutes. Melt butter, blend in flour, slowly add cream, and cook, stirring frequently until thickened. Add Worcestershire, salt, pepper, celery salt, cayenne, onion, and crabmeat. Heat mixture thoroughly. Remove vinegar and garlic from avocados. Peel avocados and fill with creamed mixture. Sprinkle with cheese, place in a baking dish, and add about ¼ inch water in bottom of dish. Bake at 350° for 15 minutes or until cheese melts. *Avocados may be garnished with pimiento stuffed olives and served on a bed of lettuce or in toast "boats".*

*Toast "boats" Butter 6 thin slices bread with crusts removed. Place each slice into an individual baking dish large enough for avocados. Bake at 350° until lightly toasted and firm. Place avocado into toast "boat". Garnish with parsley and thin slices of tomato, being sure tomato does not touch toast. Serves 6.
Mrs. Richard Knight, Jr. (Darleen)

Scallops Brittany

⅔	stick butter, melted	1	pound scallops or ½ pound
2	teaspoons minced parsley		scallops and ½ pound cubed,
2	teaspoons minced chives		sweet boneless fish such as turbot
¼	clove garlic, crushed		or flounder
⅔	cup dried bread crumbs		Lemon wedges

Butter 4 large baking shells. Combine butter, parsley, chives, garlic, and bread crumbs. Spread some of crumb mixture in center of shells, top with scallops, and sprinkle with remaining crumb mixture. Place shells on a baking sheet. Bake at 350° for 25-30 minutes. Serve with lemon wedges. *It is delicious!* Serves 4.
Mrs. Willis E. Brown, Jr. (Elizabeth "Ann" Bliedung)

Scallops and Green Beans

2   10 ounce packages frozen green beans, cooked according to package directions and drained
¾   cup white wine
1½ pounds scallops or cooked and cubed chicken
½   stick margarine, divided
3   green onions, chopped
1   4 ounce can mushrooms, drained

1   teaspoon dried parsley
¼   teaspoon marjoram
¼   teaspoon thyme
½   teaspoon salt
¼   teaspoon pepper
3   tablespoons flour
1⅔ cups milk
2   slices bread

Place beans in a greased 1½ quart casserole. Heat wine, add scallops, and simmer 3-4 minutes. Remove scallops, reserving liquid, and place scallops over beans. Sauté onions in 3 tablespoons butter until tender. Add mushrooms and seasonings. Stir in flour. Gradually add reserved liquid and milk, stirring constantly, and bring to a boil. Pour over scallops. Whirl bread in blender to make crumbs. Melt remaining margarine, add crumbs, and sprinkle over casserole. Bake at 350° for 10-15 minutes.

Mrs. Edward C. Held (Joan McMartin)

Coquille St. Jacques

2   cups scallops
¾   stick butter or margarine, divided
¼   cup flour
1   teaspoon prepared mustard
1   teaspoon salt
Dash of cayenne pepper

2   cups milk
1   teaspoon Worcestershire sauce
⅔   cup grated Parmesan cheese, divided
1   teaspoon minced shallots
1   cup cooked, peeled shrimp
1   tablespoon minced parsley

Simmer scallops in water to cover for 5 minutes and drain. Melt ½ stick butter and stir in flour, mustard, salt, and cayenne. Gradually add milk, stirring until thickened. Remove from heat and add Worcestershire and ⅓ cup cheese. Sauté shallots in remaining butter until tender. Stir in scallops, shrimp, parsley, and cheese sauce. Spoon into 6 baking shells or ramekins, sprinkle with remaining cheese, and broil until browned. *I entered this recipe in the Home and Hobby Show a few years ago, and won a self-cleaning Westinghouse stove!*

Variation   For Coquille Diable, substitute dry mustard for prepared mustard and 4 cups crab or lobster meat for scallops and shrimp, and add 2 tablespoons white wine to sauce.
Serves 6.
Mrs. Frank Haegelin

Shrimp Victoria

1	pound raw shrimp, peeled and cleaned	¼	teaspoon salt
1	small onion, finely chopped		Dash of pepper
½	stick butter	½	cup sour cream
½	cup sliced fresh mushrooms	1	tablespoon vermouth
1	tablespoon flour		Juice of ½ lemon
			Cooked rice

Sauté shrimp and onion in butter for 10 minutes or until shrimp are pink. Add mushrooms and cook for 5 more minutes. Sprinkle in flour, salt, and pepper. Stir in sour cream, vermouth, and lemon, and cook gently for 10 minutes, being sure mixture does not boil. Serve over rice.
Serves 4.
Mr. William A. Jeffers, Jr.

Shrimp or Chicken Casserole

1	pound shrimp, cooked and peeled, or chicken breasts, cooked and cubed	1	cup milk
		1	cup heavy cream
1	14 ounce can artichoke hearts, drained and quartered	1	teaspoon salt
		½	teaspoon pepper
¼	pound fresh mushrooms, sliced and sautéed	2	teaspoons Worcestershire sauce
		¼	cup sherry
½	stick butter	¼	cup grated Parmesan cheese
5	tablespoons flour		Paprika to taste
			Cooked rice or noodles

In a lightly greased baking dish, layer shrimp, artichoke hearts, and mushrooms. Melt butter, stir in flour, and add milk gradually, stirring until thickened. Add cream, salt, pepper, Worcestershire, and sherry and pour over casserole. Sprinkle with cheese and paprika. Bake at 375° for 30 minutes. Serve over rice or noodles.
Serves 6. Freezes.
Mrs. John Robert Beauchamp (Francis Ann Drake)

Shrimp and Rice Cantonese

¼	cup chopped onion	2	tablespoons soy sauce
1	stick butter or margarine		Salt to taste
3	cups cooked rice, chilled	1	pound shrimp, cooked and peeled
2	eggs, beaten		

Sauté onion in butter and add rice. Gradually stir in eggs and soy sauce. Season with salt and cook over low heat for 10 minutes. Stir in shrimp to heat and serve immediately. *Leftover rice may be reheated by adding a beaten egg for moisture.*
Serves 8.
Mrs. John Ragland Harrison (Frances Bates)

Fried Shrimp

¼ pound saltine crackers
¼ teaspoon pepper
3 pounds medium or large raw shrimp, peeled and cleaned
½ teaspoon salt

½ teaspoon pepper
1 tablespoon milk
5 eggs, beaten
Cooking oil
Tartar or red sauce

Crush saltines in blender and add ¼ teaspoon pepper. Slice the shrimp lengthwise almost to the vein. Spread and flatten to form a butterfly shape. Add salt, ½ teaspoon pepper, and milk to eggs, mixing well. Dip shrimp into egg mixture, then into crackers. Fry in oil heated to 375°-400°F until golden brown. Serve with tartar or red sauce.
Serves 10-12.
Mrs. Melvin M. Mitchell (Yeola Steed)

Shrimp Boiled in Beer

3 pounds raw shrimp in shells
3-4 cans beer
2 teaspoons dried dill or sprigs of fresh dill
Celery leaves

1 bay leaf
8-12 peppercorns
1 small onion, sliced, optional
1 lemon, sliced, optional

Place the shrimp in a pan with enough beer to cover. Add remaining ingredients and bring to a boil, cover, and simmer for 5 minutes. Drain and chill. *Serve cold with additional slices of lemon.*
Serves 4.
Mrs. Alex Weil, III (Penny Speier)

Canlis Shrimp

2 tablespoons olive oil
2 pounds raw jumbo shrimp, peeled and cleaned
2 tablespoons butter
1 small clove garlic, crushed

¼ teaspoon salt, or more to taste
¼ teaspoon freshly ground pepper
Juice of 2 lemons
¼ cup dry vermouth

Heat oil and add shrimp, cooking and stirring 2-3 minutes or until the shrimp are pink. Reduce heat and stir in butter, garlic, salt, and pepper. Increase heat, add lemon juice and vermouth, and cook for 1 minute stirring constantly. *This recipe, served at the Fairmont Hotel in San Francisco, may be used as an appetizer or as an entrée when served over rice.*
Serves 6.
Mrs. Walter O. Baker (Susan Wolff)

Shrimp Casserole

2½ pounds fresh shrimp, cooked
 and peeled
1 tablespoon lemon juice
3 tablespoons salad oil
¾ cup uncooked rice
¼ cup chopped green pepper
¼ cup chopped onions
2 tablespoons butter or margarine
1 10¾ ounce can tomato soup

1 teaspoon salt
⅛ teaspoon pepper
⅛ teaspoon mace
1 cup heavy cream
½ cup sherry
Dash of cayenne pepper
¾ cup slivered almonds
Paprika

Place shrimp in a 2 quart casserole, sprinkle with lemon juice and oil, and refrigerate. Cook rice and refrigerate. About 70 minutes before serving, sauté green pepper and onions in butter for 5 minutes. Combine all ingredients except 8 shrimp, ¼ cup almonds, and paprika. Bake at 350° for 35 minutes or until bubbly. Top with reserved shrimp, almonds, and paprika and continue to bake for 20 minutes.
Serves 8.
Mrs. Jack Beretta (Mary Austin Perry)

Shrimp in Avocado with Mustard Sauce

1 lemon slice
Salt to taste
½ bay leaf
2 sprigs parsley
1 rib celery, cut into thirds
10 peppercorns
½ teaspoon dried thyme
2 quarts water
36 medium raw shrimp in shells
1 tablespoon Dijon mustard

1 teaspoon anchovy paste
3 tablespoons lemon juice
¾ cup olive oil
1 tablespoon chopped fresh tarragon
 or dill, or ½ teaspoon dried
 tarragon or dill
2 tablespoons capers
3 ripe avocados
Lemon wedges

Add lemon, salt, bay leaf, parsley, celery, peppercorns, and thyme to water and bring to a boil. Add shrimp, bring to a boil, and cook 4-6 minutes. Remove shrimp with a slotted spoon and chill. Peel and clean shrimp. Beat mustard, anchovy paste, and lemon juice with a wire whisk, adding the oil gradually. Add salt, tarragon, and capers. Pour over shrimp and marinate 1-2 hours. Peel and halve avocados. Fill avocados with shrimp and serve with lemon wedges. *The liquid that remains after boiling the shrimp is a wonderful stock to use for soup or gumbo.*
Serves 6.
Mrs. Edgar M. Duncan (Linda Wyatt)

Shrimp Tetrazzini

1   stick butter, divided
1   bunch green onions, sliced
½   cup cold water
5   tablespoons flour
2½ cups chicken broth
½   cup clam juice
½   cup dry white wine
½   cup heavy cream
1   teaspoon oregano
2   ounces fresh Parmesan cheese, grated, or ½ cup

2   tablespoons vegetable oil
2   cloves garlic, peeled and split
½   pound small mushrooms, thinly sliced
2   pounds cooked, peeled medium shrimp
8   ounces spaghetti, cooked and drained
Salt to taste

Melt ½ stick butter in a heavy saucepan. Add the onions and water, bring to a boil, reduce heat, and cook until all the water has boiled away and the onions are soft. Stir in flour until smooth, cook about 3 minutes, but do not brown. Add the broth, clam juice, wine, cream, and oregano. Cook, whipping constantly with a whisk, until the sauce begins to boil. Stir in half the cheese and remove from heat. Melt remaining butter with oil, add garlic and mushrooms, and shake the pan over high heat for 4-5 minutes until mushrooms have browned. Remove from heat, discard garlic, and add shrimp. Combine shrimp mixture, spaghetti, and salt in a large, shallow casserole and sprinkle with remaining cheese. Bake at 375° for 15 minutes or until the sauce is bubbly and the top is brown. *This may be prepared ahead of time.*
Serves 6-8. Freezes well before baking.
Mrs. Daniel J. Sullivan, IV (Ruth Eilene Butler)

Sherried Shrimp Rockefeller

2   10 ounce packages frozen chopped spinach, thawed
1   10¾ ounce can cream of shrimp soup
4   ounces sharp Cheddar cheese, grated, or 1 cup

3   tablespoons sherry
2   slices bread
3   tablespoons butter, melted
¾-1 pound peeled, cleaned shrimp
Paprika to taste

Squeeze out as much liquid as possible from spinach and spread in the bottom of a 2 quart casserole. Over low heat mix soup, cheese, and sherry, stirring until cheese melts. Whirl bread in blender to make coarse bread crumbs and combine with butter. Place shrimp over spinach, add cheese mixture, top with bread crumbs, and sprinkle with paprika. Bake at 350° for 45 minutes. *This recipe is ideal for microwave cooking. Bake, uncovered, 12-14 minutes, giving dish ½ turn after 6 minutes. Cover and let stand 5 minutes before serving.*
Serves 4. May be prepared a day ahead.
Mrs. Charles Ralph Hardinge (Anne Kennerly Rumsey)

Argyle Shrimp Congeglia

3	hard-boiled eggs		Salt to taste
2	dill pickles		White pepper to taste
1	4 ounce jar pimientos		Lemon juice to taste
2	medium green peppers	2	pounds cooked, peeled, and
⅓	bunch parsley		cleaned fresh shrimp
1	quart mayonnaise		Parmesan cheese
4	ounces catsup		Paprika

Grind the first 5 ingredients and combine with mayonnaise and catsup. Season with salt, white pepper, and lemon juice. Place shrimp in a shallow casserole or individual shells, cover with sauce, and top generously with cheese. Sprinkle with paprika and bake at 400° for 7 minutes or until heated and cheese is toasted.

Mr. Mel Weingart

Baked Shrimp

1	pound cooked, peeled shrimp	¼	cup cream
1	tablespoon olive oil	1	tablespoon Worcestershire sauce
1	tablespoon butter		Dash of Tabasco sauce or cayenne
½	cup chili sauce		pepper

Mix ingredients thoroughly. Place in individual ramekins and bake at 350° for 20 minutes.
Serves 4 as an entrée, 6-8 as an hors d'oeuvre.
Mrs. James L. Ewing (Alice Grehan Witherspoon)

Shrimp Orleans

1	tablespoon butter or margarine	¼	cup catsup
1	medium onion, thinly sliced	1	4 ounce can broiled, sliced
1	clove garlic, crushed		mushrooms, drained
1	10¾ ounce can cream of	2	cups cooked, peeled shrimp
	mushroom soup		Cooked rice
1	cup sour cream		

Melt butter in a chafing dish or skillet. Add onion and garlic, cooking until tender but not brown. Combine soup, sour cream, and catsup and stir into onions. Add mushrooms and shrimp. Cook over low heat only until mixture is thoroughly heated. Serve over fluffy hot rice. *Leftover shrimp mixture may be puréed in blender and used as a dip served either hot or cold. Fast, easy, delicious, and different.*
Serves 4.
Mrs. Frank B. Vaughan, Jr.

Shrimp in Butter Sauce

1½ sticks butter
1-2 tablespoons chopped onion
1-2 cloves garlic, chopped

1 tablespoon minced parsley
1½ pounds shrimp, cooked and peeled
Bread crumbs

Mix together butter, onion, garlic, and parsley and allow mixture to stand 30 minutes. Place shrimp in individual baking dishes, sprinkle with bread crumbs, and add a spoonful of the butter mixture. Bake at 350° for 15 minutes.
Serves 4.
Mrs. Kenneth Reed Wynne (Paula Gay Edwards)

Shrimp Creole

1 onion, chopped
2 cloves garlic, minced
½ pound link hot sausage with casing removed, sliced
1 green pepper, chopped
2 ribs celery, chopped
2 tablespoons bacon drippings

2 14½ ounce cans stewed tomatoes
3 tablespoons Pace Picante Sauce
2 tablespoons tomato paste
3 tablespoons A-1 sauce
1 teaspoon sugar
1 pound shrimp, cooked and cleaned
Cooked rice

Sauté onion, garlic, sausage, green pepper, and celery in bacon drippings for about 10 minutes. Add tomatoes, picante sauce, tomato paste, A-1 sauce, and sugar and simmer for 10 minutes. Add shrimp and cook for 15 minutes. Serve over rice. *A creole with a Texas twist.*
Serves 4-6.
Mrs. Robert R. Archer (Marian Lindsay)

Shrimp Conchiglia

1 10¾ ounce can tomato soup
½ cup milk
¼ cup Worcestershire sauce
Juice of 1 lemon
1 tablespoon sugar

Pinch of oregano
2 pounds cooked shrimp, peeled and cleaned
1 cup grated Parmesan cheese, divided

Combine all ingredients, except shrimp and ½ cup cheese, and heat slowly. Do not boil. Arrange shrimp in baking shells. Top with sauce and remaining cheese. Broil 2-3 minutes until heated and cheese is lightly browned.
Serves 4 as an entrée, 10-12 as an hors d'oeuvre.
Mrs. O'Neill Munn (Sandy)

Shrimp and Eggplant Casserole

1   large eggplant, peeled and cubed
1   tablespoon sugar
1   large onion, chopped
1   green pepper, chopped
2-3 tablespoons butter
1   10¾ ounce can cream of
    mushroom soup
1   4 ounce can sliced mushrooms,
    drained
1   pound raw shrimp, peeled

1   pound New York sharp cheese,
    grated and divided
1   teaspoon Worcestershire sauce
Dash of cayenne pepper
2-3 drops Tabasco sauce
Pepper to taste
¼   teaspoon garlic salt
1   cup cracker crumbs
Paprika

Cook eggplant in boiling water with sugar until tender. Sauté onion and green pepper in butter until tender but not brown. Add soup, mushrooms, eggplant, shrimp, ½ of cheese, and seasonings. Place mixture in a 9 x 15 casserole, top with cracker crumbs and remaining cheese, and sprinkle with paprika. Bake at 350° for 1 hour or until almost dry. *This is very attractive served in the eggplant shell.*
Serves 8-10.
Mrs. J. Fletcher Lee

Bar-B-Qued Shrimp

5   pounds large raw shrimp with
    heads if possible
1   pound butter or margarine, melted
2   tablespoons pepper
1   jar French's or McCormick's
    Italian seasoning

2   tablespoons soy sauce
2   tablespoons Worcestershire sauce
Juice and rind of 2 lemons
1½ tablespoons salt

Place shrimp in a large shallow baking pan. Combine remaining ingredients and pour over shrimp. Bake at 350° for 20-30 minutes. *This recipe is from Manale's Restaurant in New Orleans where the shrimp are served hot in the sauce and peeled at the table.*
Serves 6-8.
Mrs. Samuel Earl Maclin (Jane Emerson)

Barbecued Shrimp

¼ cup vegetable oil
¼ cup soy sauce
3 tablespoons Worcestershire sauce
5 ounces La Choy Sweet and Sour Sauce

Juice of ½ lemon or 2 tablespoons vinegar
¼ teaspoon garlic salt or to taste
1 pound raw, peeled shrimp

Mix ingredients and marinate at least 2 hours. Skewer shrimp and heat remaining sauce. Cook shrimp over hot coals for 10 minutes on each side. Remove shrimp and cover with sauce.
Serves 2 as an entrée, 4 as an hors d'oeuvre.
Mrs. Ed Pfefferling

Barbecued Shrimp with Dip

1½ cups vegetable oil
¼-½ cup lemon juice
½ clove garlic, minced
1 onion, sliced
2 pounds shrimp, peeled
1 cup sour cream

1 6 ounce can tomato paste
Juice of 1 lemon
1 tablespoon grated onion
Pinch of garlic salt
Pinch of cayenne pepper
2 drops Tabasco sauce

Combine oil, lemon juice, garlic, and onion. Marinate shrimp in this mixture for several hours. Prepare dip by combining remaining ingredients, and refrigerate. Place shrimp on aluminum foil in which holes have been pierced and grill over hot coals for 10-15 minutes or until shrimp curl and turn pink. Serve hot shrimp with dip.

Mrs. David Starks (Laura Ann Thomas)

Curried Shrimp Boats

2 4½ ounce cans small shrimp or 2 cups small shrimp, cooked and peeled
¾ cup mayonnaise
2 tablespoons finely chopped onion
2 tablespoons finely chopped parsley

1 cup chopped celery or 1 cup peeled, seeded, chopped cucumber
1½ teaspoons curry powder
¼ teaspoon ground ginger
Crisp salad greens
8 hot dog buns, cut down top center, to use as "boats"

Combine all ingredients except salad greens and buns. Arrange salad greens in buns and stuff with shrimp mixture. *This recipe is a good shrimp salad without the buns.*
Yields 6 sandwich "boats".
Mrs. Emmett B. Dawson

Scampi Guadalajara

1	stick butter, at room temperature	1	tablespoon lemon juice
2	green onions, finely chopped, or 3 tablespoons	¼	teaspoon salt
		¼	teaspoon coarse black pepper
2	cloves garlic, crushed	8	raw, peeled, cleaned jumbo shrimp with tails
1½	tablespoons A-1 sauce		

Combine all ingredients, except shrimp, in a saucepan and cook over low heat stirring occasionally until thoroughly heated but not brown. Slice the shrimp lengthwise almost to the vein. Spread and flatten to form a butterfly shape. Place shrimp, split sides up, in a greased baking pan and broil 4 inches from heat for 5 minutes. Pour hot butter sauce over shrimp and serve. *These shrimp are good with prosciutto wrapped melon, sliced tomatoes sprinkled with basil, and buttered spaghetti. This recipe is so quick and easy you will find it helpful for entertaining in a hurry.*
Serves 2.
Mrs. Charles P. Mueller, Jr.

Shrimp Italian

1	pound jumbo shrimp, peeled and cleaned	2	tablespoons finely chopped onion
2½	teaspoons salt, divided	6	cloves garlic, finely minced
1	teaspoon pepper, divided	1	teaspoon finely chopped pimiento
Cayenne pepper to taste		½	cup lemon juice
2	tablespoons lemon juice	¼	cup grated Provolone cheese
¾	stick butter, divided	⅛	cup sherry
4	tablespoons cornstarch	1	teaspoon Italian seasoning
2	cups light cream	1	cup flour
		Cooking oil	

Season shrimp with 1 teaspoon salt, ½ teaspoon pepper, cayenne, and 2 tablespoons lemon juice. Melt ½ stick butter and stir in ½ teaspoon salt and cornstarch. Add cream gradually, stirring until thickened. Sauté onion and garlic in remaining butter. Add cream sauce, pimiento, ½ cup lemon juice, cheese, sherry, and Italian seasoning. Roll shrimp in flour seasoned with remaining salt and pepper. Fry shrimp until golden brown in deep fat heated to 375°F. Place shrimp on a heat proof platter, cover with sauce, and broil for 2-3 minutes. Serve immediately. *The sauce portion of this recipe may be prepared ahead and heated before pouring over shrimp. Serve with green salad, garlic bread, and a dry white wine.*
Serves 4.
Mrs. Ferd C. Meyer, Jr. (Marcia Marron)

Fat Man's Shrimp

½ pound fresh mushrooms, sliced
½ stick butter
1 cup sour cream
2 10¾ ounce cans cream of mushroom soup
½ cup grated Parmesan cheese

½ teaspoon dry mustard
1 pound fresh shrimp, cooked, or 2 cups
2 10 ounce packages frozen chopped spinach, cooked and drained
Buttered bread crumbs

Sauté mushrooms in butter. Mix sour cream, soup, cheese, and mustard. Add to mushrooms, heat, and add shrimp. In a 2 quart casserole, layer spinach and shrimp twice. Sprinkle with bread crumbs and bake at 350° for 15 minutes. *This recipe may be made with 2 pounds of shrimp without increasing the amounts of the other ingredients.*
Serves 4.
Mrs. William B. Culverwell (Sally Powell)

Louisiana Shrimp

1½ sticks butter
1 bay leaf
¼ cup lemon juice
1 teaspoon garlic powder

1 teaspoon cayenne pepper, optional
1½ teaspoons lemon-pepper seasoning
½ cup water
1 pound raw shrimp with shells

Combine all ingredients, except shrimp, and simmer until the butter is melted. In a single layer place shrimp in a casserole and cover with butter mixture. Bake, uncovered, at 350° for 1 hour. *Serve with lots of hot French bread for dunking in the butter sauce and peel the shrimp as you eat them. It's nice to have a finger bowl near!*

Mrs. Benjamin F. Swank, III (Susie Schroeder)

Shrimp Virginia

1 stick butter
1 teaspoon garlic juice
1 ounce orange juice

1 ounce lime juice
¼ teaspoon Lawry's seasoned salt
1½ pounds raw shrimp, peeled

Melt butter and add garlic juice, orange juice, lime juice, and salt. Place shrimp in a baking pan and cover with butter mixture. Broil in a preheated oven for 3½ minutes or until shrimp curl.
Serves 6.
Judge John H. Wood, Jr.

Shrimp Étouffée

1 medium onion, chopped
2 green onions, chopped
3-4 cloves garlic, crushed
¼ cup chopped celery
1 stick butter
2 tablespoons flour
2½ cups water
1¼ cups tomato juice
2 bay leaves

1 tablespoon Worcestershire sauce
4 drops Tabasco sauce
1 teaspoon salt
½ teaspoon thyme, crushed
⅛ teaspoon pepper
1½ pounds peeled, raw shrimp
Cooked rice
2 hard-boiled eggs, sliced

Sauté onion, green onions, garlic, and celery in butter. Stir in flour and cook until light brown. Add water, tomato juice, bay leaves, Worcestershire, Tabasco, salt, thyme, and pepper. Simmer for 25 minutes, stirring occasionally. Add shrimp and cook 15 minutes longer. Serve over rice with sliced eggs for garnish.
Serves 4.
Mrs. Earl Daniels

Shrimp Curry

5 tablespoons margarine
1 apple, peeled and chopped
½ cup chopped onion
6 tablespoons flour
2 teaspoons curry powder
1 teaspoon salt
¼ teaspoon ground ginger
1½ teaspoons sugar

2 chicken bouillon cubes, dissolved in 1 cup boiling water
2 cups light cream
4 cups cooked, peeled shrimp
1 teaspoon lemon juice
6 cups hot cooked rice
Condiments (see index)

In a double boiler, melt margarine and cook apple and onions about 30 minutes or until tender. Stir in flour, curry powder, salt, ginger, and sugar. Add dissolved bouillon cubes and cream and cook slowly, stirring constantly until smooth and thickened. Add the shrimp and lemon juice and heat thoroughly. Serve over rice with condiments. *Delicious with mango salad and stuffed squash.*
Serves 6. Best if prepared same day. Does not freeze well.
Mrs. Marion Olson (Martha Pancoast)

Crab and Shrimp Ramekins

1½ cups fresh crabmeat or frozen crabmeat, drained well	1 10¾ ounce can cream of shrimp soup
1½ cups cooked shrimp, cut in large pieces	1 cup sour cream
½ cup homemade French dressing*	2 tablespoons Sauterne or dry white wine
1 tablespoon chopped green onions	1 cup grated Swiss cheese
1 tablespoon diced pimiento	½ cup grated Parmesan cheese

Marinate seafood in French dressing 1-2 hours. Do not drain marinade and add green onions and pimientos. Carefully fold in soup, sour cream, and wine. Spoon into buttered ramekins or casserole dish. Mix cheeses and sprinkle over top. Place in a cold oven and bake at 450° for 20 minutes or until bubbly and browned.

*French dressing Combine ⅔ cup vegetable oil, ⅓ cup white wine vinegar, 1 teaspoon sugar, 1 teaspoon salt, ½ teaspoon paprika, and ¼-½ teaspoon black pepper to make approximately 1 cup dressing.
Serves 6 as an entrée or 12 as an hors d'oeuvre.
Mrs. Ernest L. Brown, III (Connie Lentz)

Spaghetti and Oysters

1 stick butter	1 cup chopped green onions
¼ cup flour	1 tablespoon Worcestershire sauce
2 dozen small oysters	1 teaspoon Accent
4 cups oyster liquor or oyster liquor and water	Salt and pepper to taste
½ cup chopped parsley	1 pound spaghetti, cooked and drained

Melt butter slowly. Blend in flour and cook until foam appears, but do not brown. Boil the oysters in oyster liquor until the edges curl. Remove oysters. Gradually add boiling liquor from oysters to the flour mixture, stirring rapidly over medium heat, and cook for 10 minutes. Reduce heat to low and add parsley, green onions, Worcestershire, Accent, salt, and pepper. Continue to cook for 15 minutes. Add oysters and serve over hot spaghetti.
Serves 4.
Mrs. Marshall T. Clegg (Patricia "Trish" Pennington)

Glenwood Oysters Farcis

3 dozen oysters
½ cup finely chopped celery
¾ cup finely chopped shallots
½ cup finely chopped parsley
1 stick + 2 tablespoons butter, divided

1 tablespoon flour
¾ cup dried bread crumbs, divided
Salt to taste
Cayenne pepper to taste
1 egg, beaten

Boil oysters until plump and drain. Cut into small pieces, removing hard portions. Sauté celery, shallots, and parsley in 1 stick butter. Blend in flour, oysters, and ½ cup bread crumbs. Remove from heat, season with salt and cayenne, add egg, and cool. Place mixture into 6 buttered baking shells, sprinkle with ¼ cup bread crumbs, and dot with remaining butter. Bake at 400° for 10 minutes. Serve immediately. *This is good as a first course, followed by an entrée of beef or chicken.*
Serves 6.
Mrs. A. Tedford Barclay, Jr. (LaNelle Robertson)

Oysters Rockefeller Olé

2 10 ounce packages fresh spinach
1 bunch green onions
1 small bunch parsley
1 small bunch fresh cilantro, optional
3 cloves garlic
1 teaspoon anise seeds
1 stick butter

2 tablespoons Pace Picante Sauce
Dash of Tabasco sauce
½ tube anchovy paste or 1 can anchovies, drained and mashed
6 tablespoons Anisette liqueur or to taste
¾ cup dried white bread crumbs
2 pints oysters, drained

Wash and drain the vegetables, shaking them as dry as possible. Do not drain on paper towels. In a meat grinder or food processor, grind the first 4 ingredients. Crush garlic with anise seeds in a mortar. Simmer ground vegetables and garlic mixture in butter for about 10 minutes. Add remaining ingredients except oysters. Place oysters in a large shallow casserole or in ramekins and cover with sauce. Bake at 350° for 30-40 minutes or until thoroughly heated and the oysters curl.
Serves 6. Sauce may be made ahead and frozen.
Mrs. Reagan Houston, III (Mary Jane Lyles)

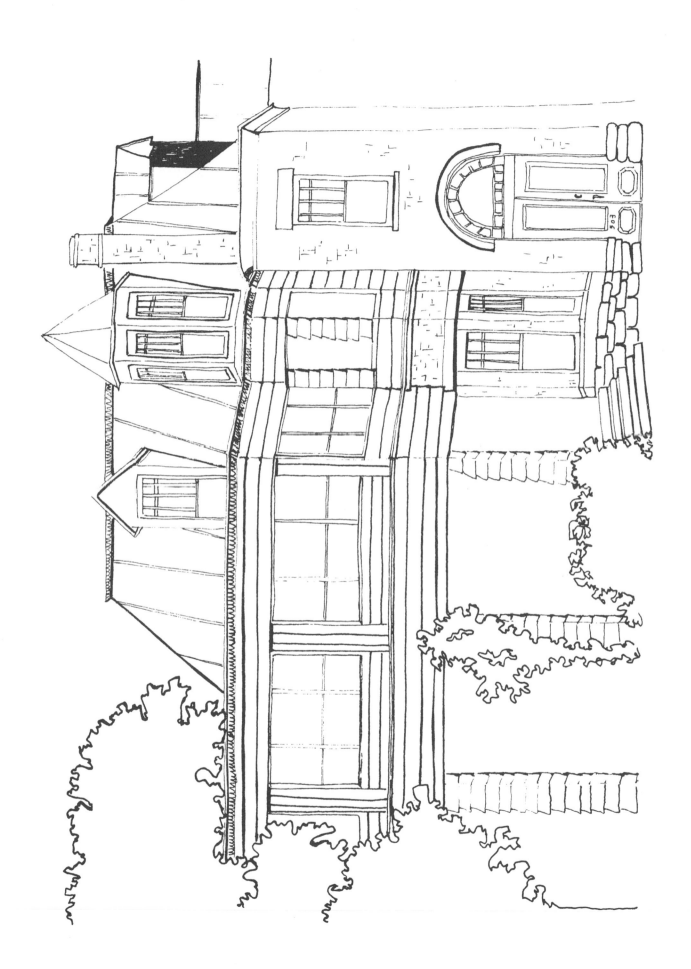

503 East Guenther Street

This red brick and limestone home on the bank of the San Antonio River was built in 1891 as the home of C.A. Stieren. Mr. Stieren was associated in the real estate business with Axel and Paul Meerscheidt. They developed the Meerscheidt River Subdivision, a portion of the Labor de Abajo or fields of Mission San Antonio de Valero.

After having two more owners, O.E. Lochausen and A.R. Byrd, the house was purchased in 1919 by J.J. and Mary Donaldson. Their daughter, Mrs. Dolly Harpham, kept the home until 1951.

reference: *Down the Acequia Madre.* Mary V. Burkholder, 1976.

Steak Su Pondre

2   small, thick steaks, club, T-bone, or filet
1   garlic clove, halved
Salt
Freshly ground or cracked pepper

2   tablespoons vegetable oil
2   slices bread
½   cup water
⅓   cup heavy cream
⅓   cup brandy

Rub steaks with garlic and sprinkle with salt. Press pepper into steaks with heel of hand. Let stand refrigerated for 2 hours or at room temperature for 1 hour. Heat oil until very hot, sear steaks on both sides to seal the juices, reduce heat, and cook slowly until done. Remove steaks from pan, sauté bread in the drippings, and set aside. Add water to pan and stir until all brown bits are dissolved. Add cream. To serve with flair, top bread slices with steak and place on a warmed serving platter. Heat brandy, ignite, and pour over steaks. Serve cream sauce separately.
Serves 2.
Mrs. Monte D. Tomerlin (Jacqueline R. Beretta)

Steak and Bacon Tournedos

1-1½ pounds beef flank steak
Instant unseasoned meat tenderizer
½   pound bacon
1   teaspoon garlic salt
½   teaspoon ground pepper

2   tablespoons parsley
1   1¾ ounce package hollandaise sauce mix
¼   teaspoon crushed, dried tarragon

Pound tenderizer into steak, sprinkle with garlic salt and pepper, and score steak diagonally. Fry bacon until almost done but not crisp, and place on steak. Sprinkle with parsley and roll in jelly roll fashion. Skewer with wooden sticks 1 inch apart, cut in 1 inch slices, and grill over medium coals. Prepare hollandaise sauce adding tarragon. Pour over steaks or serve separately.
Serves 4.
Ms. Jessica Bell

Earl's Steak Secret

Sirloin steak, 1½ inches thick
Prepared mustard

Salt and pepper to taste

Rub steak completely with prepared mustard. Sprinkle with salt and pepper. Grill over charcoal. *This same idea is good for pork chops and they may be grilled or pan fried.*

Mr. Earl Hobbs Chumney, Jr.

Steak Picante

1½	cups sliced fresh mushrooms	1	cup tomato sauce
½	cup chopped onion	1	teaspoon salt
¼	cup chopped green pepper	¼	cup sliced ripe olives
¼	cup shortening	1¼	pounds round steak, 1 inch thick
2	teaspoons chili powder		

Sauté mushrooms, onions, and green pepper in shortening for 5 minutes. Add chili powder, tomato sauce, salt, and olives. Place steak in a shallow baking dish. Pour sauce over steak. Cover and bake at 350° for 1½ hours or until meat is tender.
Serves 6.
Mrs. John Watson

Dip an ice cube into natural gravy to remove fat.

Pepper Steak

1	2 pound flank steak	3	tablespoons flour
Salt and pepper to taste		½	pound mushrooms, sliced
1	tablespoon bacon drippings	2	large green peppers, sliced
2	small onions, finely chopped	2	tomatoes, cut into eighths
1	10½ ounce can beef consommé	½	cup red wine
3	tablespoons butter	1	tablespoon chopped parsley

Slice meat across the grain into ¼ inch strips. Season with salt and pepper. Sauté meat in bacon drippings until brown. Add onions and sauté about 5 minutes or until brown. Add consommé, bring mixture to a boil, cover, and simmer over low heat for 10 minutes. Blend butter and flour into a smooth paste and gradually stir into mixture, and cook, stirring until thickened. Add mushrooms, green peppers, tomatoes, and red wine, cover, and simmer over low heat about 25 minutes or until green peppers are tender. Mixture may be turned into a 2 quart casserole and baked at 300° for 25 minutes or until green peppers are tender. Before serving, sprinkle with chopped parsley. *Serve over rice.*

Mrs. Carl R. Olson (Polly Westbrook)

Individual Beef Wellington

Beef
4   beef filets, 4 ounces each
1   clove garlic, halved
Salt and pepper to taste
½   stick butter

4   tablespoons brandy
½   cup fresh mushrooms, finely minced
1   4 ounce tin liver pâté

Mushroom Sauce
¼   cup onion, minced
6   large mushrooms, sliced
3   tablespoons flour
½   cup red wine

1   10½ ounce can beef broth
1   bay leaf
Salt and pepper to taste
1   teaspoon Worcestershire sauce

Pastry
1   package Pepperidge Farm Patty Shells, 6 per package, defrosted; or any pie crust dough enough for a 2 crust pie

1   egg, beaten
Butter

Beef   Rub each filet with garlic and sprinkle with salt and pepper. Saute filets in butter 3-4 minutes on each side. Flame brandy, pour over filets. Remove filets and chill. In the same skillet, saute chopped mushrooms and chill. Mix pate with chilled mushrooms, spread over filets, and refrigerate.

Mushroom Sauce   Using the same skillet over medium heat, combine onion and sliced mushrooms, stir in flour, and gradually add wine, broth, and bay leaf. Stir until sauce bubbles and is thickened. Season with salt, pepper, and Worcestershire.

Pastry   Roll out patty shells or dough and trim into four 6 inch squares. Brush with egg. Place each filet, pâté side down, on pastry. Fold dough completely over filets and seal edges with butter. Place seam down on a greased baking sheet and brush again with egg. Pastry may be garnished with small flowers or leaves made from extra dough and attached by using butter or beaten egg. Bake at 425° for 20-25 minutes or until crust is richly browned. Serve with heated mushroom sauce. *May be prepared, covered, and kept in refrigerator for 2 days before baking.*
Serves 4. Freezes well before baking for 1 month.
Mrs. Earl Hobbs Chumney, Jr. (Barbara Sue Christian)

Beef Birmingham

1 clove garlic, minced
1 cup sliced onion
1 cup sliced celery
1 pound round steak or sirloin tip, cut in thin strips
2 tablespoons oil

2 tablespoons peanut butter
2 tablespoons soy sauce
½ teaspoon sugar
1 cup beef stock or bouillon
1 4 ounce can mushrooms

Sauté garlic, onion, celery, and beef in hot oil. Add remaining ingredients, cover, and simmer about 1 hour or until meat is tender. Add additional liquid during cooking if necessary. *Serve over hot cooked rice with chopped peanuts and green onions sprinkled on top.*
Serves 4.
Mrs. Wallis M. Paul (Jo)

Teriyaki

3-4 pounds sirloin steak or arm roast
1 cup Japanese soy sauce
1 cup dry wine, red or rosé
2 teaspoons ground ginger

1 clove garlic
½ cup brown sugar
¼ cup water
½ teaspoon pepper

Partially freeze meat and slice as thinly as possible, 2-3 inches long and ½ inch wide. Combine remaining ingredients and marinate meat for 6-8 hours. Remove meat and heat marinade. Grill meat over hot coals on each side for 1-2 minutes. Combine meat and marinade in a covered casserole. Keep warm in oven until ready to serve.
Serves 6.
Mrs. Courtenay R. Atkins (Jan)

Asticciole alla Calabrese

12 filets of beef, cut ½ inch thick
12 thin slices mozzarella cheese, or more to taste
3 Italian sausages, sliced and sautéed in their juices

1½ teaspoons salt
½ teaspoon freshly ground black pepper
1 teaspoon crushed bay leaves
3 tablespoons olive oil

Pound the filets very thin. On each filet place a slice of cheese and a few sausage slices. Roll the filets and fasten with toothpicks. Season with salt, pepper, and bay leaves and brush with oil. Broil for 15 minutes, turning the rolls to brown all sides.
Serves 6.
Mrs. T. William Cothren (Laurin Dawson)

Beef à la Mode

1	8-10 pound bottom round of beef, boned and rolled	1	package Pepperidge Farm herb-seasoned stuffing mix
3	tablespoons saltpeter (available at drug stores)	1	onion, chopped
8	ounces dark brown sugar, or ½ box	4-5	ribs celery, chopped
2½	tablespoons salt		Salt and pepper to taste
1	teaspoon cayenne pepper		Dash of nutmeg
10-12	slices raw bacon		Beef broth
		2	cups dry sherry
			Parsley and red apple rings

Step 1 Begin preparation for this recipe 6 days before serving. Untie round of beef. Partially slice through thicker parts, if necessary, to make meat lie fairly flat. Mix the saltpeter, brown sugar, salt, and cayenne pepper in a small bowl. Rub entire piece of meat well with about ⅓ of saltpeter mixture, place meat in a bowl, cover, and refrigerate. Repeat process 2 more days. On the fourth morning, wash beef thoroughly with clear water and discard juices from bowl.

Step 2 Place meat fat side down, top with a few slices of bacon, and add ½-1 cup stuffing. Roll the meat back into shape, being careful to keep as much stuffing in the middle as possible, and tie securely with string in about 5 places. Using a sharp, serrated knife, make 3-4 slits in rolled meat at both ends, as deep as you can, and stuff these slits with more bacon and stuffing. Return to bowl, cover with sherry, and refrigerate overnight.

Step 3 Place beef on rack in roasting pan and cover with juices from bowl. Bake at 500° for 15 minutes. Reduce heat to 300° and continue to bake for 3½-4 hours. Cool slightly and refrigerate overnight. Serve cold, garnished with parsley and red apple rings and sliced very thin. *This recipe is from my grandmother who, at age 84, wrote it in a cookbook that she and my aunt prepared for me when I was married. Beef à la Mode was served on "state" or special occasions, and was a Christmas Day necessity. It is also good for biscuit sandwiches with hot mustard, and is literally good for 3 weeks when kept in refrigerator.*
Serves 12-16. Freezes.
Mrs. W. J. Lyons, Jr. (Martha "Molly" Collett)

New Ro Fan Chieh
Anlin's Stirred Steak with Tomatoes

3 tablespoons soy sauce	1 teaspoon M.S.G.
1 tablespoon cornstarch	1 onion, sliced
2 teaspoons sugar, divided	2-3 tomatoes, cut in wedges
4 teaspoons sherry, divided	1 tablespoon water
2-3 tablespoons vegetable oil, divided	
1 pound flank steak or tenderized sirloin or chuck steak, thinly sliced against the grain in 1½ x ½ inch strips	

Combine soy sauce, cornstarch, 1 teaspoon sugar, and 1 teaspoon sherry. Let stand for about 5 minutes. Place sliced steak in marinade and add 1-2 drops of the oil. Heat remaining oil in a skillet, preferably teflon. When hot, stir in onion to season the oil and quickly stir in beef slices. Sprinkle with M.S.G. and remaining sherry. When meat begins to cook, stir in tomatoes, sprinkle with remaining sugar, and add water. Remove from heat and serve immediately.

Mrs. Harry Brusenhan (Laura)

The truest Texas sandwich is made by spreading a flour tortilla with refried beans, and filling with the thinnest possible slices of brisket, guacamole, a sprinkle of finely chopped onion, and a healthy amount of picante sauce.

Barbecued Brisket

4-5 pound lean brisket	2 tablespoons Worcestershire sauce
1 tablespoon salt	1 cup water
½ teaspoon pepper	2 tablespoons chili sauce
3 tablespoons brown sugar	½ cup vinegar
¼ cup catsup	2 sticks butter, melted
3 tablespoons French's brown mustard	

Place brisket, fat side up, in a roasting pan. Brown slightly under broiler and reduce heat to 225°-300°. Mix remaining ingredients in the order given, using a rotary beater, and simmer slowly until slightly thickened. Keep warm and baste meat every 15 minutes for 3-5 hours or until well done. When meat is slightly cooled, thinly slice and serve with remaining sauce.

Mrs. Frank Steed

Barbecued Beef Brisket

6-8 pound lean boneless brisket
1 4 ounce bottle liquid smoke
Garlic salt to taste
Onion salt to taste
Celery salt to taste
Worcestershire sauce to taste
Salt and pepper to taste
1 14 ounce bottle Heinz catsup
½ cup brown sugar
½ tablespoon salt

½ teaspoon dry mustard
3 cloves garlic
1 catsup bottle of water
¾ tablespoon Worcestershire sauce
⅛ teaspoon cayenne pepper
¼ tablespoon liquid smoke
½ teaspoon vinegar
¼ teaspoon pepper
½ tablespoon A-1 sauce

Place meat in a long shallow pan. Cover with liquid smoke and sprinkle generously with garlic salt, onion salt, and celery salt. Refrigerate overnight. Sprinkle generously with Worcestershire, salt, and pepper. Cover with foil and bake at 275° for 5 hours. Combine remaining ingredients to make barbecue sauce and simmer 30-40 minutes. Cover brisket with barbecue sauce and bake 1 hour. Cool before slicing.
Freezes.
Mrs. Robert Ownby

Erskine's Brisket

4-5 pound boneless brisket
2 onions, sliced or diced
2 tablespoons vegetable oil
1 cup dry red wine
1 cup strong coffee

1 slice stale rye bread, crumbled
2 cloves garlic, minced
1 bay leaf
2 teaspoons sugar
3 tablespoons catsup

In a roasting pan, brown brisket and onions in oil over medium heat. Combine remaining ingredients and pour over meat. Cover and bake at 300° for 3-4 hours or until meat is tender.

Mrs. John Oppenheimer (Evelyne Ehrich)

Sherried Beef

3 pounds boneless chuck roast
1 package dry onion soup mix
2 10¾ ounce cans cream of
   mushroom soup

¾ cup dry sherry
1 4 ounce can whole mushrooms

Trim fat from roast, cut into 1 inch cubes, and place in a 3 quart casserole. Combine remaining ingredients and pour over roast. Cover and bake at 325° for 3 hours.
Serves 6.
Mrs. Clement Richard DiBona (Ina Fleishel)

Roast Peppered Rib-Eye of Beef

5-6	pound rib-eye beef roast, fat removed	1	teaspoon paprika
½	cup coarsely cracked pepper	1	cup soy sauce
1	tablespoon tomato paste	¾	cup red wine vinegar
½	teaspoon garlic powder	1	tablespoon cornstarch

Rub pepper over beef and press in with heel of hand. Place in a shallow baking dish. Shake remaining ingredients in a jar. Carefully pour over roast and marinate overnight. Remove marinade and bake roast at 325° for 17-20 minutes per pound for rare. For best results, use a meat thermometer. Add 1 cup water to meat juices after baking for "au jus", or thicken this gravy with 1 tablespoon cornstarch mixed with ¼ cup cold water.
Serves 10-12.
Mrs. James M. Cavender, III (Judith Gosnell)

Pot Roast with Sour Cream Gravy

3	tablespoons shortening	1½	teaspoons paprika
3-4	pound pot roast	½	cup hot water
2	medium onions, sliced	2	tablespoons flour
1	8 ounce can water chestnuts, sliced	½	cup sour cream
1	tablespoon salt		

Melt shortening in a Dutch oven and brown meat on all sides. Slip rack under meat. Add onions, water chestnuts, salt, paprika, and hot water. Cover and simmer 2½ hours or until meat is fork tender. Remove roast and rack. Skim fat from drippings. Fold flour into sour cream. Gradually add sour cream mixture to drippings, and cook until thick. Slice meat and serve with gravy.

Mrs. Robert E. Fawcett, Jr. (Ann Ingrum)

Pot Roast

3-4	pound Pike's Peak roast	1	onion, sliced
3	cloves garlic, slivered	1	stick margarine
1¼	teaspoons Lawry's seasoned salt	1	cup water
	Pepper to taste		Potatoes, peeled
2	teaspoons chili powder		Carrots
1	tablespoon grated Parmesan cheese		

Make slits in roast and insert garlic slivers. Cover the roast with salt, pepper, chili powder, and Parmesan cheese. Place onion on top. Put margarine and water in pan with the roast. Bake, covered, at 325° for 4 hours, basting the roast every 30 minutes. After 3 hours add potatoes and carrots. *The carrots are tastier with the peeling left on.*

Mrs. Benjamin F. Swank, III (Susie Schroeder)

Chipped Beef with Artichoke Hearts

¾	stick butter	½	cup dry white wine
6	tablespoons flour	1	cup shredded chipped beef
1½	cups milk	1½	cups ripe olives, chopped
½-1	teaspoon salt or to taste	2	packages frozen artichoke hearts,
2	cups sour cream		cooked

Melt butter in saucepan, add flour, and stir with wire whisk. Bring milk to a boil and add to butter mixture, stirring vigorously with whisk. When mixture is thick and smooth, add salt, sour cream, wine, beef, olives, and artichokes and heat, but do not boil. *Serve hot with rice.*
Serves 4. Easily doubled.
Mrs. Jack Beretta (Mary Austin Perry)

Fricandeaux "Mémé"

6	breakfast steaks	½	cup water
Salt and pepper to taste		½	cup red Burgundy
½	cup finely chopped fresh parsley	1	bay leaf
6	slices smoked bacon	1	8 ounce can mushrooms

Pound steaks and season with salt and pepper. Place 2 teaspoons parsley in center of each steak. Form a roll with each steak and wrap 1 slice bacon around it. Secure bacon with a length of white thread. Brown steak rolls carefully in an 8-9 inch frying pan. No need to add any fat. When well browned, remove and set aside. Add water to pan, stirring to remove brown bits. Stir in wine, bay leaf, and mushrooms. Return beef to pan, cover, and cook over low heat for 20 minutes. Check often, adding water or wine if necessary. *This is numed after my wonderful 91 year old grandmother who taught me a lot about cooking back home in Geneva, Switzerland.*
Serves 6.
Mrs. Melvin Baden

Hunter's Stew

42	ounces Wolf Brand chili	2	onions, chopped
44	ounces hominy, drained	10	ounces Cheddar cheese, grated

Layer chili, hominy, and onion in a casserole, and top with cheese. Bake at 325° for 30 minutes or until thoroughly heated. *Cook in a slow oven for as long as you wish.*

Mrs. John K. Walters, Jr. (Lucy Masterson Yerly)

Green Tomato Stew

1 pound ground beef
2 teaspoons vegetable oil
1 medium onion, chopped
6 pods fresh green chilies or 1½ chiles serranos, finely chopped
2 large zucchini or yellow squash, cubed

4 medium green tomatoes, sliced
3 ears fresh corn, with kernels sliced from cob, or 1 cup whole kernel canned corn

Brown beef in oil. Add onion and chilies and sauté 5 minutes. Add squash, tomatoes, and corn. Simmer, uncovered, over low heat for 30 minutes.
Serves 4.
Mrs. Harry E. Brown (Carolyn Carlisle)

Saltimbocca Naples

1½ pounds sirloin tip or veal, sliced paper thin
½ cup flour
⅔ cup freshly grated Parmesan cheese, divided
1 teaspoon salt
½ stick butter, divided
2 tablespoons olive oil
½ pound thinly sliced prosciutto ham

½ cup finely chopped green onions
½ pound fresh mushrooms, sliced
½ cup beef bouillon
2 tablespoons lemon juice
¼ cup Marsala wine (no substitution)
1¼ pounds fresh spinach, stems removed
Salt to taste

Step 1 Dredge sirloin slices in flour that has been mixed with ⅓ cup cheese and 1 teaspoon salt. In a large skillet, melt ¼ stick butter, add olive oil, and brown the sirloin on both sides, adding additional butter and oil if necessary. Drain the browned sirloin on paper towels. Quickly heat ham on both sides in the same skillet. Place ham over sirloin.

Step 2 In the skillet used for browning sirloin, melt ¼ stick butter to begin making the Marsala sauce. With a wooden spoon, loosen browned bits from bottom of pan, add onions and mushrooms, and sauté until tender. Slowly add bouillon and lemon juice, cook until slightly thickened, and add wine. Return meat and ham slices to the skillet, cover, and simmer about 30 minutes. It is important to check mixture to make certain it does not become dry. If dry, add a proportionate mixture of wine, bouillon, and lemon juice.

Step 3 Cook spinach over high heat in the water that clings to the leaves after washing. When steam begins to rise from bottom of pan, lower heat, and cover. Cook about 3-4 minutes or until spinach appears wilted and add salt. Arrange spinach on a large platter and cover with sirloin and ham. Pour remaining sauce over meats and sprinkle with remaining cheese. *Great served with garlic buttered pasta.*
Serves 6.
Mrs. Edgar M. Duncan (Linda Wyatt)

Italian Meat Sauce for Spaghetti

½ pound bacon, diced
2½ pounds lean ground beef
2 cups finely chopped onion
1 cup finely chopped green pepper
6 garlic cloves, minced
3 2 pound 3 ounce cans Italian plum tomatoes
3 6 ounce cans tomato paste
1½ cups dry red wine, divided
5 teaspoons oregano, divided
5 teaspoons basil, divided

1½ cups water
½ cup chopped fresh parsley
2 teaspoons thyme
1 bay leaf, crumbled
2 tablespoons salt
1 tablespoon sugar
Freshly ground pepper
Spaghetti, cooked 8-10 minutes and drained
Parmesan cheese, freshly grated

Fry bacon until crisp. Remove bacon and all but 2 tablespoons drippings. Add ground beef and brown. Stir in onion, green pepper, and garlic and cook 10 minutes. Mash plum tomatoes or whirl in a blender. Add tomatoes, tomato paste, crumbled bacon, 1 cup wine, 4 teaspoons oregano, 4 teaspoons basil, and remaining ingredients, except spaghetti and cheese, to meat mixture. Bring to boil, reduce heat, and simmer for 3 hours, stirring occasionally. May be frozen at this point. Thirty minutes before serving add remaining basil, oregano, and wine. Flavor improves with age. Serve over hot spaghetti with generous amounts of Parmesan cheese.
Serves 12-14. Freezes. Easily doubled.
Mrs. Jimmie V. Thurmond, Jr. (Melissa Strock)

Use toasted English muffins as a base for individual pizzas.

Party Pizza

6 tablespoons vegetable or olive oil
1 onion, finely chopped
1 heaping tablespoon finely chopped garlic
2 28 ounce cans Progresso peeled crushed tomatoes with added purée
1 12 ounce can Progresso tomato paste
1 tablespoon oregano
1 teaspoon dried basil

1 bay leaf
1½ pounds lean ground beef, browned
4 large pizza crusts
½ -¾ pound mushrooms, sliced
Mozzarella cheese
Parmesan cheese, grated
Olives
Capers
Pepperoni sausage

Combine the first 8 ingredients and simmer about 30 minutes to make tomato sauce. Cover each pizza crust with tomato sauce, sprinkle with browned meat, and any combination of the remaining ingredients. Top with Parmesan cheese and bake at 400° for 15-20 minutes. *This recipe is perfect for a "do-it-yourself" pizza party. Give each couple a pizza crust in a pan to garnish as they wish. Use your imagination for added ingredients with which to top pizzas.*
Serves 8.
Mrs. Ben Foster, Jr. (Raye Boyer)

Trittini

2	pounds lean ground beef	¼	teaspoon pepper	
½	cup minced onion	2	3 ounce cans sliced mushrooms, drained	
2	6 ounce cans tomato paste			
2	8 ounce cans tomato sauce	3	10 ounce packages frozen chopped spinach, thawed or cooked	
2	teaspoons dried basil			
2	teaspoons dried parsley	1	pound creamed cottage cheese	
1	teaspoon salt	Dash of salt		
1	teaspoon oregano	1	8 ounce package mozzarella cheese	
Dash of garlic salt		¼	cup grated Parmesan cheese	

In a large skillet, sauté ground beef and onion until meat is no longer pink and onion is transparent. Add tomato paste, tomato sauce, basil, parsley, 1 teaspoon salt, oregano, garlic salt, and pepper. Add mushrooms, reserving 15 slices. Simmer over low heat for 10 minutes or until thickened, stirring often. Mark off meat mixture into 5 equal portions. Squeeze out as much liquid as possible from spinach. In a medium bowl, combine spinach, cottage cheese, and a dash of salt. Mark off spinach mixture into 5 equal portions. Cut 12 strips, 2½ x ½ x ½ inches, from mozzarella cheese. Dice remaining mozzarella cheese. In a 13 x 9 x 2 baking dish, arrange alternately in lengthwise strips 3 portions of spinach mixture and 2 portions of meat mixture, covering bottom of baking dish. Sprinkle with diced mozzarella and Parmesan cheese. Make a second layer arranging alternately in lengthwise strips 3 portions of meat mixture and 2 portions of spinach mixture. Using mozzarella cheese strips, make 4 crosswise rows over meat and spinach mixtures using 3 strips, placed end to end, for each row. Garnish meat portion with reserved mushroom slices. Bake at 375° for 25-30 minutes or until bubbly. *May be prepared ahead.*
Serves 8-10.
Mrs. Richard Tide Coiner, III (Charlotte Turner Watson)

Italian Cutlets

1	pound ground beef	¼	cup vegetable oil
Salt and pepper to taste		3	slices mozzarella cheese, halved
2	tablespoons chopped parsley	1	1⅝ ounce package Lawry's spaghetti sauce mix, prepared according to package directions
Flour			
2	eggs, beaten		
½	cup bread crumbs	½	cup grated Parmesan cheese

Combine meat, salt, pepper, and parsley. Shape into 6 cutlets. Dredge cutlets in flour, dip in eggs, and roll in crumbs. Sauté cutlets in oil until brown and place in a baking dish. Put mozzarella slices on each cutlet, cover with sauce, and sprinkle with Parmesan cheese. Bake at 400° for 20-25 minutes.

Mrs. Bertrand O. Baetz, Jr.

Eggplant-Hamburger Dish

1 medium eggplant, peeled and sliced
2 chicken bouillon cubes, dissolved in enough water to cover eggplant
½ cup diced green onions
1-2 cloves garlic, pressed
1 tablespoon olive oil
1 pound ground round steak
1 teaspoon oregano
½ teaspoon Italian herbs
Salt and pepper to taste

1 14½ ounce can peeled, whole tomatoes, drained and chopped
Tabasco sauce to taste, optional
3-4 fresh mushrooms, sliced
2 teaspoons butter
1 4½ ounce can chopped ripe olives, drained
1½ cups grated yellow cheese
½ cup grated Parmesan cheese
1 8 ounce can tomato sauce

Boil eggplant in chicken broth until tender and drain thoroughly. Sauté green onions and garlic in oil until tender. Add meat, cook until no pink remains, and drain fat. Add oregano, Italian herbs, salt, and pepper. In a large, shallow baking dish, layer eggplant, meat, and tomatoes. Sprinkle with Tabasco. Sauté mushrooms in butter until tender and add to casserole with olives. Top with a mixture of yellow cheese and Parmesan, drizzle with tomato sauce, and bake at 350° for 30 minutes.
Serves 6.
Mrs. Alex Weil, III (Penny Speier)

Beef Stew Bordeaux

6 slices bacon, diced, or 1 cup
2-3 pounds lean sirloin or chuck, cubed
1 tablespoon salt
Pepper to taste
12-15 small onions
6 carrots, sliced
2 shallots, chopped
1 clove garlic, crushed
2 tablespoons flour

2 cups red wine
1 cup beef stock or water
Bouquet garni:
5 sprigs parsley
2 ribs celery, chopped
1 bay leaf
pinch of thyme
½ pound mushrooms, sliced
½ stick butter

In a large stew pot, fry bacon until crisp. Remove bacon, drain, and crumble. Reserve 1 tablespoon drippings. Season beef with salt and pepper and brown in drippings with onions and carrots. Add shallots, garlic, and flour, mixing well. Bake at 250° about 45 minutes or until brown. Add red wine and stock, being sure meat is covered with liquid. Place ingredients for bouquet garni in a cheesecloth and tie securely, add to stewpot, bring to boil, and cook slowly for 2 hours on top of stove. Sauté mushrooms in butter. Just before serving, add mushrooms and crumbled bacon to beef. *Serve with potatoes or noodles. This recipe was given to me by Mrs. Rollins Wofford.*
Serves 6-8.
Mrs. W. L. Myers (Bettie Townsend)

Best Meat Loaf — Do It Your Way

2-3 pounds lean ground beef	½ of a small bottle catsup
No bread crumbs	Curry powder, optional
No egg	Ingredients you especially like such as:
No tomato sauce	mushrooms
Lots of:	chives
Worcestershire sauce	olives
Parmesan cheese, grated	green pepper
garlic	oregano
salt and pepper	chutney
minced onion	Sherry or wine to taste

Mix all ingredients except sherry or wine. Do be daring — this is your chance! Shape into a loaf. Spread with additional catsup and bake at 350° for 50 minutes. Pour sherry or wine over loaf and bake 10 minutes.
Serves 4-6.
Mrs. J. Ross Crawford (Judith Claire Bennett)

To perk up Monday night meatloaf, place ½ of a peeled and seeded avocado in the center of the meat mixture. Fill the cavity of the fruit with a tablespoon or more of Cheez-Whiz, cover generously with meat mixture, and bake.

German Meatballs with Caper Sauce

1 cup finely chopped onion	½ teaspoon pepper
¾ stick butter or margarine, divided	2 teaspoons Worcestershire sauce
2 pounds boneless veal or beef, ground with ¼ pound pork fat	¼ cup + 2 tablespoons chopped parsley, divided
1 cup packaged herb-seasoned stuffing mix	2 eggs, beaten
1 teaspoon grated lemon peel	3 10½ ounce cans beef bouillon
1½ teaspoons anchovy paste, divided	1 cup dry white wine
1 teaspoon salt	¼ cup flour
	¼ cup drained capers

Sauté onion in ¼ stick butter about 3 minutes or until tender. In a large bowl, combine onion with veal, stuffing mix, lemon peel, 1 teaspoon anchovy paste, salt, pepper, Worcestershire, ¼ cup parsley, and eggs, mixing well. With moistened hands, shape mixture into 2 inch meatballs. In a large kettle, bring bouillon and wine to boiling. Drop meatballs into boiling liquid. Return mixture to boiling, reduce heat, and simmer, covered, for 20 minutes. Remove meatballs and keep warm. Strain liquid, reserving 3 cups. Melt ½ stick butter in large kettle, remove from heat, and add flour, stirring until smooth. Gradually stir in reserved liquid and bring to a boil. Add capers and ½ teaspoon anchovy paste. Add meatballs to sauce, cover, and return the mixture to boiling. Remove from heat and stir in 2 tablespoons parsley. *Serve meatballs with cooked noodles or hot, boiled potatoes.*
Serves 6-8.
Mrs. Benjamin Wyatt

Sweet and Sour Meatballs

1   pound ground beef
1   egg
1   slice bread, moistened with ¼ cup milk
½   tablespoon salt
Butter
1   13 ounce can pineapple chunks in heavy syrup
½   cup brown sugar

3   tablespoons cornstarch
1   beef bouillon cube, dissolved in 1 cup water, or 1 cup beef broth
⅓   cup cider vinegar
1   tablespoon soy sauce
1   green pepper, cut in strips
1   8 ounce can water chestnuts, drained

Combine the first 4 ingredients and form into small balls the size of walnuts. Sauté lightly in butter. Drain pineapple and reserve ½ cup syrup. Mix brown sugar and cornstarch in a saucepan. Blend in syrup, bouillon, vinegar, and soy sauce. Cook, stirring until thick and bubbly. Stir in meat balls, pineapple, green pepper, and water chestnuts. Heat, stirring to prevent scorching. *Serve over rice or as an appetizer.*
Serves 6. Better prepared ahead. Freezes.
Mrs. Ed Baker (Ruth)

Stuffed Cabbage

Cabbage
1   head cabbage
3   eggs, well beaten
1   3½ ounce package soda crackers, crumbled

2   tablespoons butter
Salt and pepper to taste
2   cups cooked, diced ham or beef

Hollandaise Sauce
3   tablespoons butter
2   tablespoons flour
⅛   teaspoon salt
¼   teaspoon paprika
1¼ cups boiling water

½   tablespoon mustard, optional
Juice of 1 lemon or 1 tablespoon vinegar
Chopped parsley
3   egg yolks, well beaten

Cabbage   Arrange a large napkin or cheesecloth square in a mixing bowl. Remove outer leaves of cabbage and arrange overlapping inside of bowl. Boil remaining cabbage in a large pot of salted water until barely tender. Drain and chop in squares. Add eggs, crackers, butter, salt, pepper, and ham or beef. Mix well and pour into arranged cabbage leaves. Tie cloth together in a ball. Drop in a kettle of boiling water and boil about 20 minutes. Drain, cover with Hollandaise Sauce, and slice to serve. *Browned butter may be substituted for the Hollandaise Sauce.*

Hollandaise Sauce   Blend butter and flour. Add seasonings and water and cook about 4 minutes. Remove from heat and add mustard, lemon, parsley, and eggs. Serve hot or cold.
Serves 8.
Mrs. R. H. Wagenfuehr

Pirog with Dill Sauce

Cheese Crust
2   cups sifted flour
1   teaspoon salt
1   stick butter

3   ounces cream cheese
1   egg, beaten

Filling
2   cups chopped onion
4   tablespoons butter, divided
1   beef bouillon cube, crumbled
1½ pounds ground round steak
1   egg, beaten

1   tablespoon chopped parsley
1   teaspoon salt
1   teaspoon pepper
1   tablespoon fine corn flake crumbs

Dill Sauce
1   cup sour cream
⅓ cup finely chopped dill pickle, or
    more to taste

½ cup mayonnaise
2   tablespoons dill pickle liquid

Cheese Crust   Sift together flour and salt. Cut butter and cream cheese into flour with a pastry blender until mixture resembles coarse cornmeal. Add egg and mix until moistened. Form into a ball, wrap, and refrigerate.

Filling   Sauté onion until tender in 3 tablespoons butter, stir in bouillon, and cool. Combine onion mixture, ground beef, egg, parsley, salt, and pepper. Shape into an 8 x 4 inch oval loaf. Roll dough on lightly floured surface into a 12 x 6 inch oval. Center meat loaf on dough. Cut dough around loaf into 1½ inch strips starting 1 inch from meat and cutting to outside edge of dough. Fold strips up over loaf, joining them at center top, and pressing dough firmly against meat. Seal ends together at top of loaf. Melt remaining 1 tablespoon butter and brush over crust. Sprinkle with crumbs. Bake on a baking sheet at 375° for 1 hour. Cool 10 minutes and serve with dill sauce.

Dill Sauce   Combine ingredients and heat slowly, stirring constantly.
Serves 8.
Mrs. Robert L. Cook (Sandra Mueller)

Copenhagen Cabbage Casserole

1½ pounds ground beef
¼ cup minced onion
1   15½ ounce can tomato sauce
1   teaspoon salt

⅛ teaspoon cinnamon
⅛ teaspoon ground cloves
4   cups shredded cabbage

Brown meat and onion and drain. Blend tomato sauce, salt, cinnamon, and cloves and add to meat. Put ½ of the cabbage in a 2 quart casserole and top with ½ of the meat sauce. Repeat layers. Cover and bake at 350° for 45 minutes.
Serves 4-5.
Mrs. William R. Campbell, Jr. (Mary Gail Thomas)

Baboetie

1	large onion, finely chopped	1	cup whole almonds, toasted and broken into pieces
½	stick butter, divided	2	tablespoons apricot jam
½	pound ground beef, lamb, or venison		Juice of 1 lemon
½	pound ground pork	1	tablespoon curry powder
1	thick slice white bread	⅛	teaspoon oregano
¾	cup milk, divided		Salt and pepper to taste
⅓	cup raisins	1	egg

Sauté onion in ¼ stick butter until soft. Add meats and bread which has been soaked in ¼ cup milk. Add raisins, almonds, jam, lemon juice, curry powder, oregano, salt, and pepper. Cook for 5 minutes, stirring constantly. Place the mixture in a shallow, buttered casserole. Beat ½ cup milk with the egg, pour ½ of this mixture over meat, and punch in. Dot with remaining butter and bake at 325° for 30 minutes. Add remaining milk mixture and bake 5 minutes or until set. May be served hot or cold.

Mrs. Frates Seeligson (Martita Rice)

K-Bobs

1	16 ounce bottle Wishbone Italian dressing	32	ounces Del Monte whole new potatoes
	Juice from one 7 ounce can Clemente Jacques mild jalapeño peppers	16	cherry tomatoes or 4 large tomatoes, quartered
2	chopped jalapeño peppers, optional	4	6 ounce cans B in B whole mushrooms or 18 fresh mushrooms
3	pounds sirloin steak, cut in 1¼ inch cubes		Squash, optional
16	small onions or 4 regular onions, quartered		Salt and pepper to taste
4	large green peppers, cut in large pieces	1	stick butter or margarine

Combine first 4 ingredients and marinate at least 1 hour. Parboil onions and green peppers for 5 minutes and drain. Remove meat and reserve marinade. Place vegetables and meat on skewers, spacing colors apart, and using meat more frequently than vegetables. Salt and pepper liberally. Add butter to marinade and heat. Grill K-Bobs over hot coals, basting frequently with marinade. *Marinade browns meat before it is cooked, so a hot grill and a short cooking period are recommended for tender meat and firm vegetables.*
Serves 6.
Mr. Chick Mueller

Anticuchos Peruanos

1½ pounds lean chuck roast
1   cup water
¼   cup red wine vinegar
1   tablespoon tomato paste
1   teaspoon garlic salt
½   teaspoon salt

1   teaspoon pepper
1   bay leaf
½   cup chopped jalapeño peppers, seeds and stems removed
1   cup chopped onion

Cut meat in 1 inch squares. Cutting meat while partially frozen makes this very easy. Combine remaining ingredients in a large glass or plastic bowl. Stir in meat, cover tightly, and marinate at least 24 hours, stirring occasionally. When ready to cook, place 5-6 cubes of meat on a skewer and grill over hot coals, basting with ½ cup marinade. Simmer remaining marinade about 15 minutes and serve with anticuchos. *This was traditionally served as an hors d'oeuvre in Lima, Peru and is similar to the anticuchos served during Fiesta Week at "A Night in Old San Antonio"*.
Serves 4.
Mrs. Jacob M. Huffman, Jr. (Dotty)

Veal Parmigiana

½   cup chopped onion
2   tablespoons olive oil
Dash of garlic salt
1   17 ounce can Italian tomatoes
2   teaspoons sugar
¾   teaspoon salt
½   teaspoon dried oregano
¼   teaspoon dried basil
¼   teaspoon pepper

1   pound veal, thinly sliced, or veal cutlets
2   eggs, beaten
1   cup seasoned dry bread crumbs
½   cup olive oil, divided
1   6 ounce package sliced mozzarella cheese
¼   cup grated Parmesan cheese

Sauté onion in oil with garlic salt for 5 minutes. Add tomatoes, sugar, salt, oregano, basil, and pepper. Mix well, mashing tomatoes with fork and bring to a boil. Reduce heat and simmer, covered, for 10 minutes. Wipe veal with damp paper towels. Dip veal in eggs, then bread crumbs. Brown veal in ¼ cup oil about 3 minutes on each side, adding oil as needed. Place veal in a baking dish. Add ½ the tomato sauce and ½ the cheeses. Repeat layers. Cover and bake at 350° for 30 minutes.
Serves 4-6.
Mrs. John A. Bitter, III (Karen Akard)

Veal Scaloppine

3   pounds veal or sirloin, sliced ¼ inch thick
½   cup flour
1   cup freshly grated Parmesan cheese, divided
1   teaspoon salt
⅛   teaspoon pepper
2   teaspoons paprika
1   clove garlic
3   tablespoons olive oil

1   6 ounce can sliced mushrooms or 1⅓ cups sliced fresh mushrooms
1   beef bouillon cube or 1 cup canned bouillon
½   cup white wine
1   tablespoon lemon juice
½   stick butter
¼-½ cup chopped green pepper
Parsley

Cut meat into 2 inch wide strips. Combine flour, ½ cup cheese, salt, pepper, and paprika. Dredge meat in flour mixture and pound thoroughly. In a skillet, crush garlic; then add olive oil and meat. Brown meat and place in a baking dish. Drain mushrooms and reserve liquid. Add water to mushroom liquid to make 1 cup, heat to boiling, add bouillon cube, and dissolve. Remove from heat, add wine and lemon juice, and pour over meat. Bake at 350° for 30 minutes. Sauté green pepper and mushrooms in butter, pour over the meat, and sprinkle with remaining Parmesan cheese. Bake 15 minutes. Garnish with parsley. *Serve with buttered green noodles.*
Serves 8. May be frozen before or after the first baking.
Mrs. Kenneth L. Farrimond (Susan Redwine)

Veau Orloff

1   veal roast, ½ pound per person
Butter
Salt and pepper to taste
½   medium onion, finely chopped, per person
½   cup finely chopped fresh mushrooms, per person

½   stick butter
¼   cup flour
2   cups milk
2-3 egg yolks
¾-1 cup grated Gruyère, New York sharp, or Old English cheese, divided

Rub veal with butter, salt, and pepper and roast at 375° for 1 hour. Sauté onions and mushrooms in ½ tablespoon butter per person for 2-3 minutes and set aside until meat is cooked. Melt ½ stick butter in a heavy saucepan, stir in flour, and gradually add milk, stirring constantly. Bring to a boil, stirring with a whisk, add salt and pepper, and remove from heat. Add egg yolks and ½ cup cheese, bring to boil, and remove from heat. Thinly slice veal and arrange on a heat resistant platter. Spread a layer of mushroom mixture on each slice, cover with sauce, sprinkle with remaining cheese, and brown in oven. Serve very hot.

Mrs. Arthur Gill (Ellen Frances McCamish)

Veal Piccalilli

1½ pounds veal cutlets or top round steak
¼ cup flour
Salt and pepper to taste
6 tablespoons olive or vegetable oil
6 ounces sliced mozzarella cheese
⅓ pound fresh Parmesan cheese, grated
½ cup dry white wine
1 6 ounce jar Progresso Pepper Piccalilli

Cut meat into serving pieces. Meat must be thin to be tender and may be flattened with a mallet if necessary. Dredge meat in flour seasoned with salt and pepper and brown in oil. Place a slice of mozzarella on each portion and sprinkle with Parmesan. Add wine and peppers and simmer about 20 minutes or until tender. Remove to a warm serving dish and top with remaining Parmesan.
Serves 4.
Mrs. John Kampmann Meyer (Betty Taylor)

Marinate steaks for several hours in Wishbone Italian or Herb and Garlic salad dressing. For a south of the border twist, remove steaks from grill or broiler about 5 minutes before they are done, top with sombreros of chopped green chilies and grated Monterey Jack cheese and return to broiler until cheese is melted. Olé!

Gorditas Rellenas

2 pounds lean ground beef
½ onion, chopped
2 cloves garlic, pressed
2-3 potatoes, peeled and cubed, or 3 cups
3 cups Masa Harina
6 tablespoons flour
Salt and pepper to taste
2-2¼ cups water
Shredded lettuce
Chopped tomatoes
Picante sauce to taste
Hot vegetable oil

Brown beef, onions, and garlic. Add potatoes, cover, and cook over low heat until the potatoes are just done. Combine masa, flour, salt, pepper, and water, mixing to form a soft dough. Shape the dough into flattened balls approximately 1¾ ounces each. This size will fit in the palm of your hand. Press between 2 plastic storage bags to form a circle approximately 3½-4 inches in diameter. A tortilla press may be used, but the masa dough should not be pressed as thin as for tortillas. Place each masa circle into hot oil and spoon the oil over until it puffs. When the masa circle is puffy and the bottom is brown, gently turn circle over to brown other side. Remove with a slotted spoon to colander. Using a sharp knife, slit the masa circle or gordita at the outer edge half way around so that a pocket is formed. Spoon meat into puffed gorditas, filling about ⅔ full, add lettuce, tomato, and picante sauce.
Yields 15 gorditas.
Miss Juanis Terrazas Garcia

Chili con Carne

5 pounds lean beef, cubed
1 pound pork, cubed
1-2 tablespoons bacon drippings
½ pound chili pods, soaked and scraped
1 4 ounce can chopped green chilies
1 10 ounce can Rotel tomatoes and green chilies
1 31 ounce can Hunt's tomatoes

2 green peppers, chopped
2 cups chopped onion
4 cloves garlic, minced
1 tablespoon cumin
1 tablespoon salt
1 tablespoon oregano
4 tablespoons flour, mixed with 1 cup cold water

Brown meats in bacon drippings. Add remaining ingredients and simmer 2 hours. *Serve in soup bowls with shredded lettuce on top.*
Yields 4 quarts.
Mrs. Richard T. Coiner, Jr. (Helen Nix)

Try picadillo for stuffing green peppers or top with Swiss cheese for a change in taste.

Chili Cheese Jubilee

1 pound ground chuck
2 tablespoons shortening
2 tablespoons butter
1 medium onion, chopped
1 8 ounce can tomato sauce
½ cup water
1 1¼ ounce package chili seasoning mix

2 eggs
1 cup light cream
1 11 ounce package Fritos
8 ounces Monterey Jack cheese, grated
1 cup sour cream
1-1½ cups Cheddar cheese, grated

Brown meat in shortening. In a separate skillet, melt butter and sauté onion. Add tomato sauce, water, and chili seasoning and simmer 5 minutes. Lightly beat eggs with cream and add to tomato mixture. In a 2 quart casserole layer ½ of the Fritos, meat, Monterey Jack cheese, and sauce. Repeat layers, top with sour cream, and sprinkle with Cheddar cheese. Refrigerate if desired. Bake at 325° for 30 minutes.
Serves 6-8. Freezes before baking.
Mrs. Pierce Sullivan (Mary Wallace Kerr)

Bandana Bandwagon Chili

1	pound Jimmy Dean pork sausage	1	tablespoon paprika
8-9	pounds lean chuck roast, chopped, or 10 cups	2	teaspoons red pepper flakes
2	medium onions, finely chopped	2	teaspoons cayenne pepper
2	cups tomatoes, finely chopped	1	tablespoon salt
2	4¾ ounce cans or 1 10½ ounce can tomato purée	3	teaspoons pepper
6	tablespoons Spice Island Chili Con Carne mix	5	cloves garlic, pressed
2½	tablespoons ground cumin	2	teaspoons Fox Hollow Herbs or Spice Island Fines Herbes
		2	bottles Heinekins beer

Brown sausage slightly and add beef. When browned, add onions and cook until golden. Add remaining ingredients and 1 bottle beer. Cook for 3 hours over low heat. Add remaining beer as the liquid cooks down. *This recipe won third place in the Luckenbach Women's Chili Cooking Contest. The prize was a trip to Terlingua.*

Mrs. Richard L. Killian (Carol Ann Moore)
Mrs. Douglas W. Smith, Jr. (Sally Ann Mayfield)

To substitute venison for beef when making beef enchiladas, simply remember to pour off the liquid that accumulates when browning the meat. This eliminates any strong flavor of the venison.

Cheesy Beef Enchiladas

1	pound ground beef	½	pound longhorn cheese, grated
2	10 ounce cans enchilada sauce	½	pound mozzarella cheese, grated
1	package taco seasoning mix, prepared according to package directions	12	corn tortillas
			Cooking oil, ½ inch deep in skillet
		1	medium onion, chopped

Brown beef and pour off fat. Add 1 can enchilada sauce and taco seasoning mixture, simmering for 20 minutes. Combine cheeses. Heat remaining enchilada sauce. Dip each tortilla into hot oil for 2-3 seconds, then into enchilada sauce. Fill each tortilla with some onion, beef mixture, and cheese mixture, reserving ½ of the cheese mixture and some onion for topping. Roll tortilla and place seam side down in a 9 x 13 casserole. Pour remaining enchilada sauce evenly over enchiladas, sprinkle with onion, and top with cheeses. Bake at 350° for 15-20 minutes.

Mrs. James L. Drought (Joane Bennett)

Cay Fry's New Mexico Enchiladas

½   cup chopped onion
2   tablespoons margarine
1   pound ground beef
1   teaspoon salt
½   teaspoon pepper
1   6 ounce can tomato paste
3   tablespoons water
1   14½ ounce can Hunt's whole
    tomatoes

½   teaspoon basil
10 corn tortillas
1   4 ounce can green chilies, seeded
    and diced
1   10¾ ounce can golden mushroom
    soup
12 ounces Cracker Barrel mellow
    cheese, grated

In large skillet, sauté onion in margarine. Add ground beef and brown. Season with salt and pepper. Add tomato paste, water, tomatoes, and basil. Allow to simmer while preparing other ingredients. Soften tortillas quickly in hot oil. Set aside on foil. In a 2-3 quart casserole, place a layer of tortillas, a layer of meat mixture, a layer of chilies, ½ can mushroom soup, and a layer of grated cheese. Repeat layers. Bake at 350° for 25-30 minutes or until bubbly. Serve immediately.
Serves 4-6.
Mrs. John Flannery, Jr. (Caroline Olson)

Lupe's Super Enchiladas

1   onion, diced
1½-2 pounds ground beef
Cooking oil
2   cups water
2   tablespoons chili powder
2   tablespoons flour

1   16 ounce can tomato sauce
Salt and pepper to taste
10-12 red tortillas
1   pound Cheddar cheese, grated
Grated onion, optional

Brown onions and beef in oil and set aside. Combine water and chili powder and set aside. Heat 3 tablespoons of oil and add flour, stirring until browned. Slowly add chili powder mixture, stirring until thickened. Add tomato sauce, salt, and pepper and simmer about 5 minutes. Soften tortillas by dipping in enough hot oil to cover, quickly remove, and drain. Place some of the meat mixture in each tortilla, top with cheese, and roll. Place seam side down in a baking dish, cover with tomato sauce, any remaining meat mixture, cheese, and grated onion. Bake at 350° for 30 minutes or until hot and bubbly.

Mrs. Charles Schreiner Nelson (Shawn Adele Carpenter)

Tamale Pie

1   24 ounce can chili without beans
1   8 ounce can tomato sauce
2   dozen tamales, fresh or frozen
1   16 ounce can whole kernel corn,
     drained

1   cup seedless raisins
1   cup chopped onions
2   cups grated cheese

Combine chili and tomato sauce. Line a baking dish with ½ of the tamales. Add ½ of the chili mixture, corn, raisins, onions, and cheese. Repeat layers. Bake at 350° until bubbly.
Serves 8. Freezes.
Mrs. William Hammond (Ruth Dyer)

Tongue 'n Noodles

1   fresh tongue, about 3 pounds
2   bay leaves
½   teaspoon vinegar
½   pound fresh mushrooms, sliced
1   large onion, chopped
1   green pepper, chopped

1   7 ounce can sliced pimientos
1   stick butter or margarine
1   10¾ ounce can chicken broth
1   8 ounce package egg noodles,
     cooked and drained
Salt to taste

Boil tongue in water with vinegar and bay leaves about 2½ hours or until done. Cool and remove skin. Slice into bite-sized pieces. In a large frying pan, melt butter and sauté the mushrooms, green pepper, onions, and pimientos until tender. Combine tongue, sautéed vegetables, chicken broth, noodles, and salt in a 3 quart casserole. Cover and bake at 350° for 30 minutes.
Serves 6.
Mrs. Orvis Meador, Sr.

California Tongue

1   fresh beef tongue
1½   cups chopped onion
1   clove garlic
⅓   cup vegetable oil
⅓   cup chopped green pepper

3   cups tomatoes, fresh or canned
½   cup sliced pimiento stuffed green
     olives
1½   teaspoons salt
1   cup seedless raisins

Boil tongue about 2 hours or until tender. Cool and remove skin. Fry onions and garlic in oil. Add pepper, tomatoes, olives, salt, and raisins, cooking until mixture boils. Pour over tongue and bake at 350° for 30-45 minutes. This may be prepared a day in advance. Slice before serving. *Excellent with rice.*
Serves 6.
Mrs. Garland M. Lasater (Carolyn Kampmann) .

Sweetbreads

1	pound sweetbreads	½	stick butter
1	bay leaf	1	tablespoon chopped onion
2-3	peppercorns	10	medium mushroom caps, sliced
1	small onion, quartered	1½	tablespoons flour
1	rib celery, cut in large pieces	½	cup chicken stock
Flour		½	cup white wine or dry vermouth
Salt and pepper to taste			

Parboil sweetbreads 20 minutes in water with bay leaf, peppercorns, quartered onion, and celery. Cool, remove sweetbreads from stock, trim, and dry. Dredge in flour seasoned with salt and pepper. Sauté in butter until golden brown, remove, set aside, and keep hot. Sauté chopped onion and mushrooms in pan drippings until tender. Stir in 1½ tablespoons flour, chicken stock, and wine until smooth. Serve sweetbreads with wine sauce.

Mrs. Jack T. Williams, II (Jane Yeaton)

Liver 'n Onions

8	slices bacon	¼	teaspoon pepper
2	onions, sliced and separated	1	pound beef liver, thinly sliced
¼	cup flour	⅓	cup wine vinegar
¾	teaspoon salt		

Fry bacon in large skillet until crisp. Remove, crumble, and set aside. Add onion to bacon drippings, cook slowly until tender, remove, and set aside. Mix flour, salt, and pepper. Coat liver with seasoned flour. Sauté liver quickly in same skillet over high heat. Do not overcook. When liver is still pink in center, remove to a serving platter. Add wine vinegar to pan, stirring to remove browned bits and blend flavors together. Top liver with crumbled bacon and onion rings. Spoon wine vinegar glaze over each serving of liver.

Mrs. Joe Carroll Rust (Margie Cape)

King William Area Houses

"For Sale — A beautiful residence fronting one hundred yards on the River opposite the Arsenal embracing the falls. It has a fine water power, suitable for a mill seat. A good stone house on the place and a garden with plenty of shade."
San Antonio Herald. September 12, 1865.

Leg of Lamb

French

½	cup chopped parsley	¼	teaspoon pepper
½	clove garlic, crushed	1	6-8 pound leg of lamb, boned and
½	teaspoon basil		flattened
4	tablespoons olive oil or melted		Olive oil or butter
	butter		Salt to taste
⅛	teaspoon ginger		Cracked pepper to taste
1	teaspoon salt		

Persian

⅓	cup chopped pitted dried prunes	¼	teaspoon coriander
⅓	cup chopped pitted dates	⅛	teaspoon pepper
⅓	cup chopped dried figs	1	6-8 pound leg of lamb, boned and
¼	cup chopped onion		flattened
⅔	cup bulgur (cracked wheat)		Olive oil or butter
4	teaspoons chopped parsley		Salt to taste
1⅓	cups stock or bouillon		Cracked pepper to taste
1	teaspoon salt		

French   Combine the first 7 ingredients, mix well, and spread on lamb.

Persian   Combine the first 10 ingredients, reserving ⅓ cup stock to baste lamb while cooking, mix well, and spread on lamb.

Roasting instructions   Roll lamb, tuck in edges, and secure with skewers or tie with string. Rub with additional olive oil or butter and sprinkle with salt and cracked pepper. Roast at 450° for 10 minutes, reduce heat to 325°, and roast 2-2½ hours.
Serves 10.
Mrs. Ralph H. Winton

Stuffed Roasted Leg of Lamb

3	cups chopped parsley	2	tablespoons butter
2	cups chopped green onions	1	5 pound leg of lamb, boned and
1	clove garlic, minced		flattened
4	ounces dried apricots, finely	Salt to taste	
	chopped	Freshly ground pepper to taste	

Sauté parsley, onions, garlic, and apricots in butter until soft. Sprinkle lamb with salt and pepper. Spread vegetable and fruit mixture on lamb, roll, tuck in edges, and secure with skewers. Roast at 400° for 30 minutes. Reduce heat and bake at 325° until done. Roast 15-18 minutes per pound for a medium rare lamb roast. Water may be added to the roasting pan during cooking for gravy. Serves 10.

Mrs. Robert Buchanan (Sara "Sally" Ware Matthews)

Lamb Shanks

6	lamb shanks, about 4 pounds	2	tablespoons grated orange rind
¼	cup vegetable oil	1	teaspoon rosemary, crumbled
1	teaspoon paprika	1	teaspoon salt
2	cups diced onion	¼	teaspoon pepper
2	cups diced mushrooms	1	cup sour cream
2	cups vermouth or dry white wine	1	teaspoon dill
1	tablespoon horseradish	Cooked rice	

Brown lamb shanks in oil in a Dutch oven. Remove shanks and pour off drippings. Return shanks to pan and sprinkle with paprika. Add remaining ingredients except sour cream, dill, and rice. Cook, covered, over medium heat for 2-3 hours or until tender, turning shanks occasionally. Remove shanks. Add sour cream and dill to pan and heat, but do not boil. Serve shanks on a bed of rice and top with sour cream sauce. *The sauce may be increased with a good gravy mix, if necessary; and 4 teaspoons of curry powder add a new flavor, if desired.*

Serves 6.

Mr. V. W. Brinkerhoff

Couscous

1	package couscous	3	tomatoes, peeled and chopped
¼	cup olive oil	2	teaspoons salt
1	stick butter	1	teaspoon pepper
2	cups chopped onions	½	teaspoon cayenne pepper
4	pounds lamb, cut in 1 inch cubes	¼	teaspoon saffron
5	pounds chicken, cut into serving pieces	2	cups raisins
3	cups chicken broth	1	pound green peas, fresh or frozen
2	carrots, sliced	1	stick butter, melted
2	green peppers, sliced lengthwise		

Prepare couscous according to package directions and set aside. Heat oil and 1 stick butter in a couscousière or a large soup kettle into which a colander lined with cheesecloth will fit. Brown onions, lamb, and chicken. Add broth, carrots, green peppers, tomatoes, salt, pepper, cayenne, and saffron. Place couscous in lined strainer or colander and set over meat and vegetables in kettle. Cover tightly with foil and simmer over low heat 1½ hours. Add raisins and peas, cover, and cook 45 minutes or until chicken is tender. Stir 1 stick melted butter into couscous with a fork. Serve couscous on a large platter surrounded by meat and vegetables. *Couscous, a well known regional dish in Morocco and Algeria, has many variations. Ingredients may be added or subtracted according to the needs of the family.*
Serves 8-10.
Mrs. Robert Buchanan (Sara "Sally" Ware Matthews)

Lamb Curry with Rice

1	cup chopped onion	1⅓	tablespoons Worcestershire sauce
½	cup chopped green pepper, optional	3	cups cubed, cooked lamb
¾	cup diced celery	2⅔	cups stock made from lamb bones
3	tablespoons butter	4	tablespoons flour
1	teaspoon curry powder	¼	cup water
1½	teaspoons salt	1½	cups rice, cooked

Brown onion, pepper, and celery in butter. Stir in curry powder, salt, and Worcestershire. Add meat and stock and cook over low heat for 30 minutes. Make a smooth paste of flour and water. Stir into meat mixture and cook 10 minutes. Serve with rice.
Serves 6.
Mrs. Mary H. Hanks

Greek Meat Balls Kapamá

1	pound lean ground lamb	¼	cup flour
1-2	cloves garlic, crushed	¼	teaspoon cinnamon
1½	teaspoons salt, divided	½	teaspoon salt
¼	teaspoon pepper	2	tablespoons butter
¾	teaspoon cinnamon, divided	1	6 ounce can tomato paste
¼	cup red Burgundy	1	6 ounce can wine or water

Mix meat, garlic, 1 teaspoon salt, pepper, ½ teaspoon cinnamon, and Burgundy. Shape into balls. Combine flour, ¼ teaspoon cinnamon, and ½ teaspoon salt. Roll meatballs in flour mixture. Sauté in butter until well browned. Add tomato paste diluted with wine. Simmer, covered, 45-60 minutes. *Use as cocktail meatballs or serve over spaghetti with grated cheese.*

Mrs. S. Peter Lambros

Between King William Street and Yturri - Edmunds Mill

"Fred Stous, who resides on Presa Street, went below Guenther's mill to watch some young ladies shoot turtles with a revolver, when one of the balls glanced off the water and struck him on the ankle, making an awkward wound. Drs. Herff and Graves searched for the ball but failed to find it. They dressed the wound and report that Mr. Stous is doing well."

San Antonio Light. May 8, 1883.

Spicy Pork Chops

4	lean pork chops, at least 1 inch thick	1	teaspoon nutmeg
2	tablespoons oil	¼-½	cup lemon juice
1	teaspoon salt	4	thin slices lemon

In a heavy skillet, brown pork chops in oil over medium heat for about 15 minutes. Season with salt and nutmeg. Add lemon juice, cover, and simmer for 30-40 minutes or until tender. Arrange a lemon slice on each chop and cook, uncovered, for 5 minutes.
Serves 4.
Mrs. John Kampmann Meyer (Betty Taylor)

Pork Chops Flambé

6-8	large pork chops	1	large onion, thinly sliced
1½	teaspoons salt	1½	teaspoons tomato paste
¼	teaspoon pepper	1	cup white wine
1	teaspoon dry mustard	3	tablespoons orange juice
5½	tablespoons butter, divided	⅓	cup warmed brandy

Dust pork chops with a mixture of salt, pepper, and dry mustard. Brown pork chops on both sides in 1½ tablespoons of butter and remove from pan. Add 3-4 tablespoons of butter and brown sliced onion. Stir in tomato paste, wine, and orange juice. Return pork chops to pan and simmer, covered, for 45 minutes or until done. Place pork chops and sauce on a serving platter, add brandy, and flame.
Serves 6.
Mrs. Charles Schreiner Nelson (Shawn Adele Carpenter)

Stuffed Pork Chops

6	pork chops, 2 inches thick	1	large green apple, peeled, cored, and thinly sliced
1	teaspoon salt, divided		
⅛	teaspoon pepper	5	tablespoons seedless grapes, halved, or raisins
5	tablespoons chopped onion		
2	slices dry bread, crumbled, or 1½ cups	½	teaspoon nutmeg
		¼	teaspoon cinnamon
3	tablespoons butter	2-3	tablespoons water

Split the chops through the middle from the outer edge toward the bone, leaving meat attached to the bone. Spread open and pound thin. Season with ½ teaspoon salt and the pepper. Sauté onion and bread crumbs in butter in a heavy skillet. Add apple slices, grapes, ½ teaspoon salt, nutmeg, cinnamon, and water, and mix lightly. Spread dressing evenly inside chops, fold over, and fasten with picks. Place chops in a shallow roasting pan. Bake at 350° for 1½ hours, turning once and draining excess fat. *An excellent gravy may be made after chops are removed by adding ¾-1 cup water to the drippings and stirring over medium heat until the brown bits are dissolved.*
Serves 6.
Mrs. Jack Grieder (Nancy Bickham)

Tortilla Dogs

Hot dogs	Thick corn tortillas
Sliced cheese	Vegetable oil

Slit the hot dogs lengthwise halfway through and put cheese in the slits. Wrap tortillas around hot dogs and secure with a toothpick. Place in hot oil and fry until cheese is melted and tortilla is crisp.

Mrs. Juanita Bartlett

Jambon en Croûte

Duxelles

1	cup finely chopped onion	2	tablespoons butter
¼	pound fresh mushrooms, finely chopped, or 1 cup	½	teaspoon salt
		⅛	teaspoon pepper

Lemon Butter Sauce

3	tablespoons butter	¼	cup fresh lemon juice
1	tablespoon flour	½	teaspoon salt
½	cup milk		

Pastry and Filling

2	10 ounce packages Peppridge Farm Patty Shells, thawed overnight in refrigerator	4	thin slices boiled ham, finely diced
		6	tablespoons grated Cheddar or Swiss cheese
1½	cups cooked, cooled long grain and wild rice mix	1	egg, beaten with 1 teaspoon cold water

Duxelles Sauté onions and mushrooms in butter over moderate heat until dry, stirring frequently. Season with salt and pepper. Yields ½ cup.

Lemon Butter Sauce Melt 1 tablespoon butter in small saucepan. Remove from heat and stir in flour. Add milk gradually while stirring. Return to medium heat. Bring to a boil, stirring constantly. Stir in remaining ingredients. Yields ¾ cup.

Pastry and Filling Roll each patty shell large enough to make two 4½ x 5½ inch ovals. On 6 of them, place ⅙ of the rice, ⅙ of the ham, ⅙ of the duxelles, 1 tablespoon lemon butter sauce, and 1 tablespoon cheese. Top with another oval and press edges together to seal securely. Brush with egg and prick top with a fork. Place on baking sheet and chill for 15 minutes before baking. Decorate with flowers and ribbons cut from pastry trimmings and brush again with egg. Bake at 375° for 25-30 minutes. Serve hot. These may be prepared ahead of time and frozen. Thaw at room temperature 2-3 hours and bake. *Many other fillings could be used, such as sliced turkey or chicken and broccoli with cheese sauce; substitute salmon for the ham and cheese; or make a Reuben of sauerkraut, thinly sliced corned beef, and Swiss cheese.*
Serves 6. Freezes.
Mrs. Joe McFarlane, Jr. (Nancy Jane Arnot)

Ham Jambalaya

3	onions, sliced or diced	3½	cups canned tomatoes
1	green pepper, diced	½	teaspoon thyme
1	garlic clove, minced	½	teaspoon basil
½	stick butter	½	teaspoon paprika
2	cups diced ham	½	teaspoon Tabasco sauce
½	cup dry white wine	1	cup uncooked rice

Sauté onions, green pepper, and garlic in butter for 10 minutes. Add ham, wine, tomatoes, and seasonings, mixing well. Bring to a boil and add rice gradually, stirring constantly. Reduce heat, cover, and simmer for 25 minutes or until rice is done. This keeps well in the refrigerator for at least a week. *Also good with shrimp instead of ham.*
Serves 6.
Mrs. John Robert Beauchamp (Francis Ann Drake)

Ham Soufflé

8	cups diced French bread	4	eggs
4	cups diced ham	3	cups light cream
1¾	cups grated sharp Cheddar cheese, divided	1	teaspoon salt
4	tablespoons chopped green onions		Pepper to taste
1½	sticks butter, diced		Paprika

Grease a 3-4 quart casserole. Combine bread, ham, 1¼ cups cheese, onions, and butter. This may be done ahead of time. Beat eggs, cream, salt, and pepper and pour over bread mixture. Mix and let stand 15 minutes. Place mixture into casserole, sprinkle with ½ cup cheese, and dust with paprika. Bake at 350° for 40-50 minutes or until bubbly and crispy on top.
Serves 10.
Mrs. George V. Burkholder (Gretchen Schneider)

Bourbon Baked Ham

1	cup bourbon	¼	teaspoon ground cloves
1	cup packed light brown sugar	1	5-6 pound cooked ham
	Grated rind of 1 orange		

Combine bourbon, sugar, orange, and cloves. Let stand at least 30 minutes, stirring frequently to dissolve sugar. Pour over ham and bake, uncovered, at 325° for 1½ hours, basting frequently. This may be served hot or cold, but should be served the same day as prepared.
Serves 12.
Mrs. Thomas H. Snider

Ham with Cherry Sauce

1   8-10 pound cooked ham
2   10 ounce jars guava or apple jelly
2   tablespoons prepared mustard
⅔   cup unsweetened pineapple juice

¼   cup dry white wine
2   21 ounce cans cherry pie filling
1   cup light raisins

Place ham fat side up on rack in shallow pan and bake at 325°. It takes about 2¾ hours for a 10 pound ham. Thirty minutes before end of baking time, remove ham from oven and score fat in a diamond pattern. In a medium saucepan, combine jelly and mustard. Stir in pineapple juice and wine, bring to a boil stirring constantly, and simmer 2-3 minutes. Pour ⅓ of the glaze over ham and continue baking for 10 minutes. Repeat this step twice at 10 minute intervals. In saucepan, heat cherry pie filling and raisins to boiling, stirring occasionally. Remove ham to serving platter. Add glaze from baking pan to cherry sauce and bring to a boil. Spoon some sauce over ham and serve remainder in a bowl.
Serves 20-24
Mrs. Hubert W. Green, Jr. (Leah Tritt)

Ham and Chicken Roulades

1   large onion, chopped
½   stick butter
1   tablespoon Dijon mustard
1   cup Pepperidge Farm corn bread stuffing mix, crushed
Chicken stock

Salt to taste
Freshly ground pepper to taste
12   thin slices ham
12   thin slices cooked chicken
1   cup apple purée or applesauce
¼   cup horseradish

Sauté onion and mushrooms in butter in a heavy skillet until soft. Add mustard, stuffing, and enough stock to moisten. Season with salt and pepper. Place a slice of chicken over each ham slice and spoon some filling in the center. Roll and tie. Bake at 350° for 20-30 minutes. If frozen, bake at 350° for 40-45 minutes. Serve immediately with English applesauce made by heating apple purée and combining with horseradish.
Serves 6. Freezes.
Mrs. Robert Hausser (Maurine Sasser)

Ham Stroganoff

4	tablespoons butter or margarine, divided	3	tablespoons flour
2	cups cubed, cooked ham	1½	cups chicken stock
½	pound mushrooms, thinly sliced	½	cup sour cream
½	teaspoon prepared mustard	Dill to taste	
		Cooked peas or steamed rice	

Melt 3 tablespoons of the butter in a large heavy skillet. Add ham and mushrooms and sauté until lightly browned. Add remaining butter and mustard, mixing well. Blend in flour. Add stock and stir until mixture begins to boil. Cover and simmer at least 5 minutes to allow flour to blend well. Slowly stir in the sour cream and mix thoroughly. Sprinkle with dill and serve immediately over peas or rice.

Variation   Chicken liver stroganoff can be made by increasing the butter by 1 tablespoon, sautéing the livers separately and then flaming them with ¼ cup brandy. Decrease the flour 1 tablespoon and stir with ¼ teaspoon dry mustard, instead of prepared mustard, into the livers. Add salt and pepper, combine with mushrooms, and proceed as above.
Serves 4.
Mrs. Keith O'Gorman (Eleanor Law)

Cumin Cabbage and Sausage

3	tablespoons butter	1	8 ounce can tomato sauce
1	medium cabbage, cored and finely shredded, or 10 cups	1	teaspoon Dijon mustard
2	teaspoons ground cumin	3	medium-sized tart apples, peeled and finely diced
1	teaspoon salt	1½	pounds fully cooked smoked or Polish sausage
⅛	teaspoon pepper		

Melt butter in a Dutch oven over medium heat. Add cabbage and cook, stirring until it is just limp. Stir in cumin, salt, pepper, tomato sauce, mustard, and apples. Cover and simmer for 15 minutes. Arrange sausage on top, cover, and cook 10 minutes or until sausage is hot.
Serves 6.
Mrs. Lewis Tucker (Marjorie Stephenson)

Yturri – Edmunds Mill

"An old grist mill, constructed during the Spanish regime and run by water power furnished through one of the laterals of the old Pajalache Ditch, the ruins of which are still standing at 105 Concepcion Road, is the only evidence of such an enterprise."

A Chronology of Events in San Antonio.   Edward W. Heusinger, 1951.

Chasen's Chili

½ pound pinto beans
2 medium green peppers, seeded and chopped
2 large onions, chopped
4 cloves garlic, crushed
½ cup finely chopped parsley
¾ stick butter, divided

2 16 ounce cans tomatoes, drained and juice reserved
3½ pounds ground venison or lean chuck
½ cup chili powder
Salt and pepper to taste
½ teaspoon cumin

Cover beans with water 2 inches over beans and soak overnight. Sauté peppers, onions, garlic, and parsley in ¼ stick butter until tender and add tomatoes. Sauté venison in remaining butter and add seasonings. Combine vegetable mixture and venison mixture with beans in water and simmer 2-3 hours. Add reserved tomato juice as needed for right consistency. Correct seasoning. *Chili is better when prepared ahead and heated just before serving.* Serves 8-10.
Mrs. Robert Callaway

Chili

1 pound ground beef
2 pounds venison chili meat
1 large onion, chopped
1 package chili seasoning mix
1 tablespoon brown sugar
2 large cloves garlic, minced
Salt and pepper to taste

3 tablespoons chili powder
1 16 ounce can tomatoes or ½ Rotel tomatoes and green chilies and ½ plain tomatoes
2 cups water
1 pound brick of Goas' Chili con Carne

Brown meat. Add remaining ingredients, except Goas' chili, and cook until meat is tender. Add Goas' chili and water if needed, and continue to cook until blended.

Mrs. William W. Beuhler

Venison Pepper Steak

2 pounds venison steak or backstrap
1 stick butter
1 clove garlic, minced
Dash of ground ginger
½ cup soy sauce
1 cup canned beef bouillon

Pepper to taste
3 green peppers, sliced in strips
5 green onions with tops, sliced
3-4 tablespoons cornstarch
½ cup white wine or water
Rice or Chinese noodles

Remove all tendons and connective tissue and slice steak into thin strips. This is easy if meat is partially frozen. Cook over medium heat in butter with garlic and ginger until well browned, adding more butter if necessary. Add soy sauce, bouillon, and pepper. Cover and simmer about 30 minutes or until tender. Add peppers and onions and cook only until tender. Mix cornstarch with wine, simmer separately until clear, and add to meat mixture. When thickened, serve over rice or Chinese noodles.
Serves 6.
Mrs. Fred W. Middleton (Barbara Ann Loffland)

Smothered Venison Backstrap

Venison backstrap, cut into filets about ¾-1 inch thick
Salt and pepper to taste
Flour
4 tablespoons bacon drippings
2 cups minced onions
½ cup minced green pepper

3 cloves garlic, minced
⅛ teaspoon thyme
⅛ teaspoon sage
3 cups beef stock or consommé
1⅓ cups sherry
⅛ teaspoon Tabasco sauce

Season filets with salt and pepper. Pound flour into filets. In a Dutch oven brown the filets in bacon drippings, remove, and set aside. Add the onions, green pepper, garlic, thyme, and sage and sauté 20 minutes or until onions are transparent. Return the filets to Dutch oven and add beef stock, 1 cup sherry, and Tabasco. Cover and cook over low heat for 1½-2 hours. Just before serving add ⅓ cup sherry.
Serves 6-8.
Mrs. Charles Schreiner Nelson (Shawn Adele Carpenter)

Venison Marsala

1½ pounds venison, backstrap or ham, sliced ¼ inch thick
½ cup flour
⅓ cup grated Parmesan cheese
1 teaspoon salt
½ stick butter
¼ pound fresh or canned mushrooms, sliced

2 green onions with tops, chopped
½ cup consommé or beef broth
1-2 tablespoons lemon juice
¼ cup Marsala wine
Chopped parsley

Trim meat and cut slices into 3-4 inch pieces. Combine flour, cheese, and salt. Dredge meat into flour mixture, shaking off as much as possible. In ¼ stick butter, brown meat 1 minute on each side. Set aside and keep warm. Add remaining butter to skillet and sauté mushrooms and onions until tender. Add consommé, lemon juice, and wine, stirring well. Return meat to skillet and simmer, covered, for 15 minutes or until tender. To serve, pour pan juices over meat and sprinkle with parsley.
Serves 6-8.
Mrs. Jack Harvey, Jr. (O'Linda Boggess)

Texas Venison in Wine Sauce

1½ pounds venison with tendons removed, thinly sliced
¾ cup flour
Salt and pepper to taste
1 stick butter, divided

½ cup chicken broth
1 cup dry white wine
½ teaspoon salt
Freshly ground pepper
1 lemon, thinly sliced

Dredge venison slices in flour seasoned with salt and pepper to taste, shaking off excess flour. Melt ¼ stick butter in a skillet over medium heat. Sauté venison quickly a few pieces at a time, adding remaining butter as needed. Remove venison and keep warm. Pour broth into skillet, stirring well to remove browned bits. Add wine and salt and cook 1 minute. Return venison to sauce and cook 2-3 minutes until bubbly. Sprinkle with pepper. Arrange meat on a serving platter, pour wine mixture over, and top with lemon slices.
Serves 6.
Mrs. Walter J. Buzzini, III (Minnette London)

Backstrap Tournedos

2	pounds venison backstrap or flank steak	1	teaspoon pepper
½	cup wine vinegar	2	bay leaves
½	cup salad oil	1	tablespoon chopped parsley
½	teaspoon garlic salt	1½	tablespoons minced onion
			Partially cooked bacon strips

Butterfly backstrap and pound to tenderize. Combine remaining ingredients, except bacon, and marinate backstrap at least 4 hours. Remove backstrap and reserve marinade. Place strips of bacon to cover on 1 side of backstrap. Roll up lengthwise, secure with toothpicks, and slice 1 inch thick. Grill slices over hot coals, basting frequently with marinade. For medium rare, grill 5 minutes on each side.
Serves 4.
Mrs. J. Charles Hollimon, II (Nancy Smith)

Venison Diane

3	tablespoons butter, divided	1	tablespoon chopped parsley
1	tablespoon chopped shallots	1	tablespoon Worcestershire sauce
½-1	pound venison ham or backstrap, trimmed and thinly sliced	1	tablespoon A-1 sauce
		Salt	and pepper to taste
1	tablespoon chopped chives	2	tablespoons cognac

In a heavy skillet melt 2 tablespoons butter and sauté shallots until golden. Add venison and sear on both sides. Add chives, parsley, Worcestershire, A-1, and 1 tablespoon butter, mixing well. Sprinkle with salt and pepper and continue to cook about 10 minutes or until done. Flame with cognac.
Serves 2.
Mrs. Jack Harvey, Jr. (O'Linda Boggess)

Russian Rechauffé

2   pounds venison or round steak,
     cubed
1   large onion, chopped
1   clove garlic, chopped
¼   cup bacon drippings
1   4 ounce can sliced mushrooms
     with liquid

1   cup sour cream
1   8 ounce can tomato sauce
1   tablespoon Worcestershire sauce
1   teaspoon salt
¼   teaspoon pepper
Flour
½   cup sherry

Brown venison, onion, and garlic in bacon drippings. Add mushrooms with liquid, sour cream, tomato sauce, Worcestershire, salt, and pepper. Cook slowly for 1½ hours. If gravy is not thick enough, stir in a small amount of flour. May be prepared ahead, but add sherry just before serving.
Serves 6. Freezes before adding sherry.
Mrs. Martin Weilbacher (Jakey Price)

Chinese Style Venison with Oysters

1½-2 pounds venison backstrap,
      partially frozen
¾   cup peanut oil, divided
½   pint oysters and liquor
½   pound snow peas

8-10 green onion tops, finely chopped
1½   cups chicken broth
2   tablespoons cornstarch
Soy sauce to taste

Thinly slice the venison against the grain. In a wok or skillet heat 2 tablespoons oil and quickly brown venison a few pieces at a time, adding more oil as needed. Remove venison and set aside. Drain oysters, reserving liquor, and sauté in oil until edges curl. Wipe out pan and using 2 tablespoons fresh oil, sauté snow peas and green onion tops until crisp-tender. In a saucepan, combine broth with cornstarch and heat until slightly thickened. Add all ingredients including oyster liquor to broth and season with soy sauce. *Serve with Chinese fried rice or steamed rice.*
Serves 6.
Mrs. Willard Simpson, Jr. (Betsy Johns)

Venison Bourguignonne

2	pounds venison stew meat	1	teaspoon rosemary
4	tablespoons bacon drippings	1	tablespoon dried parsley
1	onion, diced	1-2	tablespoons butter, softened
2	cloves garlic, minced	1-2	tablespoons flour
2	teaspoons powdered beef bouillon	½-1	pound fresh mushrooms, sliced
2	cups red wine	1	stick butter, divided
1	bay leaf	12	small onions
1	tablespoon tomato paste	1	tablespoon water
1	teaspoon thyme		Chopped fresh parsley

Brown meat in drippings. Add diced onion and garlic cooking until golden. Add bouillon, wine, bay leaf, tomato paste, thyme, rosemary, and dried parsley. Simmer, covered, for 2 hours or until meat is tender. Mix 1 tablespoon butter with 1 tablespoon flour and add gradually to mixture to thicken. Use additional butter and flour if necessary. Sauté mushrooms in ½ stick butter. Simmer onions, covered, in remaining butter and 1 tablespoon water until tender. Add mushrooms and onions to meat mixture. Garnish with fresh parsley.
Serves 6.
Mrs. Ernest L. Brown, III (Connie Lentz)

Venison Sauerbraten

1	venison ham, trimmed, or 1 4 pound boneless lean roast	½	teaspoon thyme
1	cup vinegar	½	cup ginger snap crumbs or flour, divided
1½	cups water, divided	2	tablespoons shortening
½	cup chopped onions, divided	¼	cup chopped celery
2	bay leaves	¼	cup sliced carrots
1	teaspoon paprika	2	teaspoons salt
2	cloves	¼	cup dry red wine

Marinate meat in a mixture of vinegar, 1 cup water, ¼ cup onions, bay leaves, paprika, cloves, and thyme. Cover and refrigerate several days, turning once daily. Drain meat and reserve marinade. Coat meat with ¼ cup crumbs and sear in shortening. Add celery and remaining onions and cook 5 minutes, stirring constantly. Pour marinade over meat and add carrots. Cover and simmer 3 hours or until meat is tender. Remove meat and keep hot. Mix remaining crumbs, salt, and ½ cup water. Stir into sauce and cook until thickened. Add wine and serve over meat.

Mrs. Scott Petty, Jr. (Louise James)

Pita's Venison Roast

1	venison shoulder roast or ham	2	onions, quartered
10	chili petins or chopped jalapeño	1	green pepper, chopped
Salt to taste		1	cup olive or vegetable oil
Lemon-pepper seasoning to taste		1	cup water
3	cloves garlic, crushed	1	cup wine vinegar or red wine
2	tomatoes, quartered	3	tablespoons Worcestershire sauce

Make holes with a knife in the roast and fill each with a chili petin or a piece of jalapeño. Season with salt and lemon-pepper. Rub meat with garlic. In a deep roasting pan place vegetables on meat. Pour remaining ingredients over meat. Marinate meat for 10-12 hours or overnight, basting occasionally. Bake at 350° for 25 minutes per pound for medium and 30 minutes per pound for well done.

Mrs. Kip McKinney Espy (Sally Searcy Kleberg)

Venison Pâté

1   venison ham

Marinade

2	cups vegetable oil	1	tablespoon basil
2	cups lemon juice	1	tablespoon tarragon
1	cup Worcestershire sauce	4	cloves garlic or 3 teaspoons garlic powder
2	tablespoons cracked pepper		
2	tablespoons marjoram		

Pâté

5	pounds of the ground venison	¼	cup Worcestershire sauce, or to taste
3	pounds Monterey Jack cheese, grated	5	cloves garlic, minced, or 3 teaspoons garlic powder
1	tablespoon dry mustard	1-2	cups mayonnaise
1	cup drained capers		Tabasco sauce to taste
1	cup drained dill relish or 2 large dill pickles, finely chopped		Ripe olives
			Pimientos
½	cup finely chopped onion		Hard-boiled egg slices

Marinade Combine ingredients and marinate ham for several days. Drain marinade and reserve, as it may be used again. Bake ham at 325°-350° for 3 hours. Cool and grind.

Pâté Combine ingredients, except olives, pimientos, and eggs, and mix well. Mold or shape pâté. It will thicken slightly when refrigerated. Garnish with olives, pimientos, and egg before serving.

Mrs. Ricks Wilson (Barbara Koch)
Mrs. George Fischer (Carolyn Carter)

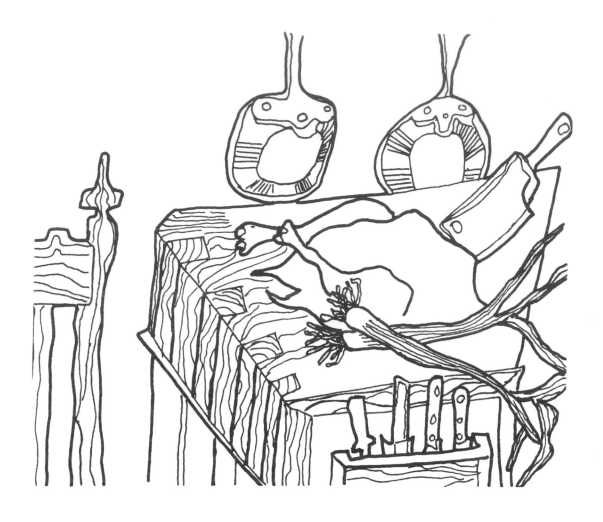

Doves Delicious

8-9 doves
⅓   cup olive oil
Garlic salt to taste
Celery salt to taste
Curry powder to taste

Dry mustard to taste
Black pepper to taste
1   6 ounce can mushrooms
Wine, bouillon, water or a combination

Place doves in a casserole and sprinkle with olive oil. Season generously with salts and curry powder and sparingly with mustard and pepper. Add mushrooms with juice and enough liquid to measure 1 inch. Cover and bake at 350° for 1 hour or until tender.

Mrs. L. Lowry Mays (Peggy Pitman)

Smothered Doves

10 doves
Salt and pepper to taste
Flour
Vegetable oil
¾ cup chopped celery

3 10½ ounce cans beef bouillon
⅓ cup chopped onions
1 3-4 ounce can chopped mushrooms
1 bay leaf, crushed

Wash birds and season lightly with salt and pepper. Shake birds 2-3 at a time in a sack with flour. Brown in hot oil, remove, and drain. In a roasting pan lined with foil, place birds with remaining ingredients, salt, and pepper. Bake, covered, at 350° for 1 hour. Turn birds and bake for 1 hour, adding water if needed. Pour gravy over birds to serve.
Serves 4-6.
Mrs. Stanton P. Bell (Jean Todd)

Texas Doves

12 doves
½ cup flour
1 tablespoon Jane's Krazy Mixed-Up Salt
1 teaspoon lemon-pepper seasoning
Bacon drippings
½ cup chopped onion
½ cup chopped celery

¼ cup chopped green onions with tops
2 tablespoons chopped parsley
1 green pepper, chopped, optional
1 10½ ounce can beef bouillon, divided
1 whole jalapeño pepper, optional
½ can beer

Wash and dry doves. Combine flour, salt, and lemon-pepper. Shake doves two at a time in a paper bag with seasoned flour. If more seasoned flour is needed, increase ingredients proportionately. Brown doves in ½ inch bacon drippings. Remove doves and set aside. Remove all but 2-3 tablespoons bacon drippings, add vegetables, and sauté until tender. Return birds to pan, add ½ can beef bouillon and the jalapeño, cover, and simmer 20 minutes. Add ½ can beer and remaining bouillon. Cover and simmer 40 minutes or longer, depending on age of birds. Remove jalapeño before serving. May be made 1 day ahead.
Serve with brown or wild rice.
Serves 4.
Mrs. Huard Hargis Eldridge (Earl Fae Cooper, Jr.)

Doves Picante

3   doves per person
Salt and pepper to taste
Equal parts of flour and red chili
    powder

Bacon drippings, butter, margarine, or
    vegetable oil
Bouillon cubes
Hot peppers to taste

Rinse doves and pat dry with paper towels. Season each bird with pepper and very little salt. Put flour and chili powder in a small paper bag and shake. Put a few doves at a time in bag and shake well to coat. Heat ½ inch of drippings in a cast iron pot or skillet. Brown birds a few at a time and set aside. Dissolve bouillon cubes in boiling water, add to the drippings, and stir well. You should have enough liquid to slightly more than half cover the birds. Return birds to pot, add hot peppers, and cover. Bake at 300° for 1½-2 hours. This can be prepared and refrigerated 1-2 days ahead. The gravy will be thicker when heated the second time.

Mrs. Joe Straus, Jr. (Jocelyn Levi)

Paula's Dove Pie

Filling
12-15 doves
Salt and pepper to taste
Garlic powder to taste
¾   stick margarine
½   cup chopped parsley
1   cup chopped onion
1   cup chopped celery
½   cup chopped green pepper
2   heaping tablespoons flour

1   6 ounce can sliced mushrooms
    with juice or fresh mushrooms
1   8½ ounce can tiny English peas,
    drained
2   tablespoons Wyler's instant
    chicken bouillon
Dash of Tabasco sauce
2   tablespoons Sauterne

Pastry
2   cups sifted flour
1   teaspoon salt

⅔   cup shortening
6-8   tablespoons cold water

Filling   Wash doves and sprinkle with salt, pepper, and garlic powder. Wrap tightly in foil and cook at 300° for 3 hours. Turn oven off and let cool. Remove meat from bones and reserve. Sauté in margarine the parsley, onion, celery, and green pepper. Stir in flour and add mushrooms, peas, bouillon, Tabasco, and Sauterne. Mixture should be thick. Add dove meat. Put in a deep casserole and place pastry on top. Brown and serve.

Pastry   Sift the flour and salt together. Cut in the shortening quickly and lightly with a pastry blender. Stir in cold water as quickly as possible to form a ball. On a lightly floured pastry cloth, roll out pastry in the shape to fit casserole. This makes more than enough pastry for a 2 crust pie.

Mrs. Alex Weil, III (Penny Speier)

Dove, Quail, or Chicken with Rice

8　whole doves or quail or 1 chicken, cut into parts
Salt and pepper to taste
¼　cup flour
1　stick butter, divided
½-1 cup chopped onion
1　teaspoon dried parsley
½　cup chopped mushrooms
½-1 cup white wine or sweet red wine

Wash birds and dry well. Combine salt, pepper, and flour in a plastic bag and shake birds in mixture. Sauté birds in ½ stick butter and remove to a casserole. Add onions, parsley, mushrooms, remaining butter, and wine to pan drippings. Cook a few minutes to blend flavors and pour over birds. Bake at 350° for 1 hour and 15 minutes, basting 2-3 times during baking. *Serve with rice cooked in bouillon.*

Mrs. Fred C. Lepick, Jr. (Morgia Howard)

Game Birds in Wine Marinade

Doves, duck, or goose
Salt and pepper to taste
¾　cup rosé wine
¼　cup vegetable oil
¼　cup soy sauce
2　tablespoons water
1　teaspoon oregano
1　teaspoon ginger
1　tablespoon brown sugar
1　clove garlic
1　cup canned mushrooms with liquid

Season birds with salt and pepper. Combine remaining ingredients and marinate birds 6-12 hours. Bake, covered, at 375° for 1½ hours; or brown birds in additional oil, pour marinade over, and cook, covered, on top of stove for 2 hours.
Yields 2½ cups marinade.
Mrs. Tom Stolhandske (Betsy)

Fried Quail

12　quail
3　cups water
1　tablespoon salt
1　cup Pioneer Pancake or Biscuit Mix
2　teaspoons onion powder
2　teaspoons seasoned salt
¼　teaspoon seasoned pepper
2　envelopes instant chicken broth

Cover quail with water to which 1 tablespoon salt has been added. Chill at least 1 hour. Combine remaining ingredients in a paper bag. Remove quail from water a few at a time and do not dry. Shake in mix. Fry in deep, hot oil only until quail float and are golden brown.
Serves 4.
Mrs. Pierce McGrath (Beatrice Findlater)

Sesame Fried Doves or Quail

3 eggs
1 cup milk
2 cups flour
2 tablespoons seasoned salt

2 tablespoons seasoned pepper
4 tablespoons sesame seeds
12 doves or 8 quail
Vegetable oil

Combine eggs and milk and beat lightly with fork. Mix flour, salt, pepper, and sesame seeds. Dip each bird in egg mixture, then in sesame flour. In a deep pot filled with vegetable oil, fry birds only until they float and are golden brown.

Mrs. Joe Frost (Marianna)

Tasty Quail

Wild quail, 3 per person
Italian salad dressing, Good Seasons or
  Wishbone

Bacon slices, cut in half
Lemon-pepper seasoning to taste

Marinate quail, breast-side down, in salad dressing for 4 hours. Remove from marinade and sprinkle generously with lemon-pepper. Wrap each bird with ½ slice of bacon and secure with toothpick. Broil over charcoal until done.

Mrs. Fred W. Middleton (Barbara Ann Loffland)

Oven Baked Doves or Quail

12-18 doves or 6-12 quail
1 stick butter
1 cup chopped onion
2 cloves garlic, minced
½ teaspoon thyme

Salt and pepper to taste
¼ cup dry sherry
1 13¾ ounce can chicken stock
½ pound fresh mushrooms, sliced
2 tablespoons fresh parsley, chopped

In a skillet, brown birds in butter. Remove birds to a covered roasting pan. In drippings, sauté the onion and garlic until golden. Stir in thyme, salt, pepper, sherry, and stock and pour over birds. Cover and bake at 350° for 1 hour or until tender. Add mushrooms and parsley during the last 15 minutes of cooking.
Serves 6.
Mrs. Ernest L. Brown, III (Connie Lentz)

Quail with Raisins

2	large or 4 small quail	½	stick butter
Butter or margarine		12	tiny white onions, peeled
Salt and pepper to taste		2	teaspoons meat glaze or extract
½	cup golden seedless raisins, soaked in warm water to cover for 2 hours	8	button mushrooms
		3	tablespoons pine nuts, optional
3	ounces salt pork, diced	¾	cup beef bouillon

Rub quail with butter or margarine and season with salt and pepper inside and out. Drain raisins and dry well. Put salt pork into boiling water for 1 minute, remove, and dry. Melt butter in an oven proof casserole, add salt pork and onions, and brown lightly. Add meat glaze and stir to dissolve. Cover the casserole and simmer for 15 minutes. If the onions stick, add a few drops of water. Add the quail, turning them to brown evenly. Add mushrooms, raisins, and pine nuts. Cover and cook 7-8 minutes. Add bouillon, stirring to remove browned bits, and simmer for 8 minutes.
Serves 2.
Mrs. Paul R. Snow (Mary Lynn "Mimi" Fariss)

Quail for Company

8	quail	1	clove garlic, chopped
½	teaspoon Accent	2	tablespoons chopped carrot
½	cup flour	1	cup chicken broth
Salt and pepper to taste		1	cup dry white wine
½	cup vegetable oil	1	tablespoon grated orange rind
2	tablespoons chopped onion	1	teaspoon Worcestershire sauce
2	tablespoons chopped green pepper	1	cup sour cream, heated

Wipe quail dry, sprinkle with Accent, and let stand 15 minutes. Mix flour, salt, and pepper in a paper bag. Drop quail in bag, two at a time, and shake well. Heat oil and quickly brown birds on all sides. Remove to a covered casserole. Lightly sauté onion, green pepper, and garlic in pan drippings. Stir in carrots, broth, and wine and simmer 15 minutes. Strain broth mixture over birds. Add orange rind and Worcestershire, cover, and bake at 350° about 45 minutes. Turn off heat and let birds remain in oven 30 minutes. Stir in sour cream and serve at once.
Serves 4.
Mrs. Charles A. Westbrook (Mary Frances)

Sautéed Quail

6-8 quail
1 stick butter
2 shallots, finely chopped
2 cloves garlic, minced
½ bay leaf
2 whole cloves

2 cups white wine
1 pint heavy cream
½ teaspoon salt
⅛ teaspoon pepper
1 teaspoon chopped chives
Pinch of cayenne pepper

Melt butter and add shallots, garlic, bay leaf, and cloves, stirring constantly. Sauté quail in butter mixture until well browned. Add wine and simmer 30 minutes. Remove quail; strain sauce into a casserole and slowly add cream, salt, pepper, chives, and cayenne. Add the quail, cover, and heat to boiling.

Mrs. John K. Walters, Jr. (Lucy Masterson Yerly)

Wild Duck in Cream

2-3 wild ducks
Salt to taste
1 cup flour

1 stick butter
Light cream to cover ducks

Sprinkle ducks inside and out with salt, truss, and dust with flour. In a large, heavy, flameproof casserole, brown ducks on all sides in butter. Add enough boiling cream to cover ducks. Simmer, covered, at 350° for 1 hour and 40 minutes or until almost tender. Remove cover and simmer for 20 minutes. *This recipe is also excellent for doves and quail.*

Mrs. James L. Hayne (Roxana Catto)

Chinese Roast Duck

3 wild ducks
3 tablespoons + ⅓ cup soy sauce, divided
2 tablespoons ginger, divided

2 tablespoons + ½ cup honey, heated, divided
1 tablespoon dry sherry
1 clove garlic, minced

Brush ducks thoroughly inside and out with a mixture of 3 tablespoons soy sauce, 1 tablespoon ginger, 2 tablespoons honey, and sherry. Roast ducks, covered, at 350° for 1½ hours. Combine remaining soy sauce, ginger, honey, and garlic to make a basting sauce. Roast ducks 1 more hour, basting with sauce every 15 minutes.
Serves 6.
Mrs. Ernest L. Brown, III (Connie Lentz)

Smoked Wild Duck

Duck	Onion, quartered
Salt and pepper to taste	½ - ¾ bottle Kraft barbecue sauce
Apple, quartered	2 tablespoons lemon juice
Orange, quartered	¼ teaspoon Evangeline hot sauce

Season duck inside and out with salt and pepper. Stuff each cavity with pieces of apple, orange, and onion. Combine lemon juice and hot sauce with barbecue sauce and brush generously on all sides of duck. Place on a rack and put in smoker with water pan for at least 4 hours. *Serve in thin slices as an hors d'oeuvre with rye bread.*

Mr. George Bristol

Filé should always be served at the table, never cooked with gumbo.

Duck Gumbo

6	ducks	1-2	10 ounce packages frozen cut okra
1	cup flour	2	tablespoons Worcestershire sauce
1	cup bacon drippings	½	teaspoon Tabasco sauce
3	medium onions, chopped	1	tablespoon salt
2	cloves garlic, minced	1	teaspoon pepper
4	ribs celery, chopped		Cooked rice
1	8 ounce can tomato sauce		Filé powder

Simmer ducks in water over low heat for several hours until tender. Bone meat and reserve 3 quarts stock, adding water if necessary. In a large, heavy pot, make a roux by slowly browning flour in bacon drippings until it is the color of a walnut, stirring constantly. This takes approximately 30-45 minutes. Add onion, garlic, and celery. Cook over medium heat for 5 minutes, stirring occasionally. Add warm stock gradually, stirring until smooth. Add tomato sauce, okra, Worcestershire, Tabasco, salt, pepper, and duck. Simmer about 1 hour. Serve gumbo over a bed of mounded rice with filé to taste.
Makes approximately 4 quarts.
Mrs. William Scanlan, Jr. (Cecil Collins)

For an extra special gumbo, in the last 15 minutes of cooking time add 1 pound peeled, uncooked shrimp and in the last 5 minutes add 1½ pints raw oysters with liquor.

Wild Duck

2 large wild ducks	1 cup orange juice concentrate
Salt to taste	½ cup sherry
½ apple, cut in wedges	1¼ cups water, divided
½ onion, cut in wedges	3 tablespoons flour
Bacon slices	

Salt each duck and stuff with apple and onion wedges. Put strips of bacon across the breasts and bake at 450° for 15 minutes or until ducks are slightly brown and bacon is crisp. Reduce heat to 350°. Combine orange juice, sherry, and ½ cup water, pour over ducks, cover, and bake 2½-3 hours. Remove ducks, stir in flour and add remaining water, stirring over medium heat until mixture is the desired consistency for gravy. *A delicious duck and gravy!* Serves 4.

Mrs. Cary Stratton (Joan Whitelaw Browning)

Duck à la Middleton

Wild ducks, 1 per person	½ cup glaze per duck made with:
Salt	2 tablespoons apple jelly
Orange slices	2 tablespoons currant jelly
Lemon slices	2 tablespoons plum jelly
Salt and pepper to taste	2 tablespoons sherry
1 46 ounce can apple juice	Grated orange or lemon rind
Orange liqueur, optional	

Heavily salt outside of each duck and refrigerate 24 hours to draw out blood. Wash off salt and blood thoroughly. Bake on a rack at 325° for about 1 hour or until fat has dripped out. Fill each cavity with lemon and orange slices. Salt and pepper ducks, place in a Dutch oven, and fill ⅓ full with apple juice. Add any leftover fruit slices and orange liqueur to taste. Bake, covered, at 350° for 2½ hours. Melt over low heat enough apple, currant, and plum jelly, sherry, and grated orange or lemon rind to make ½ cup glaze for each duck. Place ducks in shallow baking dish, baste with glaze, and bake at 325° for 15 minutes.

Mrs. Fred W. Middleton (Barbara Ann Loffland)

Roast Wild Turkey in Foil

1	wild turkey	¼	cup dry white wine
Salt to taste		¼	cup brandy
Lemon-pepper seasoning to taste		1½	teaspoons thyme
Butter to taste		1½	teaspoons basil
½	stalk celery with leaves, cut in chunks	½	teaspoon salt
2	large onions, quartered	1	teaspoon lemon-pepper seasoning
		1	stick butter, melted

Line a large roasting pan with enough heavy foil to cover the turkey. Clean turkey inside and out extremely well. Sprinkle inside with salt and lemon-pepper. Rub skin with butter. Fill turkey cavity with chunks of celery and onions. Place turkey in pan. Mix wine, brandy, thyme, basil, salt, 1 teaspoon lemon-pepper, and butter, and pour over turkey. Close foil tightly and cover pan. Roast at 350° for 3½ hours or until tender. Fold foil back and roast 30 minutes to brown.

Mrs. Scott Petty, Jr. (Louise James)

Wild Turkey Marinade

1	wild turkey	¼	cup soy sauce
¼	teaspoon Accent per pound	Salt and pepper to taste	
½	cup vegetable oil	1	tablespoon poultry seasoning
½	cup white wine vinegar	Herb or corn bread dressing, optional	
½	cup lemon juice		

In cavity of turkey, sprinkle ½ of the Accent. Combine remaining ingredients, except Accent, and marinate turkey in a covered roasting pan for 2 hours, turning or basting every 30-45 minutes. Stuff turkey with dressing if desired and sprinkle remaining Accent on outside of turkey. Bake breast side down, covered, on the lowest oven rack at 350° for ½ of the baking time.* Turn turkey breast side up for remainder of time. Baste frequently throughout baking. Remove cover and brown during last 45 minutes.

*Baking time

6-8	pounds — 2-2½ hours	12-16	pounds — 3-3¼ hours
8-12	pounds — 2⅓-3 hours	24	pounds — 4½-5½ hours

Use your favorite herb or corn bread dressing to which you have added sautéed onion, celery, giblets, and raw egg.

Mrs. Frederick C. Groos, Jr. (Martha Grace Bailey)

Turkey with Tamale Stuffing and Enchilada Gravy

1   12-16 pound wild or domestic
turkey

Gravy
2½ 10 ounce cans Gebhardt's mild
enchilada sauce
2   cans water
2   13¾ ounce cans Swanson's
chicken broth
2   teaspoons chili powder

½   teaspoon poultry seasoning
1   teaspoon salt
1   medium onion, quartered
1   clove garlic, sliced
Turkey liver, gizzard, and neck

Stuffing
8   ounces bulk seasoned sausage
1   large onion, chopped
½   stick butter
48   tamales, broken into pieces
1   recipe day-old corn bread to fill a
9 x 9 x 2 inch pan

2   eggs, beaten
½   10 ounce can Gebhardt's mild
enchilada sauce
¼   teaspoon cayenne pepper
½   teaspoon ground cumin
Salt and pepper to taste

Gravy   Combine all ingredients and simmer 3-4 hours, adding more water if necessary. Strain before serving. *Best made a day ahead.*

Stuffing   Brown sausage and drain if necessary. Sauté onions in butter. Crumble tamales and corn bread into a large bowl. Add sausage, onions, and remaining ingredients and mix gently. Loosely stuff turkey and truss before baking.

Turkey   Bake wild turkey according to chart on page 205 or domestic turkey according to package instructions, basting frequently with enchilada gravy until done.

The Cookbook Committee

Mission Nuestra Señora de la Purisima Concepcion de Acuña

"One league south of San Antonio and on the east side of the river is the mission of Nuestra Señora de la Purisima Concepcion de Acuña, first founded in the land of the Texas in 1716, and later removed to its present site... The church is beautiful. It is thirty-two varas long and eight wide, built of stone and mortar, with vaulted roof, transept, cupola, and two belfries."

History of Texas 1673-1779. Fray Juan Augustin Morfi.

Texas Chicken Spaghetti

1   2½ pound chicken, cut into parts
Salt and pepper to taste
Flour
Shortening
1   large onion, chopped
1   medium can tomatoes, drained
1   6 ounce can tomato paste
Cayenne pepper to taste

Pepper to taste
1   tablespoon chili powder
1   teaspoon salt
1   pound spaghetti, cooked and
      drained
½   pound cheese, grated
Parsley

Season chicken with salt and pepper and dredge in flour. Heat shortening in an iron skillet and fry chicken until lightly browned and partially done. Drain on paper. Remove all but 2-3 tablespoons shortening from skillet, add onion, and sauté. Add tomatoes, tomato paste, and seasonings. Cook for a few minutes and return chicken to sauce. Put in oven, cover, and bake 30-40 minutes or until chicken is tender. Arrange chicken over spaghetti, cover with sauce, and sprinkle with cheese. Garnish with parsley and serve at once.
Serves 6.
Mrs. Anne Covington Phelps

Pineapple Chicken

1   pound chicken, beef, or pork, cut
      into 1 inch pieces
1   tablespoon cornstarch
1   teaspoon salt
2   teaspoons cold water
1   tablespoon soy sauce
1½ cups chopped onion

4   tablespoons vegetable oil, divided
1   cup diagonally cut celery
10   water chestnuts, sliced
4   canned pineapple slices, cut in
      wedges
4   tablespoons pineapple juice
Cooked rice

Dredge chicken in a mixture of cornstarch, salt, water, and soy sauce. Sauté onions in 1 tablespoon oil for 2 minutes, and remove from pan. Sauté celery and water chestnuts in 1 tablespoon oil for 2 minutes, and remove from pan. Sauté chicken in 2 tablespoons oil until brown. This may be prepared ahead. Add vegetables, pineapple, and pineapple juice. Simmer until thoroughly heated and serve with rice. *I took a Chinese cooking class from the Benedictine sisters in Tokyo and this was one of their recipes. The vegetables should be crisp-tender.*
Serves 6.
Mrs. Dan C. Peavy, Jr. (Harriet Williams)

Chicken Excelsior House

6	whole chicken breasts, halved and boned		Salt to taste
Garlic salt to taste		2	4 ounce cans mushrooms, drained
1	stick butter	½	10¾ ounce can chicken broth
1	teaspoon paprika	2	cups sour cream, at room
Dash of cayenne pepper			temperature
3	tablespoons lemon juice	¼	cup sherry

Sprinkle chicken with garlic salt. Melt butter and add paprika, cayenne, and lemon juice. Roll chicken breasts in butter mixture, place on a baking sheet, and bake at 375° until tender. Salt mushrooms lightly, add to broth, and stir in sour cream. Place chicken in a casserole, cover with the sour cream mixture, and add sherry. Bake 30-35 minutes or until bubbly. *This is from my friend who runs the Excelsior House in Jefferson, Texas. Their food is famous.*

Mrs. Virginia P. Sinclair (Virginia Phillips)

Cashew Chicken

3	whole chicken breasts, boned and skinned	½	pound fresh mushrooms, sliced
½	pound snow peas or 2 packages frozen snow peas, partially thawed	1	cup chicken broth
		1	15 ounce can bamboo shoots, drained and sliced
4	green onions	¼	cup Kikkoman soy sauce
¼	cup vegetable oil, divided	2	tablespoons cornstarch
1	4 ounce package cashew nuts	½	teaspoon sugar
		½	teaspoon salt

Slice chicken horizontally in ⅛ inch thick slices; then cut in 1 inch diamonds. Remove the ends and strings from fresh peas. Cut the green part of the onions into 1 inch lengths and slash both ends several times; slice the white part ¼ inch thick. Heat 1 tablespoon oil over moderate heat, 350°F, add nuts, and cook 1 minute, shaking pan, until lightly toasted. Remove from pan and set aside. Add remaining oil to pan, add chicken, and cook quickly, turning until it turns opaque. Add peas, mushrooms, and broth. Cover and simmer 2 minutes. Add bamboo shoots. Mix soy sauce, cornstarch, sugar, and salt, and add to pan juices. Cook until sauce is thickened, stirring constantly. Simmer 1 minute, stir in green onions, and sprinkle with nuts. *Serve with Chinese Fried Rice (see index).*
Serves 8.
Mrs. Huard Hargis Eldridge (Earl Fae Cooper, Jr.)

Chicken Wino

2-3 pounds chicken breasts
1 tablespoon flour
2 teaspoons salt
1 teaspoon pepper
2 cups chopped onions
6 tablespoons olive oil
1 cup dry white wine

2 tablespoons tomato paste
1 beef bouillon cube, dissolved in 1 cup boiling water
¼ cup wine vinegar
2 cloves garlic
1 teaspoon capers
2 tablespoons chopped parsley

Dredge chicken in flour seasoned with salt and pepper. Sauté onions in oil in a large skillet. Add chicken to onions and brown. Pour wine over chicken and cook on high heat for 5 minutes. Combine tomato paste and bouillon, pour over chicken, and stir. Reduce heat to medium, cover, and cook about 45 minutes or until chicken is tender. Remove chicken and keep warm. Add vinegar to skillet and boil 1 minute; then add garlic, capers, and parsley and cook 1 minute, mixing well. Pour sauce over chicken and serve.
Serves 6-8.
Mrs. James R. Hardy, Jr.

Swiss Chicken

3 whole chicken breasts, halved, skinned, and boned
1 teaspoon M.S.G.
½ cup flour
¼ cup vegetable oil
6 thick slices French bread
6 slices Swiss cheese

1 tablespoon butter
½ pound mushrooms, sliced
⅔ cup white wine
1 teaspoon salt
¼ teaspoon pepper
Flour, optional

Sprinkle chicken with M.S.G. and roll in flour. Brown chicken in oil over medium heat. Reduce heat, cover, and cook 15 minutes or until a fork can be inserted with ease. Top bread slices with cheese, place on a baking sheet, and bake at 200° until heated. Remove chicken from pan and add butter. Sauté mushrooms about 3 minutes and add wine, stirring to loosen browned bits. Add salt, pepper, and chicken and simmer until the sauce has thickened. If necessary, add a sprinkle of flour to thicken sauce. Place chicken over bread slices and top with mushroom sauce.
Serves 6.
Mrs. Charles E. Cheever, Jr. (Sarah "Sally" McKinney)

Chicken with Duck Sauce

2-3	pounds chicken thighs and breasts	2	envelopes Lipton Onion Soup Mix
1	8 ounce bottle Russian dressing	8	ounces apricot jam or preserves

Place chicken in a roasting pan lined with aluminum foil. Mix remaining ingredients and spread over chicken. Bake at 300° for 2 hours, basting chicken several times. Watch carefully so sauce does not burn.
Serves 8.
Mrs. Ralph L. Marx

Fiesta Chicken

1	3-3½ pound chicken, cut into parts	1	teaspoon salt
¼	cup vegetable oil	1	20 ounce can pineapple chunks
1	tablespoon chili powder	3	ripe bananas, peeled and quartered
¼	teaspoon pepper	1	ripe avocado, peeled and sliced
¼	teaspoon cinnamon	½	pound fresh white grapes or ½ cup
1½	tablespoons grated onion		golden raisins

Brown chicken in oil. Sprinkle with the next 5 seasonings. Pour pineapple and juice over chicken. Add raisins at this time if they are to be substituted for grapes. Cover and cook 30-35 minutes or until tender. If necessary, add a small amount of water during cooking. Remove chicken to a serving platter. Garnish with bananas, avocado, and grapes separated into small bunches. Cover with pineapple sauce.
Serves 4-6.
Mrs. Richard Knight, Jr. (Darleen)

Chicken Breast Supreme

4	whole chicken breasts	4-5	tablespoons margarine
½	teaspoon poultry seasoning	½	cup hot water
1	teaspoon McCormick Season All	½-1	cup white wine
1	teaspoon salt	4	whole cloves
1	teaspoon pepper	Parsley	
¼	cup flour, divided		

Rub chicken with a mixture of poultry seasoning, Season All, salt, and pepper. Lightly flour chicken and brown in heated margarine in a heavy skillet. Place in a baking dish. Add 1 tablespoon flour to skillet and brown slightly, stirring constantly. Slowly add hot water and mix well. Remove from heat, stir in wine, and pour over chicken. Add cloves, cover, and bake at 325° for 45-60 minutes. Remove cover the last 15 minutes to crisp. Garnish with parsley.
Serves 4.
Mrs. James R. Armstrong (Fay Lawrence)

Chicken in Bourbon

3	whole chicken breasts, halved and boned	Pinch of tarragon
1	stick + 2 tablespoons butter, divided	Pinch of ginger
4	shallots, finely chopped	Pinch of garlic powder
2	jiggers bourbon	12 whole mushrooms, halved
½	cup red wine	Salt and pepper to taste
½	cup chicken broth	1½ teaspoons cornstarch
1	chicken bouillon cube	Juice of ½ lemon
Pinch of thyme		2 tablespoons finely chopped parsley

Brown chicken in 1 stick butter and remove. Add remaining butter, sauté shallots for 2 minutes, add the chicken breasts, and heat. Add bourbon, giving it time to heat, then ignite the bourbon and let it flame until it burns out. Add the wine, broth, bouillon cube, herbs, garlic, mushrooms, salt, and pepper. Simmer for about 10 minutes or until the liquid is reduced slightly, stirring occasionally with a wooden spoon. Blend in cornstarch, stirring until the sauce thickens. Add lemon juice and parsley. *Serve over wild or plain rice or over chestnut purée. This may be cooked at the table by browning the chicken ahead and cooking the remainder of the recipe in a chafing dish without a bain-marie.*
Serves 10. Freezes.
Mrs. Thomas A. Taylor, Jr.

Little Red Hen

1	2½ pound fryer, cut into parts	1	tablespoon seasoned salt
½	cup chopped green pepper	1	tablespoon pepper
½	cup chopped onion	¼	cup vinegar
1	10¾ ounce can tomato soup	1	tablespoon Worcestershire sauce
2	tablespoons brown sugar	1	6 ounce can mushrooms

Place chicken in a 3 quart baking dish. Combine remaining ingredients, mix well, and pour over chicken. Bake at 325° for 1½ hours.
Serves 4-6.
Mrs. Jon Grant Ford (Nancy Archer)

Chicken Cacciatore

2	2½-3 pound chickens	3	large cloves garlic, minced
2	chicken bouillon cubes	2	medium green peppers, seeded and cut into ½ inch squares
1	large onion, quartered		
1	large carrot, sliced	2	tablespoons flour
1	cup sliced celery with tops	1	16 ounce can Italian plum tomatoes
6	tablespoons minced parsley, divided	1	cup dry red wine
1	bay leaf	1	cup chicken stock
1½	teaspoons thyme, divided	½	teaspoon salt
10	peppercorns	1	teaspoon sugar
4	tablespoons olive oil, divided	2	cups freshly grated Parmesan cheese
¾	stick butter or margarine, divided	1	16 ounce package spaghetti or vermicelli, cooked and drained
1	pound fresh mushrooms, sliced		
3	medium onions, chopped		

In a large kettle, place enough water to cover the chickens. Add bouillon cubes, onion, carrot, celery, 2 tablespoons parsley, bay leaf, 1 teaspoon thyme, and peppercorns. Bring the mixture to a simmer, add the chickens, cover, and simmer 45 minutes or until done. Cool, bone, and cube chickens. Strain the stock, cool, and skim fat. In a large frying pan, heat 2 tablespoons olive oil with ¼ stick butter over medium heat. Add mushrooms and sauté about 5 minutes or until slightly brown and juices evaporate. Remove from pan and set aside. Add remaining oil and ¼ stick butter to pan. Sauté onions and garlic for about 5 minutes or until onions are wilted. Add green peppers and cook about 3 more minutes or until onions are golden. Sprinkle flour over onion mixture and stir until blended. Add tomatoes, breaking them with a fork. Stir in wine, stock, salt, remaining thyme, and sugar. Reduce heat and simmer for about 20 minutes, stirring often. Add mushrooms and 2 table-spoons parsley and continue simmering about 10 minutes or until sauce is thick. Place ½ the sauce in a shallow 3 quart baking dish, add the chicken, and cover with remaining sauce. If making ahead, cover dish tightly and re-frigerate. Before serving cover the casserole tightly with foil, and bake at 350° for 30 minutes or 45 minutes if refrigerated. Remove foil and bake for 15 minutes. Sprinkle with 1 cup of the cheese and bake 15 minutes or until thoroughly heated. Toss spaghetti with ¼ stick melted butter and remaining parsley. Serve chicken with spaghetti and remaining cheese.
Serves 8. Freezes.
Mrs. John Harrison Berry (Sally Martindale)

Chicken Tarragon

½ stick butter
1 broiler or fryer, quartered
½ teaspoon salt
½ teaspoon tarragon

¼ teaspoon pepper
¾ cup sour cream
¼ cup grated Parmesan cheese
2 cups sliced fresh mushrooms

Melt butter in a 13 x 9 x 2 baking pan. Dip both sides of chicken in butter and place skin side up in pan. Sprinkle with salt, tarragon, and pepper. Bake at 375° for 45-50 minutes. Combine sour cream and cheese. Stir drippings from pan into sour cream mixture. Add mushrooms to chicken. Spoon sour cream mixture over chicken and bake 10 minutes. Serve immediately.
Serves 4.
Mrs. Chris Kopecky (Linda Fischer)

To give Paella a South Texas twist, substitute chorizo for ham.

Paella

1 2½ pound chicken, cut into parts with whole breast cut into 6 pieces
½ pound ham, cut into small pieces
½ cup olive oil
1½ pounds shrimp, peeled
1 cup chopped onion
1 clove garlic, minced
2 cups short-grained rice
1 cup peeled, chopped tomatoes
1 10 ounce package frozen peas

1 10 ounce package frozen artichoke hearts
1 can clams in shells with juice
2½ teaspoons salt
1½ teaspoons saffron
1 teaspoon paprika
1 2 ounce jar pimientos, sliced in strips
Ripe olives

Sauté chicken and ham in olive oil until golden brown and remove from skillet. Sauté shrimp in remaining oil until pink and remove from pan. Sauté onion and garlic lightly. Add rice, stirring until all grains are coated with oil. Transfer to a 12-14 inch paella pan or flameproof casserole. Arrange chicken, ham, shrimp, tomatoes, peas, and artichoke hearts over rice. Drain clams and add enough water to the juice to equal 4½ cups. Bring to a boil, add salt, saffron, and paprika and pour over rice mixture. Bake at 350° for 30 minutes. Arrange clams in shells and pimiento over the top and heat a few more minutes. Garnish with olives. May be prepared in advance. *Serve with sangria, gazpacho, crusty homemade French bread, and flan.*
Serves 8.
Miss Helen Hogan

Skillet Chicken

1 chicken, cut into parts	¼ cup chopped green pepper
Salt and pepper to taste	2 tablespoons soy sauce
¼ cup flour	1 tablespoon molasses
¼ cup shortening	1 teaspoon prepared mustard
1 cup orange juice	1 teaspoon garlic salt
½ cup chili sauce	

Season chicken with salt and pepper and lightly coat with flour. Heat shortening in an electric skillet to 300°F. Brown chicken and drain shortening. Combine remaining ingredients and pour over chicken. Cook in a covered skillet at 250° for 1 hour.
Serves 4.
Mrs. Hal Motheral

Chicken Casserole

7 chicken breasts	½ pound sharp cheese, grated
Salt to taste	½ teaspoon Tabasco sauce
Poultry seasoning to taste	2 teaspoons soy sauce
Onion pieces	1 teaspoon salt
Celery pieces	½ teaspoon pepper
1 medium onion, chopped	1 teaspoon M.S.G.
1 stick butter	2 tablespoons pimiento, chopped
1 10¾ ounce can cream of mushroom soup	2 cans asparagus
1 10¾ ounce can cream of chicken soup	1 8 ounce can sliced mushrooms, drained
1 5 ounce can evaporated milk	½ cup slivered almonds

Boil chicken breasts in water seasoned with salt, poultry seasoning, onion, and celery until tender. Cool, bone, and cut into bite-sized pieces. Sauté chopped onion in butter and add remaining ingredients except asparagus, mushrooms, chicken, and almonds. In a casserole, layer chicken, asparagus, mushrooms, and sauce. Repeat layers ending with sauce and top with almonds. Bake at 350° for 45-60 minutes.
Serves 8-10.
Mrs. James F. Huff (Virginia "Scootie" Ann Day)

For an excellent "Goodbye Turkey" casserole, substitute 3-4 cups cubed turkey for the chicken, adding rice if desired.

Barbecued Chicken Casserole

Chicken thighs and breasts, 20-24 pieces
Shortening
1½ cups sliced onions
1½ cups sliced green peppers
1 stick + 1 tablespoon butter
3 cups sliced mushrooms

3 cups catsup
2 cups water
6 tablespoons Worcestershire sauce
3 tablespoons brown sugar
¾ teaspoon salt
¾ teaspoon paprika

Fry chicken in hot shortening and drain. Bone and skin chicken. Sauté onion and green pepper in butter. Add mushrooms and cook until tender. Stir in remaining ingredients and bring to a boil. Pour mixture into a large casserole dish and add chicken pieces. Cover and bake at 350° for 45 minutes. *Serve warm over rice. It is best to make the whole recipe even if the casserole is to be used for a small family meal. The remainder can be frozen.*
Serves 10-12. Freezes.
Mrs. Charles G. Crumley

Chicken and Chipped Beef

1 2½-3 ounce jar chipped beef
2 whole chicken breasts, halved and boned
6 large chicken thighs

10 slices bacon
2 cups heavy cream
1 10¾ ounce can cream of mushroom soup

Cut beef into small pieces with scissors and place in bottom of baking dish. Wrap chicken with bacon slices and place on beef. Combine cream with soup and pour over chicken. Bake at 275° for 3 hours or until chicken is tender. You may want to baste with pan drippings as chicken cooks.
Serves 6-8. Freezes.
Mrs. Ralph L. Marx

Chi Cola

4 whole chicken breasts, halved, or other parts
Flour
Vegetable oil

¼ cup finely chopped green onions
1 cup catsup
1 cup Coca-Cola
Parsley

Sprinkle chicken with flour. In a skillet, lightly brown chicken in oil. Remove chicken to a roasting pan and add the onion, catsup, and Coca-Cola. Cover and bake at 325° until tender. Garnish with parsley. *Bite-sized chunks instead of breasts may be placed in a chafing dish and covered with sauce to serve for a buffet dinner.*
Serves 4-6. Freezes.
Mrs. Albert M. Biedenharn, Jr. (Betty Osborn)

Chicken Hollandaise

6 whole chicken breasts, boned and skinned
Salt and pepper to taste
¼ cup flour
3-4 tablespoons butter

1 pound fresh mushrooms, stems removed and caps quartered
1½ cups white sauce
2 cups hollandaise sauce (see index)

Season chicken with salt and pepper. Lightly flour chicken and sauté in butter until lightly browned. Place chicken in a buttered casserole. Sauté mushrooms in remaining butter, adding more if necessary, until the liquid has evaporated. Add mushrooms to chicken. Combine white sauce and hollandaise sauce and pour over chicken. Bake at 350° for 20-25 minutes until chicken is hot and bubbly. *Serve with Savory Rice (see index).*
Serves 6.
Mrs. Paul A. Braymen (Judith Barnard)

Chicken Superb with Lemon Cream Sauce

3 large chicken breasts, boned and cut into ½ inch strips
½ cup milk
¾ cup flour, divided
3 teaspoons salt, divided
2¼ teaspoons paprika, divided
4 cups hot rice

Peanut oil, ½ inch deep in skillet
½ stick butter or margarine
2 chicken bouillon cubes
1½ cups water
1 cup heavy cream
2 teaspoons lemon juice

Dip chicken into milk and roll in ½ cup flour seasoned with 2 teaspoons salt and 2 teaspoons paprika. Fry chicken strips in hot oil until golden brown, set aside, and keep warm. Melt butter in a saucepan. Blend in remaining flour, salt, paprika, and bouillon cubes. Gradually add water and cook, stirring constantly, until mixture thickens and comes to a boil. Stir in cream and heat; then add lemon juice. Mound rice on a warm platter. Pour lemon cream sauce over rice and top with fried chicken strips.
Serves 8.
Mrs. J. Maurice Smith

Coq au Vin

3	whole chicken breasts, halved	1	large onion, chopped
1	cup flour	½	bottle white wine such as
4	tablespoons paprika		vermouth
1	stick butter, divided	1	pound fresh mushrooms, sliced

Dredge chicken breasts in flour seasoned with paprika. Brown chicken in ½ stick butter and remove. Sauté onions in the same butter, adding more if necessary. Return chicken to pan and add wine. Simmer for 1 hour, adding more wine if it appears dry. Before serving, sauté mushrooms in ¼ stick butter, add to chicken, and simmer 15 more minutes. *The taste of the wine used determines the flavor so be sure to use a wine you like.*
Serves 4.
Mrs. William Scanlan, Jr. (Cecil Collins)

Mock Wiener Schnitzel

1 pound whole chicken breasts, halved, boned, and skinned	Salt and pepper to taste
	Olive oil
1 2 eggs, beaten	Lemon wedges
Flour	

Pound chicken breasts until less than ¼ inch thick. Dip in egg and then in flour seasoned with salt and pepper. Heat ¼ inch olive oil in skillet and fry chicken breasts until golden brown. Drain on paper toweling and serve immediately with lemon wedges.

Variation for Pizza Chicken Substitute seasoned Progresso crumbs for flour, omit lemon wedges, and proceed as before. Remove cooked chicken to a greased, shallow casserole. Top each breast with a slice of mozzarella cheese and cover with your favorite Italian tomato sauce. Sprinkle with Parmesan cheese and bake at 350° until bubbly.
Serves 8.
Mrs. Edgar M. Duncan (Linda Wyatt)

Chicken Mandarin

1   2-2½ pound chicken, cut into
    parts, or chicken breasts
½   cup flour
1   teaspoon salt
⅛   teaspoon pepper
½   cup vegetable oil

⅓   cup sliced onion
¼   cup water
1   6 ounce can frozen orange juice
    concentrate
Mandarin orange sections

Shake chicken pieces, one at a time, in a small paper bag of flour seasoned with salt and pepper. Heat oil in a heavy skillet and brown chicken over low heat. Place chicken in a 1½ quart casserole. Sauté onion until tender in the same skillet. Add water, bring to a boil, and stir to loosen browned bits. Pour over chicken, add orange juice, cover, and bake for 1 hour or until chicken is tender. Garnish with mandarin orange sections.
Serves 4-6.
Mrs. Joe Carroll Rust (Margie Cape)

Hawaiian Luau Chicken

1   5 pound hen
⅓   cup chopped onion
⅓   cup chopped green pepper
2   cups sliced celery
1   8 ounce can water chestnuts, sliced
¼   cup flour
1   tablespoon salt

1   3 ounce package slivered almonds
¼   stick butter
1½ cups pitted ripe olives, sliced
1   6 ounce can bamboo shoots
1   4 ounce jar pimientos
2   cups grated Cheddar cheese
Cooked rice

Cover chicken with water, simmer until almost tender, and cool in the broth. Remove chicken and chill broth. Bone and skin chicken and set aside. Skim ½ cup fat from broth and reserve fat and broth. Sauté onion, green pepper, celery, and water chestnuts in ¼ cup fat until onions are transparent and set aside. In a Dutch oven, make a roux by slowly browning flour in remaining fat until it is the color of a walnut, stirring constantly. Add salt and gradually stir in 2 cups chicken broth, cooking until thickened. Add chicken and sautéed vegetables. Heat until steaming. Brown almonds in butter. The recipe may be done ahead to this point. Just before serving add almonds, olives, bamboo shoots, pimientos, and cheese to heated mixture, stirring until cheese is melted. Serve over rice with condiments (see index).
Serves 12.
Mrs. Wilbur L. Matthews (Helen Pruit)

Indian Curry

4   slices bacon, diced
¼   cup sliced celery
¼   cup chopped onion
½   clove garlic, minced
2   tablespoons vegetable oil
¼   cup flour
½   cup applesauce
¼   cup curry powder
3   tablespoons tomato paste

1   tablespoon sugar
1   tablespoon lemon juice
1   teaspoon salt
2   chicken bouillon cubes, dissolved
     in 1¼ cups boiling water
2   cups light cream
2   chickens, cooked, boned, and cubed
Cooked rice

In a saucepan, sauté bacon, celery, onion, and garlic in oil for 10 minutes. Sprinkle in flour and cook the mixture over low heat, stirring frequently for 5 minutes. Add applesauce, curry powder, tomato paste, sugar, lemon juice, salt, and bouillon cubes dissolved in water. Cover and cook over low heat for 45 minutes. Cool and refrigerate or freeze. This makes about 2 cups of base to which you add 2 cups light cream and the chicken. Serve over rice with condiments (see index). *It may also be made with beef, shrimp, or smoked turkey. Real curry lovers may not find this spicy enough and may wish to add more curry powder or use a hot curry powder.*
Serves 6-8. Freezes.
Mrs. Albert E. Riester (Sally Krusen)

Exotic Condiments for Curry

Chopped crisp bacon
Grated egg yolks
Grated egg white
Chopped green pepper
Toasted grated coconut
Dark raisins
Golden raisins
Sliced banana
Kumquats
Chopped radishes

Crushed potato chips
Halved peanuts
Guava jelly
Chopped olives
Preserved ginger
Sliced watermelon pickles
Chopped chives
Chopped baked ham
Major Grey's Sunshine Chutney
Chopped tomato

A curry party is one of the most exciting and colorful dinner parties possible. Served buffet, each guest "creates" his own feast by choosing his favorite condiments. The more selection the more fun! A delicate tossed green salad, buttered and toasted English muffins, and your favorite dessert served with steaming coffee — a magnificent experience!

Mrs. J. Travis Richardson (Jeanie Travis)

Cheesy Chicken Tetrazzini

6	pounds chicken	2	cups milk
1	green pepper, diced	2	cups chicken stock
1	large onion, diced	½	pound Old English cheese, diced
1	6 ounce can sliced mushrooms with stems and pieces	½	pound American cheese, diced
2½	sticks butter, divided	½	pound spaghetti, cooked in chicken stock
⅔	cup flour		

Boil chicken and drain, reserving stock. Remove bones and cube chicken. Sauté green pepper, onion, and mushrooms in ½ stick butter and set aside. Melt 2 sticks butter and stir in flour. Add milk and stock gradually, stirring until thickened. Add cheeses. Combine spaghetti, chicken, sautéed vegetables, and cheese sauce in a large bowl, mixing well. Pour into three 9 x 12 casseroles and bake at 350° until bubbly. *Good made with smoked turkey.*
Serves 12-14. Freezes well.
Mrs. Gerry Allan Solcher (Sally Sethness)

Green Enchilada Casserole

3	large onions, chopped, divided	2	4 ounce cans mild green chilies, drained and chopped
1	large clove garlic, minced	2	dozen corn tortillas, cut in pieces
3	tablespoons olive oil	3	cups cooked, boneless, diced chicken
3	pounds fresh tomatillos verdes (green tomatoes), peeled, cored, and cut into eighths	1	pound mozzarella cheese, grated
1	tablespoon snipped fresh cilantro or 1 teaspoon dried coriander		Sour cream to taste
1	teaspoon salt		Picante sauce to taste

Sauté 1 chopped onion and garlic in olive oil until wilted but not brown. Add tomatillos, cover, and simmer until soft. Add cilantro, salt, and chilies. Purée in blender. This sauce may be prepared and frozen ahead of time. Grease a casserole with olive oil. Layer ½ the tortillas, chicken, remaining onion, cheese, and sauce. Repeat layers ending with sauce and cheese. Bake at 325° for 1 hour or until the cheese is melted and casserole is bubbly. Serve with sour cream and picante sauce.
Serves 12. Sauce freezes well.
Mrs. Reagan Houston, III (Mary Jane Lyles)

This recipe may be translated to true green enchiladas by softening each whole tortilla in oil, dipping in the sauce, filling with chicken, onion, cheese, and a little sour cream, covering with remaining sauce, and baking. Top with sour cream, broil, and serve with picante sauce.

Mexicali Chicken

1   10¾ ounce can cream of
    mushroom soup
⅔   cup milk
½   teaspoon salt
1   cup cream style cottage cheese
6   ounces cream cheese, crumbled
½   teaspoon poultry seasoning
⅓   cup chopped onion
1   4 ounce can mild green chilies,
    chopped

3   cups cooked, diced chicken
1   6¾ ounce bag Doritos
2   cups grated mild Cracker Barrel
    cheese
Grated Parmesan cheese
Bread crumbs
Pimiento strips

Heat together soup, milk, and salt. Stir in cottage cheese and cream cheese. Add poultry seasoning, onion, chilies, and chicken. In a casserole, layer Doritos, chicken mixture, and Cheddar cheese. Repeat layers and sprinkle with Parmesan and bread crumbs. Garnish with pimientos. Bake at 350° for 30 minutes.
Serves 8.
Mrs. Murray L. Johnston, Jr. (Anne Whittenburg)

Tamale Pie — estilo México, D.F.

1   dozen tamales, shucked
1   3 pound chicken, boiled, boned,
    and shredded
1   onion, chopped
1   clove garlic, minced
½   green pepper, chopped

Olive or vegetable oil
1   16 ounce can tomato sauce
1   4 ounce can chopped ripe olives
2   tablespoons chili powder
1   14 ounce can creamed corn
½   pound Cheddar cheese, grated

Line a 13 x 8 x 2 casserole with tamales. Cover with a layer of chicken. Sauté onion, garlic, and pepper in oil. Add tomato sauce, olives, chili powder, and corn. Pour sauce over chicken and top with cheese. Bake at 300° for 1 hour or until cheese is bubbly.
Serves 6-8. Freezes.
Mrs. Jean B. McCormick (Jean Brittingham)

Tona's Arroz con Pollo

1	medium chicken	1½	tomatoes
1½	cloves garlic, divided	¼	cup vegetable oil
Salt to taste		1	cup rice
¼	teaspoon peppercorns	1	green onion, chopped
¼	teaspoon cumin seeds	1	tablespoon Pace Picante Sauce

Boil chicken in about 1 quart of water with 1 clove garlic and salt for 30 minutes. Reserve 2½ cups chicken stock. Cool chicken, bone, cut into small pieces, and set aside. Mash together peppercorns, cumin seeds, and ½ clove garlic. Add tomatoes and mash. Heat oil in saucepan, add rice, and stir continuously until brown. Add onion and cook for 1-2 minutes; then stir in tomato mixture. Add chicken, reserved stock, and salt. Mix well, cover, and simmer for 30 minutes. Stir in picante sauce and serve.
Serves 6.
Mrs. Christopher Goldsbury, Jr. (Linda Pace)

For a South American touch to Arroz con Pollo, garnish with pimiento strips and green peas.

Brandied Chicken Livers in Grapefruit

1	grapefruit, halved and seeded	1	tablespoon butter
1	teaspoon cinnamon	2	large chicken livers, sautéed in
2	tablespoons brown sugar		butter
2	tablespoons dry sherry	2	tablespoons warmed brandy

Section grapefruit and remove center membrane from each half. Mix together cinnamon and brown sugar and sprinkle on top. Pour sherry over grapefruit and add butter. Bake grapefruit halves at 450° for 10-12 minutes, then broil just until brown. Place a warm chicken liver on a toothpick in the center of each grapefruit. Pour brandy over grapefruit and flame. *An exotic combination.*
Serves 2.
Mrs. Donald M. Greer, Jr. (Anne Lindsay)

San Antonio River

"...we camped for the night near the eastern springs of the San Antonio River under some fine peccans, profitably amusing ourselves shooting wild turkies as they would come to roost for the night. Last year the peccans (were) in abundance. This year they will be scarce. This is a pretty general rule..."

Travels in the Republic of Texas, 1842.   Francis S. Latham.

Dinde Farcie Ma Façon
Stuffed Turkey My Own Way

1	turkey liver and gizzard or substitute chicken livers and gizzards	½	pound pitted prunes
2	tablespoons chopped parsley	2	eggs
2	cloves garlic		Small glass of cognac
1	onion		Salt and pepper to taste
3	ounces French bread	1	stick butter
1½	pounds bulk sausage	1	10 pound turkey
			Softened butter

Grind together or finely mince the liver, gizzard, parsley, garlic, onion, and bread. Add the sausage, prunes, eggs, cognac, salt, and pepper. Mix ingredients well, and sauté in butter over low heat. Spoon stuffing into the turkey cavities. Truss with heavy white thread and rub softened butter over entire surface of turkey. Cover with foil, and bake at 375° for approximately 3 hours, basting frequently. One hour before cooking time is complete, remove foil, and continue basting. *A bottle of Champagne Brut is recommended as an accompaniment.*
Serves 10-12.
Mr. Guillermo Ardid

Roasted Turkey

1	turkey, approximately 12 pounds	Parsley	
5	tablespoons dry mustard	1	onion, halved
2	tablespoons Worcestershire sauce	2	slices bacon
2	tablespoons olive oil	1	stick butter, cut into small pieces
Salt and pepper to taste		1	cheesecloth, soaked in olive oil
1	tablespoon vinegar	2	cups rich chicken stock
2	ribs celery		

The day before baking rub the turkey inside and outside with a paste made from dry mustard, Worcestershire, oil, salt, pepper, and vinegar. For a larger turkey increase the amounts proportionately for the paste. Just before roasting place celery, parsley, and onion inside the turkey. Lay bacon across the breast. Insert small pieces of butter between the drumstick and the body of the turkey. Soak a cheesecloth in olive oil and place over the turkey. Put turkey in a roaster, add stock, and roast at 300° for 20 minutes per pound for a 10-12 pound turkey, 18 minutes for 15-18 pounds, and 15 minutes for 18-20 pounds. Baste several times while roasting. Remove cheesecloth the last 30 minutes of roasting to brown turkey.

Mrs. Earl Hobbs Chumney, Jr. (Barbara Sue Christian)

Corn Bread Dressing

1	cup hot canned broth or broth from cooking giblets and neck	½	cup chopped onion
8	slices stale bread, torn into pieces, or 2 cups	2	eggs, beaten
		¾	teaspoon salt
1	cup packed crumbled corn bread	¼	teaspoon pepper
1	stick butter or margarine	1	teaspoon poultry seasoning
½	cup chopped celery	4	hard-boiled eggs, chopped

Pour broth over bread crumbs and corn bread, and let stand until soft. Sauté celery and onions in butter until tender. Combine bread mixture, celery, onions, beaten eggs, salt, pepper, and seasoning. Mix well and add the hard-boiled eggs. Place dressing in a buttered casserole and bake at 350° about 25-30 minutes. *This dressing may also be stuffed into the cavity of the bird.* **Serves 8-10.**
Mrs. Stanton P. Bell (Jean Todd)

The poultry section of a cookbook from the Southwest would not be complete without a recipe for corn bread dressing. Many variations can be made by adding oysters sautéed in butter, toasted Texas pecans, fresh chopped parsley, or whatever is your favorite.

Granary — Mission San José y San Miguel de Aguayo

"In the granary there were twenty-five hundred bushels of corn and beans. They had thirty yokes of oxen and all the necessary implements and tools for the cultivation of the fields. These were all irrigated. It is of interest to note that sugar cane was being cultivated and that here was the first place in Texas where it was made into sugar by the Indians."

Our Catholic Heritage in Texas, 1519-1936. Volume IV: The Province of Texas in 1762. Carlos E. Castañeda.

Mission San José y San Miguel de Aguayo

"Three miles further and on the west bank of the river stands the Mission of San José, the church of which is still in good preservation, built of stone — the limestone of the country — but the images of saints and other ornamental parts have been sadly mutilated by the soldiery during the wars. The ornaments on the doorway and window of the sacristy or vestry still show much exquisite work and labour that had been bestowed upon them."

William Bolleart's Texas. William Bolleart, 1842-1844.

Artichokes Florentine

2   15 ounce cans artichoke bottoms
2   10 ounce packages frozen creamed
     spinach

Lemon juice, optional
Seasoned bread crumbs or Parmesan
     cheese, optional

Heat artichoke bottoms in liquid from the can. Cook spinach according to package directions and season with lemon juice. Spoon spinach into drained artichoke bottoms. Top with seasoned bread crumbs or Parmesan cheese. *A dramatic vegetable with which to surround a beautiful roast.*
Serves 8.
Mrs. Pierce Sullivan (Mary Wallace Kerr)

Soufflé with Asparagus

¼   stick butter or margarine
2   tablespoons flour
¾   cup hot milk
½   teaspoon salt
Dash of cayenne pepper

1   8 ounce package Old English
     cheese
4   egg yolks, beaten
4   egg whites, stiffly beaten
1   16 ounce can asparagus tips

Melt butter, add flour, and stir until bubbly. Add milk slowly and stir until thickened and smooth. Add seasonings and cheese and stir until cheese is melted. Add egg yolks and cool. Fold in egg whites. Arrange asparagus in 1½-2 quart casserole or individual ramekins and fill with the soufflé mixture. Bake at 315° for 30 minutes. Serve at once for best results. If necessary it may be kept warm a short while in a 200° oven. *I have been serving this recipe for 41 years and have never had a flop or a fall. This is hearty enough for a main dish and grand enough for company.*
Serves 4-6.
Mrs. Marion Wallace McCurdy

Green Beans Parmesan

2   pounds green beans, fresh or canned
1   small onion, minced
¼   cup wine vinegar
½   cup vegetable oil

¼   teaspoon pepper
1   teaspoon salt
¼-½ cup grated Parmesan cheese
2   tablespoons chopped anchovies

Cut beans into 2 inch diagonal pieces and cook for 15-20 minutes if they are fresh. Marinate beans and onion in vinegar for at least 1 hour. Mix with remaining ingredients. Serve hot or cold. The flavor increases the longer it stands.
Serves 6.
Mrs. John K. Walters, Jr. (Lucy Masterson Yerly)

Episcopal Green Beans

2	16 ounce cans whole green beans	2	tablespoons prepared mustard
Garlic salt to taste		2	tablespoons Worcestershire sauce
1	stick butter, melted		

Drain half the liquid from beans. Place beans and remaining liquid in a saucepan. Season generously with garlic salt, cook on medium heat about 20 minutes, and drain. Combine butter, mustard, and Worcestershire and add to beans. Marinate 6-12 hours. Warm before serving. *This vegetable was served annually at the Thanksgiving dinner at the Episcopal Church in Brenham, Texas. It's the perfect combination with turkey, dressing, and sweet potatoes.* Serves 6-8.
Mrs. Benjamin F. Swank, III (Susie Schroeder)

Green Bean Casserole

2	pounds canned French cut green beans, or 2 packages frozen, cooked	½	teaspoon pepper
		1	tablespoon sugar
		1	tablespoon grated onion
3	tablespoons butter, divided	1	cup sour cream
2	tablespoons flour	½	pound Swiss cheese, grated
½	teaspoon salt	1	cup corn flakes, crumbled

Drain green beans, rinse, and let stand in ice water. Melt 1 tablespoon butter over low heat. Add flour and stir. Mix in remaining ingredients, except beans and corn flakes, and heat thoroughly. Mix sauce lightly with the drained beans. Put into a buttered 1½ quart casserole. Sprinkle crumbs over the beans and dot with remaining butter. Bake at 325° for 20-30 minutes.
Serves 4-6.
Mrs. William R. Campbell, Jr. (Mary Gail Thomas)

Mei Mei's Barbecued Green Beans

3	slices bacon	½	cup chili sauce
½	onion, chopped	1	16 ounce can cut green beans

Fry bacon and remove from pan. Drain and crumble. Sauté chopped onion in bacon drippings and add chili sauce. Drain half the liquid from beans. Add remaining liquid and beans to pan. Cover and cook 45 minutes. Just before serving, sprinkle bacon over beans.
Serves 6.
Mrs. Fred C. Lepick, Jr. (Morgia Howard)

Best Baked Beans

1	pound ground beef	¼	cup prepared mustard
2	medium onions, chopped	½	cup brown sugar
½	stick margarine	¼	cup maple syrup
3	15 ounce cans Ranch Style beans	1	cup catsup
2	16 ounce cans pork and beans		

Brown beef and onions in margarine and combine with remaining ingredients. Refrigerate overnight. Bake at 300° for 1½ hours. *For a delicious one dish meal, increase beef to 2 pounds.*
Serves 10-12. May be doubled or tripled.
Mrs. Jack T. Williams, II (Jane Yeaton)

Birch Point Baked Beans

4	31 ounce cans pork and beans	1	teaspoon oregano
6	ounces mushroom stems and pieces, drained	1	tablespoon dry mustard
		1	tablespoon powdered horseradish
6	ounces whole mushrooms, drained	½	teaspoon coriander
9	ounces Major Grey's chutney	½	cup chopped green onions
2	tablespoons Worcestershire sauce	½	cup chopped fresh parsley
1	tablespoon Tabasco sauce	1	tablespoon dried minced onion
3	tablespoons brown sugar	6	ounces blackstrap molasses
½	teaspoon cumin		

Mix all ingredients in a large bowl. Bake in a covered bean pot or ceramic casserole at 300° for 2-3 hours.
Serves 36.
Mr. Orval A. Slater

Lively Oaks Ranch Beans

½	cup diced salt pork	1	14½ ounce can tomatoes
⅔	cup coarsely chopped onion	1	level teaspoon chili powder
½	cup chopped celery	½	teaspoon cayenne pepper, or more to taste
½	cup finely chopped green pepper		
3	quarts water	1	tablespoon Worcestershire sauce
1	pound package pinto beans, washed		Salt or garlic salt to taste

Bring salt pork, onion, celery, and green pepper to boil in 3 quarts water. Reduce heat and simmer for 30 minutes. Add beans, tomatoes, chili powder, cayenne, and Worcestershire. Simmer for 4-5 hours. Add more water if necessary and stir occasionally. Add salt or garlic salt.
Serves 12.
Mr. Earl Fae Cooper

Refried Beans

4   slices bacon, diced
½   medium onion, chopped
2   1 pound cans Old El Paso Refried
     Beans; or 4 cups cooked and drained
     pinto beans; or 4 cups Ranch Style
     beans, rinsed and drained

½   teaspoon ground cumin seed
½   teaspoon coriander
1   clove garlic, pressed
½   teaspoon salt

Fry bacon until almost done; add onions and continue cooking until onions are slightly browned and bacon is crisp. Add the beans and mash well. Add seasonings and heat slowly. *In a hurry? Mash beans into heated bacon drippings.*
Serves 6.
Mrs. Thomas M. Porter (Flo)

Frijoles Poblanos

1   pound dried pinto beans
1   pound Monterey Jack cheese,
     divided
Salt to taste

10 large fresh chiles poblanos
     (the small poblanos are hot)
Vegetable oil
1   pint sour cream

Step 1   Clean and wash beans. Soak overnight for faster cooking. Drain and put in a pot with fresh water to cover. Bring to a boil, cover, and simmer slowly until soft. As liquid is absorbed, add more water, always hot. Mash beans well. Cube ½ pound cheese and add to beans, then add salt and blend until cheese melts.

Step 2   Grease poblanos with oil. Place the poblanos directly over the flame of an open burner or under the broiler and let the skin blister and char slightly, turning them from time to time. Place them immediately in a damp dish towel or plastic bag and let them sweat for about 20 minutes. Peel skin from poblanos, slit each one down the side, and remove core, seeds, and as much of the vein as possible. Stuff beans into poblanos. Place in a shallow buttered casserole. Bake at 325° for 30 minutes if dish is at room temperature. More time will be needed if dish is chilled. *If your hands get hot peeling the poblanos, rub them with sugar.*

Step 3   Grate remaining cheese. Spread sour cream over filled poblanos. Top with cheese and bake 10 minutes or until cheese is melted. *Good served with green enchiladas and guacamole salad.*
Serves 10.
Mrs. Comer M. Alden, Jr. (Barbara Burgher)

Cherokee Beets

5	medium fresh beets	2	tablespoons vinegar
¼	cup boiling water		Sour cream or yogurt for topping
½	teaspoon salt	1	teaspoon horseradish, optional
¼	stick butter		

Peel beets and shred on coarse grater. Place in pan with boiling water to which salt has been added. Simmer about 10-15 minutes or until most of the water disappears. Add butter and vinegar. Place a dollop of warmed sour cream mixed with horseradish over hot beets. Chilled yogurt mixed with horseradish may be used to top cold beets. *A garnish of chopped walnuts makes this a fancier dish.*

Mrs. Reagan Houston, III (Mary Jane Lyles)

Creamed Broccoli

2	10 ounce packages frozen broccoli, cooked and drained	1	cup sour cream
		2	tablespoons lemon juice
¼	teaspoon salt	¼	teaspoon crushed oregano leaves
¼	teaspoon pepper	½	stick butter, melted

Season broccoli with salt and pepper. Add remaining ingredients, mix thoroughly, and serve immediately.
Serves 8.
Mrs. Houston Munson (Genevieve Hollman)

Broccoli 'n Cheese Puffle

4	slices bread, cut into triangles		Dash of Tabasco sauce
1	10 ounce package frozen chopped broccoli, cooked and drained	2	teaspoons instant minced onion
		3	eggs
¼	stick margarine	1	cup instant milk powder
1	cup grated Swiss cheese	1½	cups hot water
½	teaspoon salt		

Line a greased 9 x 9 pan with bread. Combine broccoli with margarine, cheese, salt, Tabasco, and onion. Spoon over bread. Beat eggs, add milk powder and water, mix well, and pour over broccoli. Bake at 375° for 20-25 minutes.
Serves 4.
Mrs. Orvis E. Meador, Jr. (Jo Lynn Musselman)

Broccoli Pie

2	10 ounce packages frozen chopped broccoli, cooked and drained	1	egg, beaten with ¼ teaspoon milk
2	cloves garlic, minced	½	teaspoon salt
2	tablespoons vegetable oil	¼	teaspoon pepper
1	pound mozzarella cheese, grated	2	9 inch frozen pastry shells
2	ounces sliced Genoa salami or pepperoni, cut into small pieces		

Place baking sheet on bottom shelf of oven and preheat to 350°. Sauté broccoli and garlic in oil. Mix with remaining ingredients and pour into pastry shell. Top with second pastry shell. Make "B" on top pastry with fork. Bake pie on baking sheet for 50 minutes. *May be served as an appetizer or a main dish.*

Mrs. Charles H. Way

German Red Cabbage

½	cup shortening	1	tablespoon salt
1	onion, chopped	1	teaspoon pepper
1	apple, chopped		Dash of cinnamon
2-3	pounds red cabbage, sliced		Dash of cloves
¾	cup sugar	½	cup white vinegar
3	bay leaves	2	cups beef bouillon

Melt shortening and add all remaining ingredients. Simmer 30-40 minutes, turning slices of cabbage occasionally.
Serves 10.
Mrs. Alfred Shepperd (Honey Inglish)

New Mexico Cabbage Casserole

4	cups shredded cabbage	½	cup water
1	10¾ ounce can cream of potato soup	2	cups grated Cheddar cheese
			Buttered bread crumbs or croutons

Place cabbage in a greased 7 x 11 casserole. Mix potato soup and water. Pour over cabbage. Cover with grated cheese. Bake at 350° about 30 minutes. Sprinkle with bread crumbs and bake an additional 15 minutes.
Serves 6-8.
Mrs. Lee Quincy Vardaman (Jane McCurdy)

Stuffed Cabbage

1	medium cabbage	3	eggs, well beaten
6	crackers	¼-½	cup onion, sautéed
¼	cup hot milk		Salt and pepper to taste
1	tablespoon butter	½	stick butter, browned

Remove and save 6 outer leaves of the cabbage. Finely slice remainder of cabbage. Boil sliced cabbage until barely tender in lightly salted water. Drain well. Soak 6 crackers in hot milk and wring dry. Add to cooked cabbage along with butter, eggs, onion, salt, and pepper. In a round bowl, place a clean cloth. Arrange 6 outer cabbage leaves in cloth. Pour in cabbage mixture. Tie up tightly. Place in pot of boiling, salted water. Boil gently for 45 minutes to 1 hour, turning once. Remove cabbage from cloth and place on serving platter. Serve slices with browned butter. *This is my husband's Grandmother Eckhardt's German recipe. This is easy and fun to make and tastes better than you'd expect.*
Serves 6.
Mrs. Richard H. Eckhardt (Mary Webb)

Baked Carrot Ring

2	cups peeled, chopped carrots	½	cup light cream
¼	stick butter, melted	2	teaspoons brown sugar
2	eggs		Salt and pepper to taste

Cook carrots in boiling water until tender and drain. Put carrots and remaining ingredients in blender. Blend until smooth. Pour mixture into a well greased 5 cup ring mold, place in a pan of water, and bake at 350° for 30 minutes or until firm. Unmold on platter. *This is pretty served with minted green peas in center of ring.*
Serves 6.
Mrs. William A. Myers (Ellen Howell)

Add cognac to your favorite glazed carrot recipe for an easy company treat.

Company Carrots

1	stick butter	1	bunch green onions with tops, chopped
1	pound carrots, peeled and sliced		

Melt butter in pan. Add carrots and green onions, cover tightly, and cook 1 hour. Do not add water. Cook slowly over low heat.
Serves 6.
Mrs. Frederick C. Groos, Jr. (Martha Grace Bailey)

Stuffed Carrots

6	large round carrots	1	teaspoon Worcestershire sauce
2	cups grated Cheddar cheese	⅓-½	cup mayonnaise
1	teaspoon sugar		Buttered bread crumbs

Scrape carrots. Boil in lightly salted water until tender and drain. Scoop out more than half of carrot, discarding yellow vein and leaving a shell. Mix together cheese, sugar, Worcestershire sauce, and enough mayonnaise to make a paste. You may add some of the carrot pulp to the mixture. Stuff carrot shells and cover with buttered bread crumbs. Bake at 325° for 15 minutes.
Serves 6.
Mrs. C. A. Beall, Jr.

Carrot Casserole

1	small onion, minced	4	cups diagonally sliced carrots, cooked and drained
½	stick butter		
¼	cup flour	6	slices American cheese
1	teaspoon seasoned salt	2	cups fresh bread crumbs
¼	teaspoon seasoned pepper	⅔	stick butter, melted
2	cups milk		

Sauté onion in ½ stick butter. Stir in flour, salt, and pepper. Gradually add milk, stirring constantly until thickened. Arrange a layer of carrots in a 2 quart buttered casserole. Place 3 slices of cheese over carrots. Repeat layers. Pour sauce over carrots. Mix bread crumbs with ⅔ stick butter and sprinkle over casserole. Bake at 350° for 25 minutes.
Serves 6-8.
Mrs. Hugh Halff, Jr. (Marie Mahone)

Creamy Carrots

1	pound carrots, peeled and diced	¼	cup heavy cream
1	4 ounce can diced green chilies with liquid	¼-½	cup chopped fresh parsley
			Salt to taste
3	ounces cream cheese, cubed		

Simmer carrots in salted water until tender but still firm. Drain. Stir in chilies, cheese, cream, and parsley. Stir over low heat until cheese is melted and sauce is smooth. Season with salt.
Serves 4-6. May be prepared ahead.
Mrs. Lee Quincy Vardaman (Jane McCurdy)

Orange Carrots

6   oranges
2   pounds carrots, peeled
3   tablespoons butter, divided
½   teaspoon salt

¼   teaspoon ground cloves
½   cup sugar
¼   cup water

Cut tops from oranges and scrape out pulp. Reserve pulp from 2 oranges. Grate rind of orange tops. Cook carrots until tender, drain, and mash. Add 2 tablespoons butter, salt, cloves, and grated rind. Fill orange shells with carrot mixture and dot with remaining butter. Heat reserved pulp with sugar and water. Place shells in baking dish and pour hot orange syrup over them. Bake at 400° for 15 minutes, basting often.
Serves 6.
Mrs. Virginia P. Sinclair (Virginia Phillips)

TikChik Celery Casserole

4   cups celery, cut in 4 inch diagonal pieces
1   8½ ounce can water chestnuts, sliced
¼   cup slivered almonds

¼   cup chopped pimiento
1   10¾ ounce can cream of chicken soup
½   cup buttered and toasted bread crumbs

Cook celery in boiling water for 4 minutes, drain, and place in a buttered baking dish. Mix remaining ingredients, except crumbs, and pour over celery. Top with crumbs and bake at 350° for 30 minutes. *Discovered while on a fishing vacation at the TikChik Narrows Lodge in Alaska.*
Serves 6.
Mrs. Frates Seeligson (Martita Rice)

Cauliflower and Peas

1   medium or large cauliflower
1   10 ounce package frozen green peas

½   stick butter or margarine
2   tablespoons lemon juice

Trim outer leaves of cauliflower. Boil cauliflower in lightly salted water until tender, but do not overcook. Prepare peas according to package directions, omitting butter. Melt butter and add lemon juice. When cauliflower is tender, lift whole into a round serving dish; then cut in wedges, as a pie. Pour prepared peas over the cauliflower. Pour lemon butter over vegetables. Serve immediately.

Mrs. J. Maurice Smith

Zesty Cauliflower con Queso

1	large cauliflower, broken into medium flowerets	1	4 ounce can chopped green chilies, drained
¼	stick butter or margarine	1	teaspoon salt
¼	cup chopped onion	¼	teaspoon Tabasco sauce
2	tablespoons flour	4	ounces Monterey Jack or mild Cheddar cheese, cubed or grated
1	16 ounce can tomatoes		
1	bay leaf		

Cook flowerets about 10-15 minutes in salted water or until just crisp-tender. Drain. Melt butter in medium saucepan. Add onion and cook until tender, about 5 minutes. Blend in flour. Stir in tomatoes. Cook, stirring constantly, until mixture thickens and comes to a boil. Add bay leaf, green chilies, salt, and Tabasco. Cook 5 minutes. Add cheese and stir until melted. Drain flowerets and serve with sauce. *This sauce is good on other vegetables and meats. Also good served over scrambled eggs.*
Serves 4-6.
Mrs. Elkin McGaughy (Barbara Crossette)

Corn Pudding

¼	stick margarine	Salt and pepper to taste
1	16 ounce can creamed corn	2 eggs
2	tablespoons sugar	1 5 ounce can Carnation evaporated milk
1	heaping tablespoon flour	

Melt margarine in a 1½ quart casserole at 350°. Pour corn into casserole and add sugar, flour, and seasonings. Stir in eggs and milk. Mix well. Bake for 1-1¼ hours, until knife inserted in center comes out clean. *Delicious served with steak instead of baked potatoes.*
Serves 6.
Mrs. Clifton F. Anderson (Betty King)

Corn Roasted in Romaine

½	stick butter or margarine, softened	6	ears corn, husked
1	teaspoon dried rosemary	1	head romaine lettuce
½	teaspoon dried marjoram		

Blend butter, rosemary, and marjoram, and spread on corn. Wrap each ear in 2 or 3 leaves of romaine. Place in a shallow baking dish and cover tightly with foil. Bake at 450° for 20-25 minutes.

Mrs. Edgar M. Duncan (Linda Wyatt)

Fresh Corn Oysters

2	ears fresh corn	¾	teaspoon salt
2	eggs, separated	½	teaspoon baking powder
1	tablespoon finely minced onion	⁄₁₆	teaspoon pepper
¼	cup sifted flour		

Remove husks and silk from corn. Cut kernels from cobs (about 1 cup). In a medium bowl, combine kernels with egg yolks and onion. Mix well. Sift flour with salt, baking powder, and pepper. Stir into corn mixture. Beat egg whites until stiff, but not dry, and gently fold into corn mixture. Drop by the teaspoonful into deep fat preheated to 350°F. Cook until golden, about 3 minutes, turning once. Drain on absorbent paper. Serve immediately.
Yield 36.
Mrs. George Rice, Jr. (Martha Lewis)

Baked Cushaw

6	cups cushaw, boiled and drained*	½	tablespoon nutmeg
2	cups sugar	½	tablespoon allspice
1	tablespoon cinnamon	½	stick butter or margarine

Spoon half the cushaw into a buttered baking dish. Mix sugar and spices and sprinkle half of mixture over cushaw. Dot with half of butter. Repeat layers. Bake at 350° for 1½ hours.

*To prepare cushaw   Halve cushaw, remove seeds and rind, and cut in medium cubes. Place in a pan of salted, boiling water and boil 5-10 minutes or until tender. Do not overcook. *To freeze, drain boiled cushaw, saving water. Place cushaw into freezing container and cover with reserved water.*

Mrs. D. Gregg Francis (Mattie B. Craig)

Braised Cucumbers

3	medium cucumbers	1	tablespoon boiling water
¼	stick butter		Salt and pepper to taste
1	chicken bouillon cube	3	tablespoons grated Cheddar cheese

Peel cucumbers and cut once lengthwise and crosswise. Brown lightly in butter. Add chicken bouillon cube dissolved in water. Cook, covered, over low heat for about 5 minutes. Season with salt and pepper. Just before serving, sprinkle with cheese.
Serves 4.
Mrs. Harry Brusenhan (Laura)

Cucumbers in Cream

4	8 inch cucumbers, peeled	4	tablespoons chopped green onions
2	tablespoons wine vinegar	¼	stick butter
1	teaspoon salt	⅓	cup heavy cream
1	teaspoon sugar	1-2	tablespoons chopped fresh parsley

Cut cucumbers in half lengthwise and scoop out the seeds with a spoon. Cut each half into 4 strips and each strip into 2 inch pieces. Place in glass bowl and sprinkle with wine vinegar, salt, and sugar; toss. Marinate 1-2 hours. Drain and pat dry with a towel. Sauté onions in butter until tender, but not brown. Increase heat and add cucumbers, stirring and cooking until crisp-tender. Add cream and continue to cook until cream is reduced slightly and coats the cucumbers. Remove from heat and garnish with chopped parsley. Serve immediately. *Toss an extra cucumber into the marinade for a low calorie snack to have while preparing dinner.*
Serves 8.
Mrs. Frank H. Williams, Jr. (Martha)

Eight Goal Eggplant

1	large eggplant, peeled and thinly sliced	2	cans Rotel tomatoes and green chilies, drained
2	cups corn flake crumbs	2	tablespoons minced onion
1	teaspoon garlic salt	⅓-½	cup freshly grated Parmesan cheese
1	teaspoon pepper		Oregano to taste, optional
2	eggs, beaten		Basil to taste, optional
½-1	cup olive oil		
1	8 ounce can tomato sauce		

Soak eggplant in salted water for 30 minutes. Drain and pat dry. Mix corn flake crumbs with garlic salt and pepper. Dip eggplant in egg, then corn flake crumbs, and fry in olive oil until golden brown. Whirl tomato sauce, tomatoes, and onion in blender. Layer deep casserole with eggplant, tomato sauce mixture, and cheese 3 times. Bake at 350° for 35-45 minutes. *This recipe has been used by polo players' wives all over the country. It was Tim Leonard's mother's recipe, and his wife, Patricia, is famous for it.*
Serves 8-10.
Mrs. Patricia Beveridge (Patricia Preis)

Eggplant au Gratin

4	small eggplants, peeled	1	pound sharp Cheddar cheese, grated
2	large onions, sliced		Salt and pepper to taste
1	stick butter, divided	½	cup cracker crumbs
2	eggs, beaten		

Boil eggplant in salted water until tender. Drain and mash, and drain again if necessary. Sauté onions in half of the butter. Combine eggplant, onions, eggs, cheese, salt, and pepper. Place in greased casserole. Top with crumbs and dot with remaining butter. Bake at 350° for 45 minutes.
Serves 8-10.
Mrs. James L. Hayne (Roxana Catto)

To fry leftover grits, chill in a loaf pan, and slice ½ inch thick. Dip slices in beaten egg, then in flour. Fry in hot fat until golden, turning once. Serve immediately. Good for a real ranch style breakfast.

Garlic Cheese Grits

4	cups water		Pressed garlic, optional
1	cup grits	1	egg, slightly beaten
1	stick butter	1	scant cup warm milk
1	6 ounce roll garlic cheese	½	cup grated Cheddar cheese

Boil water, add grits, and continue to boil for 3 minutes. Add butter, garlic cheese, and garlic. Boil until butter and cheese are melted. Put egg into a measuring cup, fill to 1 cup with milk, and slowly add to cheese mixture. Place in a greased casserole and sprinkle with cheese. Bake at 350° for 1 hour. *Creamed turkey or chicken may be spooned over grits for brunch or luncheon.*
Serves 8-10.
Mrs. W. W. McAllister, III (Lida Suttles)

Quien Sabe Grits Casserole

5 cups cooked grits or 4 cups
cooked rice, seasoned with
2 tablespoons butter
1 teaspoon salt
¼ teaspoon pepper
4 cups sour cream
10½ ounces mild jalapeño peppers,
drained, seeded, and chopped; or
peeled green chilies, chopped; or
half jalapeños and half green chilies

1 pound Monterey Jack or mozzarella
cheese, cut in thin strips
¾ cup grated Cheddar cheese,
optional with rice

Season grits with salt and pepper. Blend sour cream with peppers. In a 3 quart greased casserole, layer the grits, sour cream-pepper mixture, and strips of cheese. Repeat layers, finishing with grits on top. Bake at 350° for 35-40 minutes, or until bubbly throughout. Just before serving, sprinkle with grated cheese, and broil 4-6 inches from source of heat until cheese melts.
Serves 14-16.
Mrs. Frates Seeligson (Martita Rice)

Heaven and Earth

2 pounds potatoes, peeled and cubed
1 teaspoon salt
2 pounds McIntosh apples, pared
and sliced

7 slices bacon
1 cup chopped onions
Buttered, toasted bread crumbs,
optional

In a large covered saucepan, cook potatoes in 1 cup boiling water with salt until almost tender. Add apples and continue cooking over low heat, stirring occasionally until apples are crisp-tender. Fry bacon until crisp, remove, drain, and crumble. Sauté onions in bacon drippings until light brown. Drain and keep warm. Mash potato mixture with a large spoon or fork until well mixed, but a bit lumpy. Toss with some of the onions and bacon. Place in a deep serving dish. Garnish with remaining bacon and onions or with crumbs. *This was my great grandmother's, Johanna Steves, recipe. The Germans call it "Himmell und Erde"*.
Serves 8.
Mrs. Jimmie Dick Ansley (Johanna Belle Steves)

Elva's Hot Hominy

1   medium onion, chopped
1   medium green pepper, chopped
1   15 ounce can tomatoes
2   tablespoons Rotel tomatoes and
    green chilies, or more to taste

1   28 ounce can white hominy,
    drained and rinsed
1-1½ cups American cheese, grated
Salt and pepper to taste

Sauté onion and green pepper until soft; add tomatoes and simmer about 15 minutes. Add hominy, half of the grated cheese, salt, and pepper. Mix well. Pour into a greased 1½ quart casserole and sprinkle remaining cheese on top. Bake at 350° for 45 minutes.
Serves 6.
Mrs. Lamoine Holland (Carol Jean Fulton)

Hot Cheese Hominy

¾   cup chopped onion
¼   stick butter
2   14½ ounce cans hominy
2-4 ounces canned green chilies

8   ounces sour cream
1   teaspoon chili powder
Salt and pepper to taste
½   pound grated Cheddar cheese

Sauté onion in butter. Mix onion and all other ingredients, except cheese, in a greased casserole. Sprinkle cheese on top. Bake at 400° for 20-30 minutes. Serve hot. *May be prepared ahead.*
Serves 6-8.
Mrs. Kenneth R. Bell

Hopping Johnny

1   cup rice
2   15¼ ounce cans Trappey's
    Jalapeño Black Eye Peas

6-8 slices bacon
½   medium onion, chopped

Cook rice according to package directions. Cook peas separately and drain well. Fry bacon until crisp. Drain and crumble. Sauté onion in bacon drippings until soft. Remove onion with a slotted spoon and add to rice. Add peas and bacon and a little more of the bacon drippings to taste.
Serves 8.
Mrs. Lewis Jefferson Moorman, III (Nancy Clark Wood)

Huitlacoche

1 medium to large onion, diced	Pinch of cayenne pepper or paprika
2 cloves garlic, crushed	1 4 ounce can huitlacoche
2 tablespoons oil	(cuitlacoche) or sliced mushrooms
1 tomato, diced	6 corn tortillas or crêpes
1 rib celery, diced, optional	Sour cream or cream sauce
Salt and pepper to taste	

Brown onions and garlic in oil. Add tomatoes and celery and continue cooking 5-10 minutes on medium heat. Add seasonings and huitlacoche, stirring well. Cook for approximately 15 minutes. Steam tortillas or soften them in oil as you would for enchiladas. Spoon mixture into tortillas and roll. Place seam side down in a greased casserole and bake at 350° until thoroughly heated. Top with sour cream or cream sauce and broil for a few minutes. *Huitlacoche, the corn fungus, may have been the ambrosia of the Aztec gods. Truly "comida de los dioses", this is a specialty of the Hacienda de los Morales in Mexico City. Charles de Gaulle became enamored with this inky appearing delicacy. His appreciation of the mushroom-like flavor is responsible for its availability in cans.*

Mrs. Harold Vexler (Esther)

A hard-boiled egg slicer may be used to slice mushrooms quickly and evenly.

Mushrooms Berkley

1 onion, chopped	2 tablespoons Worcestershire sauce
2 sticks butter	2 tablespoons Dijon mustard
1 pound fresh mushrooms, thickly sliced	Salt to taste
2 green peppers, cut in 1 inch squares	Cracked black pepper to taste
½ cup dark brown sugar	¾ cup mellow red wine

Sauté onions in butter until transparent. Add mushrooms and peppers and cook until mushrooms turn brown. This takes only a few minutes. Prepare a sauce by mixing together the brown sugar, Worcestershire sauce, mustard, pepper, salt, and wine. Add to the mushrooms and cook over medium heat until sauce thickens. *Serve as a vegetable or as a sauce over rice or roast beef. To vary this recipe, mix with cooked yellow and zucchini squash. These mushrooms will look dark, but the taste and aroma should not be missed.*
Serves 12.
Miss Frances F. Chamberlain

Stuffed Mushrooms

8	whole mushrooms	2	teaspoons flour
1	stick butter, divided	½	cup milk
2	shallots, chopped	2	ounces Gruyère or Swiss cheese,
2	ounces chopped mushrooms		grated
2	ounces cooked ham, diced	Salt and pepper to taste	
2	teaspoons parsley		

Sauté whole mushrooms in half of butter about 2 minutes on each side. Remove and place in shallow baking dish. Sauté the shallots, mushrooms, and ham. Add the parsley and stir in flour. Cook over low heat, continuing to stir for about 2 minutes. Remove from heat and add milk. Return pan to heat and cook the mixture, stirring until it is thickened and smooth. Fill each mushroom with about 1 tablespoon of the mixture. Sprinkle with grated cheese and dot with butter. Season with salt and pepper. Bake at 350° for 10-15 minutes or until cheese is melted and lightly browned. *This mixture is also delicious as a filling for artichoke bottoms.*
Serves 4.
Mrs. Edward D. Hodge, III (Almeda Doughty)

Spicy Okra Gumbo

2	strips bacon, cut in pieces	1	5½ ounce can tomato juice
½	medium onion, chopped	Salt and pepper to taste	
1½	cups cut okra	2	tablespoons Pace Picante Sauce
1	tomato, chopped		

Sauté bacon in saucepan, add onions, and cook until onions are transparent. Add okra, tomato, tomato juice, salt, pepper, and picante sauce. Reduce heat, cover, and simmer about 15 minutes or until tender.
Serves 4.
Mrs. Christopher Goldsbury, Jr. (Linda Pace)

Onion Pie

2	cups thinly sliced onions	2	eggs, slightly beaten
⅔	stick butter	1	teaspoon salt
1	cup scalded milk	1½	cups grated sharp Cheddar cheese

Sauté onions in butter. Mix with remaining ingredients and put into greased casserole. Bake at 350° for 45 minutes. *Good with ham.*
Serves 6.
Mrs. Thomas R. Benesch (Jane Bickham)

Baked Onion

1	large white onion, peeled	1	teaspoon brown sugar
1	teaspoon jalapeño juice		Salt and pepper to taste

Cut onion in quarters stopping before it is sliced all the way through. Place on a square of foil, add remaining ingredients, and seal. Bake at 350° for 1 hour. *Leave in foil to serve picnic style. These are a delicious surprise to serve with steak or barbecue.*
Serves 1.
Mrs. Howard Hasting

Chow Ching Tou
Fried Green Peas

1	large onion, diced	1	teaspoon dry sherry
1	tablespoon peanut, vegetable, or sesame oil	¼	teaspoon Accent
		1	teaspoon cornstarch
2	cups green snow peas, fresh or frozen	½	cup soup stock
		1	tablespoon soy sauce
½	teaspoon salt	6	slices bacon, fried and crumbled
1	teaspoon sugar	½	cup diced onion

Using a large skillet, sauté large diced onion in oil until light brown and remove from pan. Pour peas into pan with remaining ingredients, except bacon and ½ cup onion, and cook over high heat for 3 minutes. Add bacon and onion, and serve immediately. Do not overcook. Vegetables should be crunchy.
Serves 4.
Mrs. Harry E. Brown (Carolyn Carlisle)

Vegetable Cooking

Cut, slice, chop, or break any vegetable into uniform pieces. This includes broccoli, cauliflower, carrots, squash, asparagus, etc. In a skillet with a tight fitting cover, melt the butter, olive oil, or margarine that you would ordinarily use for seasoning. Add any other seasonings you desire such as Beau Monde, chopped parsley, chives, pepper, or sugar, except for salt which should be added later. Use very little water or wet a few lettuce leaves and place on bottom of skillet for moisture. One-fourth head of Boston lettuce chopped in chunks may be used for moisture. Spread vegetables evenly and uniformly, but don't overload. It's better to use an extra frying pan. Cover vegetables and steam until no water remains. Do not uncover or stir. Vegetables will be cooked in 5-10 minutes.

Mrs. Patricia Beveridge (Patricia Preis)

Dauphine Potatoes

5	medium potatoes, peeled	2	eggs, beaten
Salt and pepper to taste		1	cup water
½-⅔	cup milk	1	stick butter or margarine
1	rounded tablespoon + 1 stick	1	cup flour
	butter or margarine, divided	4	eggs
¼	teaspoon nutmeg	Peanut oil	

Boil potatoes until tender. Drain, mash, and season with salt, pepper, milk, and 1 rounded tablespoon butter. Add nutmeg and the beaten eggs. Set this mixture aside. Combine water and 1 stick butter and bring to a rolling boil. To this, add flour and remove pan from heat. Stir until mixture leaves sides of pan. Add 4 eggs, one at a time, beating well after each addition. Stir in the mashed potato mixture (this may be made ahead and refrigerated). Just before serving, drop by teaspoonful into hot peanut oil and fry until golden brown. Serve immediately. *This recipe may be varied by adding finely minced onion, green pepper, crabmeat, shrimp, parsley, chives, etc. to potatoes.*
Serves 8-10.
Mr. Don Strange

Pommes Gruyère

4-5	large potatoes, peeled	½	pound bacon, fried crisp and
1	cup thinly sliced onion		crumbled
1	cup finely chopped celery	¾	stick butter
10	ounces processed Gruyère cheese,	1	tablespoon flour
	grated	⅓	cup milk
1½	teaspoons salt	⅔	cup heavy cream
⅜	teaspoon pepper		

Slice potatoes ⅛ inch thick. Soak in ice water ½-1 hour. Drain well and pat dry. This process is the secret to making potatoes crisp. Grease a deep 9 x 13 x 3 casserole and line with ⅓ of the potatoes. Top with ⅓ of the onions, celery, cheese, ½ teaspoon salt, and ⅛ teaspoon pepper. Make 2 more layers, ending with cheese on top. Sprinkle with bacon. In a saucepan, melt butter, and stir in flour. Gradually add milk and cream, stirring constantly. Pour over potatoes, cover, and bake at 400° for 30 minutes. Reduce heat to 350°. Uncover and bake 25-30 minutes. Cover casserole during final minutes of baking if it begins to get too brown.
Serves 10-12.
Mrs. Van Henry Archer, Jr. (Edna Moody Myrick)

Fiesta Potatoes

6   large baking potatoes
Light cream to taste
Butter to taste
Salt to taste

½   pound American cheese, grated
3-5   ounces Rotel tomatoes and green chilies, drained

Prepare approximately 6 cups hot, fluffy mashed potatoes mildly seasoned with cream, butter, and salt. Combine cheese and tomatoes. Swirl cheese and tomato mixture through potatoes and turn into greased casserole. Bake at 350° for 15-20 minutes until heated and brown on top.
Serves 6-8.
Mrs. Howard Hasting

Mint Potatoes

4   large potatoes, peeled and quartered
1   cup chicken stock
1   bay leaf
1   stick butter or margarine
⅓   cup heavy cream

½   cup milk, optional
⅛   teaspoon nutmeg
1   tablespoon finely chopped fresh mint
Salt to taste
White pepper to taste

Cook potatoes in chicken stock with bay leaf, adding enough water to barely cover potatoes. When done, drain, and remove bay leaf. Mash the potatoes, and beat in butter and cream. If not fluffy, add some or all of the milk. Stir in nutmeg and mint. Season with salt and pepper. Heat in double boiler until piping hot.
Serves 6-8.
Mrs. Middleton S. English (Shirley Fitch)

Potatoes Supreme

4   baking potatoes, boiled
1½   cups light cream
1   stick margarine
½   pound yellow cheese

½   pint sour cream
½-¾   cup chopped green onions
6   strips bacon, fried and crumbled

Peel cooled potatoes and grate. Combine cream, margarine, and cheese in a double boiler and stir until melted. Add cheese mixture to grated potatoes and put in a casserole. This may be done ahead. Bake at 350° for 30 minutes or until bubbly. Top with sour cream, onions, and bacon. Bake about 5 minutes.
Serves 8.
Mrs. Frederick C. Groos, Jr. (Martha Grace Bailey)

Pommes Anna

4-5 baking potatoes, peeled
½   stick butter or margarine, melted
2   cloves garlic, crushed
2   onions, thinly sliced

Salt and pepper to taste
Paprika to taste
¾   cup grated Parmesan cheese

Slice potatoes in ⅛ inch thick rounds and soak in ice water for at least 30 minutes. Drain slices and pat dry with paper towels. Combine butter and garlic. In a deep 10 inch greased pie plate or casserole, arrange ⅓ of the potato slices in slightly overlapping fashion, beginning with the outside edge and continuing the circle design to center of dish. Layer ⅓ of onion slices, broken into rings, on top of potatoes, then ⅓ of butter mixture, salt, pepper, paprika, and cheese. Repeat this process 2 more times, ending with cheese on top. Bake, covered, at 400° for 1 hour. If cheese is not brown on top, place under broiler for 4-5 minutes. Cut in wedges to serve.
Serves 6.
Mrs. Edgar M. Duncan (Linda Wyatt)

Crab Stuffed Potatoes

4   medium baking potatoes
1   stick butter
½   cup light cream
1   teaspoon salt
½   teaspoon pepper

4   teaspoons grated onion
1   cup grated sharp yellow cheese
6½   ounces crabmeat
½   teaspoon paprika

Bake potatoes at 425° for 1 hour or until they can be pierced with a fork. Cut potatoes lengthwise and scoop out centers, reserving shells. Whip potatoes with butter, cream, salt, pepper, onion, and cheese. With a fork, mix in crabmeat and fill potato shells. Sprinkle with paprika before serving. Bake at 400° for about 15 minutes.
Serves 4. Freezes.
Mrs. J. Fletcher Lee

Sweet Potatoes and Apricots

1	16 ounce can sweet potatoes or yams	¼	teaspoon salt
1	16 ounce can peeled apricots, pitted	¼	stick butter
¼	cup pecan halves	⅛	teaspoon cinnamon
1¼	cups brown sugar	1	teaspoon grated orange peel
1½	tablespoons cornstarch	½	cup juice from apricots

Drain sweet potatoes and apricots, reserving juice from apricots. Layer sweet potatoes and apricots in a casserole. Sprinkle with pecan halves. In a saucepan, combine remaining ingredients, bring to a boil, and continue to cook for 2 minutes, stirring constantly. Pour sauce over casserole and bake at 375° for 25 minutes. *To double this recipe you need only 1½ recipes of sauce to twice the amount of potatoes, apricots, and pecans. This is my mother's recipe which she has used successfully for many years.*
Serves 6-8.
Mrs. Albert E. Riester (Sallie Krusen)

Sweet Potato Soufflé

2	cups mashed sweet potatoes	½	teaspoon nutmeg
2	eggs, beaten	½	teaspoon cinnamon
1¼	cups sugar	¾	cup crushed corn flakes
1½	sticks butter or margarine, melted and divided	½	cup brown sugar
1	cup milk	½	cup chopped nuts

Mix potatoes, eggs, sugar, half of the butter, milk, nutmeg, and cinnamon. Pour into a greased casserole. Bake at 400° for 20-25 minutes. Mix the corn flakes, brown sugar, nuts, and remaining butter. Spread over casserole and bake 10 minutes. *Many who have never eaten sweet potatoes go back for seconds.*
Serves 10-12. May be doubled.
Mrs. Leslie D. Maurer

Baked Sweet Potato Casserole

1	1 pound, 14 ounce can whole sweet potatoes		Raisins, optional
4	slices canned pineapple in syrup	1	cup light brown sugar
3	bananas, sliced lengthwise	1	stick butter
1	large apple, cored and thinly sliced	½	teaspoon cinnamon
		½	cup orange brandy or Cointreau

Drain potatoes and pineapple, reserving liquid. Layer potatoes, pineapple, bananas, apple, and raisins in a baking dish, and sprinkle each layer with brown sugar. Mix half of the liquid from potatoes with 1 cup liquid from pineapple and add butter, cinnamon, and brandy or Cointreau. Boil until liquid is reduced and pour over casserole. Bake at 350° for 35 minutes. *This recipe is easily doubled and is a favorite from my grandmother, Mrs. J.T. Bowman, first President of the Austin Junior League.*
Serves 6-8.
Mrs. John Korbell (Bonnie Bowman)

Sweet Potatoes with Pecan Topping

3	pounds sweet potatoes, cooked and peeled	1	teaspoon salt
2	eggs	1	teaspoon cinnamon
¾	cup light brown sugar, divided	½-1	cup fresh orange juice
1	stick butter, melted and divided	1	cup pecan halves

Mash potatoes. There should be approximately 6 cups. Beat in eggs, ½ cup brown sugar, and ½ the butter. Add salt and cinnamon. Beat in enough orange juice to make potatoes moist and fluffy. Place in a 1½-2 quart casserole. Refrigerate if you wish. Just before baking, arrange pecans to completely cover top. Sprinkle with remaining brown sugar and drizzle with remaining butter. Bake at 375° for 20 minutes or until thoroughly heated. *A very good casserole of fluffy, sweet, mashed yams to serve with Thanksgiving turkey.*
Serves 8-10.
Mrs. Charles H. Randall (Jane)

Cheesy Spinach

2   10 ounce packages frozen chopped spinach
16   ounces cottage cheese
2½   cups grated sharp cheese
3   eggs, beaten

3   tablespoons flour
1   stick butter, melted
¼   teaspoon garlic salt
¼   teaspoon lemon-pepper seasoning
¼   teaspoon onion salt

Defrost spinach and squeeze out water. Mix spinach with remaining ingredients and place in a greased casserole. Bake at 325° for 1 hour. *Casserole may be made a day ahead and baked when ready to serve.*
Serves 6.
Mrs. John Henry Tate, II (Toby McClelland)

Elegant Spinach Casserole

2   10 ounce packages frozen chopped spinach
1   14 ounce can artichoke hearts packed in water, drained
1¼   sticks butter, divided

8   ounces cream cheese
8   ounces water chestnuts, sliced
Dash of garlic salt, optional
½   cup fresh bread crumbs

Cook spinach according to package directions. Cut artichoke hearts in half. Melt 1 stick butter in a large saucepan. Add cream cheese, spinach, water chestnuts, and garlic salt. Line a greased baking dish with artichoke hearts. Cover with spinach mixture. Sprinkle with bread crumbs. Dot with remaining butter. Bake at 400° for 20-25 minutes.
Serves 8.
Mrs. Thomas R. Benesch (Jane Bickham)

German Style Spinach

2   10 ounce packages fresh spinach
⅓   cup small egg noodles
½   cup milk

1   tablespoon margarine
Salt and pepper to taste
1   hard-boiled egg, optional

Wash spinach and remove stems. Cook in just the water that clings to the leaves after washing. Spinach is cooked when the leaves may be cut with a fork. Drain well, pressing all possible water from spinach, and chop. In a 2 quart pot, cook noodles in milk slowly until tender and all milk is absorbed. Add spinach, margarine, salt, and pepper. Garnish with slices of hard-boiled egg. *This is an old German recipe used by my grandmother.*
Serves 4.
Mrs. George E. Dullnig (Margaret Rolle)

Spinach and Eggs with Cheese Sauce

4	slices bacon, finely chopped	Salt and pepper to taste	
1	pound fresh spinach, chopped, or two 10 ounce packages frozen chopped spinach, thawed	¼	stick butter
		2	tablespoons flour
		1	cup milk
4	eggs, hard-boiled and quartered	½	pound sharp Cheddar cheese, grated

Fry bacon until crisp and drain on paper towels. Place spinach in a buttered casserole and arrange a layer of hard-boiled eggs on top. Sprinkle with salt and pepper. In a saucepan, melt butter and blend in flour. Slowly add milk and more salt and pepper. Stir until smooth and thickened. Add the cheese and cook slowly until the cheese is melted. Pour over eggs and spinach. Sprinkle with bacon and bake at 350° for 25 minutes. *For a variation in flavor, omit hard-boiled eggs and cheese. Stir spinach into sauce and bake.*
Serves 4-6.
Mrs. James L. Hayne (Roxana Catto)

To stir-fry spinach, melt ⅔ stick butter in a large skillet. Add 2 pounds washed and drained fresh spinach with stems removed. Cook over high heat stirring constantly for 1 minute. Add salt, pepper, and lightly toasted sesame seeds.

Peggy's Fresh Spinach Soufflé

1	stick butter	4	heaping cups chopped fresh spinach with stems removed
½	cup flour		
3	cups light cream	2	teaspoons grated onion
2	teaspoons salt	7	eggs, beaten
½	cup grated Longhorn cheese		

In a large saucepan, melt butter, add flour, and stir until well blended. Slowly add cream, stirring constantly. When this mixture comes to a boil, cook for 3 minutes, continuing to stir. Add salt and cheese and mix well. Fold in spinach and onion; then fold in eggs. Pour into a well buttered 2 quart ring mold or casserole and bake at 350° for 30 minutes. *May be prepared ahead and baked just before serving.*
Serves 8.
Mrs. Huard Hargis Eldridge (Earl Fae Cooper, Jr.)

Spinach Rice Soufflé

1	10 ounce package frozen chopped spinach	2	eggs
¼	stick butter	⅓	cup milk
½	cup uncooked Minute rice or 1 cup cooked rice	2	tablespoons chopped onion
1	cup shredded American cheese	½	teaspoon Worcestershire sauce
		½	teaspoon salt
		¼	teaspoon thyme

Cook spinach slightly, without water. Do not drain. Add butter, rice, and cheese. Blend eggs, milk, onion, Worcestershire sauce, salt, and thyme in blender. Combine with spinach mixture. Place in greased 1 quart casserole or soufflé dish. Bake at 350° for 30 minutes.
Serves 4.
Mrs. Kenneth Reed Bentley (Carol Jane Case)

To thaw frozen filo, wrap in a moistened tea towel and refrigerate for at least 8 hours. Sheets tend to stick together if refrozen.

St. Anthony Hotel's Famous Spinach Pudding

1	10 ounce package fresh spinach	3	eggs
½	cup chopped celery	1	cup white bread crumbs
¼	cup chopped parsley	½	stick butter, softened
1	small clove garlic, minced, or ¼ cup finely chopped onion		Salt and pepper to taste
			Additional butter and bread crumbs

Step 1 Remove stems from spinach and wash thoroughly. In the water that clings to the leaves, cook the spinach until just tender. Press spinach in a colander, reserving liquid, to get it completely dry. Put spinach, celery, parsley, and garlic or onion through a grinder. This yields approximately 1 cup of spinach mixture. Mix spinach with eggs, crumbs, butter, salt, and pepper.

Step 2 Cut several thicknesses of cheesecloth approximately 8 x 18 inches. Spread cheesecloth with additional butter, then sprinkle with enough bread crumbs to cover butter. Spoon spinach on cheesecloth lengthwise along the edge. Gently roll the cheesecloth around the spinach. Tie both ends and also the center if necessary. Bring the reserved spinach liquid and enough water to cover the spinach roll to a boil. Add spinach roll and boil for 30 minutes. Cool. Spinach roll may be frozen at this point. When ready to use, slice, place in a buttered casserole, cover, and heat at 350° about 10 minutes. *This is a very old recipe, tried and proven many times.*
Serves 12.
Mrs. Richard E. Morrison (Susan Browning)

Spanakopites
Spinach Rolls

2   10 ounce packages fresh spinach
1   tablespoon salt
½   pound Feta cheese
3   tablespoons grated Parmesan
    cheese
1   medium onion, chopped
¼   cup chopped parsley

Several sprigs fresh dill, chopped, or ½
    teaspoon dried dill
¼   cup olive oil
3   eggs, beaten
1   pound filo or strudel pastry
2   sticks butter or margarine, melted

Step 1   Wash spinach and drain well. Cut spinach finely with kitchen scissors, place in a bowl, and sprinkle with salt. Rub salt into spinach and set aside for 15 minutes or longer. Rinse Feta cheese in cold water, drain well, and crumble into a large bowl. Add Parmesan cheese, onion, parsley, and dill. Then take handfuls of spinach, squeeze dry, and add to cheese mixture. Pour olive oil over mixture and fold in eggs.

Step 2   Unfold pastry sheets and cut so that you have sheets measuring approximately 8 x 13 inches. Cover sheets with a towel so they will not dry out. Gently brush each sheet as it is used with butter. Place 1 tablespoon spinach mixture 1 inch away from the edge on the shorter side. Fold 1 inch margin over mixture, then fold longer sides in toward the middle, butter pastry, and roll compactly to end. Place in large pans and bake at 400° for 20-30 minutes or until golden brown. Serve hot. This can be used as an appetizer by cutting the filo smaller.

Alternate Method   This recipe may also be made in layers rather than individual rolls. In a greased casserole place 6-8 sheets of filo brushing each with butter, add the spinach mixture, and top with 6-8 more sheets of filo brushed with butter. Using a sharp razor blade or knife, score the top layers in squares. Lightly sprinkle with water and bake. Cut all the way through before serving.
Yields 40-45. Freezes well up to 2 months after cooking.
Mrs. Arthur Sockler

Spinach Crêpe Filling

2   10 ounce packages frozen chopped
    spinach
½   stick butter
¼   cup flour
1   teaspoon salt

Dash of pepper
2   cups light cream
1   cup grated Swiss cheese
Pinch of nutmeg
12 crêpes

Cook spinach slightly and drain well. Melt butter and stir in flour, salt, and pepper. Add cream gradually and stir until smooth. Add spinach, cheese, and nutmeg. Fill crêpes and bake at 350° until thoroughly heated.
Fills 12 crêpes.
Mrs. Jack Grieder (Nancy Bickham)

Spinach Loaf

2 cups chopped cooked spinach	4 slices bacon, diced
2 eggs, beaten	2 tablespoons chopped onion
¾ cup finely diced Cheddar cheese	2 tablespoons flour
2 tablespoons bacon drippings	1 cup strained tomatoes
1 cup toasted bread crumbs	2 tablespoons chopped green pepper
1 tablespoon vinegar	Salt and pepper to taste

Combine the first 6 ingredients and place in a greased 8 x 4 loaf pan. Bake at 350° for 30 minutes. Fry bacon with onion until slightly browned. Remove onion and bacon from pan and set aside. Stir flour into bacon drippings, add tomatoes, and cook until thick, stirring constantly. Add bacon, onion, green pepper, salt, and pepper. Cook 5 minutes. Serve this sauce over hot sliced spinach loaf.
Serves 6-8.
Mrs. William Terry O'Daniel (Billie)

Spinach Pie

1 9 inch deep dish pastry shell	1 10 ounce package frozen chopped spinach, well drained
3 ounces cream cheese, softened	
1 cup light cream	½ stick butter or margarine
½ cup soft bread cubes, lightly packed	1 large onion, finely chopped
	½ pound mushrooms, finely chopped
¼ cup grated Parmesan cheese	1 teaspoon tarragon
2 eggs, slightly beaten	½ teaspoon salt

Prebake pastry shell at 400° for 8 minutes. Mash cream cheese with a fork and gradually blend in cream. Add bread cubes, cheese, and eggs. Beat with wire whip to break up bread pieces. Stir in spinach. Melt butter in a frying pan and add onion and mushrooms. Cook until lightly browned, stirring frequently. When vegetables are soft, add the tarragon, blend with spinach mixture, and add salt. Pour filling into pastry shell. Bake at 400° on lowest rack in oven for 25 minutes or until crust is well browned. Let stand 10 minutes. May be served hot or at room temperature. *Good with fried chicken, fruit salad, and a light dessert.*
Serves 6-8. Freezes.
Mrs. George R. Bristol (Patricia Peterson)

Chili con Queso Squash

10-12 yellow squash, cubed
2   tablespoons bacon drippings
3   4 ounce cans chopped green chilies
¼   teaspoon salt
2   cloves garlic, minced

1   pound Velveeta cheese, grated
1¼ cups light cream
Salt and pepper to taste
Bread crumbs or corn flake crumbs

In a small amount of water, cook squash until tender and drain. In a separate pan, melt the bacon drippings, add the chilies and salt, and simmer. Add garlic and stir well. Add cheese and continue to stir until cheese is completely melted. Slowly add the cream to the cheese sauce, using more cream if the sauce becomes too thick. Season squash with salt and pepper, mash, and place a thick layer in the bottom of a 9 x 13 casserole. Top with cheese sauce and continue to layer squash and sauce until all the squash and sauce are used. Cover with crumbs and bake at 325° for 30 minutes.
Serves 14.
Mrs. Austin Wright Moore (Martha Marks)

Squash and Peas

4-5 white scalloped squash
Onion powder to taste
1   8 ounce can tiny English peas

Butter to taste
Salt and pepper to taste

Select squash that are full and have a good hump. Boil whole squash until just tender. Scoop out seeds and sprinkle each squash with a little onion powder. Heat peas, drain, and season with butter, salt, pepper, and onion powder. Fill each squash with peas. This may be prepared ahead and kept warm in a baking pan with a cover. *This easy, delicious recipe came from a famous hotel in Mexico.*
Serves 4.
Mrs. Frank Steed

Acorn Squash — Variations for Stuffing
Green Stuffing

1 tablespoon butter	½ cup chopped onions
2 tablespoons flour	½ cup chopped celery
½ teaspoon dry mustard	2 tablespoons chopped parsley
Salt and pepper to taste	3 whole acorn squash, halved and seeded
½ cup milk	Parmesan cheese, optional
2 eggs, lightly beaten	Paprika, optional
1 package frozen chopped spinach, thawed and drained	

Melt butter and stir in flour, mustard, salt, and pepper. Add milk and eggs and stir until smooth. Fold in spinach, onions, celery, and parsley. Spoon into squash halves. Bake at 350° for 40 minutes or until squash is tender. Parmesan cheese and paprika may be sprinkled over top of filling for color.
Serves 6.

Sausage Stuffing

½ cup finely chopped onion	1 tablespoon finely chopped pecans
½ cup finely chopped zucchini	1 cup herb seasoned stuffing mix
2 tablespoons finely chopped parsley	Salt and pepper to taste
Butter	2 whole acorn squash, halved and seeded
¼ pound pork sausage, cooked and drained	Canned onion rings for topping

Sauté onion, zucchini, and parsley in butter. Add sausage, pecans, and stuffing to sautéed vegetables. Add salt and pepper and toss lightly. Spoon stuffing into squash halves. Put squash in a shallow dish that has been filled with ½ inch of water. Bake at 350° for 35 minutes. Crumble onion rings, sprinkle over squash, and continue baking 10 minutes.
Serves 4.

Walnut Cheese Stuffing

1 egg	1 cup chopped walnuts
1 cup milk	1 cup grated cheese
1 cup bread crumbs	3 whole acorn squash, halved and seeded
Pinch of nutmeg	

Beat egg and milk together and stir into bread crumbs. Add nutmeg, walnuts, and cheese. Spoon into squash halves and bake at 350° for 40 minutes.
Serves 6.
The Cookbook Committee

Squash Tuscaloosa

2 pounds small, white scalloped squash	1 cup grated Swiss cheese
1 cup finely chopped onion	1 tablespoon cream
1 cup finely chopped celery	Salt and pepper to taste
½ stick butter	8 saltine crackers, coarsely crumbled

Parboil squash until barely tender. Remove centers and mash. Reserve shells. Sauté onion and celery in butter until clear, and add mashed squash, cheese, cream, salt, and pepper. Fill shells with mixture and sprinkle crumbs on top. Bake at 350° until light brown. *Mixture may also be mashed together, placed in a casserole, and topped with crumbs.*
Serves 6-8.
Mrs. William R. Campbell (Cynthia Rote)

Butternut Squash

1 butternut squash, halved	4 teaspoons butter
4 tablespoons cajeta de leche (quemada)	Pinch of salt

Remove seeds from squash. Fill each half with 2 tablespoons cajeta, 2 teaspoons butter, and a pinch of salt. Place halves in a casserole filled with ½ inch water and bake at 350° for 45 minutes.
Serves 4.
Mrs. John McCamish (Tita Loughborough)

Cajeta de leche is sold in glass jars in Mexico and in some cities near the border. It is usually the consistency and color of caramel sauce and is sweet. It comes in many flavors: envinada (wine), vainilla (vanilla), and quemada. The most popular flavor is quemada, similar to caramel, and for which there is no literal translation. It may be served over ice cream and topped with chopped, salted peanuts. You may also spread it on toast as you would jam or jelly.

A substitute for cajeta may be made by the following method. Pour one 14 ounce can sweetened condensed milk into an 8 inch glass baking dish, cover with aluminum foil, place in a shallow pan of water, and bake at 425° for 1 hour or until thick.

Leche Quemada Pie may be made by pouring the cooked milk into a baked pastry shell. Chill; then top with whipped cream and nuts before serving.

Zucchini Casserole

4 medium zucchini, sliced
¾ cup shredded carrots
½ cup chopped onion
¾ stick butter, divided

1-2 cups herbed stuffing cubes
1 10¾ ounce can cream of chicken soup
½ cup sour cream

Cook zucchini and drain. In a saucepan, sauté carrots and onion in ½ stick butter until tender. Remove from heat. Stir in ¾-1½ cups stuffing cubes, soup, and sour cream. Gently stir in zucchini. Turn into a 1½ quart buttered casserole. Toss remaining cubes or enough to cover casserole with ¼ stick melted butter and sprinkle over squash mixture. Bake at 350° for 30-40 minutes. *This may be prepared ahead.*
Serves 6-8. Does not freeze.
Mrs. Jack Grieder (Nancy Bickham)

For a flavor change in acorn or butternut squash, use mace or light brown sugar combined with butter to season before baking.

Calabacitas con Jitomate

1½ pounds calabaza or zucchini, chopped
1 tablespoon minced onion
1 clove garlic, minced
5 tablespoons butter, divided

1 16 ounce can tomatoes, chopped
½ cup grated Swiss cheese
4 eggs, beaten
Salt and pepper to taste
½ cup bread crumbs

Steam squash until tender. Sauté onion and garlic in 2 tablespoons butter until tender. Add tomatoes and cook 5 minutes. Add squash and cheese. Remove from heat and add eggs. Season with salt and pepper. Pour into a buttered casserole. Cover with bread crumbs and dot with remaining butter. Bake at 350° for 30 minutes.
Serves 6-8. Freezes well after cooking.
Mrs. Robert Jones (Bettina Blair)

Fried Zucchini à la Josef

4 medium zucchini
1 cup flour
Salt and pepper to taste

2 eggs, beaten
1 cup fine bread crumbs
Shortening or vegetable oil

Slice ends from each zucchini and cut lengthwise into 6 strips. Mix flour, salt, and pepper. Dust zucchini strips with flour mixture, dip into egg, and roll in bread crumbs. Preheat oil to 350°F and fry zucchini until golden. Drain and serve immediately.
Serves 4.
University Club of San Antonio

Italian Stuffed Zucchini

4 medium zucchini
½ stick butter or margarine, melted
Salt to taste
⅓ cup finely chopped onion or
2 tablespoons dehydrated onion mixed with 2 tablespoons water
2 tablespoons minced parsley

8 saltine crackers, crumbled
2 tablespoons grated Parmesan cheese
½ teaspoon salt
Pinch of pepper, optional
½ teaspoon oregano, optional
Paprika

Parboil zucchini until just tender. Rinse with cold water immediately to stop the cooking process. Cut the squash in half lengthwise and scoop out the center, saving the pulp. Brush the shells with 1 tablespoon butter and lightly sprinkle with salt. Sauté onions in 2 tablespoons butter until tender and slightly brown. Add pulp, parsley, cracker crumbs, cheese, salt, pepper, and oregano and continue cooking 3 minutes. Fill shells with this mixture and brush with remaining butter. Sprinkle with paprika and place in a baking dish. Bake at 375° for about 20 minutes or until thoroughly heated. For scalloped summer squash, use the same procedure as above, leaving out the oregano and adding 4 slices crisp bacon, crumbled. *This recipe may be prepared early in the day and baked just before serving.*
Serves 8.
Mrs. William A. Parker (Camilla Mueller)

Sausage Zucchini Boats

4	medium zucchini	½	teaspoon M.S.G.
½	pound sausage	¼	teaspoon salt
¼	cup chopped onion	¼	teaspoon thyme
½	cup fine cracker crumbs	¼	teaspoon garlic salt
1	egg, slightly beaten	½	cup grated Parmesan cheese

Boil whole zucchini 7-10 minutes or until barely tender. Cut lengthwise, scoop out centers, and mash. Reserve shells. Brown sausage and onion in skillet. Drain. Stir in mashed squash and remaining ingredients except the cheese. Stuff shells with mixture and top with cheese. Bake in a 9 x 13 pan at 350° for 25-30 minutes. *This can be prepared and refrigerated before baking.* Serves 8.
Mrs. Elaine H. Wagener

Zucchini, Corn, and Cheese

1	pound zucchini	4	ounces grated Swiss, Old English, or Cheddar cheese
¼	cup chopped onion		
¼	stick butter or margarine, melted	¼	teaspoon salt
2	eggs, beaten	¼	cup fine, dry bread crumbs
1	10 ounce package frozen whole kernel corn, cooked and drained; or 2 cups fresh corn; or 1 can whole kernel corn, drained	2	tablespoons grated Parmesan cheese
		Parsley and cherry tomatoes	

Slice zucchini 1 inch thick and cook, covered, in a small amount of salted water 15-20 minutes. Drain and mash with fork. Sauté onion in 1 tablespoon butter until tender. Combine eggs, squash, onion, corn, grated cheese, and salt, and put in a greased casserole. Mix bread crumbs, Parmesan cheese, and 1 tablespoon butter, and sprinkle over squash mixture. Place casserole on a baking sheet and bake at 350° until knife inserted in center comes out clean. Bake 40 minutes for a 1 quart casserole and 25-30 minutes for a square baking dish. Let stand 5-10 minutes before serving. *Garnish with parsley and cherry tomatoes.*
Serves 6.
Mrs. Kip McKinney Espy (Sally Searcy Kleberg)

Chile Cheese Tomatoes

3   large, firm tomatoes, or 4 medium
1   cup sour cream
½   teaspoon salt
¼   teaspoon pepper
1   tablespoon flour

2   tablespoons chopped green onions
1-2 tablespoons chopped, canned green chilies
1   cup grated Longhorn cheese, about ¼ pound

Peel tomatoes and cut in thick slices. Mix remaining ingredients, except cheese, in a small bowl and stir until well blended. Place tomato slices in a broiler pan or shallow glass baking dish. Spoon sour cream mixture evenly over tomato slices. Top with grated cheese. This may be done early in the day and refrigerated. Just before serving, broil tomatoes about 4 minutes or until cheese is bubbly and golden brown. The tomatoes will be just warm.
Serves 8.
Mrs. William McNeel (Amy Lillian McNutt)

Tomato Mushroom Cup

1   medium tomato
4   large mushrooms, coarsely chopped
1   teaspoon margarine

Salt and pepper to taste
⅛   teaspoon dried tarragon
1   tablespoon minced fresh parsley

Hollow out tomato, discard center, and drain. In a teflon pan sauté mushrooms in margarine and add seasonings. Fill tomato with mushroom mixture, and bake at 350° for 30 minutes or until heated. *This is very low in calories and delicious.*
Serves 1.
Mrs. Howard E. Lancaster, (Betty Lain)

Creole Tomatoes

4	large, firm tomatoes	½	cup water
1	small onion, finely chopped	2	tablespoons flour
1	small green pepper, chopped	1	cup light cream
	Salt to taste	4	slices dry toast, cut in half
	Cayenne pepper to taste		diagonally
½	stick butter, divided		

Core tomatoes, cut in half crosswise, and place cut side up in a shallow baking dish. Sprinkle onion, green pepper, salt, and cayenne pepper over tomato halves. Place a small amount of butter on top of each tomato. Pour water in dish and bake at 375° for 20-30 minutes or until tender. Melt remaining butter in skillet, add flour, and cook until brown as you would for a roux. Stir occasionally. Add cream slowly, then cook about 3 minutes, stirring constantly. Place tomatoes on toast and pour sauce over them.
Serves 8.
Mrs. J. Maurice Smith

Escalloped Tomatoes

1	small onion, finely chopped	1	28 ounce can tomatoes
1	stick butter or margarine	1	teaspoon salt
1¼	cups toasted dry bread cubes	⅛	teaspoon pepper
½	cup loosely packed brown sugar		

Using a heavy skillet, sauté onions in butter. Add bread cubes and sugar. Cook slowly for a few minutes until bread cubes are well coated. Stir in tomatoes, breaking into pieces, and add seasonings. Place mixture in a buttered 8 x 8 casserole. Bake at 350° for 45 minutes.
Serves 6-8. May be prepared ahead.
Mrs. William B. Schiller

Tomato Pie

5	medium tomatoes, sliced	½	cup grated Parmesan cheese
1	9 inch pastry shell	¼	teaspoon pepper
½	cup mayonnaise	6	crackers, crumbled
1	clove garlic, crushed	2	teaspoons butter

Drain tomatoes on paper towels and place in pastry shell. Mix mayonnaise, garlic, cheese, and pepper. Spread over tomatoes. Sprinkle cracker crumbs on top and dot with butter. Bake at 425° for 20-25 minutes. Let stand 10-15 minutes before cutting.
Serves 6-8.
Mrs. Walter Hale, III (Janin Sinclair)

Pomodoro con Riso

6   large, medium ripe tomatoes
1½ cups cooked rice
1   tablespoon chopped parsley
1   clove garlic, mashed
½   teaspoon pepper

½   teaspoon sugar
1   tablespoon chopped basil or 2 teaspoons dried basil, crushed
¾   teaspoon salt
¼   cup olive oil

Cut tops off tomatoes and set them aside. Scoop out pulp and seeds and put through foodmill or coarse strainer. Mix with rice and seasonings and let this mixture stand for 30 minutes. Fill tomatoes with rice mixture and cover with the tops which were reserved. Pour olive oil over tomatoes and sprinkle lightly with salt. Bake at 350° for 45-60 minutes. Beware of overcooking or they will get too soft. *These can be prepared a few hours ahead and served at almost room temperature. One summer when I was studying in Rome, I found these to be a popular item in the many corner "delis" where students ate; they were also served in the best restaurants.*
Serves 6.
Mrs. Rapier Dawson (Polly Butte)

Turnip Puff

2   cups cooked turnips, drained well and mashed
1   tablespoon minced onion
½   teaspoon salt
½   teaspoon seasoned salt

Pepper to taste
3   tablespoons butter
2   eggs, separated
¼   cup milk
Parsley, finely chopped

Mix turnips, seasonings, and butter and cool slightly. Beat egg yolks, combine with milk, and add to turnip mixture. Fold in stiffly beaten egg whites and pour into a buttered 1 quart soufflé or baking dish. Set in a pan of hot water and bake at 350° for 40 minutes or until firm and golden brown. Garnish with parsley and serve at once.
Serves 4.
Mrs. Frates Seeligson (Martita Rice)

Bulgarian Vegetable Bake

½ cup each:
    corn
    chopped cabbage
    diced carrots
    chopped green beans
    diced okra, fresh or frozen
    cubed eggplant
    chopped tomatoes

2   small onions, sliced
3   tablespoons chopped parsley
1   raw potato, diced
½   teaspoon salt
½   cup water
¼   teaspoon pepper
½-1 cup olive oil

Mix all ingredients together except olive oil. Put in a baking dish and add oil. Bake, covered, at 300° for 1 hour.
Serves 6-8.
Mrs. Harry E. Brown (Carolyn Carlisle)

Vegetable Casserole

1   10 ounce package frozen baby lima beans, cooked and drained
1   9 ounce package frozen cut green beans, cooked and drained
1   10 ounce package frozen green peas, cooked and drained
Salt and pepper to taste

Butter to taste
1-2 green peppers, thinly sliced
8   ounces cream cheese, softened
2   tablespoons mayonnaise
3-4 tablespoons light cream
Paprika

Season each vegetable with salt, pepper, and butter. Layer vegetables with green pepper in a 2 quart casserole. Make a sauce with the cream cheese, mayonnaise, and cream, and pour over vegetables. Heat at 325° for 10-15 minutes and sprinkle with paprika before serving.
Serves 8.
Mrs. Burleson Smith (Constance Ball Terrell)

Mushroom Ratatouille

2 medium green peppers
2 medium zucchini
½ cup salad oil, divided
1 medium onion, thinly sliced
2 cloves garlic, minced
1 pound small mushrooms, halved

4 medium tomatoes, peeled and quartered
1½ teaspoons salt
¼ teaspoon pepper
½ teaspoon thyme

Halve peppers and remove seeds. Cut crosswise into ¼ inch slices. Cut zucchini into ½ inch slices. Place ¼ cup oil in a large skillet or Dutch oven. Sauté green pepper, onion, and garlic about 5 minutes or until tender and remove using a slotted spoon. Add remaining ¼ cup oil and sauté zucchini, mushrooms, and tomatoes about 5 minutes or until tender. Add the other sautéed vegetables, salt, pepper, and thyme and mix gently. Cover and simmer a few minutes until hot and bubbly. Add more seasonings if desired. *This recipe can be made ahead of time but does not freeze well.*
Serves 10-12.
Mrs. Robert Lee Brusenhan, Jr. (Lollie Wright)

Ratatouille Filling for Crêpes

1 onion, finely chopped
1 clove garlic, crushed
2 tablespoons olive oil
1 green pepper, chopped
1 zucchini, diced
3 slices eggplant or 1 small eggplant, peeled and diced
2 medium tomatoes, peeled, seeded, and chopped
¼ teaspoon basil

¼ teaspoon oregano
¼ cup tomato purée
1 teaspoon cornstarch, dissolved in 1 tablespoon water
Salt and pepper to taste
Chopped parsley, tomato wedges, and pitted ripe olives
Parmesan cheese, optional
Crêpes

Sauté onion and garlic in oil until soft and transparent. Add green pepper, zucchini, and eggplant. Cover and simmer over low heat for 15 minutes. Add tomatoes and herbs and continue cooking, uncovered, for another 10 minutes. Remove vegetables with a slotted spoon and put into another bowl. Make a sauce by adding tomato purée and cornstarch dissolved in water to the pan juices. Cook until thick, add salt and pepper, and adjust seasonings. Fill each crêpe with vegetable mixture and roll. Place crêpes with the seam side down in a buttered casserole and bake at 400° for 10 minutes. Pour sauce over crêpes and garnish with parsley, tomato wedges, and ripe olives. *May be sprinkled with Parmesan cheese and run under broiler to brown. Fabulous!*
Fills 18-20 crêpes.
Mrs. Pierce Sullivan (Mary Wallace Kerr)

Ratatouille

1	medium eggplant	½	cup olive oil
2-3	small zucchini		Salt and pepper to taste
2-3	yellow squash		Sugar to taste
3-4	tomatoes		Pinch of herbs such as:
1	large or 2 small yellow onions		dill weed
2	cloves garlic		sweet basil
1	small green pepper		tarragon
1	fresh jalapeño pepper		parsley

Step 1 Thinly slice but do not peel eggplant, zucchini, yellow squash, and tomatoes. Thinly slice onion and garlic. Seed and thinly slice green pepper. Seed and finely chop jalapeño.

Step 2 Place ⅛ cup olive oil in the bottom of a 2-3 quart heavy pan or casserole with a tight fitting lid. Place a layer of each in the following order: eggplant, onion, green pepper rings, tomato, a few slices of garlic, and a bit of jalapeño pepper. Sprinkle with salt, pepper, and a pinch of sugar. Dribble a bit of oil over the layer and add a pinch of one of the herbs.

Step 3 Repeat Step 2 using the zucchini instead of the eggplant and a different herb.

Step 4 Repeat Step 3 using yellow squash instead of the zucchini and a different herb.

Pile the vegetable layers high as they reduce while cooking. Cover and place on top of stove or in oven. Cook on lowest heat for 2-2½ hours or until the vegetables are soft. It is very important that you do not stir. *This recipe is easily prepared and is also delicious cold with a dash of lemon juice added. The principal vegetables and herbs may be varied. Choose whatever is plentiful at the market, or whatever you have on hand. This is a very pungent and strongly flavored dish. It is best served with boiled, broiled, or roasted meats.*
Serves 6-8.
Mrs. Reagan Houston, III (Mary Jane Lyles)

Mission San Juan Capistrano

"We also visited the third mission, San Juan, which lies three miles farther down on the left bank of the river. Here the church can be traced only by its foundation walls, but the encircling wall which enclosed the square courtyard, and against whose inner walls several buildings, such as the houses of the Indians, lean, were in almost perfect state of preservation."

Roemer's Texas.   Ferdinand Roemer, 1845-1847.

"The San Juan Mission, situated seven miles southeast of the city, on the San Antonio river and Aransas Pass railroad, comprising one thousand acres, is owned by Mr. Charles L. Dignowity, and is a magnificent and important estate in itself."

San Antonio: Her Prosperity and Prospects.   Andrew Morrison, 1887.

Baked Pineapple

4 eggs, slightly beaten
1 stick butter or margarine, slightly softened
½ cup sugar

1 16 ounce can crushed pineapple
5 slices white bread, broken into fine pieces

Combine eggs with butter, sugar, and crushed pineapple in a medium bowl. Add bread and mix until all ingredients are blended. Pour into a 2½ quart casserole. Bake at 325° for 30 minutes. *A great replacement for potatoes, especially when serving ham.*
Serves 8-10.
Mrs. Wayne Tatman (Pat)

The canned peach half is so very versatile! Fill it with orange marmalade, chutney, or currant jelly. Broil until bubbly. Good for a morning coffee klatch and especially good with chicken.

Cheese Baked Pineapple

1 20 ounce can pineapple chunks
½ cup sugar

½ cup flour
½ pound sharp cheese, grated

Blend juice from pineapple with sugar, flour, and cheese. Pour over pineapple and bake at 400° for 45 minutes.

Mrs. Edward Snyder (Gloria)

Spiced Pineapple Chunks

1 29 ounce can pineapple chunks
¾ cup vinegar
1¼ cups sugar

Pinch of salt
6-8 whole cloves
1 4 inch cinnamon stick

Drain pineapple and combine syrup with vinegar, sugar, salt, cloves, and cinnamon stick. Simmer for 10 minutes. Add pineapple chunks and bring to a boil. Remove from heat and cool. Refrigerate. *Make 3 days before serving. Nice for a brunch.*
Serves 8. Keeps well.
Mrs. Richard H. Eckhardt (Mary Webb)

Baked Apricots

4　large cans peeled, halved apricots, drained
1　16 ounce box light brown sugar
1　medium-sized box Ritz crackers, coarsely crumbled
2　sticks butter

Drain apricots on paper towels. In buttered baking dish, place a layer of the apricot halves; sprinkle with brown sugar and then cracker crumbs. Dot with butter. Repeat layers until ingredients are used. Bake at 300° for 1 hour or until thick and crusty on top. *May be used to accompany ham or served à la mode for dessert.*
Serves 10-12.
Mrs. Walter Hale, III (Janin Sinclair)

Copper Kitchen Banana Fritters

½　cup rum
½　cup orange juice
6　bananas, each split lengthwise and crosswise to make 4 pieces
2　tablespoons flour
2　tablespoons cornstarch
2　egg whites
1　stick butter
¼　cup sugar

Mix rum with orange juice. Marinate bananas in mixture for ½ hour. Make a batter of flour, cornstarch, and egg whites. Dip banana pieces in batter and brown in butter. Remove to a platter. Add marinade and sugar to pan, bring mixture to a boil, and pour over bananas. Keep in a warm oven until ready to serve.
Serves 8.
Mrs. V. H. McNutt

New England Fresh Cranberry Granite

4　cups fresh cranberries
2　cups water
¼　teaspoon salt
2　cups sugar
¼　cup fresh lemon juice

Place cranberries in a saucepan with water and salt. Cover and cook 8-10 minutes or until skins pop. Remove from heat immediately and strain through a ricer. Dissolve sugar in cranberry mixture and cool. Stir in lemon juice and pour into ice cube trays. Freeze until cubes will retain shape, but are not solid. *Serve as an accompaniment to fowl.*
Yields 2 cups.
Mrs. Porter Fearey

Hawaiian Cereal

¾ cup water
¾ cup vegetable oil
2 teaspoons vanilla
4 cups regular rolled oats
½ cup brown sugar

2 cups wheat germ
1 cup broken nuts, pecans, walnuts, or almonds
1 cup sunflower seeds

Mix water, oil, and vanilla. Combine dry ingredients and mix with liquid until well blended. Spread in a shallow pan. Bake at 325° for 45 minutes, stirring every 10 minutes. *Serve with milk for breakfast. Also good as topping for ice cream or as after school snack.*
Makes 2 quarts.
Mrs. Richard F. Halter (Beverly Francis)

Fresh peach halves may be stuffed with a mixture of 12 crumbled macaroons, 1 egg yolk, 2 tablespoons sugar, and ½ stick butter and baked at 325° for 30 minutes. Serve à la mode if desired.

Anne Barnes' Brew

1 quart pineapple juice
1 quart water
1 quart apple cider
4 pieces ginger

3 3 inch sticks cinnamon
16 whole cloves
1 teaspoon allspice
½ teaspoon pickling spice

Combine ingredients and boil for several minutes. Reduce heat to low. The aroma fills the air as long as the mixture simmers. *This is not to drink. It makes the house smell like Christmas and is fun for a party.*

Mrs. Walter Mathis Bain (Sue Howell)

Peach halves are delicious filled with jalapeño or other pepper jelly, broiled until bubbly, and served with game.

Agarita Jelly

Agarita berries   **Sure-Jell**
Sugar   **Lemon juice**

Boil berries in enough water to cover for 30 minutes. Strain juice but do not mash berries. Discard berries and add 1 cup of sugar for each cup of juice. Stir in one 1¾ ounce package of Sure-Jell for every 6½-7 cups of liquid. To this add 1 teaspoon of lemon juice for each quart of juice mixture, and bring to a boil in a stainless steel pan for 20-30 minutes or until the mixture begins to gel. Remove from heat. Skim top of mixture if desired. In the top of a double boiler, melt paraffin. Never attempt this over a direct heat. Fill jars within ½ inch of the top with jelly mixture and top with 1 tablespoon of melted paraffin. Cool slightly but cover jars while jelly is still warm.

Mrs. Eleanor Weed

Pepper Jelly

⅛-¼ cup chopped red or green hot peppers or to taste
1 cup chopped green pepper
1½ cups apple cider

1 cup apple cider vinegar
6½ cups sugar
1½ 6 ounce bottles Certo

Bring all ingredients, except Certo, to hard rolling boil. Boil 1 minute, remove from heat, and let stand 5 minutes. Add Certo and stir well. Strain if clear jelly is desired. Pour into jars and seal. *Great with meats, especially venison.* **Yields 4 pints.**
Mrs. Fred W. Middleton (Barbara Ann Loffland)

Maraschino Honey Jelly

3 cups honey
1 cup maraschino cherry juice

6 ounces liquid fruit pectin

Combine honey with juice in a large saucepan and mix well. Place over high heat and bring to a boil, stirring constantly. Immediately stir in pectin and bring to a full rolling boil. Boil 1 minute, stirring constantly. Remove from heat, skim off foam with a metal spoon, and pour quickly into jars or glasses. Immediately cover with ⅛ inch hot paraffin.

Mrs. J. Sherrel Lakey

When making jam, stir in a bit of butter after removing from heat. The foam will disappear.

Pyracantha Jelly

1 pint pyracantha berries, sorted and washed
2 pints water
Juice of 1 grapefruit, strained

Juice of 1 lemon, strained
1 1¾ ounce package Sure-Jell
5½ cups sugar

Boil berries in water for 20 minutes. Strain juice into a large pot and discard berries. Add enough water to make 4½ cups juice. Then add grapefruit juice, lemon juice, and Sure-Jell. Bring to a boil, quickly add the sugar, and boil several minutes to gel. Test with a spoon or in small dish. Pour into jars or glasses and seal with paraffin.
Yields 3-4 pints.
Mrs. Kaye E. Wilkins (Sidney Howell)

Sherry Jelly

5	cups sugar	1	tablespoon grated orange rind
1	quart good sherry	1	6 ounce bottle Certo

Combine sugar and wine in an enamel pan. Bring to a boil. Add orange rind and Certo. Bring to a rolling boil. Pour into sterilized jars. *Good with meats, especially game.*
Yields 4 pints.
Mr. William B. McMillan

Banana Jam

1	pound ripe bananas	Juice of 4 sweet oranges
1½	cups sugar	Juice of 1 lemon

Slice bananas ¼ inch thick. Put into a heavy saucepan with sugar and juices. Simmer about 1 hour or until the jam thickens. Pour into jars and seal while warm. *An Australian recipe from ranching friends in Queensland.*
Yields 3 small jars.
Mrs. Frates Seeligson (Martita Rice)

Peach Jam

3-4	pounds peaches	4 cups sugar

Trim off any bad spots from peaches, but do not peel. Cut in chunks and whirl briefly in blender about 2 cups at a time. Measure 4 cups peaches and pour into a large heavy pan with the sugar. Stir over low heat until sugar is dissolved. Turn heat to high and boil 12-15 minutes, stirring frequently, until syrup is clear and mixture has thickened. Pour into hot sterilized jars and seal. Jam has a beautiful color and taste from the skins.
Yields 5½ pints.
Mrs. William McNeel (Amy Lillian McNutt)

Strawberry Lime Jam

1	quart fully ripe strawberries, stems removed	4	cups sugar
½	teaspoon grated lime rind	¾	cup water
2	tablespoons lime juice	1¾	ounce box powdered fruit pectin

Crush strawberries 1 layer at a time and measure 2 cups into a large bowl or pan. Add rind, lime juice, and sugar, mixing well. Let stand 10 minutes. Combine water and fruit pectin in a small saucepan, bring to a boil, and boil 1 minute, stirring constantly. Stir into fruit mixture, and continue stirring about 3 minutes. A few sugar crystals will remain. Ladle quickly into sterilized jars no larger than 1 pint. Cover at once with tight lids. Let stand at room temperature until set. This may take up to 24 hours. Store in freezer. If jam will be used within 2-3 weeks, it may be stored in refrigerator.
Yields 5½ cups. Freezes.
Mrs. Middleton S. English (Shirley Fitch)

Fig Strawberry Preserves

3	cups peeled, mashed figs	3	cups sugar
1	6 ounce package strawberry or raspberry gelatin		

Combine figs, gelatin, and sugar in a large saucepan and mix well. Bring to a boil over medium heat and continue boiling 3 minutes, stirring occasionally. Pour quickly into sterile jars and seal. Allow flavors to blend for several days before serving.
Yields 5 small jars.
Miss Nancy Law

Strawberry Preserves

4	cups strawberries	5	cups sugar

Place strawberries in a 6 quart pan over low heat. When hot, gradually add sugar, stirring gently. When mixture reaches a full rolling boil, cook for 12 minutes. Skim off foam and let cool overnight in pan. Pour into sterilized jars, cover with melted paraffin, and seal. The berries will remain whole and will not rise to top of jar.

Mrs. Earl Fae Cooper (Gladys)

River Below San Antonio

"The river San Antonio takes its rise about four or five miles above the city from four large springs which gush from the side of a mountain, and after running twenty miles, it unites with the Medina. The water is clear as crystal and runs through the valley with a current of not less than five or six miles an hour, over a bed of rocks...The country along the valley is handsome beyond description, especially in the vicinity of some of the missions, and justifies all that has been said of its extraordinary beauty and fertility."

Texas In 1837. Anonymous.

Spiced Grapes

4 quarts purple grapes, seeded	½ teaspoon cinnamon
½ pint cider vinegar	½ teaspoon nutmeg
3 pounds sugar	½ teaspoon allspice

Combine ingredients and boil for 30 minutes or until 230°F is reached on a candy thermometer. *This recipe was used at my great-grandmother's plantation on Hilton Head Island in South Carolina. It originally called for a thick-skinned grape that is not usually available in this area, but the thin-skinned grapes substitute beautifully and are equally tasty.*

Mrs. D. W. Eisenhart (Anne)

Cranberry Relish

| 2 | oranges | 2 | cups sugar |
| 1 | pound cranberries | | |

Quarter oranges and remove seeds, but do not peel. Put berries and oranges through a food grinder. Stir in sugar. Chill and serve.
Yields 1 quart.
Mrs. Alfred E. McNamee (Josephine McClelland)

Pear Relish

18	hard pears, peeled, cored, and sliced	½	teaspoon cayenne pepper
4	green peppers, sliced and seeded	2	tablespoons onion flakes
4	lemons, sliced and seeded	1	cup cider vinegar
1	cup seedless raisins	1	tablespoon salt
1	cup brown sugar	1	tablespoon ground ginger
2	cups sugar	1	tablespoon dry mustard

Place ingredients in a large kettle, and simmer gently about 2 hours or until pears are translucent and tender and the syrup is thick. Seal in sterile jars. *This is a rather unusual, but delicious chutney-type relish. Serve with steak, roasts, or curries.*
Yields 5 pints.
Mrs. Middleton S. English (Shirley Fitch)

Chirmol
Salvadorian Spicy Relish

4	medium tomatoes, peeled, chopped, and drained	2	tablespoons olive oil
½	cup chopped onion	4	teaspoons lemon juice
½	medium green pepper, chopped	1	teaspoon oregano
5	chiles serranos, seeded and chopped, optional	1	teaspoon salt
		¼	teaspoon pepper

Combine tomato, onion, green pepper, and serranos. Add olive oil, lemon juice, oregano, salt, and pepper. Chill. *Very good with beef or venison.*

Mrs. Frates Seeligson (Martita Rice)

Prune Relish

2	pounds extra large, dried prunes	1	quart red port wine

Place prunes in wide-mouthed jars and pour wine to top of jar. Check occasionally to see that wine is up to top of jar. Keeps indefinitely in refrigerator. *Serve with ham or poultry.*

Ann M. Rogers

Sweet Red Pepper Relish

12	sweet red peppers, seeded	3	cups sugar
2	green peppers, seeded	1	cup white vinegar
1	tablespoon salt		

Put peppers through the fine blade of a food chopper. Add salt and let stand 3-4 hours. Strain under running water to remove salt. Place peppers in an enamel pan, add sugar and vinegar, and bring to a boil. Boil 25 minutes, stirring occasionally. Store in glass jars in refrigerator.
Yields 1 pint.
Mrs. Franklin C. Davis, Jr. (Virginia Armitage)

Honey's Tomato Relish

18	ripe tomatoes, chopped	2½	cups vinegar
6	onions, chopped	2	teaspoons salt
6	green peppers, chopped	½	teaspoon ground cloves
2-3	hot peppers, chopped	1	teaspoon cinnamon
1	whole stalk celery, chopped	1	teaspoon allspice
1	cup sugar	1	teaspoon nutmeg

Combine vegetables and add remaining ingredients. Cook until tender and thick, stirring constantly. If you cannot stir constantly, place mixture in a covered kettle in slow oven. Relish must be tender, but not overcooked. Seal while hot.

Mrs. Alfred E. McNamee (Josephine McClelland)

Bread and Butter Pickles

1   gallon cucumbers, thinly sliced
8   small onions, shredded or thinly sliced
2   green peppers or 1 green and 1 red pepper, sliced
½   cup salt
1   quart cracked ice

5   cups sugar
½   teaspoon ground cloves
1-2   teaspoons celery seed
1½   teaspoons turmeric
2   tablespoons mustard seed
5   cups vinegar

Combine vegetables with salt and ice and let stand refrigerated for 3 hours. Drain and wash thoroughly. Blend sugar and spices with vinegar. Pour over vegetables, place on low heat, and bring just to boiling point. Remove from heat, place in hot jars, and seal.
Yields 8 pints. Cannot be doubled.
Mrs. William E. Fitch (Patrice Gilbreath)

Pickles

3   cups sugar
2   cups cider vinegar
⅓   cup salt
1   teaspoon celery seed
8-10 cucumbers, peeled and sliced, or 3 quarts

2   medium onions, sliced
1   green pepper, sliced
1   red pepper, sliced, optional

Bring sugar, vinegar, salt, and celery seed to a boil. Let cool, stirring occasionally. Mix cucumbers, onions, and peppers. When liquid is cool, pour over cucumber mixture. Marinate in refrigerator at least 24 hours. Store in covered jars in refrigerator.
Yields 5 pints.
Mrs. Jimmy Raines (Judy)

Pickled Okra

3   pounds tender fresh okra
12-14 chili petins
12   peppercorns
6-7 cloves garlic
4   cups vinegar

2   cups water
½   cup salt
1   teaspoon sugar
1   teaspoon oil

Pack 6-7 pint jars with okra. Add 2 chili petins, 2 peppercorns, and 1 clove garlic to each jar. Combine vinegar, water, salt, sugar, and oil in a saucepan, bring to a boil, and pour over okra. Seal jars. Store in a cool place for 2 weeks before serving.
Yields 6-7 pints.
Mrs. Frederick C. Groos, Jr. (Martha Grace Bailey)

Lucinda Trippe's Crisp Watermelon Pickles

4½ pounds watermelon rind, peeled	1¼ cups vinegar
3 tablespoons salt	1 teaspoon ground mace
2½ tablespoons powdered alum	3 sticks cinnamon
8 cups sugar	1½ tablespoons whole cloves

Remove most of pink from the rind, but not all, as a little pink adds color. Cut all outer green peeling from rind. Cut rind in ½ x 2 inch pieces or in triangles. Add salt and rind to 3 quarts of water, and let stand overnight. Drain and rinse well. Add alum and rinds to 3 quarts of fresh water. Bring to a boil, reduce heat, and simmer for about 30 minutes. Drain and rinse very well. Simmer in 3 quarts of fresh water for about 30 more minutes. Add enough water to cover rind if needed, add the sugar, and cook briskly until rind appears transparent. Add vinegar and cook 30 minutes. Add spices and cook only 5 minutes as longer cooking darkens the syrup. Pack rinds, spices, and syrup into sterilized pint or quart jars and seal while hot. Store for 2 weeks before using.

Mrs. Arthur M. Eldridge

Market Gardens

"The market-gardens, belonging to Germans, which we saw later in the season, are most luxuriant. The prices of milk, butter, and vegetables are very high, and the gains of the small German market-farmers must be rapidly accumulating."

A Journey Through Texas. Frederick Law Olmstead, 1857.

Magic Marinade

Tang	2 parts sherry
1 part soy sauce	

Sprinkle Tang heavily on meat. Cover with generous amounts of soy sauce and sherry. Marinate in refrigerator for at least 4 hours. *Fabulous on steak but delicious for any grilled meat.*

Mrs. J. Ross Crawford (Judith Claire Bennett)

Marinade for Steak

1½ cups vegetable oil
¾   cup soy sauce
¼   cup Worcestershire sauce
2   tablespoons dry mustard
2½ teaspoons salt
⅓   cup fresh lemon juice

1   tablespoon pepper
½   cup red wine
1½ teaspoons parsley
2   cloves garlic, crushed
2   pounds chuck steak

Mix all ingredients. Marinate a 2 pound chuck steak all day or overnight. Broil or grill. *This marinade does wonders to an inexpensive cut of meat.*
Serves 6.
Mrs. Robert L. Cook (Sandra Mueller)

Susie's Shish Kabob Marinade

½   cup oil
2   tablespoons jalapeño juice
Salt and pepper to taste

3   tablespoons vinegar
1   clove garlic
2-3 tablespoons chili powder

Combine ingredients and marinate squares of meat all day. This marinade will almost cook the meat. Meat may be cooked in the oven or over an open grill, but do not cook more than 15 minutes. *Any less tender cuts of meat may be used with this marinade. Especially good for venison.*

Mrs. Harry Brusenhan (Laura)

Broiled Chicken Marinade

1   cup soy sauce
1   cup grapefruit juice or sake
1   teaspoon sugar
½   teaspoon ground ginger

1   2½-3½ pound fryer or
    8 drumsticks
¼   cup vegetable oil or margarine

Mix soy sauce, grapefruit juice, sugar, and ginger in a large shallow dish. Add chicken pieces, turning occasionally. Remove chicken from marinade and brush with oil or margarine. Grill or broil about 6 inches from heat, brushing with marinade and turning frequently, 45-60 minutes or until brown and tender.
Serves 4.
Mrs. M. E. Allison, Jr. (Brooke B. Rumsey)

Barbecue Sauce

2	cups vegetable oil	8	tablespoons vinegar
4	tablespoons hickory salt	½	teaspoon chili powder
2	tablespoons pepper	½	teaspoon celery salt
6	cloves garlic, halved	1	teaspoon Tabasco sauce
8	tablespoons Worcestershire sauce	2	tablespoons soy sauce

Put all ingredients in a quart jar and shake well. Sauce will keep in refrigerator indefinitely. *This is good on all meats, ham, fowl, and game, whether baking or barbecuing. Particularly good on venison as a marinade and while baking as a baste.*
Yields 1 quart.
Mrs. Robert G. Watts (Frances Helland)

Weekend Barbecue Sauce

¼	cup vinegar	1	medium white onion, chopped
½	cup water	1	tablespoon prepared mustard
1	teaspoon salt	¼	whole lemon
½	teaspoon garlic salt	1	teaspoon chili powder
1	tablespoon sugar	¼	cup chili sauce
¼	teaspoon pepper	2	tablespoons Worcestershire sauce
1	stick margarine		

Combine first 10 ingredients in a saucepan and simmer over low heat for 20 minutes. Stir in the remaining ingredients and bring to a boil. Remove from heat. *This sauce is good for basting chicken, turkey, brisket, game, or ribs.*
Yields 1½ cups.
Dr. Orvis E. Meador, Jr.

Diet Barbeque Sauce

6	tablespoons Heinz catsup	2	tablespoons Worcestershire sauce
6	tablespoons prepared mustard		Generous shakes of Tabasco sauce
6	tablespoons vinegar	1	clove garlic, minced
20	drops Sweeta		

Combine ingredients. This may be stored in the refrigerator indefinitely. Each tablespoon of sauce contains approximately 13 calories and 1.4 grams carbohydrates.

Mrs. Reagan Houston, III (Mary Jane Lyles)

Sue's Fondue Sauce

2   tablespoons capers
½   teaspoon curry powder
1   teaspoon garlic powder
½   teaspoon Accent

1   teaspoon lemon juice
1   tablespoon horseradish
½   cup mayonnaise

Combine ingredients. *Great with beef fondue.*
Yields approximately 1 cup.
Mrs. Malcolm G. Chesney (Mary Louise Mims)

Tomato and Caper Sauce

2   6 ounce cans tomato paste
1   cup beef stock
1   teaspoon caper juice
1   tablespoon Worcestershire sauce

1   teaspoon salt
Freshly ground black pepper to taste
Dash of cayenne pepper
2   tablespoons capers

Combine all ingredients, except capers, in a saucepan. Bring to boil over moderate heat, stirring constantly. Reduce heat and simmer 10 minutes. Stir in capers. Serve hot or cold with beef fondue.

Mrs. Franklin Law (Virginia Matthews)

Herb Sauce for Beef Fondue

2   egg yolks
2   tablespoons lemon juice
1   teaspoon salt
Freshly ground black pepper to taste

1-1½ cups vegetable oil
½   cup chopped chives
½   cup chopped parsley
1   tablespoon grated or minced onion

Beat egg yolks until frothy. Add lemon juice, salt, pepper, and oil slowly. Stir in chives, parsley, and onions. Chill until ready to serve.

Mrs. Sharon Thier

Spicy Mustard

1	cup dry mustard	2	tablespoons flour
1	cup Spice Islands beef stock base	1	cup vinegar
1	cup loosely packed brown sugar	3	eggs, well beaten

Combine all ingredients in saucepan or double boiler. Cook until thickened, and strain.
Yields 3 cups.
Mr. Dale Heckmann

Horseradish Sauce

1 cup heavy cream
2-4 tablespoons prepared horseradish
Salt to taste

Freshly ground pepper to taste
Lemon juice to taste

Whip cream only until soft peaks are formed. Fold in horseradish. Season with salt, pepper, and drops of lemon juice. Serve with smoked trout, salmon, roast beef, or fondue.
Yields 1½ cups.
Mrs. Donald McGregor Jacobs (Bonnie Sue Dilworth)

Sweet and Sour Sauce

5 tablespoons orange marmalade
1 tablespoon vinegar

1 tablespoon Worcestershire sauce

Combine ingredients, mixing well. *Good on pork chops, duck, or chicken.*

Mrs. Harry Brusenhan (Laura)

Jezebel Sauce

1 18 ounce jar pineapple preserves
1 18 ounce jar apple jelly
1 5 ounce jar horseradish

1 ounce can dry mustard
1 teaspoon pepper

Combine ingredients and whirl in blender. Keeps indefinitely when refrigerated but horseradish mellows, so add more if necessary. *Excellent with lamb, venison, and beef.*
Yields 6 cups.
Mrs. John M. Smith (Jane Jordan)

Hot Sauce

4-5 large, ripe tomatoes
6-7 chiles serranos without stems, or to taste
1 large clove garlic

1 teaspoon sugar
Salt to taste

Grind tomatoes, peppers, and garlic on medium blade of grinder. Do not use a blender. Stir in sugar and salt. Keeps in refrigerator a week or more. *This is similar to the sauce served at La Fonda.*
Yields approximately 1 quart.
Mrs. Richard H. Oldfather (Jan Carter)

Blender Hot Sauce

1 tablespoon chili petins
1 tablespoon vinegar
1 teaspoon salt
1 clove garlic

1½-2 cups chopped onion
1½-2 cups chopped green pepper
1 16 ounce can tomatoes
1 8 ounce can tomato sauce

Put the first 4 ingredients in a blender and blend 5 seconds. Add onion and green pepper a little at a time, blending after each addition. Add tomatoes and tomato sauce and continue to blend. Store in a quart jar in refrigerator.

Mrs. Robert McGarraugh, Jr. (Martha Clampitt)

Ranchero Sauce

1 medium onion, chopped
1 clove garlic, minced
2 tablespoons bacon drippings
1 10 ounce can Rotel tomatoes and green chilies

Salt to taste
Oregano to taste
Cumin to taste

Sauté onions and garlic in drippings until clear. Add tomatoes, salt, oregano, and cumin. Simmer about 10 minutes. Adjust seasonings and mash any large pieces of tomatoes. *Serve hot over eggs or whatever you like.*
Yields 1½ cups.
Mrs. John M. Canavan (Suzanne Womack)

Diablo Salsa de Pancho

¼ cup finely chopped onion
Pinch of cilantro or oregano
2 teaspoons parsley
½ cup finely chopped celery
2 teaspoons curry powder
1 teaspoon Worcestershire sauce

5 drops Tabasco sauce
Salt and pepper to taste
1½ cups tomato juice or tomato purée
2 10 ounce jars oysters
Lemon slices

To make sauce, combine all ingredients except oysters and lemon slices. Fill buttered natural sea shells or ramekins with oysters. Cover with sauce and broil until bubbling and beginning to brown. Serve with lemon slices. *This sauce may also be used for shrimp and is especially good with grated cheese, yellow or Parmesan, sprinkled on top.*

Mrs. Earl Hobbs Chumney, Jr. (Barbara Sue Christian)

Plum Sauce

1 stick butter, melted
1 medium onion, quartered
2-3 jalapeños
Juice of 1½ lemons

1-2 tablespoons Worcestershire sauce
1 clove garlic, optional
2 tablespoons beer, optional

Put all ingredients, except beer, in blender and whirl until smooth. Add beer and simmer 15 minutes. Salt and pepper poultry, meat, or game and baste with the sauce frequently while barbecuing. Sauce should be thick so it will adhere to the meat. Use a fish grill when barbecuing doves and it will be easier to turn them. This amount of sauce is enough for 12 doves. Keeps well in the refrigerator. *This is called Plum Sauce because it was given to me by a friend from Plum, Texas. I never measure the ingredients but it's always good, so vary it to suit your own taste.*

Mr. Timothy Dean Word

Never Fail Hollandaise Sauce

1	stick butter or margarine	¼	teaspoon sugar
3	egg yolks	¼	teaspoon dry mustard
2	tablespoons lemon juice	¼	teaspoon bottled hot pepper sauce
¼	teaspoon salt		

Freeze butter for a few minutes. Beat together egg yolks, lemon juice, and seasonings in top of double boiler. Divide butter into 3 equal portions. Add ⅓ of butter to the egg mixture. Cook over hot water, stirring constantly, until butter is melted. Repeat this process twice, stirring constantly as butter melts and sauce thickens. Remove from heat. Serve sauce hot or at room temperature. Leftover sauce may be kept in the refrigerator.
Yields ⅔ cup.
Mrs. Middleton S. English (Shirley Fitch)

Quick 'n Easy Hollandaise Sauce

1	egg yolk, slightly beaten	Salt to taste
1-1½	tablespoons lemon juice	White pepper to taste
½	stick cold butter	Dash of Tabasco sauce, optional

Place all ingredients in a saucepan. Cook over low heat, stirring constantly until butter melts and sauce is thickened.
Yields ½ cup.
Mrs. Huard Hargis Eldridge (Earl Fac Cooper, Jr.)

Blender Hollandaise

4	egg yolks	Dash of Tabasco sauce or cayenne
2	tablespoons lemon juice	pepper
¼	teaspoon salt	2 sticks butter or margarine

Put egg yolks, lemon juice, salt, and Tabasco in blender and blend for about 3 seconds on high speed. In a saucepan, heat butter until very hot and bubbly, but not brown. Pour butter into blender in a slow, steady stream while blending. The hot butter cooks the eggs. If sauce becomes too thick, add 1 tablespoon of hot water and blend briefly. *This recipe should not be halved. It may be frozen and reconstituted over hot water.*
Yields approximately 1¼ cups.
The Cookbook Committee

Quick Bearnaise

1½ tablespoons chopped shallots
¼ teaspoon white pepper
1½ tablespoons fresh tarragon or
    2 teaspoons dried tarragon

¼ cup dry vermouth or white wine
2 tablespoons wine vinegar
1¼ cups Blender Hollandaise (see index)

Cook the first 5 ingredients until reduced by approximately half, and add to Blender Hollandaise.

Mrs. Richard Harrell Rogers (MarJo McGarraugh)

Cheese Sauce

½ stick butter
¼ cup flour
2 cups hot milk
1 cup grated Longhorn cheese
½ teaspoon salt

½ teaspoon dry mustard
¼ teaspoon seasoned salt
Dash of Accent
Dash of pepper

Melt butter over low heat. Stir in flour until smooth and bubbly. Remove from heat and add milk. Stir over low heat until thick. Add remaining ingredients and stir until cheese melts. *Serve over baked potato or green vegetable.* Yields 2½ cups.
Mrs. James W. Pressley

Supreme Sauce for Ham

3 egg yolks, well beaten
½ cup tomato soup
½ cup sugar

1 stick butter or margarine
½ cup vinegar

In the top of a double boiler, combine the egg yolks, soup, sugar, and butter. Add vinegar. Cook slowly over low heat until mixture thickens, stirring constantly. This sauce is excellent served either hot or cold.
Yields 2 cups.
Mrs. Kenneth L. Farrimond (Susan Redwine)

Remoulade Sauce

2 hard-boiled egg yolks, sieved
2 cloves garlic, minced
1½ tablespoons dark mustard, Dijon or Pom Pom
1½ cups mayonnaise
1 tablespoon paprika

1½ tablespoons horseradish
1 tablespoon Worcestershire sauce
2 tablespoons white vinegar
2 heaping tablespoons chopped parsley
Salt and pepper to taste

Combine ingredients and refrigerate at least 12 hours before serving. Yields 2 cups. Keeps well.
Mrs. Albert Steves, IV (Martha Monier)

Red Seafood Cocktail Sauce

2 cups Heinz tomato catsup
2 cups Heinz chili sauce
¼ cup cider vinegar
6 drops Tabasco sauce

2 teaspoons Worcestershire sauce
3 tablespoons lemon juice
¼-½ teaspoon prepared horseradish, optional

Combine ingredients and refrigerate 3-4 hours. *Good for all seafood cocktails.* Yields 4½ cups. Keeps well.
Mrs. Stanton P. Bell (Jean Todd)

Hot Wine Sauce

1 tablespoon butter
6 ounces currant jelly
Juice of ½ lemon
Pinch of cayenne pepper

½ cup water
3 cloves garlic
1 teaspoon salt
½ cup red port wine

Simmer all ingredients, except wine, for 5 minutes. Strain and add wine. *Serve hot over game or tongue with pan juices if desired.*

Mrs. George Bickham Grieder (Joanne Ugland)

Madeira Mushroom Sauce

Brown Sauce
1½ tablespoons butter
1½ tablespoons flour

2 cups beef consommé
Salt and pepper to taste

Mushroom Sauce
½ stick butter
1 pound fresh mushrooms, thickly
   sliced
½ teaspoon salt
Pepper to taste

1½ tablespoons finely chopped shallots
½ cup Madeira or dry sherry
1 cup Brown Sauce
½ teaspoon chopped parsley

Brown Sauce   Melt butter, add flour, and cook slowly over low heat, stirring occasionally until thoroughly blended and about the color of brown wrapping paper. Add consommé gradually and bring to a boil. Cook 5 minutes, lower heat, and simmer 30 minutes, stirring occasionally. Skim off fat and strain through a fine sieve. Season with salt and pepper.

Mushroom Sauce   Melt butter and add mushrooms, salt, and pepper. Cook, shaking pan frequently, until golden brown. Add shallots, Madeira, and brown sauce. Simmer 5-6 minutes and add parsley. Serve over broiled steaks or roast beef.
Serves 6.
Mrs. Robert Ownby

Espada Aqueduct and Acequia

"On the farms the Indians planted five fanegas of corn and raised about a thousand; two of beans which yielded about forty; and several patches of melons and pumpkins which kept the natives well supplied, and a field of cotton. All the land under cultivation was irrigated by a ditch which brought the water from the river and gave the soil greater productivity."

Our Catholic Heritage in Texas, 1519-1936. Volume III: San Francisco de la Espada in 1745. Carlos E. Castañeda.

Apricot Bread

1	pound dried apricots, chopped	2	eggs, beaten
2	cups sugar	2	teaspoons soda
2	cups apricot nectar	4	cups flour
1	teaspoon salt	½	cup chopped pecans, optional
¾	cup shortening		

Combine the first 5 ingredients and bring to a boil. Boil 5 minutes, remove apricots, and set aside. Cool liquid and add eggs, soda, flour, and pecans, mixing well. Add reserved apricots. Place in 2 greased and floured loaf pans and bake at 325° for 1 hour.
Yields 2 loaves.
Mrs. Eleanor Weed

Banana Bread

1	cup shortening	1	teaspoon salt
2	cups sugar	2	teaspoons soda
6	ripe bananas	1	teaspoon vanilla
4	eggs	1	cup chopped pecans, optional
2¼	cups whole wheat flour		

Cream shortening and sugar. Mash bananas and add to creamed mixture. Add eggs, one at a time, beating after each addition. Sift flour, salt, and soda together and add to banana mixture. Add vanilla and pecans. Pour into 2 greased and floured 9 x 5 x 2 loaf pans and bake at 350° for 45 minutes or until done.
Yields 2 loaves. Freezes.
Mrs. James D. Folbre, Jr. (Jane Shotts)

Ginger Banana Bread

⅔	cup sugar	2¾	teaspoons baking powder
⅓	cup shortening	½	teaspoon salt
2	eggs	⅞	cup mashed bananas
1⅓	cups flour	¼	cup ginger preserves

In the large bowl of mixer, cream sugar and shortening. Add eggs and beat until light and fluffy. Sift together flour, baking powder, and salt. Combine bananas and ginger preserves. Add dry ingredients to sugar mixture alternately with banana mixture and blend well. Spoon into a loaf pan, greased and lined with wax paper, and bake at 350° for about 70 minutes or until lightly browned on top. Let bread cool in pan for 20 minutes. Serve warm.
Yields 1 loaf. Freezes.
Mrs. Alex Weil, III (Penny Speier)

Date Loaf

1	teaspoon baking powder	2	cups pitted dates
1/2	teaspoon salt	1	cup sugar
1	cup flour	4	eggs, separated
4½	cups chopped pecans	1	teaspoon vanilla

Sift together baking powder, salt, and flour. Mix with nuts, dates, and sugar. Beat yolks with 1 teaspoon vanilla and add to mixture. Fold in whites, well beaten, and spread into two 9 x 9 greased pans or 1 large pan. Bake at 350° for 45 minutes. Allow to cool. Remove loaf and cut in squares. If prepared ahead of time, wrap in waxed paper and store in airtight container. *A German Christmas treat prepared by my mother, Milley Giles Beckmann, for my father, Adolph Guenther Beckmann.*
Yields 2 dozen squares. Freezes.
Mrs. W. Lee Moore (Mary Marcella Beckmann)

Mandarin Orange Bread

1	egg	1	teaspoon baking soda
1	cup sugar	1/8	teaspoon salt
5½	ounces mandarin oranges with juice	3	ounces cream cheese
1	cup flour	1	cup confectioners' sugar
1	cup chopped nuts	1	tablespoon butter
			Mandarin orange sections for garnish

Combine the first 7 ingredients with an electric mixer. Bake in a greased and floured 8 x 8 pan at 350° for 30 minutes or until browned on top. Make icing by combining remaining ingredients until smooth. Spread on bread while warm. Top with mandarin oranges for decoration.
Yields 16 squares.
Mrs. Stanley Price (Joy)

Pumpkin Piñon Bread

3	cups flour	1	cup roasted, shelled piñon nuts
2	teaspoons baking powder	1½	cups packed light brown sugar
1	teaspoon cinnamon	1/2	cup butter or shortening, melted
1/2	teaspoon nutmeg	3	eggs, lightly beaten
1/2	teaspoon salt	1¾	cups cooked pumpkin

Sift together flour, baking powder, spices, and salt and stir in nuts. Combine remaining ingredients and add to flour mixture, blending thoroughly. Pour batter into 2 greased loaf pans and bake at 350° for 1 hour or until done. Cool on rack.
Yields 2 loaves.
Mrs. Harry E. Brown (Carolyn Carlisle)

Strawberry Bread

3	cups flour	1	16 ounce package unsweetened frozen strawberries, thawed
2	cups sugar		
1	teaspoon salt	½	cup vegetable oil
1	teaspoon soda	4	eggs, well beaten
½	teaspoon cinnamon	1½	cups chopped nuts, optional

In a large bowl, sift together the flour, sugar, salt, soda, and cinnamon. In another bowl, combine strawberries, oil, eggs, and nuts. Add liquid ingredients gradually to dry ingredients, mixing well. Line two 8 x 4 loaf pans with foil and pour batter into pans. Bake at 325° for 1 hour or until done.
Yields 2 loaves.
Mrs. Helen T. Mays

Zucchini Bread

3	eggs, beaten	1	teaspoon baking soda
2	cups sugar	3	teaspoons cinnamon
1	cup oil	1	teaspoon salt
3	teaspoons vanilla	¼	teaspoon baking powder
2	cups grated zucchini	1	cup nuts or raisins, optional
3	cups flour		

Combine eggs, sugar, oil, vanilla, and zucchini. Sift together flour, soda, cinnamon, salt, and baking powder. Stir into egg mixture. Add nuts and raisins. Fill 2 greased and floured 9 x 5 x 3 loaf pans or round cans ½ full. Bake at 325° for 1 hour.

Variation   For zucchini cake instead of bread, omit 1 cup flour. Glaze with a mixture of ½ cup evaporated milk, 1 cup sugar, ¾ stick butter or margarine, and 1 teaspoon vanilla that has been boiled until thickened.
Serves 15. Freezes.
Mrs. George A. Musselman (Jo)

Crescent Caramel Swirl

1	stick butter or margarine, melted and divided	2	tablespoons water
1/2	cup chopped pecans, divided	2	8 ounce cans Pillsbury Refrigerated Quick Crescent Dinner Rolls
1	cup brown sugar		

Coat bottom and sides of a bundt pan with 1 tablespoon of the butter. Sprinkle pan with 3 tablespoons of the nuts. Add remaining nuts, brown sugar, and water to remaining butter and heat to boiling, stirring occasionally. Remove crescents from can in rolled sections and cut each section into 4 slices. Form each slice into a loose pinwheel, enlarging the circumference by pulling it apart. It does not have to look neat but must be very loose for best results. Arrange 8 slices over bottom of pan. Pour 1 tablespoon of the sugar mixture over each pinwheel. Place remaining 8 slices directly over those in pan and cover with remaining sugar mixture. Bake at 350° for 30 minutes or until golden brown. Cool 1 minute and turn onto a serving platter or waxed paper. Serve hot. *This is a revision of my grand prize winning recipe in the official Pillsbury Bake-Off Contest.*

Mrs. Bert Groves (Lois)

Sopaipillas

1½	cups flour	1	egg, slightly beaten
¾	teaspoon salt	⅓	cup water
2	teaspoons baking powder		Shortening or oil for deep frying

Combine flour, salt, baking powder, and egg with just enough water to make a stiff dough. Knead until smooth, roll out very thin, and cut into triangle or diamond shapes. Fry in deep, hot 400°F-425°F, shortening, turning several times to make them puff evenly. When brown and puffed, drain on paper towels and serve at once. *Sopaipillas were originally served as a dessert with honey, confectioners' sugar with cinnamon, or anise flavored syrup.*
Yields 1½-2 dozen.
Mrs. Chalmers Broadfoot

Bitsy's Melba Toast

| 1 | long, narrow loaf French bread, frozen | 1 | teaspoon Lawry's seasoned salt |
| | | 2 | sticks butter, melted |

Thinly slice bread. Brush each slice with a mixture of salt and butter. Place on baking sheet and toast at 300° for 1-1½ hours. Store in airtight container. *Crispy and delicious!*
Serves 10.
Mrs. Rollins Rubsamen (Florence "Bitsy" Ayres)

Golden Corn Bread

⅓ cup flour
2 teaspoons baking powder
2 tablespoons sugar
½ teaspoon salt
⅓ cup cornmeal

⅓ cup wheat germ
1 large egg
½ cup milk
2 tablespoons vegetable oil

Sift together flour, baking powder, sugar, and salt. Add cornmeal and wheat germ, mixing thoroughly. Beat egg lightly; then stir in milk and oil. Add egg mixture to flour mixture, stirring just until well mixed. Pour into a 4 x 8 lightly greased loaf pan and bake at 400° for 25-30 minutes.
Serves 2-3. Recipe may be tripled.
Mrs. William McNeel (Amy Lillian McNutt)

Jungle Oats Fritters

4 tablespoons flour
4 tablespoons cooked oatmeal, cooled
1 small onion, minced

2 eggs, well beaten
Salt and pepper to taste
1 teaspoon baking powder
Vegetable oil or bacon drippings

Mix flour and oatmeal. Add onion, eggs, salt, pepper, and then baking powder. Drop by tablespoonful into boiling oil and cook until brown on both sides. *A favorite South African recipe.*
Yields 10-12.
Mrs. Frates Seeligson (Martita Rice)

Indian Fry Bread

3 cups flour or ½ white and ½ whole wheat
1¼ teaspoons baking powder

½ teaspoon salt
1⅓ cups warm water
2 cups vegetable oil

Mix flour, baking powder, and salt. Add water and knead until dough is soft but not sticky. Stretch and pat dough until thin. Tear off 1 piece at a time, poke a hole through the middle like a doughnut, and drop into a kettle of sizzling hot oil. Brown on both sides. Serve hot.

Mrs. Harry E. Brown (Carolyn Carlisle)

Onion Corn Bread

½ cup chopped onion
¼ stick butter
1 package corn bread mix

½ cup grated sharp yellow cheese
½ cup sour cream

Sauté onion in butter until tender. Mix corn bread according to package directions, pour into a buttered 8 x 8 x 2 pan, and sprinkle with onion. Combine cheese with sour cream and spread over corn bread batter and onion. Bake at 400° according to package directions. Cool for a few minutes before cutting into squares.
Serves 6-8.
Mrs. Walter Hale, III (Janin Sinclair)

Onion Cheese Bread

½ cup chopped onion
1 tablespoon oil
1 egg, beaten
½ cup milk

1½ cups Bisquick
1 cup grated sharp cheese
1 tablespoon poppy seeds
¼ stick butter, melted

Sauté onions in oil until tender and light brown. Add egg and milk to Bisquick and stir lightly. Add onion and ½ of the cheese. Spread dough in greased pie pan, sprinkle with remaining cheese and poppy seeds, and drizzle with butter. Bake at 400° for 20-25 minutes. Serve hot.
Serves 6.
Mrs. John F. Loyd (Annette Emerson)

Oven Buttered Corn Sticks

½ stick butter or margarine
1 8¾ ounce can creamed corn

2 cups Bisquick

Melt butter in a 15½ x 10½ x 1 baking or jelly roll pan. Combine corn and Bisquick in a bowl, stirring until a soft dough is formed. Turn out on a board floured with Bisquick and knead 15 strokes. Roll into a 6 x 10 inch rectangle and cut into 1 x 3 inch strips. Place in melted butter and turn over, buttering both sides. Arrange in pan in a single layer. Bake at 450° for 10-12 minutes.
Serves 8-12. Freezes.
Mrs. William W. Coates, III (Sue Schoeneck)

Spoon Bread

1	cup white cornmeal	1	teaspoon butter
3	cups milk	4	egg yolks, beaten
1	teaspoon salt	4	egg whites, beaten
1	teaspoon sugar		Butter

In a 2 quart saucepan, combine cornmeal, milk, salt, sugar, and 1 teaspoon butter. Cook, stirring constantly, until you have a thick mush. Set aside to cool. Blend in yolks and then fold in whites. Pour into a 2 quart casserole and set in a pan of water. Bake at 350° for 1 hour or until done. Serve at once with butter.
Serves 6.
Mrs. Frank J. Siebenaler (Louise)

French Breakfast Puffs

1	cup sugar, divided	½	teaspoon salt
⅓	cup shortening	¼	teaspoon nutmeg
1	egg	½	cup milk
1½	cups sifted flour	1	teaspoon cinnamon
1½	teaspoons baking powder	¾	stick butter or margarine, melted

In mixer bowl, cream ½ cup sugar, shortening, and egg. Sift together flour, baking powder, salt, and nutmeg. Add to creamed mixture alternately with milk, beating well after each addition. Fill 12 greased muffin cups. Bake at 350° for 20-25 minutes. Combine remaining sugar and cinnamon. Remove muffins from oven and immediately dip in melted butter. Roll in the sugar mixture until coated. Serve warm.
Yields 12.
Mrs. Robert L. Cook (Sandra Mueller)

Popovers

6	eggs	¾	stick butter, melted and slightly cooled
2	cups milk		
2	cups flour	½	teaspoon salt

Combine all ingredients, stirring only slightly as batter should be lumpy. Fill buttered glass custard cups ½ full with batter and bake at 350°-375° for 45 minutes. Do not open oven until baking is complete. *Serve immediately with honey or jam and butter.*
Yields 12.
Mrs. W. Trent Harkrader, III (Bonnie)

301

Isabel's Treacle Scones

1	cup flour	½	stick butter
1	rounded teaspoon baking powder	3	tablespoons treacle or blackstrap
½	teaspoon salt		molasses
2	rounded tablespoons sugar	1	level teaspoon baking soda, dissolved
1	teaspoon ground ginger		in 1 tablespoon milk
1	rounded teaspoon cinnamon	⅓-½	cup milk

Combine dry ingredients, cut in butter, and mix in treacle. Add soda and enough milk to make a soft dough. Drop walnut-sized pieces of dough on a floured baking sheet. Bake at 350°-375° for about 10-15 minutes. Be cautious about overcooking as treacle burns easily. *This recipe was obtained from a Scottish gentlewoman.*
Serves 6.
Mrs. F. R. Veach, Jr. (Dorothy Ann)

Cottage Cheese Pancakes with Blueberries

2	cups large curd cottage cheese	1	cup flour
1	tablespoon lemon juice	1	package fresh or frozen blueberries,
¼	cup sugar		or other fruit
Pinch of salt		Sugar to taste	
2	large eggs	½	pint sour cream, optional

Beat cottage cheese until creamy. Add lemon juice, sugar, salt, and eggs, mixing well. Stir in flour. Batter may be made ahead and refrigerated. When ready to serve drop by spoonfuls onto a heated and well buttered griddle and cook on both sides until golden brown. Serve with blueberries heated with sugar. Top with sour cream. *These are elegant for breakfast or dessert.*
Serves 6.
Mrs. Charles Michael Montgomery (Gladys Fae Cooper)

Beer Batter Muffins

4	cups Bisquick	½	cup sugar
1	12 ounce can beer		

Mix all ingredients. Fill greased muffin cups ½ full and bake at 350° for 20 minutes.
Yields approximately 1 dozen.
Mrs. Helen Brooks Purifoy (Suzie)

Cherry Blossom Muffins

1 egg, slightly beaten	½ cup chopped pecans
⅔ cup orange juice	2 tablespoons flour
6 tablespoons sugar, divided	½ teaspoon nutmeg
2 tablespoons vegetable oil	1 tablespoon butter
2 cups biscuit mix	½ cup cherry preserves

In a mixing bowl, combine egg, orange juice, 2 tablespoons sugar, and oil. Add biscuit mix, beat vigorously for 30 seconds, and stir in pecans. In a separate bowl, combine remaining sugar, flour, and nutmeg. Cut in butter until mixture is crumbly and reserve for topping. Grease 12 muffin cups or fill cups with paper liners. Fill muffin cups ⅓ full with batter, place 2 teaspoons cherry preserves in the center of each, and cover with remaining batter until ⅔ full. Sprinkle with topping. Bake at 400° for 20-25 minutes.
Yields 12. Freezes.
Mrs. J. Ross Crawford (Judith Claire Bennett)

Ginger Bran Muffins

1 egg, slightly beaten	3 teaspoons baking powder
1 cup milk	½ cup sugar
¼ stick butter, melted	¼ cup brown sugar
2 tablespoons molasses	½ teaspoon salt
1 cup bran	1½ teaspoons cinnamon
1 cup flour	1½ teaspoons ground ginger

Mix egg, milk, butter, molasses, and bran in a large bowl and allow to stand 10 minutes. Sift together flour, baking powder, sugars, salt, cinnamon, and ginger. Add to liquid mixture and stir just enough to dampen flour. Spoon into buttered muffin tins. Bake at 400° for 25 minutes.
Yields 12.
Mrs. Michael Shane Brenan (Judy Kay Mason)

Prune Muffins

2 cups sugar	1 teaspoon cinnamon
1 cup oil	1 teaspoon nutmeg
3 eggs, beaten	1 teaspoon allspice
2 cups flour	1 cup buttermilk
1 teaspoon soda	2 jars baby food prunes
1 teaspoon salt	1 teaspoon vanilla

Mix sugar, oil, and eggs. Sift together flour, soda, salt, and spices. Combine buttermilk and prunes. Blend in sifted ingredients alternately with buttermilk mixture. Add vanilla. Bake in well greased and floured muffin tins at 350° for 30 minutes.
Yields about 40 muffins.
Mrs. Larry J. O'Neill (Liz Hamilton)

Tea Muffins

2½	sticks margarine	4	cups flour
1	cup sugar	¼	teaspoon ground ginger
4	eggs	½	teaspoon cinnamon
½	cup molasses	⅔	cup chopped pecans
1	cup buttermilk	¾	cup raisins
2	teaspoons soda		

Cream margarine and sugar. Add eggs one at a time. Combine molasses, buttermilk, and soda and add to the butter mixture, mixing well. Add flour and spices. Stir in pecans and raisins. Fill small greased muffin tins ½ full and bake at 425° for 20 minutes.
Yields 5 dozen small muffins.
Mrs. Eleanor Weed

Bishop's Bread

½	cup shortening	1	teaspoon soda
2	cups brown sugar	1	cup buttermilk
2	cups flour	1	egg, well beaten
2	teaspoons cinnamon		

Cream shortening and sugar. Sift together flour and cinnamon and combine with creamed mixture. Remove ¾ cup and set aside to use for topping. Dissolve soda in buttermilk and add to mixture. Stir in egg and pour into a greased 8 x 12 pan or 2 quart glass dish. Sprinkle with reserved topping and bake at 350° for 30 minutes. Cut in squares and serve hot. *A family specialty to serve for company.*
Yields 16-20 squares.
Mrs. Charles W. Harper (Margaret Biedenharn)

Cheese Biscuits

2½	cups grated sharp Cheddar cheese	2	tablespoons shortening
¾	cup flour	⅛	teaspoon salt
¼	cup water	⅛	teaspoon cayenne pepper

Mix all ingredients into a thick dough. Roll to ⅓ inch thickness and cut into biscuit shapes. Bake at 400° until light brown.
Yields 84 biscuits or 200 cheese straws. May be quadrupled.
Mrs. Arthur M. Eldridge

Sausage Biscuits

10 ounces sharp Cheddar cheese, grated	1 pound bulk sausage
	3½ cups biscuit mix

Melt cheese in a double boiler. Brown sausage until almost done and drain well. Thoroughly combine cheese, sausage, and biscuit mix. Roll out and cut with biscuit cutter. Bake at 375° for 15-20 minutes, turning once.
Yields 2-3 dozen. Freezes well before baking.
Mrs. W. J. Lyons, Jr. (Martha "Molly" Collett)

Sour Cream Biscuits

1 cup self-rising flour	½ cup sour cream
1 stick margarine	

Combine ingredients. Drop by teaspoonful onto baking sheet and bake at 350° for 18 minutes.
Yields 2 dozen.
Mrs. Tony Chauveaux (Kathryn Williams)

Sweet Potato Biscuits

¾ cup mashed sweet potatoes, fresh or canned	1¼ cups flour
⅔ cup milk	4 teaspoons baking powder
½ stick butter, melted	1 tablespoon sugar
	½ teaspoon salt

Combine sweet potatoes, milk, and butter. Sift remaining ingredients together and add to sweet potato mixture to make a soft dough. Turn out on a well floured board and knead lightly until the outside looks smooth. Roll out ½ inch thick, cut with a floured biscuit cutter, and place on a greased baking sheet. Bake at 425° for 15 minutes. Serve hot. *Excellent with game.*
Yields 16-18. Freezes.
Mrs. John H. Foster (Phoebe)

Oatmeal Coffee Cake

Cake

1½ cups boiling water	1½ cups flour
1 cup quick oatmeal	1 teaspoon soda
1 cup brown sugar	½ teaspoon salt
1 cup sugar	½ teaspoon cinnamon
2 eggs, beaten	1 tablespoon vanilla

Topping

2 egg yolks, beaten	1 cup chopped pecans
1½ cups grated coconut	1 tablespoon milk
1 cup brown sugar	1 stick butter, melted

Cake   Pour water over oatmeal and add remaining cake ingredients. Place batter into 2 greased and floured 8 x 8 pans. Bake at 350° for 25-30 minutes.

Topping   Combine the first 5 ingredients and stir in butter. Spread over hot cake, return to oven, and toast.

Mrs. Middleton S. English (Shirley Fitch)

Cream Cheese Coffee Cake

Cake

1 stick butter or margarine	2 cups flour
8 ounces cream cheese	2 teaspoons baking powder
1½ cups sugar	½ teaspoon soda
2 eggs	½ teaspoon salt
1 teaspoon vanilla	½ cup milk

Topping

½ stick butter, softened	½ cup packed brown sugar
1 cup flour	½ cup chopped nuts

Cake   Cream butter, cream cheese, and sugar. Blend in eggs and vanilla. Sift together dry ingredients and add to creamed mixture alternately with milk. Pour batter into a greased 13 x 9 x 2 pan.

Topping   Combine topping ingredients and sprinkle over batter. Bake at 350° for 30-40 minutes or until toothpick comes out clean.
Serves 20.
Mrs. Chesley Wiggins Johnston (Kathryn Wynter Wood)

Butterscotch Coffee Cake

1	18½ ounce package yellow cake mix	¾	cup water
1	3¾ ounce package butterscotch pudding mix	½	cup sugar
		1	tablespoon cocoa
4	eggs	1	teaspoon cinnamon
⅔	cup vegetable oil		Confectioners' sugar, optional

Blend cake and pudding mixes. Add eggs, oil, and water and beat well with electric mixer for 10 minutes. Pour batter into a greased and floured 10 inch tube pan. Combine sugar, cocoa, and cinnamon and sprinkle over batter. Cut mixture through batter to form marble effect. Bake at 350° for 1 hour. Cool upright 15 minutes. Loosen edges and turn cake upside down to remove. Sprinkle with confectioners' sugar.
Serves 16.
Mrs. George R. Bristol (Patricia Peterson)

Smetina Cake
Sour Cream Coffee Cake

Cake

1	cup sugar	2	cups flour
1	cup smetina or sour cream	1½	teaspoons baking powder
1	stick butter or margarine	½	teaspoon baking soda
2	eggs, at room temperature	2	1 pound cans apple, blueberry, cherry, or peach pie filling
1	teaspoon vanilla		

Topping

4	tablespoons flour	1	teaspoon cinnamon
3	tablespoons butter or margarine, softened	½	cup sugar

Cake   Cream sugar, smetina, butter, eggs, and vanilla. Sift together flour, baking powder, and soda. Add flour mixture to creamed mixture. This dough may be stored in refrigerator, covered, for up to a week. Place batter into a greased and floured 9 x 13 pan or 2 round 9 inch pans. Dough will be sticky, so use a wet spoon to spread, allowing more batter around edges. Spoon pie filling over batter just before baking.

Topping   Cut together topping ingredients and sprinkle over filling. Bake at 350° for 45-50 minutes. Dough around edges will be golden brown when done. Serve hot.
Serves 10-12.
Mrs. Thomas P. DeFossett

Alabama Biscuits

2	cups buttermilk	4	tablespoons sugar
5	cups sifted flour	1	cup shortening
1	teaspoon salt	2	tablespoons dry yeast, dissolved in
1	teaspoon soda		¼ cup warm water

Heat buttermilk until lukewarm. Sift together dry ingredients and cream with shortening. Add buttermilk and yeast mixture. Turn out on a floured board and knead well. Roll dough to ¼ inch, and cut into small biscuits using a jigger or cutter about 1½ inches in diameter. Stack 2 together to form each biscuit and place side by side in greased pans. Biscuits may be frozen at this point if desired. Let dough rise 2-3 hours. If the dough has been frozen allow more time to rise. Bake at 425° for 12-15 minutes.
Yields approximately 8 dozen.
Mrs. Jack L. Conger (Sarah Jo Williams)

Celebration Bread

1	package dry yeast	2	tablespoons brown sugar
¼	cup warm water	1	teaspoon salt
1	cup milk	4-5	cups unbleached white flour
⅔	stick butter	1	egg, beaten

Soften yeast in warm water. Heat milk and butter until milk is scalded and butter is melted. Let cool to lukewarm. Add milk, butter, sugar, and salt to yeast. Let stand for 10-15 minutes until foamy. Stir in 2 cups flour until well mixed. Let rise 1 hour or until doubled. Add remaining flour. Knead 2-4 minutes or until dough is smooth. Let rise 30-45 minutes or until doubled. Mold bread into desired shapes. Bake at 350° in a pan or on a baking sheet until bread begins to brown. Brush with beaten egg for last 5 minutes of baking. Baking time is approximately 20 minutes but depends on shape and size. *This bread is used at Learning About Learning and is often seen baked into birds, fish, Santas, or any shape desired. It is delicious and may be topped with a sugar glaze.*

Mrs. Jay Monday (Susie)

Cottage Bread

2¾	cups lukewarm water	1	tablespoon salt
2	packages dry yeast	¼	stick butter or margarine, softened
¼	cup sugar	7	cups sifted flour

In a large bowl combine water and yeast. Stir until dissolved. Add sugar, salt, and butter. Add 4 cups of flour and beat at medium speed for 2 minutes. Add remaining flour, mixing thoroughly with a large spoon. Turn into a lightly greased bowl, cover with a damp cloth, and let rise about 1 hour or until doubled. Punch down, divide, and turn into 2 well greased loaf pans. Cover and let rise again about 1 hour or until doubled. Bake at 375° for 45 minutes. Let cool in pans for 5 minutes; then turn out on cooling rack.
Yields 2 loaves.
Mrs. Michael Kangerga (Nancy Russell)

Country Loaf

1	package dry yeast	¾	pound unbleached white flour, or
Pinch of sugar			3 cups
2	tablespoons + 1¼ cups warm water, divided	¼	pound unbleached whole wheat flour, or 1 cup
2	teaspoons salt		

Dissolve yeast and sugar in 2 tablespoons water. Let stand until foamy. Dissolve salt in remaining water. Add yeast mixture and salted water to flours. Knead in a bowl until dough becomes elastic and leaves sides of bowl. Form into a ball and dust with flour. Place in a clean bowl, cover with a towel, and let rise in a warm place about 1 hour or until doubled. Turn onto a floured board and knead 5 minutes. Form into a ball and place in a well floured 8 inch banneton (French reed basket) or any tightly woven basket to give the bread a beehive appearance. Let rise until doubled, then turn out onto a greased and floured baking sheet, and bake at 450° for 15 minutes, then at 400° for 30 minutes.
Yields 1 loaf.
Mrs. Hall Street Hammond (Patricia Wilcox)

Dillon Bread

8	cups unbleached white flour	½	cup honey
1	cup whole wheat flour	¼	cup molasses, optional
1	cup powdered milk	4	cups hot tap water, 120°F-130°F
3	packages dry yeast	½	cup oatmeal, optional
1	tablespoon salt	1½	cups wheat germ
½	cup vegetable oil		

In a large bowl combine 3 cups white flour with all dry ingredients, except wheat germ and oatmeal, and blend well. Add oil, honey, and molasses, mixing well. Add water and beat until all chunks are broken. Mix in remaining flour, oatmeal, and wheat germ. Knead 5-7 minutes, place in a greased container, and cover with a towel. Let rise until doubled in bulk, but not longer than 30-45 minutes. Divide into fourths and shape into loaves. Place in greased loaf pans, cover with a towel, and let rise until doubled in bulk. Bake at 400° for 15 minutes. Reduce heat to 375° and bake for 25-30 minutes. Cool on racks. *This recipe is used by enthusiastic bread bakers at Christ Episcopal Church to raise money for the task force on hunger.*

Note The oven is a good place in which to let bread rise. Place a broiler pan full of hot water on the bottom rack. Place dough on a rack over hot water and leave oven turned off.
Yields 4 loaves.
Mrs. David Dillon (Rowena Maverick McNeel)

When cutting fresh bread, dip knife in boiling water and you can then cut thin slices.

English Muffins

1   cup milk
2   tablespoons sugar
1   teaspoon salt
3   tablespoons butter
1   cup warm water, 105°F-115°F

1   package dry yeast
1½ cups whole wheat flour
3½ cups flour
Cornmeal

Scald the milk. Stir in sugar, salt, and butter and cool to lukewarm. Put water in a large bowl, sprinkle in yeast, and stir until dissolved. Stir in milk mixture and 3 cups flour, beating until smooth. Add enough additional flour to make a stiff dough. Turn out onto a floured board and knead about 2 minutes or until dough is manageable and can be formed into a ball, though it might still be slightly sticky. Place in a greased bowl, turning dough once to grease top. Cover and let rise in a warm place about 1 hour or until doubled. Punch dough down and divide. On a board heavily sprinkled with cornmeal, pat each half into a ½ inch thickness. Cut in circles with a floured 3 inch cookie cutter. Place on baking sheet about 2 inches apart. Cover and let rise in a warm place 30 minutes or until doubled. Heat a lightly greased griddle or skillet to 350° and place muffins on griddle, cornmeal side down. Brown about 10 minutes on each side. Cool on wire racks.
Yields approximately 20 muffins.
Mrs. Hall Street Hammond (Patricia Wilcox)

French Bread

1   package dry yeast
2   teaspoons salt
2   cups warm water
2   tablespoons sugar

5-6 cups flour
1   egg, beaten
Cornmeal
Sesame or poppy seeds, optional

Mix yeast, salt, water, sugar, and flour in a bowl. Knead on a floured board and let rise in a greased bowl until doubled. May be allowed to rise in refrigerator overnight. Knead again. Divide and shape into 2 oblong loaves. Place on a greased baking sheet that has been sprinkled with cornmeal and let rise until doubled. Make diagonal slashes on top with a sharp knife. Brush with egg and sprinkle with sesame seeds just before baking. Bake at 350° for 30-40 minutes.
Yields 2 loaves.
Miss Mills Hammond

Indian Bread

3	cups whole wheat flour	⅔	stick butter
2	packages dry yeast	1½	cups regular rolled oats
2½	cups buttermilk	2	eggs
¼	cup molasses	2½-3	cups flour
¼	cup honey	¼	stick butter, melted
1	tablespoon salt		

Grease two 1½ quart round 2½ inch deep casseroles or two 9 x 5 x 3 pans. Combine whole wheat flour and yeast. Heat buttermilk, molasses, honey, salt, and butter until warm, 105°F-110°F. Pour into a 3 quart mixing bowl. Add oats, whole wheat mixture, and eggs. Blend at low speed with electric mixer until moistened. Beat 3 minutes at high speed. Stir in enough flour to make a stiff dough. Brush with melted butter. Cover and let rise in a warm place about 1 hour or until doubled. Punch down, shape into loaves, and place in baking dishes. Cover and let rise about 45 minutes or until doubled. Bake at 375° for 25-35 minutes or until loaf sounds hollow when tapped.
Yields 2 loaves.
Mrs. Robert Lull (Marianna "Penny" Mead)

Shaker Wheaton Bread

1	cup milk	1	cake yeast or 1 package dry yeast
1	tablespoon salt	2	cups flour
4	tablespoons honey or maple syrup	4	cups whole wheat flour
3	tablespoons butter		Melted butter
1	cup warm water, divided		

Scald milk and add salt, honey, butter, and ¾ cup water. Stir well and cool to lukewarm. Dissolve yeast in remaining water and add to other liquid. Add flours gradually and knead into a smooth ball, about 1 minute. Place in a buttered bowl and brush top with melted butter. Let rise until doubled. Knead lightly, shape into 1-2 loaves, and place in greased pan. Brush with melted butter and let rise until doubled. Bake at 350° for 50-60 minutes. *This recipe came from Judy Burris who lives in a large Shaker community.*
Yields 1 large or 2 small loaves.
Mrs. Edgar M. Duncan (Linda Wyatt)

Whole Wheat Bread

3	cups warm water	1	tablespoon salt
¾	cup honey	½	stick margarine
3	cakes yeast	4-6	cups whole wheat flour

In the large bowl of mixer, combine water, honey, and yeast, and let stand for 5 minutes. Add salt and margarine, mixing well. Slowly beat in the flour until dough is stiff. Continue beating for 7 minutes. Place all dough on a large, generously floured board. Knead dough until stiff. Place dough in a greased bowl and let rise for about 50 minutes in a warm place. Punch dough down and knead in bowl. Divide dough into 2-3 loaves and place in pans. Let rise 30-60 minutes. Bake at 350° for 50 minutes. *You may use all whole wheat flour or part white, part whole wheat, part stone ground, or whatever combination you prefer.*

Mrs. Hull Youngblood, Jr. (Carolee Ewing)

Travis School Bread

6	tablespoons dry yeast	1½	cups shortening, melted
1	cup warm water	2	eggs
5	cups warm milk	1	tablespoon salt
1½	cups sugar	5	pounds flour, or 20 cups

Dissolve yeast in water. Add milk, sugar, shortening, eggs, and salt. Mix well. Add flour and mix thoroughly. Put in a greased bowl. Let rise until doubled. Divide into 6 loaves and let rise again. Bake at 400° about 35 minutes.
Yields 6 loaves. Recipe may be halved.
Mrs. Arthur M. Eldridge

Sour Dough Bread

1	package dry yeast	¾	tablespoon oil or soft shortening
½	cup warm water	2	cups self-rising flour
1	cup sour dough starter		

Dissolve yeast in water and add to starter. Stir in oil and flour, mixing well. Let rise 30 minutes. Punch down and knead on floured board until smooth. Let rise 50-60 minutes, form into loaf, and bake at 325° for 30 minutes or until done. *This recipe may also be used for rolls.*

Mrs. Edward E. DeWees, Jr. (Rebecca Ruth Davis)

Swiss Cheese Bread

5	cups flour, divided	1	cup milk
3	tablespoons sugar	¼	stick butter
1½	tablespoons salt	1½	cups grated Swiss cheese
2	packages dry yeast	1	egg
1	cup water		

In bowl of mixer, combine 2 cups flour, sugar, salt, and yeast and set aside. In a saucepan, heat water and milk with butter until warm and bubbles form around the edge. Add liquid to yeast mixture, a little at a time, and beat 2 minutes. Add cheese, ½ cup flour, egg, and beat 2 minutes. Stir in remaining flour. Let dough rise, covered, for 1½ hours or until doubled. Beat dough with a wooden spoon 30 seconds and divide into 2 buttered 1 quart soufflé dishes. Bake at 375° for 40-50 minutes. *To serve, slice bread, butter, and put more grated cheese on top. Wrap in foil and heat.*
Yields 2 loaves.
Mrs. Lewis Jefferson Moorman, III (Nancy Clark Wood)

Potato Rolls

1 cake yeast	1 cup mashed potatoes
¼ cup warm water	2 sticks butter, melted
4 eggs	1 cup cold water
¾ cup sugar	6½ cups flour
1 teaspoon salt	Melted butter for dipping

Dissolve yeast in warm water. Beat eggs and add sugar, salt, and mashed potatoes. Add 2 sticks butter, cold water, and yeast mixture. Add flour and mix well with hands. Cover and refrigerate for 24 hours. Roll out ¼ inch thick on a floured board, cut with a 2½-3 inch cutter, dip in butter, and fold. Bake at 350° for 25 minutes.
Yields 9½ dozen rolls.
Mrs. James F. Huff (Virginia "Scootie" Ann Day)

Butterhorn Rolls

¾ cup milk, scalded	1 tablespoon yeast, dissolved in
1 stick butter or margarine	¼ cup water
½ teaspoon salt	4 cups flour
½ cup sugar	Melted butter
2-3 eggs, well beaten	

To milk, add 1 stick butter, salt, and sugar, cooling until lukewarm, 115°F. Add eggs, yeast, and ½ of the flour. Beat until free from lumps, then add remaining flour. Let rise until doubled. Divide dough in half and roll each to less than ½ inch thickness and as nearly round as possible. Brush with butter; then cut each into 16 pie-shaped wedges. Roll each wedge from the widest point toward the center point. Let rise for 3 hours or until desired size. Bake at 400° for 10 minutes. *This recipe was used in the Neiman-Marcus cookbook, Taste of Texas, but I gave them the recipe.*

Mrs. Rapier Dawson (Polly Butte)

Wellington Icebox Rolls

1¼	teaspoons salt	¾	cup warm water
1	stick + 3 tablespoons butter or margarine	½	cup sugar
2	cups milk, scalded	5½-6	cups flour
1½	packages dry yeast	1	egg, well beaten

Combine salt and butter with milk and let cool. Dissolve yeast in water. Add the dissolved yeast and sugar to the milk mixture. Add ½ the flour, egg, and then remaining flour, mixing thoroughly. Put in a greased bowl, cover with a damp cloth, and refrigerate for 24 hours. This will keep in refrigerator a week or more. Shape into rolls and let rise until doubled in bulk. Bake at 375° until brown.

Mrs. John Robert Beauchamp (Francis Ann Drake)

Holiday Sweet Bread

2	cups milk	½	cup warm water
1	stick butter	7-8	cups flour
1½	cups sugar	2	eggs, beaten
2	teaspoons salt	1	egg
2	teaspoons vanilla	1	tablespoon water
¼	teaspoon anise flavoring, optional	Sesame seeds	
2	cakes yeast		

Heat milk and butter just until bubbles begin to appear around edge of pan; then remove. Add sugar, salt, and flavorings, stirring well until sugar is dissolved. Cool to lukewarm. Crumble yeast into bowl of an electric mixer, add water, and mix with a spoon until dissolved. Combine ½ of milk mixture and 1 cup flour. Beat on low speed until batter is smooth. Add remaining milk mixture, 1 cup flour, and beaten eggs, beating until smooth. Add enough of the remaining flour and stir by hand until dough is no longer sticky. Knead dough for 8-10 minutes on a floured surface. Place dough in a large, greased bowl, cover, and let rise in a warm place free from draft about 1 hour or until doubled. Punch dough down and let rest 10 minutes. Divide dough into 3 parts, shaping each into a loaf. Place into greased 9 x 5 x 3 loaf pans, cover, and let rise in warm place for about 1 hour. Beat egg with 1 tablespoon water, brush loaves gently, and sprinkle with sesame seeds. Place on a rack in the lower third of oven. Bake at 400° for 15 minutes; then reduce heat to 350° and bake 15-20 minutes longer. Test by turning loaf out of pan and tapping bottom with knuckles. A hollow sound means bread is done. Cool on racks.
Yields 3 loaves. Freezes.
Mrs. Daniel J. Nichols

Christmas Stöllen

2	cups warm water, divided	1¼	cups candied mixed fruit
2	packages dry yeast	¾	cup candied cherries
½	cup sugar	1	cup raisins
2	teaspoons salt	2	tablespoons grated lemon rind
2	eggs		Soft butter
½	cup shortening		Confectioners' sugar
7-7½	cups sifted flour		Milk
1	cup slivered almonds, finely chopped		Slivered almonds, red candied cherries, and green candied fruit, for garnish

In the large bowl of an electric mixer, combine ½ cup water and yeast, stirring to dissolve. Add remaining water, sugar, salt, eggs, shortening, 3½ cups flour, almonds, fruits, and lemon rind. With spoon or hands, add enough of the remaining flour to handle easily. Turn onto a lightly floured board, and knead about 5 minutes or until smooth and elastic. Form into ball in a greased bowl and turn dough so greased side is up. Cover bowl loosely with waxed paper and a damp towel. Let rise in a warm place about 1½ hours or until doubled. Turn out and divide into fourths. Roll or pat each into an oval about 8 x 12 inches. Spread with butter, fold over lengthwise, and form into a slight crescent. Press folded edge down firmly so it will not spring open. Place crescents on 2 greased baking sheets, brush tops with butter, and cover with waxed paper and a damp cloth. Let rise again about 35-45 minutes or until doubled. Bake at 350° for 30-35 minutes or until golden and hollow sounding. Remove to racks to cool. Sift confectioners' sugar into bowl and add enough milk for a spreading consistency. Frost loaves while warm with icing. Some will probably run off but this makes it pretty. Add cherry halves, pieces of green fruit, and slivered almonds to look like poinsettias. Let cool thoroughly and wrap for freezing if desired.

Yields 4 loaves. Freezes.
Mrs. William W. Coates, III (Sue Schoeneck)

317

Danish Sweet Bread

2	cups milk	2	packages dry yeast
1	cup honey	3	eggs
2	teaspoons salt	1½	sticks butter or margarine, softened
1	teaspoon ground cardamom	7-8	cups flour, sifted

Scald milk and cool to lukewarm. Pour into a large bowl, add honey, salt, and cardamom, and sprinkle with yeast. Stir to dissolve yeast, add eggs and butter, and mix well. Add about 4 cups of flour, 1 cup at a time, beating until smooth. Gradually add remaining flour. When dough holds together and leaves the sides of the bowl, turn out on a floured board and knead 8-10 minutes, adding flour as needed to prevent sticking. When dough is smooth and resilient, shape into a ball. Place in a well greased bowl, cover, and let rise in a warm, draft free place 1½-2 hours or until doubled in bulk. Punch dough down, cover, and let rise again until doubled. Shape into 3 loaves and place in 9 x 5 x 3 loaf pans. Cover and let rise. Bake at 350° about 40 minutes or until bread is browned on top and firm to the touch. Let cool in pans on a rack 10-15 minutes. Turn out on rack to finish cooling. *This dough when wrapped in plastic wrap may be kept in the refrigerator 2-3 days and may also be used for sweet rolls and brioches.*

Yields 3 loaves. Freezes well.
Colonel Frank N. Leakey

Use your favorite sweet bread dough for sopaipillas. Simply roll the dough, cut into squares, and deep fry.

Mission San Francisco de la Espada

"One-quarter of a league from the preceding mission and three from the preceding mission and three from the presidio of San Antonio, on the west side of the river, is the mission of Nuestro Santo Padre San Francisco de la Espada... The church was demolished because it threatened to fall down, and services are being held in an ample room that has a choir and a sacristy, all very neat."

History of Texas, 1673-1779. Fray Juan Augustin Morfi.

Almond Crunch Cake

Cake

1½ cups sifted flour
1½ cups sugar, divided
8 eggs, separated
¼ cup cold water

1 tablespoon lemon juice
1 teaspoon vanilla
1 teaspoon cream of tartar
1 teaspoon salt

Almond Brittle Topping

1½ cups sugar
¼ teaspoon instant coffee
¼ cup light corn syrup
¼ cup hot water
1 tablespoon sifted soda

2-2½ cups heavy cream
2 tablespoons sugar
2 teaspoons vanilla
Almonds, blanched, halved, and
toasted

Cake Sift together flour and ¾ cup sugar. Make a well in the center, add egg yolks, water, lemon juice, vanilla, and beat until smooth. Beat egg whites, cream of tartar, and salt just until soft peaks form. Add remaining sugar, 2 tablespoons at a time, continuing to beat until stiff. Fold flour mixture gently into egg whites. Pour batter into a 10 inch tube pan or two 2 quart baking pans. Do not grease pan. Cut carefully through the batter, going around tube 5 or 6 times with a knife, to break air bubbles. Bake at 350° for 50-55 minutes or until top springs back when lightly touched. Invert pan 1 hour or until cool. Remove cake and split in 4 equal layers if using a tube pan. Make either 2 or 4 layers if using baking pans.

Almond Brittle Topping Combine sugar, coffee, syrup, and water in a saucepan, stirring well. Cook to hard crack stage, 290°F, remove from heat, and add soda. Stir vigorously until mixture blends and pulls away from sides of pan. Quickly pour into a shallow baking sheet. Do not grease sheet. Let stand until cool. Knock out of pan and crush candy with a rolling pin into small chunks. Whip cream and fold in sugar and vanilla. Spread ½ of cream between cake layers and remainder over top and sides. Cover top and sides with candy, lightly pressing into cream. Decorate with almonds. Do not press candy and almonds into cream more than 6 hours before serving. Refrigerate.

The Bright Shawl Tearoom

Eight large eggs when separated yield approximately ¾ cup yolks and 1 cup whites. The yolks and whites may be successfully frozen separately in airtight containers.

Apricot Prune Cake

1	12 ounce package prunes, chopped	½	teaspoon nutmeg
2	6 ounce packages apricots, chopped	1	teaspoon cinnamon
⅓	cup + 2½ cups sugar, divided	1	teaspoon ground cloves
1-1¼	cups boiling water	1	teaspoon soda
1	cup vegetable oil	1	teaspoon salt
3	eggs	1	teaspoon allspice
1	teaspoon vanilla	1	cup buttermilk
2½	cups flour	½	cup pecans

Combine fruit with ⅓ cup sugar. Pour water over fruit and simmer 15 minutes. In a mixer combine 2½ cups sugar, oil, eggs, and vanilla. Sift dry ingredients together. Add flour mixture and buttermilk alternately to egg mixture. Fold in pecans and fruit. Pour batter into a greased and floured 10 inch bundt pan. Bake at 350° for 1 hour.

Mrs. Wilbur F. Littleton, Jr. (Jean Richards)

German Apple Cake

2	large eggs	½	teaspoon salt
1	cup vegetable oil	4	cups peeled, thinly sliced Winesap apples
2	cups sugar		
2	teaspoons vanilla, divided	1	cup coarsely chopped pecans
2	cups flour, sifted	8	ounces cream cheese
1	teaspoon soda	3	tablespoons butter, melted
1-2	teaspoons cinnamon	1½	cups confectioners' sugar

Beat eggs and oil until foamy. Add sugar, 1 teaspoon vanilla, flour, soda, cinnamon, and salt. When mixed and smooth, add apples and pecans. Batter will be thick. Bake in a 9 x 13 greased and floured pan or 2 smaller cake pans at 350° for 45-60 minutes. Combine the remaining ingredients and spread on cooled cake.
Serves 12-14.
Mrs. W. L. Myers (Bettie Townsend)

Orange Angel Cake

6   eggs, separated
Juice of 1½ lemons
1½ cups sugar, divided
1½ cups orange juice, divided
2   tablespoons gelatin

½   cup water
1   Duncan Hines Angel Food Cake
    Mix, prepared as package directs
    and cooled
Whipped cream, optional

To well beaten egg yolks, add lemon juice, ¾ cup sugar, and ½ cup orange juice. Cook this mixture until it is thick, being very careful not to scorch. Add the gelatin which has been dissolved in water and 1 cup orange juice. When cold, add well beaten egg whites to which ¾ cup sugar has been added. Oil a tube pan and pour a small amount of custard on bottom of pan. Break up cake into bite-sized pieces. Layer cake pieces and custard until all is used. Chill overnight or until firm. When ready to serve, ice with whipped cream.
Serves 12.
Mrs. James M. Buttery

For Lemon Angel Cake   A lemon custard may be prepared by adding ¾ cup lemon juice and 1½ teaspoons grated lemon peel to the egg yolks and sugar. Cook over hot water until the mixture coats a spoon. Remove from heat and add 1 tablespoon gelatin that has been dissolved in ¼ cup water. Proceed as above.
Mrs. William W. Beuhler

Banana Cake Delight

8   ounces cream cheese
¼   cup milk
1   3¾ ounce package instant vanilla
    pudding
1   teaspoon vanilla
1   8 ounce can crushed pineapple,
    drained

⅓   cup maraschino cherries, chopped,
    or more to taste
1   cup chopped pecans
2   cups heavy cream, whipped
1   18½ ounce package banana cake
    mix, baked in 2 layers

Beat cream cheese and milk until smooth. Stir in pudding mix and vanilla. Add pineapple, cherries, and pecans. Fold whipped cream into mixture and use as filling and frosting for banana layer cake. Refrigerate.

Mrs. Murray L. Johnston, Jr. (Anne Whittenburg)

Banana Cake

Cake

1 stick butter	1 cup mashed bananas
1¼ cups sugar	1½ cups sifted flour
2 eggs, well beaten	1 teaspoon vanilla
1 teaspoon soda	¼ teaspoon salt
¼ cup sour cream	

Lemon Butter Icing

¼ stick butter	1 tablespoon milk
1 cup confectioners' sugar	1 teaspoon grated lemon rind
1 tablespoon lemon juice	

Cake Cream butter and sugar and add eggs. Dissolve soda in sour cream and beat into mixture. Stir in bananas and flour, alternately. Add vanilla and salt, mixing well. Pour into a generously buttered 13 x 9 x 2 pan and bake at 350° for 30-40 minutes or until done. Frost when cool.

Lemon Butter Icing Cream together butter and sugar. Gradually add lemon juice, milk, and lemon rind. Beat the icing until it reaches spreading consistency.
Serves 10-12.
Mrs. Robert P. Thomas, III (Sallie F. Schuchard)

Buttermilk Cake

2 cups flour	4 eggs
½ teaspoon soda	1 teaspoon vanilla
½ teaspoon baking powder	1 cup buttermilk
Pinch of salt	1 cup heavy cream
2 sticks butter	
2 cups + 2½ tablespoons sugar, divided	

Sift together dry ingredients. Cream butter with 2 cups sugar and add eggs, one at a time. Add flour mixture alternately with buttermilk and vanilla. Pour into an 11¾ x 7½ x 1¾ glass baking dish and bake at 350° for 45 minutes. Combine cream and remaining sugar in a saucepan and heat, but do not boil. Pour over warm cake. This cake must be served from the baking dish. *Special!*
Serves 8-12.
Mrs. Jim B. Criscoe (Judy)

Buttermilk Cake with Lemon Glaze

Cake

3 cups sugar
1 cup Crisco
6 eggs, separated
1 teaspoon butter flavoring
1 teaspoon lemon extract

3 cups flour
¼ teaspoon soda
½ teaspoon salt
1 teaspoon baking powder
1 cup buttermilk

Lemon Glaze

1 egg, beaten
2 tablespoons flour
½ cup water

1 cup sugar
Juice and rind of 2 lemons
½ stick butter

Cake Cream sugar and Crisco thoroughly. Add egg yolks, one at a time, beating well after each addition. Add butter and lemon flavorings. Sift together flour, soda, salt, and baking powder 3 times. Add buttermilk and flour alternately to egg mixture. Fold in stiffly beaten egg whites. Bake in a well buttered tube pan at 350° for 50-60 minutes.

Lemon Glaze Combine ingredients in a saucepan and cook over medium heat until mixture is a thin custard consistency. Pour over cooled cake.

Mrs. Jack Grieder (Nancy Bickham)

Wini's Carrot Cake

2 cups sugar
1½ cups vegetable oil
4 eggs
3 cups flour
2 teaspoons soda
½ cup buttermilk
3 cups grated carrots
1 cup chopped pecans

1 teaspoon lemon flavoring
1 teaspoon coconut flavoring
¾ cup Curaçao, triple sec, or Cointreau, optional
2 cups sugar
1½ cups fresh orange juice
2 tablespoons grated orange rind

In a mixer, combine sugar with oil and beat in eggs, one at a time. Sift flour with soda and add to sugar mixture alternately with buttermilk. Add carrots, pecans, and flavorings, mixing well. Bake at 300° for 1½ hours in a buttered and floured bundt pan. Remove from oven and while warm pour over any of the liqueurs or a sauce made by combining 2 cups sugar, 1½ cups orange juice, and 2 tablespoons grated orange rind.
Serves 12-16.
Mrs. Emil K. Moore

Christmas Cherry Cake

1 cup flour, divided
1 pound candied cherries, ½ green and ½ red, halved
1 pound pitted dates, cut into small pieces
2 slices candied pineapple, chopped
3 cups pecan halves

1 cup sugar
1 teaspoon baking powder
½ teaspoon salt
4 eggs, well beaten
1 teaspoon vanilla
Sherry

Lightly flour cherries and dates to keep them from sticking together and combine with pineapple and pecans. Combine dry ingredients and blend with eggs and vanilla. Add fruit and mix until all fruit is covered with batter. Bake in a greased and floured tube pan covered with greased brown paper to prevent cake from drying. Bake at 250° approximately 2 hours. For individual fruit cakes use chopped pecans. Place in small foil baking cups and top each with ½ cherry. Cover with greased brown paper and bake at 250° for 1 hour. When cool, and before storing in tins, add a little sherry. Can be kept for months with a little help from sherry or other spirits periodically.
Yields 1 cake or 76 individual fruit cakes.
Mrs. John M. Smith (Jane Jordan)

Cherry Pudding Cake

Cake
2 cups sugar
2 cups flour
½ teaspoon salt
2 eggs, beaten
1 16 ounce can red sour cherries, drained and juice reserved

2 tablespoons butter, melted
2 teaspoons soda
2 teaspoons hot water
1 cup chopped nuts

Topping
1½ cups brown sugar
2 tablespoons flour
2 teaspoons vanilla

2 tablespoons butter
1½ cups hot water
Whipped cream, optional

Cake   Mix sugar, flour, and salt well. Combine eggs and cherry juice. Add to dry ingredients and mix well. Add butter and soda mixed with water. Fold in cherries and nuts. Bake in a 9 x 13 pan at 350° for approximately 35 minutes.

Topping   Combine the first 5 ingredients. Cook until thick and pour over hot pudding cake. Refrigerate 12-24 hours, if possible, as flavor improves. Serve with whipped cream.
Serves 16.
Mrs. Jerry Jaeckle

Cupcake Brownies

4	ounces semi-sweet chocolate	4	eggs
2	sticks margarine	2	teaspoons vanilla
1	cup flour	2	cups chopped pecans
1¾	cups sugar		

Melt chocolate with margarine. Combine flour and sugar in a bowl and add eggs, one at a time, stirring as little as possible. Add chocolate mixture, vanilla, and pecans. Fill paper lined muffin cups half full and bake at 325° for 25-30 minutes. Cool in pans so that papers will hug cupcakes.
Yields 24.
Mrs. Howard Hasting

Marbleized Chocolate Cheesecake

Crust

1½	cups graham cracker crumbs	1	ounce semi-sweet chocolate, grated
3	tablespoons butter, melted	½	cup ground pecans
3	tablespoons sugar		

Filling

6	ounces semi-sweet chocolate chips	1	tablespoon vanilla
¼	cup rum	4	large eggs
16	ounces cream cheese, at room temperature		Sweetened whipped cream, optional
1	cup sugar		Grated semi-sweet chocolate, optional
1	cup sour cream		Chocolate sauce, optional

Crust Combine ingredients, press evenly into bottom and sides of a 10 inch spring form pan, and refrigerate.

Filling Melt chocolate with rum over hot, but not boiling water. Place cream cheese in a bowl and beat with an electric beater until fluffy. Gradually beat in the sugar, sour cream, and vanilla. Add the eggs, one at a time, beating after each addition. Divide the batter into 2 portions. Combine ½ of the batter with the chocolate mixture until smooth and pour into crust. Add remaining batter to crust and with a fork, make up and down swirls. Bake at 325° for 1½ hours or until center is firm. Remove from oven. Cool on a wire rack. Refrigerate for 12 hours. Top with sweetened cream and additional grated semi-sweet chocolate or pour heated chocolate sauce over each serving.

Mrs. Ben Foster, Jr. (Raye Boyer)

Pineapple Cheesecake

Crust and Filling

½ cup crushed graham crackers
½ stick butter or margarine, melted
2 eggs, separated
¼ cup milk
½ cup sugar, divided
Pinch of salt

½ tablespoon grated lemon rind
1 envelope gelatin
¼ cup cold water
1 cup creamed cottage cheese
8 ounces cream cheese
2 cups heavy cream, whipped

Glaze

1 tablespoon cornstarch
2 tablespoons sugar

1 8½ ounce can crushed pineapple
with juice

Crust and Filling Combine graham crackers and butter. Press into bottom of a 9 inch spring form pan. Bake at 400° for 10 minutes. Beat egg yolks in top of double boiler until thick and lemon colored. Stir in milk, ¼ cup sugar, and salt. Place over hot water and cook about 10 minutes or until thick, stirring constantly. Add lemon rind. Soften gelatin in water, add to custard, and cool. Beat cheeses and stir into custard. Add ½ of whipped cream. Beat egg whites with remaining sugar until stiff and fold into custard. Pour into crust. Top with glaze.

Glaze Combine cornstarch and sugar in a small saucepan. Gradually stir in pineapple and cook over moderate heat, stirring constantly until thickened. Remove from heat and cool, stirring occasionally. Spread on top of cheesecake and chill. Serve with remaining whipped cream.

Mrs. Marion Olson (Martha Pancoast)

Beetnik Chocolate Cake

3 eggs
1½ cups sugar
1½ cups vegetable oil
1½ cups mashed beets or baby
food beets

1½ cups flour
¾ teaspoon salt
¼ tablespoon soda
½ cup cocoa
1 teaspoon vanilla

Cream eggs with sugar. Mix oil and beets. Sift together flour, salt, soda, and cocoa, and blend into beet mixture. Stir in vanilla. Bake in a greased and floured bundt pan at 350° for approximately 30 minutes or until a toothpick comes out clean. This cake stays moist for a long time. *Ice with chocolate butter or white icing.*

Mrs. Arthur M. Eldridge

Gâteau Chocolat

Crème Fraîche
1 cup heavy cream

2½ teaspoons buttermilk

Gâteau
4 eggs
¾ cup sugar
1 cup flour, sifted

4 ounces semi-sweet chocolate, grated
¾ cup crème fraîche

Glaçage au Chocolat
4 ounces semi-sweet chocolate
2½ tablespoons butter

2 tablespoons strong coffee
½ teaspoon vegetable oil

Crème Fraîche Combine cream and buttermilk in a jar. Cover tightly and shake at least 1 minute. Let stand at room temperature for 8 hours or until thickened. Store in refrigerator. Keeps 4-6 weeks.

Gâteau Beat eggs and sugar for 5 minutes until light and thickened. Fold in flour, chocolate, and ¾ cup crème fraîche. Pour batter into a buttered and floured 9 x 1½ inch round cake pan. Bake at 325° for 40 minutes. Cool completely on a rack and frost.

Glaçage au Chocolat Melt chocolate and butter in the top of a double boiler with coffee. Remove pan from heat and beat in oil. Spread while hot over gâteau.

Mrs. Eleanor Weed

Mock Doboschtorte

1 cup sugar
¼ teaspoon cream of tartar
⅓ cup water
4 egg yolks, beaten
3 sticks butter

5 ounces semi-sweet chocolate
4 tablespoons black coffee
¼ cup crème de cacao or Kahlúa
2 Sara Lee frozen pound cakes

Boil sugar, cream of tartar, and water to thread stage, 240° F. Pour mixture in a steady stream into egg yolks, beating constantly until thickened. Beat in butter and then chocolate which has been melted in the coffee. Flavor with liqueur. Slice cakes horizontally as thinly as possible. Spread frosting on each layer, stack, and frost outside completely. Chill. *Best if made the day before.*
Serves 24. Freezes well.
Mrs. John M. Parker (Patricia Heppes)

Sour Dough Chocolate Cake

½ cup sour dough starter
¼ cup dry milk powder
1½ cups all purpose flour
1 cup water
½ cup vegetable oil
1 cup sugar
½ teaspoon salt

1½ teaspoons soda
1 teaspoon vanilla
1 teaspoon cinnamon
2 eggs
3 ounces semi-sweet chocolate, melted and cooled

Combine sour dough, milk, flour, and water and ferment 2-4½ hours in a warm place. Cream oil, sugar, salt, soda, vanilla, and cinnamon. Beat in eggs, one at a time; then add chocolate. Add fermented mixture and mix well. Pour into a greased bundt pan and bake at 350° for 30-40 minutes. Cake may be served with or without icing.

Mrs. Edward E. DeWees, Jr. (Rebecca Ruth Davis)

White Chocolate Cake

Cake
8 ounces white chocolate
½ cup boiling water
2 sticks butter
2 cups sugar
4 eggs, separated

1 teaspoon vanilla
2½ cups cake flour
1 teaspoon soda
½ teaspoon salt
1 cup buttermilk

Icing
3 egg yolks, beaten
1 13 ounce can evaporated milk
1 cup sugar
1 stick butter or margarine, melted

8 ounces white chocolate
1 cup pecans
1 cup coconut

Cake Melt chocolate in water and cool. Cream butter with sugar until light and fluffy. Add egg yolks, one at a time, beating after each addition. Add melted chocolate and vanilla to creamed mixture and set aside. Sift flour with soda and salt. Add the flour mixture and buttermilk alternately to the chocolate mixture, beating after each addition until smooth. Fold in slightly beaten egg whites. Pour into three 8-9 inch lightly greased and floured cake pans. Bake at 300° for 25-30 minutes. The cakes cannot be handled while warm. Turn over on a cloth, leaving pans on top of them until cool.

Icing Combine egg yolks and 1 cup of the milk in a double boiler. Add sugar and butter, cooking until thickened. Mixture should be light in color. Melt chocolate in a separate double boiler and add to egg mixture with remaining milk which has been heated. Stir in pecans and coconut. Spread between layers and on outside of cake.

Mrs. Benjamin F. Swank, III (Susie Schroeder)

Triple Chocolate Bundt Cake

1	box chocolate cake mix	½	cup sour cream
¾	cup water	1	6 ounce package chocolate chips
¾	cup vegetable oil		Confectioners' sugar
4	eggs		
1	3¾ ounce package instant chocolate pudding		

Combine ingredients, except chocolate chips and confectioners' sugar, in a large bowl and beat at medium speed for 10 minutes. Fold in chocolate chips and pour into a greased bundt pan. Bake at 350° for 50-60 minutes. Cool for about 20 minutes and remove from pan. Sprinkle with confectioners' sugar when cool.

Mrs. Malcolm Lauterstein (Jane)

Crème de Menthe Cake

Cake

1	18½ ounce box yellow cake mix	½	cup Wesson oil
1	3¾ ounce package instant vanilla pudding	½	cup crème de menthe
½	cup orange juice	4	eggs
		1	cup Hershey's chocolate syrup

Cream Cheese Frosting

11	ounces cream cheese, softened	2	tablespoons crème de menthe
½	stick butter		Chopped nuts, optional
1	teaspoon vanilla		Coconut, optional
1	pound box confectioners' sugar, sifted		

Cake Combine cake mix, pudding, orange juice, oil, and crème de menthe. Add eggs, one at a time, beating about 10 minutes at medium speed. Pour ⅔ of this mixture into a greased and floured 10 inch bundt pan. Add chocolate syrup to remaining batter and pour over the other batter. Bake at 350° for 1 hour. Cool and frost.

Cream Cheese Frosting Combine cream cheese and butter, mixing well. Add vanilla, stir in confectioners' sugar, and beat until smooth. Stir in crème de menthe, nuts, and coconut.

Mrs. Wilbur F. Littleton, Jr. (Jean Richards)

White Butter Cake with Caramel Icing

Cake
2	sticks butter	2½	cups sifted cake flour
1½	cups sugar	1	teaspoon salt
1	cup milk	3	teaspoons baking powder
1	teaspoon vanilla	2	eggs

Caramel Icing
1	stick butter		
1	cup heavy cream	4	cups sugar, divided

Cake Cream butter and sugar. Add milk, vanilla, flour, salt, and baking powder, alternately. Beat in eggs. Place in 2 greased and floured 9 inch cake pans. Bake at 350° for 30 minutes.

Caramel Icing In a heavy saucepan, melt butter. Add cream and 3 cups of sugar, cooking on medium heat until bubbles form around edge of pan. Set aside. In another pan, caramelize remaining sugar* and combine with butter mixture. Cook over low heat to 230°F. Remove from heat and beat until cool enough to frost cake. Frost cake in sections, never allowing icing to cool completely as this is a heavy icing and will tear cake.

***To caramelize sugar** Heat sugar in a heavy pan over low heat for 8-10 minutes, stirring constantly until sugar is melted and straw colored.

Mrs. Ernest Brumley (Betty Finnegan)

Tum Tum Cake

3	teaspoons cinnamon	½ - ¾	cup nutmeats
1	cup sugar	1	rounded teaspoon soda
1	cup water	1	scant cup flour
2	tablespoons Crisco		Pinch of salt
½	pound raisins	1	egg

Boil the first 6 ingredients for 5 minutes, stirring constantly, and cool well. This may be prepared a day ahead. Add remaining ingredients, mixing well. Bake in a pan that has been greased, floured, and lined with wax paper. Bake at 350° approximately 45 minutes or until a toothpick inserted in center comes out clean. *This recipe may be doubled and baked in a tube pan.*

Mrs. Richard Brennan Moore (Patty Lou Burns)

Gingerbread

½ cup brown sugar
½ cup shortening or margarine
1 large egg or 2 small eggs
1 cup molasses
2½ cups flour
1½ teaspoons soda

1½ teaspoons cinnamon
1½ teaspoons ground cloves
2 teaspoons ground ginger
½ teaspoon salt
¾ cup hot water

Cream sugar and shortening. Add egg and beat in molasses. Sift together dry ingredients and add to molasses mixture alternately with water. Beat until smooth. Bake in a greased and floured 8 x 8 square pan at 350° for 50-55 minutes or until a toothpick comes out clean.

Mrs. Eleanor Weed

Peach Cake

Cake
2 sticks butter
1 cup sugar
2 eggs
1 29 ounce can sliced peaches, drained
2 cups flour

1 teaspoon baking powder
1 teaspoon baking soda
1 teaspoon ground cloves
1 teaspoon cinnamon
1 teaspoon nutmeg

Icing
1 stick butter
3 cups confectioners' sugar
3 tablespoons fresh orange juice

1 teaspoon vanilla
1 teaspoon finely grated orange rind

Cake Grease and flour a 15 x 8 x 2 pan. Cream butter with sugar. Add eggs, one at a time, beating until fluffy. Purée peaches in blender to make 2½ cups. Sift dry ingredients together. Add to creamed mixture alternately with peaches. Bake at 350° for 35-40 minutes or until a toothpick tests clean.

Icing Cream butter and gradually add sugar until well blended. Add orange juice and vanilla and beat to spreading consistency. Stir in orange rind and spread on cool cake. *This recipe was given to me by Mrs. Levin Hoenecke, a fine cook of German heritage, whose husband was an owner of the IGA store on Nacogdoches Road. Our family has enjoyed this recipe for many years, and it is a special favorite of teenagers who cannot eat chocolate.*
Serves 15.
Mrs. James M. Cavender, III (Judith Gosnell)

Peanut Butter Chiffon Cake

Cake

2¼ cups Softasilk or Wondra flour
3 teaspoons baking powder
¼ teaspoon baking soda
1 teaspoon salt
1 cup packed brown sugar

⅓ cup chunky peanut butter
⅓ cup vegetable oil
1¼ cups milk, divided
2 eggs, separated
½ cup sugar

Icing

½ cup chunky peanut butter
½ stick butter or margarine

3 cups sifted confectioners' sugar
¼ cup milk

Cake Sift together flour, baking powder, baking soda, and salt. Add brown sugar, peanut butter, oil, and ½ cup milk and beat 1 minute. Add 2 egg yolks and remainder of milk and beat 1 minute. Beat 2 egg whites until frothy; gradually add sugar and continue beating until stiff. Fold into batter. Bake at 350° in greased and floured 8-9 inch layer pans or a 13 x 9 x 2 pan. Bake 8 inch layers for 30-35 minutes, 9 inch layers for 25-30 minutes, and the 13 x 9 x 2 inch layer for 40-45 minutes. Cool and frost.

Icing Mix ingredients until creamy. *A favorite of children and husbands.*

Mrs. Pamela Parks Gabbert

Graham Cracker Crumb Cake

Cake

2 sticks margarine
2 cups sugar
5 eggs
1 pound graham cracker crumbs

2 teaspoons baking powder
1 cup milk
1 3¾ ounce can Angel Flake coconut

Icing

1½ sticks margarine
1½ pounds confectioners' sugar
2 eggs

1 teaspoon vanilla
2½ cups crushed pineapple with liquid

Cake Cream margarine and sugar until smooth. Add eggs, one at a time, beating well after each addition. Mix graham cracker crumbs and baking powder together. Add crumb mixture to creamed mixture along with milk, and mix until well blended. Stir in coconut. Grease and flour three 8 inch cake pans and divide batter evenly. Bake at 350° for 30-35 minutes or until done. Cool cake in refrigerator before icing.

Icing Blend ingredients, except pineapple, to make icing. Top each layer with pineapple and then icing. Frost cake completely.
Serves 12.
Mrs. Kaye Church

Nameless Cake

Cake

¾ cup shortening
1½ cups sugar
3 eggs, well beaten
1 teaspoon vanilla
1 teaspoon lemon extract
1¾ cups flour
½ teaspoon baking powder

½ teaspoon baking soda
¾ teaspoon nutmeg
1 teaspoon cinnamon
½ teaspoon salt
¾ cup sour cream or buttermilk
3 tablespoons cocoa
½ cup toasted, chopped pecans

Frosting

¾ stick butter
1 egg yolk
3 cups confectioners' sugar

1½ tablespoons cocoa
1 teaspoon cinnamon
1½ tablespoons hot coffee

Cake Cream shortening and sugar. Blend in eggs, vanilla, and lemon extract. Sift flour, baking powder, soda, nutmeg, cinnamon, and salt together. Blend into egg mixture. Add sour cream, cocoa, and pecans. Bake in 3 well greased pans at 350° for 30 minutes. Cool and frost.

Frosting Cream butter and blend in egg yolk. Sift sugar, cocoa, and cinnamon together and add to creamed mixture alternately with coffee. Beat until smooth.

Mrs. Ivan Moore

Macaroon Icebox Cake

18 almond macaroons
⅔ stick butter
1 cup confectioners' sugar
2 eggs, separated

1 teaspoon vanilla
½ cup maraschino cherries
½ cup blanched almonds
1 cup heavy cream, whipped

Line a buttered mold with macaroons, reserving enough to cover top. Cream butter and sugar. Add yolks and beat 2 minutes. Fold in vanilla, cherries, almonds, and stiffly beaten egg whites. Pour into mold and top with remaining macaroons. Chill 24 hours. Cover with whipped cream and serve.

Mrs. Henry W. Sebesta, Jr. (Patricia Klaver)

Potato Cake

1½	sticks butter	1	teaspoon ground cloves
2	cups sugar	½	teaspoon nutmeg
1	cup mashed potatoes	2	heaping teaspoons baking powder
4	eggs, separated	½	cup light cream or milk
2½	cups flour	1	cup nuts
3	tablespoons cocoa	½	cup raisins, optional
1	teaspoon cinnamon		Whipped cream, optional
1	teaspoon allspice		

Cream butter and sugar. Add potatoes and egg yolks. Mix flour, cocoa, spices, and baking powder and add to potato mixture alternately with cream. Stir in nuts, raisins, and stiffly beaten egg whites. Pour into a greased tube pan. Bake at 350° for 1-1½ hours. Serve with whipped cream.

Mrs. Jack Beretta (Mary Austin Perry)

Potato Cake Icing

1	cup light cream	2	cups brown sugar
1	stick butter	1	teaspoon vanilla

Combine cream, butter, and sugar and cook just until it forms a soft ball in cold water. Remove from heat, add vanilla, and beat until creamy. When cool, spread on potato cake.

Mrs. Ralph H. Winton

Fresh Plum Cake

1	stick butter	¼	teaspoon salt
1	cup sugar, divided	8	fresh Santa Rosa plums, halved
2	eggs	2	teaspoons cinnamon
1	cup sifted flour		Whipped cream or ice cream
1	teaspoon baking powder		

Cream butter and ½ cup sugar until light and fluffy. Add eggs and beat thoroughly. Sift flour, baking powder, and salt and add to creamed mixture. Mix well. Spread in a buttered 8 x 8 pan. Arrange plums in cake batter, skin side down. Sprinkle with remaining ½ cup sugar and cinnamon. Bake at 350° for 40 minutes. Serve with whipped cream or ice cream.
Serves 8.
Mrs. Lester J. Laird

Coconut Pound Cake

1	pound butter	7	ounces canned coconut
3	cups sugar, divided	1	teaspoon vanilla
2	cups all purpose flour	½	cup water
6	eggs	1	teaspoon coconut flavoring

Cream butter with 2 cups of the sugar and add 1 cup flour. Add eggs, one at a time, beating after each addition. Add remaining flour mixed with coconut and vanilla. Grease and flour a tube pan; then line with waxed paper cut to fit the bottom. Bake at 350° for 1 hour and 15 minutes. After 45 minutes, test center of cake with toothpick. Do not overcook. Combine remaining sugar with water and boil only 3 minutes. Stir in flavoring and pour over cake while warm. Let stand 1 day before serving.

Mrs. Richard Brennan Moore (Patty Lou Burns)

For a crispier crust on pound cake, use Crisco.

Coffee Flavored Pound Cake

2	sticks butter	½	cup cocoa
2	cups sugar	3	tablespoons instant coffee powder
4	eggs	2	teaspoons vanilla
2¾	cups all purpose flour	1	cup sour cream
½	teaspoon baking powder		Confectioners' sugar, optional
½	teaspoon soda		

Cream butter and sugar until well blended; then beat in eggs, one at a time. Sift together flour, baking powder, soda, cocoa, and coffee. Add to creamed mixture and beat until well blended. Add vanilla and sour cream and blend well. Spoon batter evenly into a greased and floured 9-10 inch tube pan. Bake at 325° for about 65 minutes or until cake just begins to pull from sides of pan and a toothpick inserted in center comes out clean. Let stand in pan a few minutes; then invert onto a rack and remove pan. Dust with confectioners' sugar.

Mrs. M. L. Ferguson (Frances)

7 Up Pound Cake with Lemon Curd Sauce

Cake
3   sticks butter or margarine,
     softened
3   cups sugar

5   eggs
3   cups flour
¾   cup 7 Up, at room temperature

Lemon Curd Sauce
2   cups sugar
1½ sticks butter or margarine

Juice of 6 lemons
6   eggs, beaten

Cake Cream butter and sugar for 20 minutes. Add eggs, one at a time, beating after each addition. Add flour and fold in the 7 Up. Pour into a greased and floured bundt pan, and bake at 325° for 1½ hours or until brown.

Lemon Curd Sauce In a saucepan, over medium heat, stir together sugar, butter, and lemon juice. Add eggs and continue stirring until sauce has thickened and is boiling softly.

Mrs. Malcolm G. Chesney (Mary Louise Mims)

Old South Georgia Sour Cream Pound Cake

2   sticks butter, at room temperature
3   cups vanilla sugar*
1   cup sour cream
6   eggs, at room temperature,
     separated

3¼ cups sifted all purpose flour
¼ teaspoon soda
1   teaspoon vanilla
½ teaspoon lemon extract
1   teaspoon butter flavoring, optional

Cream butter well. Gradually add sugar, a little at a time, beating constantly until the mixture looks like whipped cream. Add sour cream and beat well. Remove from mixer and continue beating by hand, alternating egg yolks, one at a time, with flour that has been sifted with soda. Add flavorings. Beat egg whites until almost stiff and fold into mixture. Pour into a well greased and floured bundt pan or into a tube pan well greased and lined with wax paper. Bake at 325° for 1½-2 hours. Do not open oven door for the first hour during baking. Let cake stand when done in the bundt pan for 10 minutes before removing.

*To prepare vanilla sugar Add 1 vanilla bean to 5 pounds sugar in a covered container. Shake or stir occasionally for several days for flavor to absorb. May be kept indefinitely.
Freezes.
Mrs. Frank Steed

Party Pound Cake

1	1¾ ounce package instant lemon pudding	1½	tablespoons grated orange rind
½	cup sugar	1	16 ounce pound cake, cubed
2	egg yolks	⅓	cup apricot preserves
1½	cups milk	1½	cups frozen whipped topping, thawed
¼	cup light rum	⅓	cup slivered almonds, toasted

Prepare pudding according to package directions substituting sugar, yolks, and milk for the liquid. Stir in rum, orange rind, and pound cake cubes. Pack mixture into a 9¼ x 5¼ x 2¾ loaf pan or mold. Cover and chill for 3 hours or until set. Loosen edges of cake and turn out on a serving plate. Ice cake with apricot jelly and then with whipped topping. Garnish with almonds and chill for 1-2 hours.
Serves 8-10.
Mrs. Richard Kardys (Jessie Bell Mathis)

Pumpkin Cake Roll

3	eggs	½	teaspoon salt
1	cup sugar	1	cup finely chopped pecans or walnuts
⅔	cup pumpkin		
1	teaspoon lemon juice	1¼	cups confectioners' sugar
¾	cup flour	6	ounces cream cheese
1	teaspoon baking powder	½	stick butter or margarine
2	teaspoons cinnamon	½	teaspoon vanilla
1	teaspoon ground ginger		Whipped cream, optional
½	teaspoon nutmeg		

Beat eggs on high speed of mixer for 5 minutes and gradually beat in sugar. Stir in pumpkin and lemon juice. Combine the flour, baking powder, cinnamon, ginger, nutmeg, and salt. Fold into pumpkin mixture. Spread batter in a greased and floured 15 x 10 x 1 baking pan. Top with nuts. Bake at 375° for 15 minutes. Turn out on a towel sprinkled with ¼ cup confectioners' sugar. Starting at narrow end, roll towel and cake together, and cool. Beat until smooth 1 cup confectioners' sugar with cream cheese, butter, and vanilla to make filling. Unroll cake and spread with filling. Roll cake and chill. Serve in thin slices topped with whipped cream.
Serves 10.
Mrs. Leslie McNelis

Red Velvet Cake

4	½ ounce bottles red food coloring		1	cup buttermilk
5	tablespoons chocolate Nestle Quik		1	teaspoon vinegar
½	cup Crisco		1	teaspoon soda
1½	cups sugar		2	sticks margarine
2	eggs		8	ounces cream cheese
1	teaspoon salt		1	pound box confectioners' sugar
2½	cups cake flour		1	teaspoon vanilla

Mix food coloring with Nestle Quik and set aside. Cream Crisco with sugar and add eggs. Beat until smooth and creamy. Sift salt and flour together. Add alternately with buttermilk to creamed mixture, mixing well. Add vinegar and mix by hand. Add soda and mix by hand. Be sure to add vinegar and soda separately. Add food coloring and Nestle Quik. Bake in 9 x 13 pan at 350° for 30-35 minutes. Beat margarine and cream cheese until light and fluffy. Gradually add confectioners' sugar and vanilla. Frost cooled cake with this mixture.

Miss Marijane Gish

Blue Ribbon White Cake

Cake
1	cup butter		1	cup egg whites or 8 egg whites, stiffly beaten
2	cups sugar			
1	cup light cream		2	tablespoons baking powder
3	cups sifted cake flour			

Icing
1	cup sugar			Pinch of cream of tartar
⅓	cup boiling water		1	egg white
5	marshmallows, cut in small pieces		1	teaspoon almond flavoring

Cake Cream butter and sugar. Add cream and flour alternately. Fold in egg whites. Add baking powder. Pour into a greased bundt pan and place in a cold oven. Bake at 350° approximately 50 minutes or until toothpick inserted in center comes out clean. Cool and frost.

Icing Boil sugar and water until syrup spins a thick thread, about 240°F. Add marshmallows and cook 1 minute. Add cream of tartar to egg white and beat until very stiff. Add boiling syrup gradually to egg white mixture. Add almond flavoring and beat until cold. Spread on cake. *I won first prize at the Gonzales County Fair in the early 1920's with this recipe.*

Mrs. Edward Sweeney

Toasted Butter Pecan Cake

Cake

2 cups chopped pecans	2½ teaspoons baking powder
2½ sticks butter, divided	½ teaspoon salt
2 cups sugar	1 cup milk
4 eggs	2 teaspoons vanilla
3 cups flour	

Butter Pecan Icing

1 stick butter	⅔ cup pecans, reserved from cake recipe
2¼ cups sugar	
1½ cups evaporated milk	1 teaspoon vanilla

Cake Toast pecans in ½ stick butter at 350° for 20 minutes, stirring frequently. Set aside ⅔ cup pecans for icing. Cream sugar with remaining butter. Add eggs, one at a time, beating well after each addition. Sift flour, baking powder, and salt together and add to creamed mixture alternately with milk. Add vanilla and 1⅓ cups pecans, stirring well. Bake in 3 lightly greased 9 inch pans at 350° for 25-30 minutes. Cool before frosting.

Butter Pecan Icing Combine butter, sugar, and milk in a saucepan. Slowly bring to a boil and continue to boil for 2 minutes, stirring constantly. Remove from heat and beat until creamy. Blend in pecans and vanilla. Spread between layers and then cover cake completely.

Mrs. Jack Beretta (Mary Austin Perry)

Popcorn Cake
Rated G

4 quarts popped corn	½ cup vegetable oil
1 pound small gumdrops	1 pound marshmallows
½ pound salted peanuts	Multi-colored sprinkles, optional
1 stick butter	

In a large bowl, combine popcorn, gumdrops, and peanuts. In a saucepan, melt butter, oil, and marshmallows. Pour over popcorn mixture, and place in a generously buttered tube pan. Cool and turn out onto a tray. Decorate with multi-colored sprinkles. Must be prepared same day as served. *For children only!*
Serves 12.
Mrs. Joe L. Guinn (Nina Jane Cole)

Lammie's Cream Sponge Cake

4	eggs, separated		Flour
3	tablespoons cold water	¼	teaspoon baking powder
1	cup sugar	¼	teaspoon salt
1½	tablespoons cornstarch	1	teaspoon lemon extract

Beat yolks and water until thick and lemon colored. Gradually add sugar and beat 2 minutes. Put cornstarch in a 1 cup measure and fill with flour. Sift together cornstarch, flour, baking powder, and salt and add to egg mixture. When thoroughly mixed, carefully fold in stiffly beaten egg whites and flavoring. Bake at 350° for 30 minutes in a tube pan. *This is an excellent cake to serve with whipped cream or ice cream and fruit.*
Serves 10-12.
Mrs. Marion Wallace McCurdy

Mocha Frosting

1	stick butter, softened	1	teaspoon instant coffee, dissolved
1½	cups sifted confectioners' sugar		in 1 teaspoon water
1	egg, beaten		Sliced almonds to taste
1	tablespoon Kahlúa		

Combine all ingredients except almonds. Almonds should be patted liberally into each layer of frosting. This yields enough frosting for an 8 inch square cake divided into 3 layers. This can be easily done if cake is partially frozen. Refrigerate after icing. The recipe is easily doubled or tripled.

Mrs. Thomas Pawel (Nancy Emma Ray)

Burnt Sugar Icing

2	cups sugar, divided	⅛	teaspoon salt
¼	cup boiling water	1	teaspoon vanilla
2	tablespoons butter	1	cup chopped pecans or English
½	cup milk		walnuts, optional

Melt ½ cup sugar in a large, heavy saucepan. Stir in water until blended. Add butter, milk, salt, and remaining sugar. Boil to softball stage, 230°F. Cool slightly for 2-3 minutes. Add vanilla and nuts, beating until thick and creamy. Spread on cake. If icing begins to get too thick, add a few drops of milk until proper consistency. *Especially good on spice cake.*

Mrs. Thomas W. Folbre (Polly McShane)

Beautiful Winter Strawberries

1-1½ cups finely chopped walnuts or pecans	1 teaspoon vanilla
1-1½ cups grated coconut	Green food coloring
9 ounces strawberry gelatin	4 ounces slivered almonds
14 ounces condensed milk	⅓ cup red-colored sugar
	¼ cup green-colored sugar

Combine nuts, coconut, gelatin, milk, and vanilla. Blend until smooth. Form into a ball and chill for at least 1 hour. Mix green food coloring with water until desired color for stems is obtained. Dip almond slivers in mixture, remove, and set aside to dry. Shape chilled mixture into strawberries, using 1 tablespoon of mixture for each strawberry. Chill again if necessary. Roll in red sugar and dip ends in green sugar. Use the almond slivers for stems of strawberries. Refrigerate in an airtight container until ready to serve.
Yields 45 candies.
Mrs. John P. Houston, Jr. (Alice)

Caramels

2	cups sugar	1	stick butter
2	cups light corn syrup	1	teaspoon vanilla
2	cups heavy cream	1	cup pecans

Cook sugar with corn syrup to the firm ball stage, 245°F, and gradually add cream and butter. Stirring constantly, continue cooking rapidly to almost the same firm ball stage, 242°F. Remove from heat, add vanilla and pecans, and pour into a buttered 11¾ x 7½ x 1¾ pan. When cold, cut into squares using a sawing motion. Wrap each piece in heavy waxed paper.

Mrs. Richey Wyatt (Eloise Richey)

Cinnamon Pecans

1	cup sugar	1	teaspoon vanilla
½	cup cold water	1	teaspoon cinnamon
¾	teaspoon salt	4	cups pecans

Combine sugar, water, salt, and vanilla. Boil to 240°F or about 4 minutes. Remove from heat and add cinnamon and pecans. Stir until syrup forms a sugar coating. Place pecans on waxed paper to cool.

Mrs. Fred W. Middleton (Barbara Ann Loffland)

Creole Pralines

2	cups sugar	4	cups broken pecans
1	cup real maple syrup	1	teaspoon vanilla
⅓	cup light cream		

Combine sugar, maple syrup, and cream in a heavy saucepan. Cook to a soft ball stage, 235°F, adding pecans during the last half of cooking time. Remove from heat and add vanilla. Beat and drop immediately from a spoon onto waxed paper.
Yields 20-25 pieces.
Mrs. William Hammond (Ruth Dyer)

Date Loaf Candy

3   cups sugar
1   cup milk
1   8 ounce package dates, cut into
    pieces

½   cup candied cherries
½   cup finely chopped nuts

Bring sugar and milk to a boil and add dates. Mash with a potato masher. Cook to a soft ball stage, 228°F, stirring often. Remove from heat and stir until candy thickens. Add cherries and nuts. Pour onto a wet towel and form into a long roll. Let stand 2 hours or until hard. Slice to serve.
Yields 1 log about 18 x 2 inches.
Mrs. Jimmy Lodovic (Sharon)

English Toffee

2   cups toasted, chopped nuts,
    almonds, pecans, walnuts, or a
    combination
3½ sticks butter

3   tablespoons water
2   cups sugar
6   squares semi-sweet chocolate

Butter a shallow 10½ x 15 pan. Sprinkle nuts into pan. In a heavy saucepan greased with butter, combine butter, water, and sugar. Cook over low heat, stirring until sugar is dissolved. Slowly raise the heat, stirring until mixture comes to a full boil. Cook over moderately high heat, without stirring, until a candy thermometer registers 300°F. Immediately pour toffee into pan and cool completely. In the top of a double boiler set over simmering water, melt chocolate. Spread chocolate with a metal spatula over top of cooled toffee. When cool break in pieces and store in airtight tins.

Mrs. Garland M. Lasater (Carolyn Kampmann)

Fudge

4½ cups sugar
1   13 ounce can Pet milk
1   stick + 1 tablespoon butter
1   stick + 1 tablespoon margarine

1   pound pecans, chopped
1   teaspoon vanilla
18 ounces semi-sweet chocolate chips
1   pound miniature marshmallows

Mix the first 4 ingredients well in a large saucepan and bring to a boil. Boil for exactly 7 minutes stirring constantly. Remove from heat. Fold in remaining ingredients. Blend until chocolate and marshmallows are completely melted. Pour into a buttered 3 quart pan.
Yields approximately 100 squares.
Mrs. William W. Flannery, Jr. (Beverly Cage)

Josephine's Bourbon Candy

1½ pounds confectioners' sugar
¾ stick butter or margarine
6 tablespoons good bourbon, or more to taste
6 1 ounce squares semi-sweet chocolate

6 1 ounce squares bitter chocolate
1 teaspoon paraffin
Pecan halves, toasted

Combine confectioners' sugar, butter, and bourbon into a ball, and let set overnight. Melt chocolate and paraffin. Roll sugar mixture into small balls and dip each into chocolate mixture. While warm, press pecan halves on top of each piece.

Mrs. Anne Covington Phelps

When substituting butter for margarine in cookies, use a scant portion of butter.

Martha Washingtons

2 boxes confectioners' sugar
1 stick margarine
1 can condensed milk
1 teaspoon vanilla, Amaretto, Kahlúa, or Grand Marnier

4 cups chopped pecans
10 ounces bitter or semi-sweet chocolate
4 ounces paraffin

Cream together the first 5 ingredients. Refrigerate for 1 hour or longer. Roll into bite-sized balls. To simplify forming balls, dip hands in confectioners' sugar. Melt chocolate and paraffin over low heat in a double boiler. Using a toothpick, dip balls into chocolate mixture. Place on waxed paper until the chocolate hardens. It may be necessary to occasionally put chocolate back over hot water to keep it thin enough for a smooth coat.
Yields 5-6 dozen.
Mrs. Benjamin F. Swank, III (Susie Schroeder)

Miss Imogene's Panocha

1 16 ounce box brown sugar	3 tablespoons light Karo syrup
2 cups sugar	⅛ teaspoon salt
1½ cups milk or a 5.33 ounce can Pet milk + ⅓ cup water	2 teaspoons vanilla
	2 cups pecans, broken
3 tablespoons margarine	1 teaspoon water

Combine all ingredients, except vanilla, pecans, and 1 teaspoon water, in a large heavy saucepan. Cook, stirring to dissolve sugar; then boil slowly without stirring until it forms a soft ball, 232°F. Remove from heat. Add vanilla and nuts. Beat about 10-15 minutes with a wire whisk. If candy thickens too quickly, add 1 teaspoon water and beat again until smooth and creamy. Pour onto buttered platters. Cut into squares before it cools.

Mrs. W. Carlton Church, III (Ann Webb Schoenfeld)

Oklahoma Brown Candy

6 cups sugar, divided	1 stick butter or margarine
2 cups milk or 1 cup light cream and 1 cup milk	1 teaspoon vanilla
	2 cups or more pecans or English
¼ teaspoon soda	walnuts, broken

In a deep, heavy, buttered kettle, combine 4 cups sugar with milk and cook over low heat while beginning the next step. Pour 2 cups sugar into a heavy iron skillet and place over low heat. Begin stirring with a wooden spoon and keep the sugar moving so it will not scorch. It will take almost 30 minutes to completely melt this sugar to the color of light brown sugar syrup. At no time let it smoke or cook so fast that it turns dark. When the sugar is melted, begin pouring it in a fine stream into the kettle of boiling sugar and milk, keeping it on very low heat and stirring across the bottom of the kettle constantly. Continue cooking and stirring until the mixture forms a firm ball when dropped in cold water, 245°F. Remove from heat and immediately add the soda, stirring vigorously as it foams. When the soda is mixed, add the butter, allowing it to melt as you stir. Let stand 10 minutes, then add vanilla and beat with a wooden spoon until mixture is thick, heavy, and has lost its sheen. Add nuts and turn into square pans lined with lightly buttered wax paper. Cut into squares when slightly cooled. This keeps moist and delicious indefinitely and is most attractive.
Yields 6 pounds. May be halved.
Mrs. Opal Wilson

Patience

3 cups sugar, divided
1½ cups milk or ¾ cup light cream and ¾ cup milk

2 tablespoons light Karo syrup
2¼ tablespoons butter
1½ cups pecans, coarsely chopped

Over low heat, slowly brown 1 cup sugar in an iron skillet so it does not burn. Combine remaining sugar, milk, and syrup and heat. Stir into browned sugar until melted. Bring to a boil and continue to boil for 25 minutes. Add butter and beat constantly with "patience" until the candy begins to crystallize around the sides. Add nuts and pour into a buttered pan. Cut into squares when cooled.
Yields 2-3 dozen pieces.
Mrs. Kenneth Key Hoffman (Sally Frommeyer Cook)

Peanut Brittle

2 cups sugar
1 cup light Karo syrup
½ cup water
2 cups raw peanuts with skins

2 teaspoons butter
1 tablespoon vanilla
1 teaspoon soda

Combine sugar, syrup, and water in a heavy kettle. Bring to a boil. Just before thermometer reaches hard crack stage, 290°F, add peanuts, butter, and vanilla. Stir constantly until golden brown. Boil to hard crack stack, 300°F-310°F. Remove from heat, add soda, and pour into 2 large, buttered pans. As soon as it can be handled, turn the candy over and pull and stretch it out as thin as possible. Break into irregular pieces when cooled.

Mrs. Henry W. Sebesta, Jr. (Patricia Klaver)

Texas Taffy

3 cups sugar
½ cup vinegar
1 cup water

¼ stick butter
1 teaspoon vanilla
Food coloring, optional

In a medium saucepan, combine sugar, vinegar, and water. Stir before cooking or it will turn to sugar. Cook over low heat about 8-10 minutes until it forms a soft ball, 228°F. Add butter, vanilla, and food coloring. Pour onto a buttered platter and let cool until it can be handled. Pull until white in color. Cut with scissors into ½ inch pieces. Keep a little butter handy while pulling to keep fingers from sticking to candy. *This is a family recipe from my great-grandmother, Judith Catherine Simpson.*

Mrs. William C. Dickman (Martha Couch)

Tiger's Candy

½ cup smooth peanut butter
⅔ cup sunflower seed meal or 1 cup whole sunflower seeds, finely ground
1 tablespoon brewer's yeast

2 tablespoons dry milk powder
1 tablespoon honey
¼ cup raisins, finely chopped
¼ cup dates, finely chopped
1 cup grated coconut

In a small bowl, blend peanut butter and sunflower seed meal. Stir in brewer's yeast, dry milk, and honey. Add raisins and dates and blend. This is easiest with hands. If mixture is too dry, add liquid milk. If it is too wet, add more powdered milk. Form candy into balls the size of a pecan. Roll balls in coconut and chill.
Yields 2 dozen balls.
Mrs. Harry E. Brown (Carolyn Carlisle)

Melt 2 pounds white chocolate in a double boiler. Stir in 1 cup whole, toasted almonds and pour into a shallow, buttered pan. Press mixture to ¼ inch thickness. Refrigerate. Tap out of pan and break into pieces. Heaven! To insure success, do not double recipe.

Very Apricot Candy

1 orange
12 ounces dried apricots
1 cup sugar

Confectioners' sugar
Grated coconut

Seed the orange, squeeze, and reserve juice. Put apricots and orange halves through a grinder. Combine with sugar and juice in a saucepan. Boil slowly until stiff, stirring constantly, and then occasionally after turning heat to low. When very thick, 1 hour or more, remove from heat and allow to cool. With wet fingers form mixture into small balls and roll in confectioners' sugar and coconut.
Yields 2½ dozen.
Mrs. Napier Rogers (Mary Jean Davis)

Missions

"September 21, 1843 — Our camp in movement for a start, crossed the San Antonio at the Nogal, below the Mission of San José, and when fairly out in the prairie had a fine view of San Antonio, Concepcion, San José, La Espada, and down the river. It is reviving to the European, to behold in the far West of the New World, edifices partaking of the character of the sacred buildings he has left behind him; and we cannot withhold our praise from the Spanish ecclesiastics who designed and reared with the assistance of the Indian the churches, dwellings for the Indians, etc. forming the Missions on the San Antonio River."

William Bolleart's Texas. William Bolleart, 1842-1844.

Addadear's Oatmeal Cookies

1	cup Crisco or 2 sticks margarine, softened	½	teaspoon salt
1	cup sugar	1	teaspoon ground cloves
2	eggs	1	teaspoon allspice
1	scant cup flour	1	teaspoon cinnamon
½	teaspoon baking powder	¾	cup chopped pecans
¾	teaspoon soda	4½	cups rolled oats
		1	cup raisins

Cream Crisco and sugar. Add eggs, flour, baking powder, soda, salt, and spices, mixing well. Stir in pecans and 3 cups oatmeal. Fold in raisins and remaining oats. Drop by serving spoonfuls onto baking sheets. Bake at 350° for 20 minutes. *This recipe belonged to my grandmother, Eleanor Stevens Crane.* **Yields approximately 36 large cookies.**
Mrs. Eleanor Weed

Almond Crescents

2	sticks butter	2	teaspoons cold water
1½	cups confectioners' sugar, divided	2	cups sifted flour
1	cup finely chopped almonds	1	teaspoon vanilla

Cream butter and 1 cup sugar. Gradually add almonds, water, flour, and vanilla, mixing well. Shape into small crescents and bake on baking sheet at 350° for 15 minutes. Roll in remaining sugar while warm.
Freezes.
Mrs. Eleanor Weed

Apple Brownies

1	stick butter or margarine, melted	1	cup sifted flour
1	cup sugar	½	teaspoon baking powder
1	egg	½	teaspoon soda
3	medium or 2 large apples, cored and chopped but not peeled	¼	teaspoon salt
		1	teaspoon cinnamon
½	cup coarsley chopped walnuts		

Cream butter and sugar. Add egg, beating well. Stir in apples and nuts. Sift together dry ingredients and blend with apple mixture. Bake in a greased 9 x 9 pan at 350° for 45-50 minutes. Cut in squares. *Good for fall meetings or coffees.*
Serves 12.
Mrs. William B. Culverwell (Sally Powell)

Butterscotch Bars

1¾	cups light brown sugar	½	teaspoon salt
3	eggs, beaten	1	teaspoon vanilla
¼	cup flour	1½	cups chopped pecans
½	teaspoon baking powder		

Cream sugar and eggs. Add remaining ingredients and mix thoroughly. Pour evenly in a heavily buttered 9 x 12 pan. Bake at 350° for 20 minutes. Remove from oven and cut into 1 x 3 inch bars. In a single layer place bars on a baking sheet lined with waxed paper. Cover with foil and refrigerate. Cookie has a custard-like layer on bottom which solidifies once refrigerated.
Yields 30.
Mrs. Walter Hale, III (Janin Sinclair)

Bear Claws

Cookie

2⅓	cups flour	2	eggs
2	teaspoons baking powder	1	teaspoon vanilla
¼	teaspoon salt	¼	cup milk
2	sticks margarine	½	cup blanched almonds or peanut halves
⅔	cup sugar		
½	cup Hershey's chocolate syrup		

Icing

¼	stick butter		Pinch of salt
¼	cup water or milk	½	teaspoon vanilla
2	1 ounce semi-sweet chocolate squares	1½-1¾	cups confectioners' sugar, sifted

Cookie Sift together flour, baking powder, and salt. Cream margarine and sugar. Add syrup and eggs, one at a time, beating well after each addition. Add vanilla. Blend in dry ingredients alternately with milk. Refrigerate 1 hour. Drop by rounded teaspoonfuls onto greased baking sheet and insert 4 almond halves about halfway into one side of cookies to make claws. Bake at 350° for 10-12 minutes until edges are set and centers spring back. Spread with icing when cool.

Icing Combine butter, water, and chocolate over low heat until melted. Remove from heat and stir in salt, vanilla, and sugar. Spread on top of cookie to resemble paws. *A creative cookie to use at Scout functions or campouts.*

Mrs. Charles M. Singleton (Diane)

Butter Cookies

4	sticks butter	½	teaspoon baking powder
1½	cups sugar	1	teaspoon salt
2	eggs	1	tablespoon vanilla
4	cups flour		

Cream butter and sugar until light. Add eggs and beat well. Combine dry ingredients and add to creamed mixture. Stir in vanilla. Push through a cookie press onto baking sheet or use an Ateco Cake Decorator with a number 30 tip that has been opened by pushing a pencil through the end. Form the cookies in figure eights or 2 inch spirals. Bake at 375° for 8-10 minutes until edges are light brown.

Variations
Chocolate Butter Cookies can be made by substituting 3 tablespoons cocoa for 3 tablespoons flour.
Lemon Butter Cookies can be made by adding 1 tablespoon lemon extract.

Miss Cora Alice Perry

Caramel Cookies

1	cup + 2 heaping tablespoons flour	1½	cups light brown sugar
1	stick butter	1	teaspoon vanilla
2	tablespoons sugar	½	teaspoon baking powder
Salt		1	cup chopped nuts
2	eggs, well beaten	⅓	cup shredded coconut

Cream 1 cup flour, butter, sugar, and a pinch of salt. Spread in a 6 x 12 pan. Bake at 325° about 20 minutes, but do not brown. Mix together eggs, a pinch of salt, brown sugar, vanilla, remaining flour, baking powder, nuts, and coconut. Pour over baked dough and bake at 325° for 35 minutes. Cool before cutting.
Yields 2 dozen.
Mrs. Frates Seeligson (Martita Rice)

Chewy Southern Chess Squares

2	sticks butter or margarine	2	cups flour
1	pound light brown sugar	1	teaspoon baking powder
½	cup sugar	⅛	teaspoon salt
4	eggs	1	cup chopped pecans, optional
1	teaspoon vanilla	Confectioners' sugar	

Heat butter and brown sugar in a saucepan until butter is melted. Remove from heat and stir in sugar, eggs, and vanilla. Sift together flour, baking powder, and salt. Add to butter mixture and blend well. Stir in pecans. Spread in a greased and floured 15 x 10 jelly roll pan. Bake at 300° for 30-40 minutes. Cool 20 minutes. Cut in squares and sprinkle with confectioners' sugar while still warm.
Yields 32 squares. Freezes well.
Mrs. Blair Labatt (Gloria Bramlette)

Chocolate Crispies

2	ounces unsweetened chocolate	½	cup flour
1	stick butter	½	teaspoon vanilla
1	cup sugar	½	cup finely chopped nuts
2	eggs, beaten	Confectioners' sugar	

Melt chocolate with butter. Remove from heat and add sugar, eggs, flour, and vanilla, beating well. Spread on a baking sheet or in an 8 x 8 x 2 pan. Sprinkle with nuts. Bake at 350° for 25 minutes. Cut in squares and sprinkle with confectioners' sugar while warm.
Serves 8.
Mrs. Henry W. Sebesta, Jr. (Patricia Klaver)

Cinnamon Honey Squares

2	cups sifted flour	1	cup sugar
1½	teaspoons cinnamon	1	cup chopped pecans
1	teaspoon soda		Raisins, optional
½	teaspoon salt	1	cup sifted confectioners' sugar
1	egg, well beaten	1	tablespoon water
¾	cup vegetable oil	2	tablespoons Hellmann's mayonnaise
½	cup honey or orange honey	1	teaspoon vanilla

Sift together flour, cinnamon, soda, and salt. Combine egg with oil, honey, sugar, pecans, and raisins. Stir in sifted mixture. This makes a thick batter. Spread evenly on baking sheet with sides. Bake at 350° for 20 minutes. Combine remaining ingredients and spread over baked dough while still warm. Cut into small squares. Store in an airtight container.
Yields 3-4 dozen.
Mrs. Robert E. Howell, Jr. (Mary Zelime Lodovic)

Date Nut Bars

2	eggs	1	teaspoon vanilla
2	cups sugar	8	ounces pitted dates, chopped, or
2	sticks margarine		2 cups
1	cup flour	1	cup chopped nuts
1	teaspoon salt		Confectioners' sugar

Cream eggs, sugar, and margarine. Sift flour with salt and add to egg mixture. Fold in vanilla, dates, and nuts. Bake in a 9 x 13 greased pan at 350° for 35-45 minutes or until golden brown. Cool, cut into small bars, and dip in confectioners' sugar.
Yields 5 dozen.
Mrs. Robert Peacock ("Cyndy" Thornton)

Dutch Butter Bars

2	sticks butter, softened (no substitution)	1½	teaspoons baking powder
2	cups sugar	1	4 ounce package almond paste or 3½ teaspoons almond extract
3	large eggs	1	egg, beaten
2	cups flour		

Cream butter and sugar, add 3 eggs, and mix thoroughly. Mix flour and baking powder and add gradually to creamed mixture. Cut in almond paste. Spread into a 9 x 13 pan, brush with beaten egg, and bake at 350° for 35 minutes. Cut into bars.

Mrs. Donald M. Greer, Jr. (Anne Lindsay)

Chocolate Chip Brownies

3	squares unsweetened chocolate	1	teaspoon baking powder
2	sticks butter or margarine	1	teaspoon vanilla
4	eggs	1	6 ounce package chocolate chips
2	cups sugar	1	cup chopped nuts
1⅓	cups sifted flour		

Melt together the chocolate and butter in a double boiler. Beat eggs and sugar. When chocolate mixture is cool, add to egg mixture. Mix flour and baking powder. Slowly combine the chocolate mixture with the flour mixture. Stir in vanilla and chocolate chips. Pour into a well greased and floured shallow 8 x 12 pan. Sprinkle with nuts. Bake at 350° for 30 minutes. Leave in pan. Do not overcook brownies as they are chewy and better if left underdone.

Mrs. Frank H. Williams

Deluxe Brownies

1	package Duncan Hines Brownie Mix	Chocolate chips
Milk		Butter or margarine
½-1	cup chopped pecans	Light brown sugar

Mix brownies according to package directions for chewy brownies, substituting milk for water. Add pecans, reserving a few to sprinkle on top. Place brownie mixture in a pan. Sprinkle chocolate chips over batter. Melt equal parts butter and sugar, 2-4 tablespoons each depending on size of mix, and drizzle over batter. Bake according to package directions.

Mrs. Huard Hargis Eldridge (Earl Fae Cooper, Jr.)

Glorified Brownies

2   eggs
1   cup sugar
2   sticks butter, melted (no substitution)
1   ounce unsweetened chocolate, melted
¾   cup flour
¼   teaspoon salt

1   cup nuts, lightly floured
18 large marshmallows
¼   stick butter
4   tablespoons milk
2   cups confectioners' sugar
¼   cup cocoa
Pinch of salt
1   teaspoon vanilla

Beat eggs and sugar. Add butter, chocolate, flour, salt, and nuts. Pour into a greased 9 x 11 pan and bake at 350° for 20-25 minutes. Remove from oven, top with marshmallows, and bake for 3-5 minutes or until marshmallows are melted. Remove from oven and mash marshmallows with a spatula. Heat butter and milk just until it comes to a boil. Stir in sugar, cocoa, salt, and vanilla and beat well. Pour over marshmallows and cool thoroughly before cutting into small squares.

Mrs. Melvin Mitchell (Yeola Steed)

Easy Almond Crunch Bars

1   cup flour
1   stick butter or margarine, melted
2½   teaspoons almond extract, divided

1   package coconut-almond frosting or coconut-pecan frosting
1½   cups confectioners' sugar
2-3   tablespoons milk

Combine flour, butter, 2 teaspoons extract, and frosting mix, blending well. Press into a 13 x 9 pan. Bake at 400° for 10 minutes or until light brown. Remove from oven and cool about 15 minutes. Blend sugar, remaining extract, and milk. Drizzle over baked dough while warm. Cut into squares.
Yields 4 dozen. Freezes.
Mrs. A. R. Meador

Easy Spice Cookies

1   18½ ounce box spice cake mix
2   cups rolled oats
1   teaspoon soda
½   cup packed brown sugar

2   eggs
1   cup vegetable oil
1   teaspoon vanilla
1   cup chopped nuts, optional

Combine the first 4 ingredients. Add remaining ingredients, mixing well. Drop by teaspoonful onto baking sheet. Bake at 350° for 6-8 minutes or until done.
Yields 7-8 dozen.
Mrs. Edgar M. Duncan (Linda Wyatt)

Fat Ladies

1 roll refrigerator chocolate chip
  cookies
1 6 ounce package semi-sweet
  chocolate chips

32 light Kraft caramels
¼ cup light cream
1 cup chopped pecans

Cut cookie dough ¼ inch thick and press in a 9 x 12 x 2 pan. Bake at 375° for 20 minutes or until light brown. Cool slightly, sprinkle with chocolate chips, and spread with caramels melted in cream. Top with pecans and refrigerate. Cut into squares.
Yields approximately 24 squares.
Mrs. Robert Jones (Bettina Blair)

Frosted Devil's Food Cookies

Cookies
1 stick butter or margarine
1 cup packed brown sugar
1 egg
1 teaspoon vanilla
2 ounces unsweetened chocolate, melted and cooled

2 cups sifted flour
½ teaspoon soda
¼ teaspoon salt
¾ cup sour cream
½ cup chopped walnuts or pecans

Mocha Frosting
1 stick butter
2 tablespoons cocoa
2 teaspoons instant coffee
Dash of salt

3 cups confectioners' sugar, sifted
3 tablespoons milk
1½ teaspoons vanilla

Cookies Cream butter and sugar until fluffy. Beat in egg and vanilla. Stir in chocolate. Sift together dry ingredients and add alternately with sour cream, mixing well. Stir in nuts. Drop from teaspoon, 2 inches apart, onto greased baking sheet. Bake at 350° for 10 minutes or until done. Remove from baking sheet. Cool and frost.

Mocha Frosting Cream butter, cocoa, coffee, and salt. Slowly beat in 1 cup of the sugar. Add remaining sugar, milk, and vanilla, beating until smooth.
Yields 5 dozen.
Mrs. Julian Craven (Eleanor)

Fruit Cookies for Christmas

1	stick butter	½	cup bourbon
1	cup brown sugar	1	pound candied cherries, halved
4	eggs	1	pound candied pineapple, chopped
3	cups flour	1	pound dates, cut into pieces
½	teaspoon allspice	1	pound raisins
½	teaspoon cinnamon	1	quart pecan halves or pieces
½	teaspoon nutmeg		
3	teaspoons soda, dissolved in 2 tablespoons milk		

In a large bowl, cream butter and sugar. Add eggs one at a time. Sift flour with spices, reserving ¼ cup flour to dust fruits and pecans. Add flour to creamed mixture alternately with liquids. Mix in fruit and pecans, then drop by teaspoonfuls onto greased and floured baking sheet. Bake at 350° for 10-12 minutes. *Serve with eggnog, coffee, or wine. Nice for a coffee or brunch.*
Yields about 8-9 dozen. Freezes.
Mrs. Frank Steed

Grandmother's Teacakes

2	sticks butter	1	teaspoon baking powder
1½	cups sugar	1½	teaspoons vanilla
2	eggs, well beaten	1½	teaspoons almond extract
3	cups flour	1	egg white, beaten, optional
½	teaspoon salt	Sugar, optional	

Cream butter and sugar. Blend in eggs and dry ingredients and beat for several minutes. Stir in vanilla and almond extract. Refrigerate overnight. Roll thin on floured surface, and cut into desired shapes. Tops may be brushed with beaten egg white and sprinkled with sugar. Bake on a greased baking sheet at 375° for about 10 minutes or until golden brown. *Tops may also be iced with a mixture of confectioners' sugar, water, and food coloring which will dry to a hard glaze. A very tasty and versatile cookie recipe that may be used for "cookie jar" cookies, Christmas cookies, or giant cookies cut from a coffee can.*
Yields approximately 6 dozen.
Mrs. Jon Grant Ford (Nancy Archer)

Gumdrop Cookies

2　sticks butter or margarine, softened
1　cup sugar
½　cup packed brown sugar
1　egg
1　teaspoon vanilla

1½　cups sifted flour
½　teaspoon baking powder
½　teaspoon salt
¾　cup quick or rolled oats
1　cup chopped gumdrops

Beat together butter, sugars, egg, and vanilla until creamy. Sift together flour, baking powder, and salt. Add to creamed mixture, blending well. Stir in oats and gumdrops and drop by teaspoonfuls onto baking sheet. Bake at 375° for 10-12 minutes. *Youngsters and grown-ups alike love them!*
Yields 4 dozen.
Miss Alison English

Icebox Cookies

½　cup Crisco
1　stick butter
3　cups packed light brown sugar
2　eggs
3½　cups flour

1　teaspoon soda
½　teaspoon salt
1　teaspoon vanilla
1　cup chopped nuts

Cream the Crisco and butter. Add brown sugar and eggs, mixing thoroughly. Sift together flour, soda, and salt and add to creamed mixture. Add vanilla and nuts. Roll in waxed paper, freeze 1 hour, and slice. Place on greased baking sheet and bake at 350° for 8-10 minutes or until done.
Yields 6-8 dozen. Dough wrapped in foil will keep for weeks in freezer.
Mrs. Jo McCary

Koulourakia
Sesame Twists

2 sticks butter	1 tablespoon orange juice
¾ cup sugar	2 teaspoons vanilla
2 eggs, reserving 1 yolk for glaze	2 tablespoons water
4-5 cups flour	Sesame seeds
1 teaspoon baking powder	

Cream butter, add sugar gradually, and cream thoroughly. Add eggs and beat well. Sift dry ingredients and blend into creamed mixture. Add flavorings. Knead well until dough is smooth, adding more flour if needed. Chill 30 minutes. Pinch off pieces of dough and roll lightly by hand to desired length and shape into twists. Place on baking sheets lined with waxed paper. Mix the egg yolk with water, brush each cookie twist with mixture, and sprinkle with sesame seeds. Bake at 350° for about 15 minutes or until lightly browned. *These cookies last 2-3 weeks in an airtight container.*
Yields 6-7 dozen. Freezes.
Mrs. Daniel J. Nichols

Lace Cookies

2 cups rolled oats	2 sticks butter, melted
1 tablespoon flour	2 eggs, beaten
2 cups sugar	1 teaspoon vanilla
½ teaspoon salt	

Combine oats, flour, sugar, and salt in a large bowl and mix well. Pour very hot butter over the mixture and stir until the sugar is well blended. Add eggs and vanilla, stirring well. Drop by ½ teaspoonfuls, 2 inches apart, onto baking sheets covered with foil. Bake at 325° for 10-12 minutes. Cool completely on foil, remove, and store in an airtight container.
Yields 6 dozen.
Mrs. Arthur M. Eldridge

Lemon Whippersnaps

1 18½ ounce package lemon cake mix or other flavor	2 cups frozen whipped topping, thawed
1 egg	½ cup sifted confectioners' sugar

Combine cake mix, egg, and whipped topping in a large bowl, stirring until well mixed. Drop by teaspoonfuls into confectioners' sugar. Roll to coat. Place 1½ inches apart on greased baking sheet. Bake at 350° for 10-15 minutes or until light golden brown. Remove from baking sheet to cool.
Yields 5 dozen.
Mrs. George A. Kampmann (Wister Howell)

Macadamia Nut Crisps

2	sticks butter, softened	¾	cup chopped macadamia nuts, divided
1	cup confectioners' sugar, sifted	1	egg yolk
2	teaspoons grated orange rind	1	tablespoon water
2	cups flour		Granulated sugar

Cream butter thoroughly and gradually add confectioners' sugar, beating until light and fluffy. On low speed, gradually blend in orange rind and flour. Stir in ½ cup macadamia nuts. Shape dough into 2 balls, wrap tightly in plastic wrap, and refrigerate 30 minutes or until well chilled and firm. On a lightly floured board, roll dough ¼ inch thick, cut with a 2 inch cookie cutter, and place on baking sheet; or press out small balls of dough directly onto baking sheet with a glass dipped in water then in granulated sugar. Mix egg yolk and water and brush cookies with mixture. Sprinkle with remaining macadamia nuts and a little granulated sugar. Bake at 325° for 20-25 minutes until golden brown.
Yields 3 dozen.
Mrs. Frates Seeligson (Martita Rice)

Madeleines

2	eggs	1	teaspoon grated lemon peel
1	cup sugar		Confectioners' sugar
1	cup sifted flour		
1½	sticks butter or margarine, melted and cooled		

In the top of a double boiler, over hot but not boiling water, beat eggs and sugar at medium speed about 2 minutes as mixture heats to lukewarm. Set top of double boiler in cold water. Beat egg mixture at high speed for 5 minutes or until very light and fluffy. With a wire whisk or rubber spatula gently fold in flour until well blended. Stir in butter and lemon peel until just blended. Pour into well greased and lightly floured madeleine pans using 2-3 teaspoons batter for each mold. Bake at 350° for 12-15 minutes or until golden. Cool 1 minute; then remove from pans with a small spatula. Cool completely on wire racks. Sprinkle with confectioners' sugar.
Yields 3½ dozen.
Mrs. James Browning (Phyllis Elaine Reed)

Mexican Wedding Cakes

1	stick butter	¼	cup chopped pecans
¼	cup confectioners' sugar	1	teaspoon vanilla
1	cup flour		Confectioners' sugar

Cream butter and sugar. Add flour, pecans, and vanilla. Shape into small balls and place on well greased baking sheets. Bake at 275° for 45 minutes. When cool, roll in confectioners' sugar. Best when served fresh.
Yields about 12-16 small cakes.
Mrs. Joel B. Alexander

Molasses Cookies

¾	cup Crisco	1	teaspoon cinnamon
1	cup sugar	1	teaspoon ground ginger
1	egg	1	teaspoon ground cloves
¼	cup molasses	1	teaspoon salt
2	cups flour, sifted		Natural sugar
3	teaspoons soda		

Cream Crisco and sugar. Add egg and molasses. Stir in flour, 1 cup at a time, along with other dry ingredients. Chill ½ hour. Shape dough into marble-sized balls, roll in natural sugar, and place 1 inch apart on baking sheet. Bake at 350° for 8-10 minutes.
Yields 3-4 dozen. May be halved or doubled.
Mrs. Robert S. Boswell

Nutmeg Butter Balls

2	sticks butter	2	cups sifted flour
½	cup sugar	½	cup confectioners' sugar
1	teaspoon vanilla	2	teaspoons nutmeg
1⅓	cups chopped pecans		

Cream butter and sugar until light and fluffy. Stir in vanilla and pecans. Gradually add flour, blending well. Chill 30 minutes. Shape dough into 1 inch balls and bake on a lightly greased baking sheet at 325° for 25 minutes until light golden. Combine confectioners' sugar and nutmeg and roll warm cookies in mixture.
Yields 4 dozen. Freezes well.
Mrs. Pierce Sullivan (Mary Wallace Kerr)

Nut Squares

1	egg	½	cup sifted flour
½	cup sugar	¾	teaspoon baking powder
1	teaspoon melted butter or vegetable oil	¼	teaspoon salt
		⅔	cup chopped nuts
2	teaspoons water	1	6 ounce package chocolate chips

Cream egg and sugar with mixer. Add butter and water, mixing well. Sift together flour, baking powder, and salt and add to egg mixture. Fold in nuts and chocolate chips. Spread in a 9 x 9 pan lined with brown paper or in a greased pan lined with waxed paper and greased again. Batter is thick so must be pressed and spread into place. Bake at 325° for 25-30 minutes. Cool, remove from pan, and cut into squares.

Mrs. John M. Parker (Patricia Heppes)

Peachy Cheesies

1	cup flour	⅛	teaspoon salt
1	cup grated sharp Cheddar cheese		Peach preserves
1	stick butter		

Combine flour, cheese, and butter and mix well. Roll to ⅛ inch thick and cut in circles. Put a spoonful of peach preserves on half of the rounds. Top with remaining rounds and press edges together with a fork. Place on baking sheet and bake at 375° about 15 minutes or until light brown.
Yields 15-20.
Mrs. Edward Niehaus (Alice Lee)

Peanut Butter Cookies

½	cup shortening	2½	cups flour
1	stick margarine	1	teaspoon baking powder
1	cup peanut butter	1½	teaspoons soda
1	cup sugar	½	teaspoon salt
1	cup brown sugar	1	cup finely chopped peanuts
2	eggs, beaten		

Cream together shortening, margarine, peanut butter, sugar, and brown sugar. Add eggs, mixing thoroughly. Sift together flour, baking power, soda, and salt. Stir the flour mixture into the shortening mixture and chill the dough. Shape dough into small balls and roll in peanuts. Place on greased baking sheet and flatten each ball with a crisscross made with a fork dipped in flour. Bake at 375° for 10 minutes.
Yields 6 dozen.
Mrs. Orvis E. Meador, Jr. (Jo Lynne Musselman)

Peanut Butter Crisps

2   6 ounce packages butterscotch   ½   cup crunchy peanut butter
    chips   5   cups corn flakes

Melt chips in a double boiler. Add peanut butter and stir until smooth. Add corn flakes and mix well. Drop on wax paper. Refrigerate. *Great for children of all ages.*
Yields 5 dozen.
Mrs. M. E. Allison, Jr. (Brooke B. Rumsey)

Pecan Spice Cookies

2   egg whites   ¼   teaspoon nutmeg
⅛   teaspoon salt   ¼   teaspoon ground cloves
½   cup sugar   2   cups finely chopped pecans
2   teaspoons cinnamon

Beat egg whites with salt until stiff. Gradually add sugar mixed with spices. Fold in nuts. Drop from teaspoon onto well greased baking sheet. Bake at 250° for 35-45 minutes.
Yields 4 dozen.
Mrs. Albert C. Sien, Jr. (Almeda Towns)

Pecan Crisps

½   cup Crisco   2½ cups flour
1   stick butter   ¼   teaspoon salt
1¼ cups sugar   ½   teaspoon soda
1¼ cups brown sugar   1   teaspoon vanilla
2   eggs, well beaten   1   cup chopped pecans

Cream Crisco, butter, sugars, and eggs. Sift together flour, salt, and soda and add to creamed mixture. Stir in vanilla and pecans and drop on greased baking sheet. Bake at 350° for 12-15 minutes.

Mrs. Thomas M. Porter (Flo)

Penuche Squares

½ stick butter
1 cup brown sugar
1 egg
½ teaspoon vanilla
1 cup flour

1 teaspoon baking powder
¼ teaspoon salt
1 cup semi-sweet chocolate chips
¾ cup chopped walnuts

Melt butter and add brown sugar. Stir in egg and vanilla. Beat about 2 minutes until mixture is fluffy. Sift together flour, baking powder, and salt and stir into butter mixture. Blend in chocolate chips and walnuts. Spread evenly in a greased 8 inch square pan, and bake at 350° for 20-25 minutes or until just done. Cool and cut into squares. They should be chewy.
Yields 25 squares. Freezes well when sealed tightly.
Mrs. Dan C. Peavy, Jr. (Harriet Williams)

Praline Squares

2 eggs
2 cups light brown sugar
2 sticks butter or margarine, melted

1½ cups sifted flour
1 teaspoon vanilla
1 cup chopped pecans

Beat eggs and blend with sugar. Stir in butter and add flour gradually. Add vanilla and pecans. Pour into a greased 8 x 11 pan. Bake at 350° for 35-40 minutes. Cool on rack and cut into squares. *A delicious dessert to follow a Mexican food supper.*
Yields 3 dozen. Freezes.
Mrs. L. Gordon Dexter

Raspberry Delights

¾ cup sugar
4 sticks butter
1 teaspoon vanilla
5½ cups flour

1 cup finely chopped pecans
Raspberry jam or other flavor
Confectioners' sugar

Cream sugar, butter, and vanilla. Add flour and pecans, blending well. Pinch off small amounts of dough and form into balls. Make an indentation in each with finger, being sure it is as deep as possible because the cookie melts considerably during baking. Bake at 375° for 8-10 minutes and cool. When ready to serve, fill each cookie with a little raspberry jam and sprinkle with confectioners' sugar.
Yields 160 cookies. Freezes well without jam in an airtight container.
Mrs. John Robert Beauchamp (Francis Ann Drake)

Shortbread

2	sticks butter	¼	teaspoon salt
½	cup brown sugar	¼	teaspoon baking powder
2	cups flour		

Cream butter and sugar thoroughly. Sift together flour, salt, and baking powder. Add to butter mixture, mix well, and roll out ½ inch thick. Cut into squares, prick with a fork (making your initials if you wish), and bake at 325° for 20 minutes until lightly browned.
Yields 2 dozen cookies.
Miss Kathleen DeWees

Sugar Cookies

1	cup confectioners' sugar	2	teaspoons vanilla
1	cup sugar	⅛	teaspoon salt
2	sticks butter	4½	cups flour
1	cup Crisco	1⅛	teaspoons soda
2	eggs	1⅛	teaspoons cream of tartar

Combine ingredients in order. Refrigerate 1 hour; then roll into small balls. Press onto greased baking sheet using glass dipped in water and then in sugar. Bake at 375° for 8-10 minutes.
Yields 6 dozen.
Mrs. Robert Ownby

Triple Cereal Cookies

1	cup shortening	1	cup quick rolled oats
1½	cups sugar	1	cup corn flakes or Team flakes
2	eggs	1	cup wheat flakes, Total, Wheaties,
2	tablespoons milk		or Special K
¾	teaspoon soda	1	cup wheat germ
2½	teaspoons cinnamon	1½	cups raisins, ground
1½	cups flour		

Cream shortening and sugar. Stir in eggs and milk. Add soda, cinnamon, and flour. Mix in remaining ingredients thoroughly. Batter will be stiff. Drop by rounded spoonfuls onto baking sheets. Bake at 350° for 12-15 minutes. *A flavorful, not too sweet cookie, that is very nutritious.*
Yields 8 dozen. Freezes.
Mrs. William W. Coates, III (Sue Schoeneck)

Stained Glass Window Cookies

⅓ cup vegetable shortening
⅓ cup sugar
1 egg
⅔ cup honey
3 cups sifted flour

½ teaspoon soda
1 teaspoon salt
1 teaspoon vanilla
Clear, fruit-flavored lollypops, broken
   into small pieces

Cream shortening with sugar and add egg and honey. Combine flour, soda, and salt. Stir vanilla and flour mixture into creamed mixture and refrigerate several hours or overnight. Roll the dough between hands ¼ inch in diameter as though it were clay. On a baking sheet covered with foil, place rolls in desired outline such as Christmas trees, bells, gingerbread men, or angels. The design should be fairly large and the bigger the opening the prettier the cookie. Carefully seal the ends of dough for strength. Sprinkle crushed lollypops into design openings and bake at 375° for 8-10 minutes. When cool and firm, peel from foil, and store carefully in airtight containers. *These are impressive, especially when threaded and hung from a small tree.*

Mrs. Joe McFarlane, Jr. (Nancy Jane Arnot)

Gardens and Native Trees on the San Antonio River

"We built a strong but homely picket fence around the garden to the north and fenced the garden off from the yard. In the garden were sixteen large fig trees and many rows of old pomegranates. In the yard were several China trees, and on the river bank just below our line in the De La Zerda premises was a grand old cypress, which we could touch through our fence, and its roots made ridges in our yard. The magnificent old tree stands there today. It made a great shade and we erected our bath-house and wash-place under its spreading branches."

Samuel Maverick, Texan, 1803-1870. Samuel Maverick.

Apple Küchen

1	stick butter or margarine, softened	1	teaspoon cinnamon
1	package yellow cake mix	1	cup sour cream
1	21 ounce can apple pie filling	1	egg
¼	cup sugar		

Cut butter into dry cake mix until crumbly. Pat mixture lightly into a 13 x 9 x 2 pan, building up slight edges. Bake at 350° for 10 minutes. Arrange apple slices over warm crust. Mix sugar and cinnamon and sprinkle on apples. Blend sour cream with egg and drizzle over apples. This topping will not completely cover fruit. Bake at 350° for 25 minutes or until edges are light brown. Do not overbake. Serve warm or cold.
Serves 12-15.
Mrs. Dee Forgy (Suzanne Casmere)

Sugar Crusted Apples

6	large cooking apples	⅔	stick margarine, softened
⅓	cup flour	1	egg, slightly beaten
⅔	cup sugar	¾	cup orange juice
½	teaspoon salt		Heavy cream
½	teaspoon cinnamon		

Peel and core apples. Combine flour, sugar, salt, and cinnamon. Cut in the margarine until mixture resembles coarse cornmeal. Roll apples in egg, then in flour mixture, and arrange in a baking pan. Place any leftover flour or egg mixture over apples. Pour orange juice into pan. Bake at 350° for 1 hour or until tender. Baste twice while baking. Spoon juice over warm apples and serve with plain or whipped cream.
Serves 6.
Mrs. Napier Rogers (Mary Jean Davis)

Babas au Rhum

Babas

1	package dry yeast	¾	teaspoon salt
¼	cup warm water	4	eggs
1	stick + 2 tablespoons butter or margarine	2	cups flour
		½	cup currants
2	tablespoons sugar	½	cup seedless raisins

Syrup

2	cups sugar	½	cup orange juice, optional
1	tablespoon grated orange rind	½	cup rum, brandy, Kirsch, or your favorite liqueur
1	cup water		

Babas   Dissolve yeast in water. Add butter, sugar, salt, eggs, and flour and beat well. Stir in currants and raisins. Cover and let stand about 2 hours or until doubled in bulk. Push down and fill buttered baba tins, miniature muffin tins, or 1 large mold ¾ full. Let rise about 1 hour or until pans are full. Bake at 375° until golden brown.

Syrup   In a small saucepan combine sugar, orange rind, and water. Bring to a boil and cook over medium heat for 6 minutes. Remove from heat and add juice and rum. Pierce babas with a fork while still in molds. Turn out and pierce on opposite side. Gradually spoon syrup over babas until all has been used. Flavor improves overnight. *Babas may be placed in jars, covered with syrup, and will keep for some time when refrigerated. An excellent gift!*
Serves 6-8.
Mrs. Pressly Shafer, Jr. (Margaret Fauntleroy)

For a beautiful dessert of "Sangría con Frutas", cover fresh fruit such as melon balls, pineapple chunks, green grapes, mango cubes, or orange sections with a sangria made of ½ gallon Burgundy, 1 quart 7 Up, ¾ cup Cointreau, and ¼ cup brandy. Let stand for several hours and serve in long stemmed glasses or crystal bowl.

Banana Mango Dessert

4	bananas, peeled and sliced lengthwise	1	large can mangoes, drained, or 2 fresh mangoes, peeled

Place bananas in a shallow casserole. Whirl mangoes in a blender for a few seconds and pour over bananas. Bake at 350° for 15 minutes. Serve hot. *The perfect dessert after a Mexican dinner and also good for breakfast served with thin slices of cinnamon toast.*
Serves 4.
Mrs. William McNeel (Amy Lillian McNutt)

Fandango Mango

Canned mangoes
Large green leaves such as ivy
Fresh strawberries
Blueberries, fresh or frozen

Confectioners' sugar
Mint sprigs
Cointreau, optional

Freeze mangoes in can. Remove from freezer 15 minutes before serving, push mangoes from can, and slice into ½ inch rounds. Arrange slices on a leaf covered plate, top with strawberries and blueberries, sprinkle with sugar, garnish with mint and drizzle with Cointreau.

The Cookbook Committee

Chocolate Whipped Cream

1   cup heavy cream
3   tablespoons sugar

2   teaspoons unsweetened cocoa
½   teaspoon vanilla

Combine all ingredients in a small mixing bowl. Beat until soft peaks form. Serve chilled in parfait glasses. *Absolutely sinful served on top of fudge pie!* Serves 3-4.
Mrs. James P. Hollers (Elizabeth Cheney)

Fantastic Foosh

2   sticks butter, softened
1   cup + 1 tablespoon sugar, divided
6   eggs, separated
2   ounces unsweetened chocolate, melted
1   teaspoon vanilla, divided

½   cup chopped pecans
1   large package ladyfingers
¼-½ cup bourbon
1   cup heavy cream
Shaved semi-sweet chocolate

Cream butter with 1 cup sugar for about 10 minutes or until light and fluffy. Beat egg yolks until light and add to creamed mixture, continuing to beat. Add chocolate and beat. Stir in ½ teaspoon vanilla and pecans. Beat egg whites until stiff, but not dry, and fold into mixture. Line the bottom of a small buttered spring form pan with split ladyfingers that have been quickly dipped into bourbon. Line sides with plain ladyfingers and drink remaining bourbon. Pour chocolate mixture into pan and chill overnight. Whip cream with remaining sugar and vanilla. To serve, remove sides of pan, top with cream, and decorate with shaved chocolate.
Serves 8-10. When doubled, fills a 10 inch spring form pan.
Mrs. W. J. Lyons, Jr. (Martha "Molly" Collett)

Flan

1	cup sugar	14	ounces milk
4	eggs	2	teaspoons vanilla
1	14 ounce can condensed milk		Nuts, optional

In the top of a double boiler placed directly over heat, caramelize the sugar, rotating pan until melted sugar coats sides evenly. Set aside to cool. Whirl remaining ingredients, except nuts, in blender and add to pan of sugar. Cover and cook over water for 55 minutes or until set. Refrigerate 4-6 hours. To serve, turn flan out of pan onto a large plate. Garnish with nuts. *This was given to me by our Mexican cook when we lived in Mexico City, so it is authentic.*
Serves 6-8.
Mrs. Alfred Shepperd ("Honey" Inglish)

Floating Island

5	eggs	¼	teaspoon salt
½	cup + 6 tablespoons sugar, divided	1	quart + 1 cup milk, scalded
		1¾	teaspoons vanilla, divided

Beat 3 egg yolks and 2 whole eggs slightly in a double boiler. Continuing to beat, add ½ cup sugar and salt. Gradually add hot milk, stirring constantly. Cook until mixture coats a spoon. Add 1 teaspoon vanilla. Pour into a large pan or glass bowl. Beat remaining egg whites until foamy, gradually add remaining sugar and remaining vanilla, and continue beating until stiff peaks form. Using a large spoon, drop egg whites onto hot custard. Cover pan tightly until mixture is cool. Chill thoroughly before serving. *This recipe never fails to please and may be flavored with Grand Marnier for a more sophisticated version.*
Serves 8.
Mrs. Earl Fae Cooper (Gladys)

Fruit Pizza

1	18 ounce roll Pillsbury slice and bake sugar cookies	Fresh or canned fruits such as sliced bananas, strawberries, blueberries, seedless grapes, or mandarin oranges
8	ounces cream cheese, softened	
¼	cup confectioners' sugar	
1	teaspoon vanilla	

Slice cookie dough into ⅛ inch rounds. Overlap and press lightly in a pizza pan. Bake at 350° for 10-12 minutes or until brown. Cool. Whip cream cheese, sugar, and vanilla together until creamy and spread over crust. Decorate in a circular pattern with fruit. Chill before serving.
Serves 8-10.
Mrs. Don Strange (Frances)

Glazed Fresh Fruit

1 cup Burgundy
¼ cup sugar
⅛ teaspoon ground cloves
¼ teaspoon cinnamon

1½ teaspoons grated orange rind
Dash of ground cardamom
Pears, peaches, apricots, or nectarines,
    peeled, pitted, and halved

Combine all ingredients, except fruits, and simmer until sugar is completely dissolved. Add fruits and continue to simmer until tender but still fairly firm.

Mrs. Helen Brooks Purifoy (Suzie)

Heavenly Meringues

Meringues
3 egg whites
¼ teaspoon cream of tartar
¼ teaspoon salt

¾ cup sugar
½ cup finely chopped pecans

Lemon Brandy Filling
3 egg yolks
¼ cup sugar
1 teaspoon grated lemon rind

¼ cup lemon juice
2 tablespoons brandy
1 cup heavy cream, whipped

Penuche Topping
¼ stick butter
¼ cup sugar

½ cup coarsely chopped pecans

Meringues Beat egg whites with cream of tartar and salt until stiff but not dry. Gradually add sugar, 1 tablespoon at a time, and beat until very stiff. Fold in pecans. Cover a baking sheet with foil. Pile meringue in 6 mounds about 3 inches in diameter. Make a 2 inch depression in the center of each. Bake at 275° for 1 hour. Cool.

Lemon Brandy Filling Beat egg yolks with sugar, lemon rind, lemon juice, and brandy in the top of a double boiler. Cook over simmering water, stirring constantly until thickened. Remove from heat and chill. Fold into cream and spoon into meringues. Chill overnight. When ready to serve, sprinkle with penuche topping.

Penuche Topping Melt butter in a small skillet, stir in sugar, and add pecans. Cook over moderate heat, stirring occasionally 5-7 minutes or until sugar begins to turn golden. Turn out on foil, cool, and crumble into small pieces.
Serves 6.
Mrs. Jon Grant Ford (Nancy Archer)

Hungarian Flaky Pastry

Pastry

1½ pounds margarine, at room temperature
2   cups flour
2½ heaping cups flour

5   eggs, beaten
½-⅔ cup beer
Confectioners' sugar

Fillings

Apricot or Prune
1   16 ounce package apricots or prunes
½-¾ cup sugar
Drops of lemon juice to taste

Walnut
1   cup coarsely ground walnuts
¼   cup sugar
1   egg white, stiffly beaten

Pastry   Cream margarine and gradually add 2 cups flour to make a smooth spread. Mix remaining flour with eggs and enough beer to make a smooth dough. Roll out dough on a floured surface and cover with ⅓ of the margarine spread. Fold over and refrigerate for 30 minutes. Repeat this procedure and refrigerate 30 minutes. Repeat procedure again and refrigerate 1 hour. Roll out half of the dough at a time to ¼ inch thickness and cut in small squares. Spoon desired filling into pastry, fold over, and seal edges. Bake at 350° for 25-30 minutes. Sprinkle with sugar.

Fillings
Apricot or Prune   Cover fruit with water, add sugar to taste, and simmer until thickened. Stir in lemon juice.

Walnut   Combine ingredients.
Serves 15.
Mrs. Stephen P. Takas, Sr.

Lemon Bisque

1   13 ounce can evaporated milk, chilled
1   3 ounce package lemon gelatin
1¼ cups boiling water
¾   cup sugar

Pinch of salt
5   tablespoons lemon juice
Grated rind of 1 lemon
2   cups crushed vanilla wafers

Pour milk into an ice cube tray and freeze just until edges are set. Dissolve gelatin in hot water and cool. Whip partially frozen milk until very thick. This may take a little time. Gradually beat in sugar, salt, lemon juice, and rind. Fold in gelatin. Spread 1 cup wafers over bottom of a 9 x 13 x 2 dish and add lemon mixture. Sprinkle with remaining crumbs. Refrigerate at least 12 hours. Cut into squares and serve. *This is an easy, inexpensive, and delicious dessert to serve after a heavy meal.*
Serves 12.
Mrs. Gordon Friedrich (Ruth Caruthers)

Loukoumades
Honey Puffs

1 cup milk	¼ cup water
1¼ cups self-rising flour	Cinnamon to taste
Vegetable oil	Chopped nuts, optional
2 cups honey	

Combine milk and flour, stirring well. In a heavy saucepan or electric fryer, heat oil to 360°F. Drop flour mixture by tablespoonful into hot oil. Keep tablespoon in a container with some oil while not in use. Fry only a few at a time turning when golden brown underneath. When completely browned, drain on paper towels. Heat honey with water and skim off foam. Dip Loukoumades in honey, several at a time, and soak 1 minute. Sprinkle with cinnamon and nuts. Serve hot. *The Greeks also serve this dessert for special breakfasts.*
Yields 2-2½ dozen.
Mrs. Arthur Sockler

For extra special buñuelos or pastries made with a rosette iron, serve with a sauce made by adding brandy to heated apricot preserves. Buñuelos make an excellent hors d'oeuvre if the sugar is omitted from the batter. Sprinkle the pastry with grated Parmesan cheese or seasoned salt.

Pineapple with Pizazz

1 large ripe pineapple	¼ cup crème de menthe
¼ cup confectioners' sugar	Fresh mint
1 quart lemon or lime sherbet	

Cut pineapple in half lengthwise, retaining leaves. Remove pineapple from shell, discard core, and cut remaining fruit into chunks. Chill shells. Sprinkle pineapple chunks with sugar and chill at least 3 hours. Fill shells with pineapple, top with small scoops of sherbet, drizzle with crème de menthe, and garnish with fresh mint. *Beautiful and cool on a warm summer night.*
Serves 6.
Mrs. Pierce Sullivan (Mary Wallace Kerr)

Pear Cobbler

2	cups flour	1¼	cups sugar
½	teaspoon salt	2	teaspoons cinnamon
⅔	cup shortening	1½	teaspoons vanilla
⅓-½	cup cold water		Butter
7	pears, peeled, cored, and sliced		

Sift flour and salt together. Cut in shortening with 2 knives. Slowly add enough water until dough stays together. Roll out dough on a floured surface to ¼ inch thickness. Cut in strips about 1 inch wide. Combine pears, sugar, cinnamon, and vanilla. In a well greased, deep glass casserole, layer fruit mixture and strips of dough. Repeat layers. Dot with butter. Bake at 400° for 40-60 minutes. *Peaches may be substituted for pears. Use 10-12 peaches and add 1 tablespoon lemon juice.*
Serves 8-10.
Mrs. Scott Petty, Jr. (Louise James)

When grating lemons, limes, or oranges for a recipe which includes sugar, rub some of the sugar over the grater to absorb more of the tasty oils.

Petit Fours

2	sticks + 1 tablespoon butter, divided	½	cup chopped nuts
½	cup sugar	1	cup grated coconut
1	ounce unsweetened chocolate	2	tablespoons instant vanilla pudding
1	teaspoon vanilla	3	tablespoons milk
1	egg, beaten	2	cups confectioners' sugar
2	cups graham cracker crumbs	4	ounces semi-sweet chocolate

Combine 1 stick butter, sugar, unsweetened chocolate, and vanilla in the top of a double boiler and cook until well blended. Blend 2 tablespoons hot chocolate mixture with egg, and then slowly stir into remaining chocolate mixture and cook 5 minutes. Stir in crumbs, nuts, and coconut. Press into a 9 x 9 x 2 pan and chill 15 minutes. Cream 1 stick butter until fluffy, beat in pudding mix and milk, and add confectioners' sugar, beating until smooth and fluffy. Spread over chocolate layer. Melt the semi-sweet chocolate and remaining butter over low heat. Spread over filling. Chill until firm. Cut in 1 inch squares or diamond shapes.
Yields 50 or more. Freezes.
Mrs. Frank Steed

Plums in Flaming Vodka

1	cup sugar	2	tablespoons vodka
½	cup water	1	teaspoon vanilla
½	teaspoon powdered ginger or 1 teaspoon finely diced fresh ginger	1	teaspoon almond extract
2	pounds fresh plums, halved and pitted		

In a large saucepan combine sugar, water, and ginger and bring to a boil. Lower heat and cook 10 minutes, stirring occasionally until sugar is completely dissolved. Add plums to sugar syrup and cook 6-12 minutes or until tender but still firm. Remove plums with a slotted spoon to a deep, heat resistant serving dish. Boil down sugar syrup until slightly reduced, pour over plums, and cool to room temperature. Do not refrigerate. When ready to serve, put vodka, vanilla, and almond extract in a small saucepan, bring almost to a simmer, and ignite. Pour over plums and serve. *Peaches, apricots, or nectarines may be substituted for the plums. The flaming fruits are good served alone, in small pastries, à la mode, or with a dollop of whipped cream.* Serves 6-8.
Mrs. Benjamin Wyatt

Prune Whip with Custard Sauce

2	eggs, separated	2	cups milk, scalded
¾	cup + 3 tablespoons sugar, divided	1	teaspoon vanilla
8	prunes, stewed and puréed		

Stiffly beat egg whites and gradually add 3 tablespoons sugar, one at a time. Stir in prunes and pour into a buttered pan. Place pan in a water bath and bake at 250° for 45 minutes. Cream egg yolks with remaining sugar in a double boiler and gradually add milk, stirring constantly and cooking until thickened. Add vanilla and serve sauce over prune whip.
Serves 5-6.
Mrs. John R. Locke (Grace Walker)

Pumpkin Cheesecake Squares

12 ounces cream cheese
¾   cup + 3½ tablespoons sugar, divided
1½ tablespoons flour
1   teaspoon grated orange rind
½   teaspoon grated lemon rind
2   eggs + 2 egg yolks
8   ounces cooked pumpkin, fresh or canned

⅛   teaspoon cinnamon
⅛   teaspoon nutmeg, optional
2   recipes for graham cracker crumb crust with 1 teaspoon nutmeg and 1 teaspoon cinnamon added
2⅓ cups sour cream, divided
1   teaspoon vanilla

Combine cheese, ¾ cup sugar, flour, and rinds, blending until smooth. Add eggs and beat until smooth. Mix in pumpkin, cinnamon, and nutmeg, and continue beating until light and smooth. Press crumb mixture into the bottom and sides of an 11¾ x 7½ x 1¾ pan. Add pumpkin mixture. Bake at 350° for 40 minutes or until set. Remove and spread with a mixture of 2 cups sour cream, 3 tablespoons sugar, and vanilla and bake 10 minutes. Cool and spread with a thin layer of ⅓ cup cold sour cream combined with remaining sugar. Cut into squares.

Mrs. Lewis Faye (Linda)

Before using ladyfingers as liners, dot them with butter, and they will easily adhere to pan or dish.

Seven Layer Sour Cream Torte

3   cups sifted flour
¾   cup sugar
2   sticks butter, softened (no substitution)
1   egg
2   cups sliced fresh peaches

2   cups raspberries, strawberries, or blueberries
1½ cups confectioners' sugar
2   cups sour cream
1   teaspoon vanilla

Combine flour and sugar together and cut in butter until mixture resembles coarse meal. Stir in egg and mix with hands until dough holds together. Divide dough into 7 parts. Roll each part into a 9 inch circle. Bake each circle on the back of a cake pan or cookie sheet 10-12 minutes or until edges begin to brown. Combine fruits, reserving some for garnish, with sugar, sour cream, and vanilla. Assemble torte by alternating pastry circles and fruit mixture, beginning and ending with pastry. Refrigerate several hours before serving. For easier serving, pastry may be rolled into 3 inch circles and several individual tortes assembled.
Serves 10-12.
Mrs. William E. Fitch (Patrice Gilbreath)

Steamed Queen Pudding

Pudding

1	egg
2	tablespoons sugar
¼	stick butter, melted
¼	teaspoon salt

½	cup molasses
1½	cups flour
1	teaspoon soda, dissolved in ½ cup hot water

Sauce

2	egg yolks, well beaten
1	cup confectioners' sugar

1	cup heavy cream, whipped
1	teaspoon vanilla

Pudding Combine egg, sugar, butter, salt, and molasses. Gradually add the flour, mixing well, and stir in dissolved soda. Grease a 1 pound coffee can, and sprinkle with sugar. Pour mixture into can, and place can on a trivet in a pan with enough boiling water to halfway cover can. Cover pan and steam for 2 hours. To serve run a knife around the edges of the can and ease the pudding out onto a plate. Slice and serve with sauce.

Sauce Combine egg yolks with sugar. Fold in cream flavored with vanilla.

Mrs. Edward C. Held (Joan McMartin)

Sundae Bubble Crown

1	cup water
1	stick butter
1	cup sifted flour
4	eggs

1	quart pistachio ice cream
1	quart cherry ice cream
	Hot Fudge Sauce (see index)

Heat water and butter to a rolling boil. Add flour and stir vigorously over low heat about 1 minute or until mixture leaves sides of pan and forms a ball. Remove from heat. Add eggs, one at a time, beating after each addition until smooth and velvety. Drop by scant teaspoonfuls onto a baking sheet. Bake at 425° for 15 minutes or until golden brown. Cool. This makes about 80-90 puffs. Place a layer of puffs in the bottom of a 10 inch tube pan and cover with a layer of ice creams. Repeat layers until all puffs and ice creams are used. Drizzle with cooled sauce and freeze overnight. Remove from freezer 15 minutes before serving. Loosen edges with a spatula, push bottom up and out of pan, and place crown with pan base on a cake stand. Serve with hot sauce. **Serves 20-24.**
Mrs. Walter Capen Dunlap (Elaine Palmer)

Superb Date Pudding

1	cup chopped dates	2	tablespoons flour
1	cup chopped nuts	1	teaspoon baking powder
2	eggs, beaten	¾	cup sugar

Combine all ingredients and pour into a 1½ quart baking dish and bake at 350° for 30 minutes. Top with Caramel Sauce (see index).

Mrs. Henry W. Sebesta, Jr. (Patricia Klaver)

Syllabub

1	quart heavy cream	4	eggs
2	cups confectioners' sugar, divided	2	cups sweet white wine

Whip cream with 1 cup sugar. Beat eggs with remaining sugar and add wine. Combine with cream mixture, chill, and serve in stemmed, crystal goblets. *This recipe was handed down from Peach Point Plantation where Stephen F. Austin lived with his sister, Emily Austin Perry, and her family.*
Serves 12-14.
Mrs. Murray L. Johnston, Jr. (Anne Whittenburg)

Viennese Cheese Torte

16	graham crackers, crumbled	4	eggs
1	cup + 4 tablespoons sugar, divided	3	pounds cream cheese
1	tablespoon cinnamon	3	cups sour cream, divided
½	stick butter, melted	3	teaspoons vanilla, divided
		½	teaspoon almond extract

Combine crumbs, 2 tablespoons sugar, cinnamon, and butter. Press over the bottom and sides of a spring form pan. Bake at 350° for 5-8 minutes. Beat together eggs, 1 cup sugar, and cream cheese for 20 minutes until mixture is well blended. Fold in 1 cup sour cream, 2 teaspoons vanilla, and almond extract. Carefully pour mixture into crust and bake at 325° for 45 minutes, being sure that the top does not brown. Remove from oven and let stand 10 minutes. Combine remaining sour cream, sugar, vanilla, and spoon onto baked torte. Return to oven and bake 10 minutes. Turn oven off and allow torte to cool to room temperature. Refrigerate at least 8 hours before serving.
Serves 20.
Mrs. Robert Foard Townsend (Marian Combs Law)

Individual Coffee Soufflés

3   egg whites
2   tablespoons powdered instant
    coffee
Pinch of salt
4   tablespoons sugar, divided
2   cups heavy cream

1   teaspoon vanilla
2   tablespoons crème de cacao
2   2½ ounce Heath bars, chopped
    into tiny pieces
½   cup chopped almonds, toasted

Combine egg whites, coffee, and salt. Beat until stiff, gradually adding 2 table-spoons sugar. Whip cream, gradually adding remaining sugar and vanilla. Combine mixtures and add crème de cacao. Fold in candy and pour into pots de crèmes or demitasse cups. Refrigerate until set. Sprinkle with almonds before serving. If frozen, remove from freezer 25 minutes before serving.
Fills 14 2 ounce containers. Freezes well.
Mrs. Virginia P. Sinclair (Virginia Phillips)

Cold Sherry Soufflé

2   envelopes gelatin
½   cup cold water
1½ cups sweet sherry
6   eggs, separated

¾   cup sugar, divided
1   tablespoon lemon juice
1   cup heavy cream, whipped
Ladyfingers

Soften gelatin in water for 5 minutes. Place over boiling water and stir until dissolved. Remove from heat and add sherry. Chill for 30 minutes or until mixture begins to thicken. Beat egg whites until foamy and gradually add ½ cup sugar, beating constantly. Add lemon juice and beat until mixture is stiff, but not dry. Beat egg yolks until frothy, gradually add remaining sugar, and continue beating until yolks are thick and lemon colored. Slowly add slightly thickened gelatin mixture to yolk mixture and continue beating until thick-ened. Fold egg whites, then cream into gelatin mixture. Line a *7 inch collared soufflé dish with ladyfingers across the bottom and standing up around the sides. Chill at least 3 hours or overnight. Remove collar before serving. *Spectacular with a mound of whipped cream and sliced sugared strawberries in the center!*

*To make collar for soufflé dish   Cut a strip of wax paper 6 inches wide and long enough to fit around dish overlapping slightly. Fold the paper strip in half lengthwise, butter inside, and tie securely around dish.
Serves 12.
Mrs. Royce Moser, Jr.

Frozen Mocha Mint Parfait

½   cup sugar
½   cup water
2   teaspoons instant coffee
1   6 ounce package semi-sweet
     chocolate mint chips

2   eggs
2   tablespoons cognac
1½ cups heavy cream, whipped

Boil sugar, water, and coffee for 3 minutes. Put mint chips in blender, add coffee mixture, and whirl for 6 seconds. Add eggs and blend 1 minute. Add cognac and blend. Fold this mixture into cream. Mold or put into individual glasses or cups and freeze. Let stand at room temperature 10 minutes before serving.
Serves 6-8.
Mrs. William Scanlan, Jr. (Cecil Collins)

Cognac Crème

4   egg yolks
½-1 cup honey

1½ ounces cognac
1   cup heavy cream, whipped

Beat egg yolks until lemon colored. Beat in honey and then cognac. Fold in whipped cream. Spoon into small stemmed goblets and freeze.
Serves 6-8.
Mrs. Harry E. Brown (Carolyn Carlisle)

Frozen Mousse Grand Marnier

2   egg whites
Pinch of salt
6   tablespoons sugar
1   cup heavy cream
½   cup Grand Marnier, divided

1   10 ounce package frozen
     strawberries
1   10 ounce package frozen
     raspberries

Beat egg whites with salt until soft peaks are formed. Gradually beat in 4 tablespoons sugar until egg whites are stiff and shiny. With the same beater, whip cream until stiff; then beat in remaining sugar. Gently blend in ¼ cup liqueur. Combine with egg white mixture and turn into a 1 quart mold or individual molds. Freeze until firm. Defrost berries just enough to drain excess juice, purée in blender until smooth, strain, and add remaining Grand Marnier. Unmold mousse and serve with berry sauce.
Serves 4-6.
Mrs. Pierce Sullivan (Mary Wallace Kerr)

Avocado Sherbet

1½ cups mashed avocados	2 cups sugar
1 cup lemon juice	2 teaspoons grated lemon rind
1 cup orange juice	2 cups heavy cream, whipped

Combine avocado, fruit juices, sugar, and lemon rind, blending until sugar is completely dissolved. Pour mixture into ice cube trays and freeze 30 minutes. Remove from freezer, turn into a bowl, and stir. Fold in cream, pack into a plastic freezer container, and freeze until firm.
Serves 12.
Mrs. Harry E. Brown (Carolyn Carlisle)

Grapefruit Sherbet

1¼ cups sugar	2-3 tablespoons lemon juice
1 cup water	Drop of red food coloring, optional
2 egg whites, stiffly beaten	
2 cups unsweetened pink grapefruit juice	

Boil sugar and water about 5 minutes and pour into egg whites, beating constantly. Add grapefruit and lemon juices. Pour into a freezing tray and freeze for about 4 hours or until partially frozen. Beat until smooth and freeze overnight.
Yields 1 quart.
Mrs. William B. Lecznar

Lemon Milk Sherbet

| Juice of 7 lemons, approximately 1 cup | 2 quarts milk |
| 3 cups sugar | Ice cream salt |

Combine lemon juice, sugar, and milk, mixing thoroughly. Pour into container of ice cream freezer, cover tightly, and pack with ice and ice cream salt. This takes about 45 minutes to freeze.
Yields about 3 quarts.
Mrs. Bartlett Cocke, Jr. (Winifred Winter)

Blueberry Sherry Ice Cream

2 tablespoons cornstarch	½ cup dry sherry
½ cup sugar	¼ cup crème de cacao
¾ cup water	½ gallon vanilla ice cream, softened
2 cups fresh or frozen blueberries	

Combine cornstarch and sugar, stir in water, and ½ cup blueberries. Cook over low heat, stirring constantly until thickened. Add remaining blueberries and cool. Add sherry, crème de cacao, and ice cream. Freeze for 8 hours.
Serves 8-10.
Mrs. Donald M. Greer, Jr. (Anne Lindsay)

Cantaloupe Ice Cream

1½ cups sugar	1 quart milk
Pinch of salt	1 large ripe cantaloupe, puréed in blender
3 eggs, well beaten	
1 14 ounce can condensed milk	Ice cream salt
1 13 ounce can evaporated milk	

Add sugar and salt to eggs; stir in milks. Add cantaloupe. Pour into container of ice cream freezer, cover tightly, and pack with ice and ice cream salt. Freeze until firm.
Yields 1 gallon.
Mrs. Verner C. Koch

Ginger Pumpkin Ice Cream

36 ginger snaps	1 teaspoon cinnamon
1 #303 can solid pack pumpkin	½ teaspoon nutmeg
⅓ cup sugar	1 teaspoon vanilla
1 cup chopped pecans	½ gallon vanilla ice cream, softened
1 teaspoon salt	Whipped cream
1 teaspoon ground ginger	

Crush ginger snaps into coarse crumbs and put half of crumbs into the bottom of 9 x 13 x 2 pan. Combine pumpkin, sugar, pecans, spices, and vanilla, and fold into ice cream. Pour into pan and top with remaining crumbs. Cover and freeze. Cut into squares and serve with whipped cream. *Ideal recipe for holiday dinners.*
Serves 20.
Mrs. Armand D. Cox, Jr.

Great-Grandmother Pete's Mango Ice Cream

2   packages gelatin
2   cups milk, warmed
1   quart heavy cream
1½ cups sugar
2   32 ounce cans mangoes with
     syrup, mashed

2   32 ounce cans mangoes, drained
     and mashed
Ice cream salt

Dissolve gelatin in milk and add cream. Stir in sugar until dissolved. Blend in mangoes and pour into container of ice cream freezer, cover tightly, pack with ice and ice cream salt, and freeze until firm.
Yields 1½ gallons.
Mrs. Gerry Allan Solcher (Sally Sethness)

Coffee Ice Cream

1   pound drip coffee, mocha and java
     combination if possible
1   quart boiling water
2   cups sugar, divided
2   teaspoons malted milk powder
Pinch of salt

1   quart milk
9   egg yolks
3   egg whites, stiffly beaten
3   cups heavy cream, whipped
Ice cream salt

In a saucepan combine coffee and water. Steep 10-15 minutes and carefully strain liquid into a bowl. Add 1 cup sugar, malted milk powder, and salt, stirring well to dissolve, and cool 30 minutes. Heat milk in a double boiler. Beat egg yolks until thick and lemon colored and add remaining sugar. Add the milk in a steady stream, continuing to beat. Cool, fold in egg whites, combine with coffee mixture, and fold in cream. Pour into container of a large ice cream freezer, cover tightly, pack with ice and ice cream salt, and freeze until firm.

Mrs. Robert Buchanan (Sara "Sally" Ware Matthews)

Mint Chocolate Ice Cream

8 eggs, well beaten
2 cups sugar
2 13 ounce cans evaporated milk
⅛ teaspoon salt
4 teaspoons vanilla
⅓ cup crème de menthe

4 ounces semi-sweet chocolate, shaved, or chocolate chips whirled in blender
Green food coloring, optional
Milk
Ice cream salt

Combine all ingredients, except milk and salt, and blend thoroughly. Mixture should be colored a fairly dark green as it will be lighter in color after freezing. Pour into freezer container and add enough milk to fill about ⅔ full or according to freezer instructions. Cover tightly, pack with ice and ice cream salt, and freeze until firm. *For low calorie ice cream, substitute skimmed evaporated milk and prepare non-fat dry milk to use for filling container.*
Yields 1 gallon.
Mrs. Thomas M. Porter (Flo)

Homemade Vanilla Ice Cream

2-2½ cups sugar
6 eggs, beaten
1 14 ounce can condensed milk
2 13 ounce cans evaporated milk
2 quarts cream

1 tablespoon Mexican vanilla + 1 tablespoon water or 2 tablespoons vanilla
Ice cream salt

Combine all ingredients, except salt, mixing well. Pour into a 1½-2 gallon freezer container, cover tightly, pack with ice and ice cream salt, and freeze until firm.
Yields 1½ gallons.
Mrs. Edgar M. Duncan (Linda Wyatt)

Caramel Sauce

1   cup heavy cream   1   tablespoon butter
1½ cups sugar, divided

Heat cream in a double boiler and add 1 cup sugar. Caramelize remaining sugar in an iron skillet and add gradually to cream mixture, mixing well. Remove from heat and add butter. If mixture curdles beat until smooth. Serve hot or cold.

Mrs. Perry Shankle (Alice Stratton)

Going to Mexico? Purchase "conservas" of pasta de guayaba (guava paste) or pasta de membrillo (quince paste) to serve as a dessert or after dinner treat. It is delicious with cream cheese. Sugared slices cut into fancy shapes may decorate cakes or custards or be used as candy.

Hot Fudge Sauce

½   cup cocoa   ¼   teaspoon salt
1   cup sugar   3   tablespoons butter
1   cup light corn syrup   1   teaspoon vanilla
½   cup light cream or evaporated milk

Combine ingredients, except vanilla, in a 1½ quart saucepan. Cook over medium heat, stirring constantly until the mixture comes to a full rolling boil. Boil briskly 3 minutes, stirring occasionally. Remove from heat and add vanilla. Serve warm.
Yields 2½ cups.
Mrs. William B. Culverwell (Sally Powell)

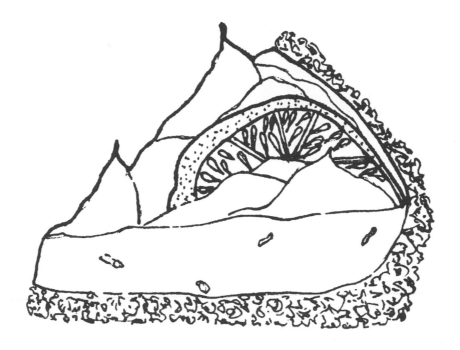

Foolproof Piecrust

4	cups flour	1	tablespoon vinegar
1¾	cups vegetable shortening	1	egg
1	tablespoon sugar	½	cup water
2	teaspoons salt		

With a fork, mix the first 4 ingredients. In a separate bowl, beat remaining ingredients. Combine mixtures, stirring with a fork until ingredients are moistened. Form dough into a ball. Chill at least 15 minutes before rolling into desired shape. Bake at 450° for 10 minutes. *Dough can be left in the refrigerator up to 3 days. It will remain soft and can be taken out and rolled at once. You can use this recipe to make great strudels and tarts.*
Yields five 9 inch shells. Freezes.
Mrs. Philip Traina

Rich Pastry

2¼	cups sifted flour	1	egg yolk
1	teaspoon salt	1	tablespoon lemon juice
1	tablespoon sugar	¼	cup milk
¾	cup vegetable shortening		

Sift flour with salt and sugar. Cut in shortening until mixture resembles fine crumbs. Beat together egg yolk and lemon juice. Blend in milk. Add to dry ingredients, tossing with a fork to form a soft dough. Divide dough in half and shape each half into a ball. Flatten each ball on a lightly floured surface and roll to ⅛ inch thickness.
Yields two 9-10 inch pastry shells.
Mrs. Walter W. McAllister, III (Lida Suttles)

Always have pie crust at hand by cutting 2 cups of shortening into 6 cups of flour combined with 3 teaspoons salt. Place in a plastic bag and refrigerate. The mixture will keep indefinitely. To make the pie crust combine 1 cup of the mixture per crust and enough cold water to form dough into a ball.

Apple Pie with Cheese Pastry

Cheese Pastry

2	cups flour	1⅓	sticks cold butter
½	teaspoon salt	4-5	tablespoons ice water
½	cup grated sharp cheese		

Filling

6-7	firm apples	½	teaspoon nutmeg
1	cup sugar	¼	cup fresh orange juice
2	tablespoons flour	¼	stick butter
½	teaspoon cinnamon		

Cheese Pastry Sift flour and salt together into a bowl and stir in cheese. Cut in butter with a pastry blender. Add ice water slowly, mixing lightly with a fork. Chill. Roll out slightly thinner than plain pastry and place in a 10 inch pie pan.

Filling Peel and slice apples. Combine sugar, flour, and spices. Arrange layers of apples over pastry alternately with sugar mixture. Drizzle with orange juice and dot with butter. Bake at 450° for 15 minutes. Reduce heat to 350° and bake about 50 minutes.

Mrs. Larry J. O'Neill (Liz Hamilton)

Apple Custard Pie

1 stick margarine	⅔ cup + ½ cup sugar, divided
1½ cups flour	1 teaspoon cinnamon
½ teaspoon salt	1 egg, beaten
3 medium apples	1 cup evaporated milk

Cut margarine into flour and salt until it resembles coarse meal. Press dough firmly on the bottom and sides of a 9 inch buttered pie plate. Peel and thinly slice apples and place over crust. Sprinkle with ⅔ cup sugar and the cinnamon. Bake at 375° for 20 minutes. Combine egg, ½ cup sugar, and milk. Pour over apples and bake 30 minutes.
Serves 6.
Mrs. Odis H. Clark, Jr.

Ranch Apple Fried Pies

Filling

1 pound dried apples	2 sticks butter
½ cup thinly sliced orange	2 cups sugar
¼ cup thinly sliced lemon	

Crust

4½ cups flour	1½ cups shortening
1½ teaspoons salt	10-12 tablespoons cold water

Filling Cover apples, orange, and lemon with water. Bring to a boil, reduce heat, and simmer 45 minutes or until the apples are tender. Remove from heat and drain. Add the butter and sugar, mixing well. Chill.

Crust Combine flour and salt. Cut in shortening until pastry is the size of small peas. Add water, 1 tablespoon at a time, until all particles are moistened and pastry can be formed into a ball. This pastry should not be delicate. Handle it as you would bread dough, so it will not flake apart while frying. Roll out pastry and cut in 4 inch circles. Add 2 tablespoons of the apple mixture to each circle, moisten the edges with water, and fold over. Press together with a fork. Fry in deep, hot fat, 360°F-370°F, until golden. Serve immediately. *These are a favorite breakfast treat or dessert served à la mode. They may also be sprinkled with cinnamon sugar.*
Freezes well before frying.
Mrs. Huard Hargis Eldridge (Earl Fae Cooper, Jr.)

Sour Cream Apple Pie

Filling

2	tablespoons flour	1	teaspoon vanilla
⅛	teaspoon salt	¼	teaspoon nutmeg
¾	cup sugar	2	cups peeled, diced apples
1	egg	1	9 inch pastry shell
1	cup sour cream		

Topping

⅓	cup sugar	1	teaspoon cinnamon
⅓	cup flour	½	stick butter, softened

Filling   Sift together flour, salt, and sugar. Beat in egg, sour cream, vanilla, and nutmeg. Stir in apples and pour into shell. Bake at 400° for 15 minutes. Reduce heat to 350° and bake for 30 minutes. Sprinkle with topping and bake at 400° for 10 minutes.

Topping   Blend ingredients until crumbly.

Mrs. Strauder Nelson, Jr. (Carolyn Moffitt)

Blueberry Cream Cheese Pie

1	14½ ounce can blueberries	6	ounces cream cheese, softened
4	tablespoons lemon juice	¾	cup confectioners' sugar
½	cup sugar	1	teaspoon vanilla
1½	tablespoons cornstarch	1	cup heavy cream, whipped
Dash of salt		1	9 inch pastry shell, baked

Drain blueberries, reserving 5 ounces of juice. In a saucepan combine blueberries, lemon juice, and reserved blueberry juice. Cook until the skins of berries pop. Combine sugar, cornstarch, and salt and stir into blueberry mixture. Cook over medium heat, stirring until mixture is thick and clear. Cool. Blend cheese, confectioners' sugar, and vanilla. Fold whipped cream into cheese mixture and spread in bottom of pastry shell. Pour blueberry mixture over the top, spreading evenly. Chill overnight.
Serves 6-8.
Mrs. Jon Grant Ford (Nancy Archer)

Concord Grape Pie

2	pounds Concord grapes	1	teaspoon flour
1	cup sugar	¼	stick butter
2	teaspoons cornstarch	Pastry for 2 crust pie	

Separate pulp from skins of grapes and reserve the skins. Boil pulp over medium heat for 15 minutes. Put through a sieve and remove seeds. Mix sugar, cornstarch, and flour. Add to pulp with butter and cook until thickened. Place skins on bottom crust, add mixture, and top with remaining crust. Bake at 350° for 50 minutes. *As a child this was a favorite dessert prepared by Beda Johnson, my aunt's Swedish housekeeper, in Joliet, Illinois.*
Serves 6.
Mrs. Carl Schenken (Ruth)

Delicious Coconut Pie

3	eggs	1	stick butter, melted
1	9 inch pastry shell	1	cup grated coconut
1½	cups sugar	Whipped cream	
1	teaspoon vanilla (Mexican vanilla is excellent)		

Brush a little egg white on pastry shell and bake at 400° about 2 minutes. This prevents having a soggy crust. Beat eggs slightly. Add sugar, vanilla, butter, and coconut. Pour into pastry shell, and bake at 375° for 45 minutes or until a knife inserted in center comes out clean. Garnish with whipped cream. *Do not use an all butter pastry as it will shrink when prebaked unless filled with rice or beans.*
Serves 8-10.
Mrs. Robert E. Schorlemer (Ann Kalb)

English Lemon Pie

6	eggs, separated	1	stick butter, melted
1½	cups sugar	1	9 inch deep dish pastry shell
Grated rind and juice of 3 lemons			

Beat egg yolks and add sugar, lemon rind, lemon juice, and butter. Stiffly beat egg whites and fold into butter mixture. Pour into pastry shell and bake at 325° for 30-40 minutes. Cool.
Serves 8.
Mrs. Jimmy Lodovic (Sharon)

Pineapple Chiffon Pie

4   eggs, separated
1   cup sugar, divided
¼   teaspoon salt
½   cup drained, crushed pineapple, divided
2   tablespoons lemon juice
½   3 ounce package lemon gelatin
½   cup pineapple juice, heated

Pinch of salt
¼   teaspoon cream of tartar
Sweetened whipped cream
2   9 inch graham cracker crumb crusts with 1-2 teaspoons cinnamon added, baked

Beat egg yolks in a double boiler and add ½ cup sugar, salt, ¼ cup pineapple, and lemon juice. Cook 15 minutes, stirring frequently, until mixture is the consistency of custard. Dissolve gelatin in pineapple juice, blend into egg mixture, and cool. Stiffly beat egg whites, gradually adding salt, cream of tartar, and remaining sugar. Fold into pineapple mixture and pour into cooled crusts. Bake at 325° for 15 minutes. Chill overnight. Top with cream and remaining pineapple.
Yields two 9 inch pies. May be doubled.
Mrs. John C. Totten (Kathy Pace)

Pumpkin Empanadas

Pastry
2   cups flour, sifted
2   teaspoons baking powder
½   teaspoon salt
⅔   cup shortening

¼   cup sugar
⅔   cup milk
½   teaspoon anise oil, optional

Filling
1   16 ounce can pumpkin or mashed sweet potatoes
¾   cup sugar
½   teaspoon anise oil, optional

1   teaspoon allspice
Egg white or canned milk
Cinnamon mixed with sugar

Pastry   Sift dry ingredients together and cut in shortening. Dissolve sugar in milk and add with anise oil to the dry ingredients, stirring just until dough follows fork around bowl. Knead 2-3 times on a floured board and roll out about ¼ inch thick. Cut in 4 inch circles.

Filling   Combine the first 4 ingredients and mix well. Place 1 heaping teaspoon pumpkin mixture on each circle of dough, fold over, and crimp edges with a fork. Brush empanadas with egg white and bake on a greased cookie sheet at 450° for 12-15 minutes or until golden brown. Sprinkle with cinnamon mixture and serve warm. *Any type of pie filling may be substituted for pumpkin. For meat or cheese and jalapeño empanadas, omit sugar from the pastry.*
Yields approximately 2 dozen.
The Cookbook Committee

Strawberry Shortcake Pie

⅔ cup + 2 tablespoons Crisco
2 cups flour
1 teaspoon salt
⅓ cup flour, stirred into ¼ cup water
1½ quarts fresh strawberries, 2-3 boxes
½ cup water
1 cup sugar
3 tablespoons cornstarch
Red food coloring
1 cup heavy cream, whipped

With a fork, cut Crisco into 2 cups flour and salt. Add moistened flour and shape into a ball. Roll out on a floured board, always rolling back and forth in the same direction. Place pastry in a 9 inch pie pan and bake at 450° for 8-10 minutes. Cool. Crush enough strawberries to make 1 cup, reserving remainder for pie filling. Make a glaze by combining crushed berries, water, sugar, and cornstarch. Bring to a boil and cook over low heat until clear. Tint to desired shade and cool. Line shell with whole berries, cover with glaze, and top with cream.
Yields one 9 inch pie.
Mrs. James Anderson (Gee)

Watermelon Chiffon Pie

1⅓ cups graham cracker crumbs
1 cup sugar, divided
⅔ stick butter or margarine, melted
¼ large watermelon
2 envelopes gelatin
⅛ teaspoon salt
1 tablespoon lemon juice
2 egg whites
1 cup heavy cream, whipped
Watermelon balls
Mint

Combine crumbs, ⅓ cup sugar, and butter. Press over bottom and sides of a 9 inch pie plate. Chill. Extract 2½ cups juice from watermelon by cutting watermelon into cubes and rubbing through a strainer to remove seeds and membrane. Sprinkle gelatin over 1 cup melon juice in a medium saucepan. Place over low heat, stirring constantly, about 5 minutes or until gelatin dissolves. Remove from heat and stir in ⅓ cup sugar, salt, remaining watermelon juice, and lemon juice. Chill, stirring occasionally, until mixture mounds slightly when dropped from a spoon. Beat egg whites until stiff but not dry. Gradually add remaining sugar, beating until very stiff. Fold with cream into watermelon mixture and turn into shell. Chill several hours or until set. Garnish with watermelon balls and mint sprigs. May be prepared no more than 1 day ahead. *After a heavy meal, this is a light, fluffy, sweet ending!*
Serves 6-8.
Mrs. Stephen B. Wilde (Elizabeth "Bibba" Jane Thomson)

"All Good" Pies

1	stick butter	1	cup finely cut dates
2	cups sugar	1	cup finely cut citron
4	eggs, separated	1	9 inch deep dish pastry shell or
3	teaspoons white vinegar		10-12 tart shells

Cream butter with sugar. Beat egg yolks until light and add to creamed mixture. Stir in vinegar, dates, and citron. Beat egg whites until stiff and fold into creamed mixture. Pour into shell. Bake at 375° for 30 minutes.
Serves 10-12.
Mrs. Alfred E. McNamee (Josephine McClelland)

Graham Meringue Pie

Pie

1	cup fine graham cracker crumbs	1	cup sugar
1	teaspoon baking powder	½	cup finely cut dates
½	teaspoon salt	½	cup chopped pecans
3	egg whites	1	teaspoon vanilla

Sauce

3	egg yolks	8	marshmallows, chopped
¼	cup sugar	1	tablespoon sherry
¼	cup milk		

Pie   Combine crumbs, baking powder, and salt. Beat egg whites until soft peaks form, and gradually add sugar. Fold into crumb mixture, and add dates, pecans, and vanilla. Pour into a lightly buttered 9 inch glass pie plate. Bake at 350° for 30 minutes.

Sauce   Stir yolks in a double boiler and add sugar and milk, blending well. Cook until thickened, add marshmallows, and stir until melted. When cool, add sherry. Serve sauce over slices of pie.
Serves 8.
Mrs. Neill Boldrick, Jr. (Dorothy Walser)

Mincemeat Pie

¼ cup self-rising flour or all purpose flour with ⅛ teaspoon baking powder
⅔ cup milk
2 egg yolks
1⅓ sticks butter, softened
⅔ cup sugar
1 teaspoon brandy extract or 2 teaspoons brandy

½ teaspoon rum extract or 1 teaspoon rum
1 9 inch deep dish pastry shell, baked and cooled
1 18 ounce jar mincemeat
Whipped cream or baked pastry cutouts

In a saucepan blend flour, a small amount of the milk, and egg yolks until smooth. Gradually add remaining milk and cook until very thick, stirring constantly. Cool to room temperature. Cream butter and sugar until light and fluffy. Add extracts and gradually blend in flour mixture, beating until light and fluffy. Place in pastry shell and spread with mincemeat. Top with dollops of whipped cream around the edges or baked pastry cutouts. *This is an original recipe created by Oma Bell Perry, one of the three Perry sisters of Big Springs Ranch located north of Leakey, Texas. They are the great-great-nieces of Stephen F. Austin.*
Serves 10.
Mrs. Murray L. Johnston, Jr. (Anne Whittenburg)

Deep South Pecan Pie

½ stick butter
1¼ cups brown sugar
Dash of salt
¾ cup dark Karo syrup
3 eggs, well beaten

1 cup pecans
1 teaspoon vanilla
1 9 inch pastry shell
Whipped cream

Cream butter and sugar. Add salt, syrup, eggs, pecans, and vanilla, mixing well. Turn into pastry shell and bake at 350° for 45 minutes. Serve with whipped cream. *This is Mohm Swallow's original recipe from her Cottage Pie Bar that was located here in the 1950's.*

Mrs. Milton Wagenfuehr (Betty Swallow)

LaNelle's Pecan Pie

2 tablespoons flour
½ cup brown sugar
½ cup sugar
2 large eggs, beaten
¼ teaspoon salt
1½ teaspoons vanilla

½ cup Log Cabin maple syrup
½ cup light Karo syrup
¼ stick butter, melted
¼ teaspoon nutmeg
¾ cup chopped pecans
1 9 inch pastry shell

Combine flour, sugars, and eggs. Add remaining ingredients, pour into pastry shell, and bake at 450° for 7 minutes. Lower heat to 275°-300° and bake 45-60 minutes or until the center is almost firm. Serve warm. *Add ¼ teaspoon salt to your favorite pie crust recipe as the extra salty crust compliments the sweet filling.*
Serves 8.
Mrs. A. Tedford Barclay, Jr. (LaNelle Robertson)

Pecan Pie

1 cup sifted flour
½ teaspoon salt
⅓ cup shortening
2 tablespoons water
5 egg yolks or 3 whole eggs
2 cups sugar

1 stick margarine, melted
½ cup milk
1 tablespoon flour
1 teaspoon vanilla
1 cup pecans

Mix flour, salt, shortening, and water with an electric mixer on medium speed 30 seconds or by hand. Roll out to ⅛ inch thickness. Place in a 9 inch pie plate. In a separate bowl, beat 5 egg yolks. Mix together sugar, margarine, milk, flour, and vanilla. Add this mixture to the beaten eggs and pour into crust. Add the pecans. Bake at 350° for 45-60 minutes or until a knife inserted in the center comes out clean. Do not overcook as pie thickens as it cools. *Very rich.*
Serves 6-8.
Mrs. Gilbert Lehne (Elvie)

Teatime Tassies

1 stick + 1 tablespoon butter, at room temperature, divided
3 ounces cream cheese, at room temperature
1 cup flour
1 egg
1 cup sifted brown sugar
1 teaspoon vanilla
Dash of salt
⅔ cup coarsely broken pecans, divided

Blend 1 stick butter with cream cheese. Stir in flour and refrigerate about 1 hour. Shape into 2 dozen 1 inch balls. Place in small muffin cups. Press dough over bottom and sides to form small shells. Beat together egg, sugar, remaining butter, vanilla, and salt until smooth. Sprinkle ⅓ cup pecans among the pastry lined cups. Add egg mixture and top with remaining pecans. Bake at 325° for 35 minutes or until filling is set. Cool and remove from pans.
Yields 24 pastries.
Mrs. Lester J. Laird

Philly Velvet Cream

1½ cups crushed chocolate wafers
⅔ stick margarine, melted
8 ounces cream cheese, softened
¼ cup sugar
1 teaspoon vanilla
2 egg yolks, beaten
1 6 ounce package semi-sweet chocolate chips, melted
2 egg whites
¼ cup sugar
1 cup heavy cream, whipped
¾ cup chopped pecans
Whipped cream for topping

Combine wafers and margarine. Press into bottom of a 9 inch spring form pan. Bake at 325° for 10 minutes. For the filling, combine cream cheese, sugar, and vanilla. Mix until well blended. Add yolks and chocolate. Beat egg whites until soft peaks form, add sugar, and fold into chocolate mixture. Fold in cream and pecans. Freeze 2 hours. Top with whipped cream.
Serves 8-12.
Mrs. Joe E. Briscoe (Gene Aubrey)

Aunt Sarah's French Silk Pie

1   stick butter
¾   cup sugar
1   square unsweetened chocolate, melted
1   teaspoon vanilla
2   eggs

1   9 inch pastry shell, baked and cooled
1   cup heavy cream, whipped
Chopped black walnuts or toasted almond slices, optional

Cream butter until fluffy. Add sugar gradually, beating thoroughly. Beat in chocolate and vanilla. Add eggs, one at a time, beating 3 minutes after each addition. Turn mixture into pastry shell. Top with cream and sprinkle with walnuts. Freeze for several hours and remove 10-15 minutes before serving. Serves 8-10.
Mrs. Robert H. Bullock (Sarah Perry)

Chocolate Fudge Pie

4   eggs
2   cups sugar
3   1 ounce squares unsweetened chocolate
⅔   stick butter
1   teaspoon lemon juice

1   scant cup pecans
½   teaspoon vanilla
2   9 inch pastry shells or a 9 inch deep dish pastry shell
Whipped cream, optional

Beat eggs and add sugar, mixing well. Melt chocolate with butter and gradually add to the egg mixture, stirring constantly. Stir in lemon juice, pecans, and vanilla. Pour into pastry and bake at 350° for 40-50 minutes or until set. Serve topped with whipped cream.

The Bright Shawl Tearoom

German Chocolate Pie

1   stick margarine
4   ounces sweet German chocolate
3   eggs
1   cup sugar

½   cup flour
½   cup broken pecans
½   teaspoon vanilla

Melt margarine and chocolate in a double boiler. Beat eggs and add sugar and flour, mixing well. Combine egg mixture with chocolate mixture and add pecans and vanilla. Pour into a greased 9 inch glass pie plate. Bake at 325° for 40 minutes. *This pie uses no crust and may be served with cream, whipped or plain, or ice cream, with or without chocolate sauce.*

Ms. Jessica Bell

Terry Davis' Chocolate Mousse Pie

1   package Keebler Fudge cookies
½   stick butter, melted
1   12 ounce package semi-sweet chocolate chips
4   egg yolks
2   eggs
3   egg whites
3   cups heavy cream, divided
1   teaspoon vanilla, rum, or Kahlúa
Chocolate shavings

Chop cookies in blender and add butter. Press cookie crumb mixture to form a pie crust on the bottom of a 10 inch spring form pan. Bake at 350° for 10 minutes. Melt chocolate chips in a double boiler. Beat 4 egg yolks and 2 eggs together and slowly add melted chocolate. Beat 3 egg whites until they form stiff peaks. Whip 2 cups cream and add vanilla. Fold together the chocolate mixture, egg whites, and whipped cream. Pour into crust. Whip remaining cream and spread over pie. Sprinkle with chocolate and refrigerate.
Serves 8-10.
Mrs. Benjamin F. Swank, III (Susie Schroeder)

Cognac Cream Pie

1   envelope gelatin
¼   cup cold water
5   egg yolks, beaten
¾-1   cup sugar
⅓-½   cup cognac or dark rum
1½   cups heavy cream, whipped
1   9 inch graham cracker crumb crust with ½ teaspoon cinnamon added, chilled
2   tablespoons shaved chocolate

Soften gelatin in cold water. Place over low heat and bring almost to a boil, stirring constantly. Beat egg yolks and sugar until light. Stir in gelatin and cool. Gradually add cognac, beating constantly. Fold cream into gelatin mixture and cool until almost set. Spoon into crust and chill until firm. Serve with chocolate.
Serves 8.
Mrs. Maury Holden

Southern Sin Chess Pie

3 whole eggs, beaten
1 cup sugar
1 stick butter
Pinch of salt

1 teaspoon vanilla or 3 tablespoons lemon juice and grated rind of 1 large lemon
1 9 inch pastry shell

Mix by hand eggs, sugar, butter, salt, and vanilla. Pour into pastry shell. Bake at 350° approximately 45 minutes or until firm.

Mrs. Charles Parish, Jr. (Betty Caldwell)

Spiced Buttermilk Pie

1 stick margarine, softened
2 cups sugar
3 eggs, beaten
3 rounded tablespoons flour
1 cup buttermilk
1 teaspoon vanilla

¼ teaspoon nutmeg
⅛ teaspoon curry powder
⅛ teaspoon ground ginger
⅛ teaspoon allspice
1 9 inch pastry shell

Cream margarine with sugar. Blend in eggs and flour. Add buttermilk, vanilla, and spices. Pour into pastry shell and bake at 350° for 45 minutes. *May be served with a dollop of whipped cream.*
Serves 8.
Mrs. Tony Chauveaux (Kathryn Williams)

When making the classic Eagle Brand lemon pie, use a crust of 1 cup finely crushed chocolate cookie crumbs, 6 tablespoons sugar, and ¼ stick melted butter or margarine.

Vinegar Pie

1 stick butter or margarine, melted and cooled
1½ cups sugar
2 tablespoons flour

1 tablespoon vanilla
3 tablespoons vinegar
3 eggs
1 9 inch pastry shell

Combine the first 6 ingredients, blending well. Pour into pastry shell. Bake at 300° for 45 minutes.
Serves 6-8.
Mrs. J. Sherrel Lakey

A Blend of Cultures

"We have no city, except perhaps New Orleans, that can vie in point of the picturesque interest that attaches to odd and antiquated foreigness with San Antonio. Its jumble of races, costumes, languages and buildings; its religious ruins, holding to an antiquity, for us, indistinct enough to breed an unaccustomed solemnity; its remote, isolated, outposted situation and the vague conviction that it is the first of a new class of conquered cities into whose decaying streets our rattling life is to be infused, combine with the heroic touches in its history to enliven and satisfy your traveler's curiosity."

A Journey Through Texas.   Frederick Law Olmstead, 1857.

Pizza Party

Antipasto Misto
Green Salad with Pasta al Pesto
Party Pizza — Make Your Own
Glazed Fresh Fruit

Chinese New Year

Mini Egg Fu Yung
Green Tea
Wonton Soup
Crystallized Ginger Salad
Cashew Chicken
Chow Ching Tou   Stir-Fry Spinach   Chinese Fried Rice
Buñuelos with Apricot Brandy Sauce

Greek Easter Sunday Buffet

Tarama
Spanakopites
Avgolemono
Tabouli
Leg of Lamb
Eggplant au Gratin
Butterhorn Rolls
Loukoumades

Pilon

Fiesta San Antonio

Ratitos
Acapulco Jicama
Puerto Vallarta Teasers
Frozen Margaritas
Sopa de Tortilla
Avocado Enchiladas
Scampi Guadalajara
Sopaipillas
Sangría con Frutas

Graduation Cookout Around the Pool

Texas Cheese Ball
Daffodil Dip with Raw Vegetables
Easy and Beautiful Salad
Anticuchos Peruanos
Potatoes Supreme   Mushrooms Berkley   French Bread
Vanilla Ice Cream

Children's Birthday Party

Peanut Butter Logs
Banana Pizazz
Honey Orange Salad
Tortilla Dogs
Lively Oaks Ranch Beans   Squash Chips
Popcorn Cake

All American Picnic
Packed in Individual Picnic Baskets

Mother's Stuffed Celery

Peach Daiquiris

Curried Apple Soup

Picnic Potato Salad

Individual Quiches

Marinated Vegetable Medley

Deluxe Brownies   Macadamia Nut Crisps

Icebox Cookies   Lemon Whippersnaps

Back to School Brunch
Celebration for Moms

Hot Cheese Cookies

Orange Blossoms

Cool as a Cucumber Soup

Mandarin Spinach Salad

Crab and Avocado Enchiladas

Celebration Bread

Minted Melon Bowl

Glorified Brownies

Picnic for Hunters
Frozen Towels*

Panamanian Shrimp Ceviche

Venison Pâté

Lettuce Tortillas

Beef à la Mode Sandwiches

Fire and Ice Tomatoes

Marbleized Chocolate Cheesecake

*Soak small towels in water, wring out, and freeze. Place
with flatware in small tin buckets and pass to each hunter.

German Octoberfest

Paresa
Vodka Wassail Bowl
Sauerkraut Salad
German Style Spinach
Venison Sauerbraten
Heaven and Earth
Mock Doboschtorte

Mexican Thanksgiving

Ceviche de México
White Sangria
Monterey Jack Cheese Soup or Black Bean Soup
Molded Gazpacho Salad with Avocado Cream
Green Beans with Jicama
Turkey with Tamale Stuffing and Enchilada Gravy
Pumpkin or Mincemeat Empanadas
Mexican Coffee

Formal Dinner for Four

Russian Caviar Mousse
Quick Delicious Clear Chicken Soup
Mushroom Sandwiches
Hot Bacon Dressing over Spinach
Individual Beef Wellington
Spiced Grapes
Baked Carrot Ring   Pommes Anna
Wellington Icebox Rolls
Fantastic Foosh

Table of Equivalents for U.S. Cooking Measures

3 teaspoons . . . . .1 tablespoon
4 tablespoons . . . . .¼ cup
5 tablespoons + 1 teaspoon .⅓ cup
8 tablespoons . . . . .½ cup
10 tablespoons + 2 teaspoons . . . . .⅔ cup
12 tablespoons . . . . .¾ cup
16 tablespoons . . . . .1 cup
2 tablespoons. . . . . .1 liquid ounce
1 cup . . . . .½ pint
2 cups . . . . .1 pint
4 cups . . . . .1 quart
4 quarts. . . . . .1 gallon

Equivalent Amounts

Flour
All Purpose, 1 pound, sifted . . . . .4 cups
Cake, 1 pound, sifted . . . . .4½-5 cups

Sugar
Granulated, 1 pound. . . . . .2¼-2½ cups
Brown, firmly packed, 1 pound . . . . .2⅛-2¼ cups
Confectioners', sifted . . . . .4½-5 cups

Cheese
American, ½ pound, grated . . . . .2 cups
Cottage, ½ pound . . . . .1 cup
Cream, 3 ounces. . . . . .6 tablespoons

Rice
1 pound, raw . . . . .2⅛ cups
1 cup, raw . . . . .about 4 cups cooked
1⅓ cups packaged, pre-cooked . . . . .3 cups cooked

Butter
½ stick. . . . . .¼ cup
⅔ stick. . . . . .⅓ cup
1 stick. . . . . .½ cup

Metric Equivalents for U.S. Cooking Measures

U.S. Measure	Metric Equivalent	U.S. Measure	Metric Equivalent
¼ teaspoon	1.25 milliliters	1 ounce	28.00 grams
½ teaspoon	2.50 milliliters	2 ounces	56.00 grams
1 teaspoon	5.00 milliliters	4 ounces	113.00 grams
2 teaspoons	10.00 milliliters	8 ounces	226.00 grams
3 teaspoons	15.00 milliliters	16 ounces	452.00 grams
1 tablespoon	15.00 milliliters	¼ pound	0.11 kilogram
2 tablespoons	30.00 milliliters	½ pound	0.23 kilogram
1 fluid ounce	30.00 milliliters	¾ pound	0.34 kilogram
2 fluid ounces	59.00 milliliters	1 pound	0.45 kilogram
4 fluid ounces	118.00 milliliters	2 pounds	0.90 kilogram
8 fluid ounces	236.00 milliliters	4 pounds	1.81 kilograms
16 fluid ounces	472.00 milliliters	6 pounds	2.72 kilograms
1 cup	0.24 liter	8 pounds	3.62 kilograms
2 cups	0.47 liter	10 pounds	4.54 kilograms

Cooking Temperatures

Heat	°F	°C
Very Slow	250-275	121-135
Slow	300-325	149-163
Moderate	350-375	177-191
Hot	400-425	204-218
Very Hot	450-475	232-246
Broil	500-525	260-274

Oven Temperatures

°F	°C	°F	°C
200	93	375	191
225	107	400	204
250	121	425	218
275	135	450	232
300	149	475	246
325	163	500	260
350	177	525	274

Bibliography

Bushick, Frank H. *Glamorous Days.* San Antonio, Texas: Naylor Printing Company, 1934.

Castañeda, Carlos E. *Our Catholic Heritage in Texas, 1519-1936. Volume III: San Francisco de la Espada in 1745.* Austin, Texas: Von Boeckmann-Jones Company, 1942.

Castañeda, Carlos E. *Our Catholic Heritage in Texas, 1519-1936. Volume IV: The Province of Texas in 1762.* Austin, Texas: Von Boeckmann-Jones Company, 1942.

Chabot, Frederick C. *Presidio de Texas at the Place Called San Antonio.* San Antonio, Texas: Naylor Printing Company, 1929.

Green, Rena Maverick, ed. *Samuel Maverick, Texan 1803-1870.* San Antonio, Texas: Privately printed, 1952.

Heusinger, Edward W., F.R.G.S. *A Chronology of Events in San Antonio.* San Antonio, Texas: Standard Printing Company, 1951.

Hollon, W. Eugene, and Ruth Lapham Butler, eds. *William Bolleart's Texas.* Norman, Oklahoma: University of Oklahoma Press, 1956.

Kendall, George Wilkins. *Narrative of the Texan Santa Fé Expedition.* London: Wiley and Putnam, 1844.

Latham, Francis S. *Travels in the Republic of Texas — 1842.* Edited by Gerald S. Pierce. Austin, Texas: Encino Press, 1971.

Lomax, Louise. *San Antonio's River.* San Antonio, Texas: Naylor Printing Company, 1948.

Morfi, Fray Juan Augustin. *History of Texas 1673-1779.* Translated by Carlos Edwardo Castañeda. Quivira Society: Albuquerque, New Mexico, 1935.

Morrison, Andrew. *San Antonio: Her Prosperity and Prospects.* circa 1887.

Muir, Andrew Forest, ed. *Texas in 1837.* Austin, Texas: University of Texas Press, 1958.

Olmstead, Frederick Law. *A Journey Through Texas.* New York, New York: Dix Edwards and Company, 1857.

Roemer, Dr. Ferdinand. *Roemer's Texas.* Translated by Oswald Mueller. San Antonio, Texas: Standard Printing Company, 1935.

San Antonio Express. Article, August 19, 1877.

San Antonio Herald. Article, September 12, 1865.

San Antonio Light. Article, May 8, 1883.

Volume of Manuscript Letters From Ursuline Nuns, 1852-1853. Daughters of the Republic of Texas Library. San Antonio, Texas.

Index

410

413

415

416

Flavors **Cookbook Information**:

The Junior League of San Antonio, Inc.
723 Brooklyn Avenue
San Antonio, Texas 78215
210 225 1861 ext 45
210 225 6832 fax
www.jlsa.org

The Junior League of San Antonio, Inc.

723 Brooklyn Avenue
San Antonio, Texas 78215
210 225 1861 ext 45
210 225 6832 fax
www.jlsa.org

YOUR ORDER	QTY	TOTAL
Flavors at $19.95 per book		$
All Texas residents add $1.47 sales tax per book		$
San Antonio residents add $0.10 MTA sales tax per book		$
Shipping and handling at $3.00 per book		$
	TOTAL	$

Name

Address

City   State   Zip

Email Address   Telephone

Method of Payment: [   ] MasterCard   [   ] VISA   [   ] Discover   [   ] American Express
                      [   ] Check(s) payable to Junior League of San Antonio

Account Number   Expiration Date

Cardholder Signature

Resellers Information: Orders of 10 or more copies are shipped direct from the manufacturer. Please contact The Junior League of San Antonio, Inc. at 210 225 1861 ext 45. If you are a reseller, furnish sales tax exemption information. There is a 40% discount to wholesalers.

Photocopies will be accepted.

The Junior League of San Antonio, Inc.
723 Brooklyn Avenue
San Antonio, Texas 78215
210 225 1861 ext 45
210 225 6832 fax
www.jlsa.org

YOUR ORDER	QTY	TOTAL
Flavors at $19.95 per book		$
All Texas residents add $1.47 sales tax per book		$
San Antonio residents add $0.10 MTA sales tax per book		$
Shipping and handling at $3.00 per book		$
	TOTAL	$

Name

Address

City   State   Zip

Email Address   Telephone

Method of Payment: [   ] MasterCard   [   ] VISA   [   ] Discover   [   ] American Express
                      [   ] Check(s) payable to Junior League of San Antonio

Account Number   Expiration Date

Cardholder Signature

Resellers Information: Orders of 10 or more copies are shipped direct from the manufacturer. Please contact The Junior League of San Antonio, Inc. at 210 225 1861 ext 45. If you are a reseller, furnish sales tax exemption information. There is a 40% discount to wholesalers.

Photocopies will be accepted.

The Junior League of San Antonio, Inc. History

Founded in 1924, the Junior League of San Antonio, Inc. has over 1,300 members trained for volunteer service. We are one of 296 Junior Leagues in the world, all of which are affiliated through The Association of Junior Leagues International.

The Junior League of San Antonio, Inc. (JLSA) has established a long list of successful community projects since its inception, including The Sunshine Cottage School for Deaf Children, The Docent Program at the San Antonio Zoo, the Non-Profit Resource Center, the Frederich Wilderness Park, and the Nature Camp at the San Antonio Botanical Society. Many of these projects continue to serve the needs of our community today.

JLSA has 500 volunteers serving our community through projects such as San Antonio Botanical Center, SA Works, Sunshine Singers, Met Opera, Project Better Future, Big Brothers/Big Sisters, St. Peter's/St. Joseph's, Provisional Works, and our own JLSA Signature Project "Walking for Women's Health." Our Signature Project increases the number of women in San Antonio who lead physically active lives, improves their physical and mental health, their quality of life, and assists in the prevention of disease. The project is "a women's preventive healthcare initiative" with two main goals: 1) Promote an educational walking program to women in San Antonio and 2) Construct a public walking path in our community.

Our Community Fundraisers Olé Marketplace, our annual Rummage Sale, and the sale of *Flavors* Cookbooks continue to contribute dollars directly to benefit our San Antonio community projects. We thank you for your support.